# Immigration, Motherhood and Parental Involvement

Library of Congress Cataloging-in-Publication Data

Names: Cibils, Lilian, author.
Title: Immigration, motherhood and parental involvement:
narratives of communal agency in the face of power asymmetry / Lilian Cibils.
Description: New York: Peter Lang, 2017.
Series: Counterpoints: studies in criticality; Vol. 439 | ISSN 1058-1634
Includes bibliographical references and index.
Identifiers: LCCN 2016043871 | ISBN 978-1-4331-3089-2 (hardcover: alk. paper)
ISBN 978-1-4331-3088-5 (paperback: alk. paper)
ISBN 978-1-4331-3921-5 (e-book pdf)
ISBN 978-1-4331-3922-2 (epub) | ISBN 978-1-4331-3923-9 (mobi)
Subjects: LCSH: Women immigrants—United States—Social conditions.
Hispanic American women—United States—Social conditions—Case studies.
Motherhood—United States—Case studies.
Parenting—United States—Case studies.
Classification: LCC HQ1421 .C53 2017 | DDC 306.874/308968073—dc23
LC record available at https://lccn.loc.gov/2016043871
DOI: 10.3726/978-1-4331-3921-5


Bibliographic information published by **Die Deutsche Nationalbibliothek**.
**Die Deutsche Nationalbibliothek** lists this publication in the "Deutsche
Nationalbibliografie"; detailed bibliographic data are available
on the Internet at http://dnb.d-nb.de/.

The paper in this book meets the guidelines for permanence and durability
of the Committee on Production Guidelines for Book Longevity
of the Council of Library Resources.

∞

© 2017 Peter Lang Publishing, Inc., New York
29 Broadway, 18th floor, New York, NY 10006
www.peterlang.com

Printed in the United States of America

To my husband and life partner, Andrés
and my daughters, Anna and Elisa

# TABLE OF CONTENTS

# ACKNOWLEDGMENTS

This work would not have seen the light had it not been for the support of many people: family members, friends, colleagues, mentors, and research participants. First and foremost, I am profoundly grateful to the wonderful women I had the privilege to get to know and interview. I will remain permanently indebted to each one of them for their trust, openness and generosity in sharing their powerful life stories. Their purpose in participating in the study was clear: they hoped that by relating their experiences they could make a difference in many immigrant mothers' lives. In retelling them here, this is my wish too.

I would like to thank Shirley Steinberg and Chris Myers for the opportunity to publish my work. Sophie Appel's diligence and support was invaluable at crucial points in the process of publication; I also thank all members of the Peter Lang team whose work made this book better. I also express my gratitude to the College of Education and the Department of Curriculum and Instruction at New Mexico State University for the generous financial support I received through graduate assistantships which allowed me to complete my research. I am grateful to Jeanette Haynes-Writer, Chair of the Department, for her interest in this project and her sustained encouragement. I would also like to thank Neil Harvey, James O'Donnell, Marisol Ruiz, and Hermán S. García for their insightful questions, comments and suggestions.

I owe thanks of a more overarching kind to role models and mentors whose timely words have sustained me beyond their knowledge and, in some cases, beyond their time. My loving mother, Alcira de Rogers, a bright and modest woman, and a tireless teacher, inspired me with her passion for making a difference through education. I was truly fortunate to be mentored by H. Patsy Boyer, a brilliant feminist scholar and translator, as well as one of the most graceful and generous teachers, who encouraged me to write and to continue my studies. María del Mar López Cabrales, whom I met as one of my professors during my MA studies at Colorado State University, has become a dear friend who throughout the years has gone out of her way to extend her unwavering support even from miles away, sometimes across continents. I would be remiss if I did not acknowledge the authors whose writings most deeply impacted this work, namely, and in no special order, Iris Marion Young, Nancy Fraser, Patricia Hill Collins, and Catherine Kohler Riessman. I would like to extend my warm thanks to friends and colleagues—especially Robin Martinez, Koomi Kim, Laura Liébana, and Heejung Chun—whose encouragement during this challenging process was invaluable.

Finally, enormous thanks go to my husband, Andrés Cibils, and to my daughters, Anna and Elisa, for their loving patience and support every step of the way. Andrés lent himself as a sounding board for ideas throughout the writing process and, more significantly, the joy of his life partnership is more than I could ask. Anna and Elisa not only inspired the research at the heart of this book in the first place but continue to inspire me daily as young adults in their active commitment to working for a more just and equitable society. Their thoughtful reading and generous feedback of drafts of the newest chapters as the text grew from dissertation to book were more helpful than they will ever know.

# ·PART I·

# THE STUDY AND ITS CONTEXTS

# INTRODUCTION

This book focuses on the experiences of seven Mexican immigrant women with their children's schooling in the Southwest of the United States as reconstructed in their narratives. Inspired by critical feminist theory, the qualitative study (Cibils, 2011) which gave rise to this book set out to gather the perspectives of this group of women in order to take a close look at instances of interaction which were expected to offer counter stories (Chase, 2005; González, 2005). Yet, a more subtle and complex relation emerged between their narratives and the official discourse of parental involvement in education.

The overarching contexts of the stories in the book are laid out in Chapter 1 through a focus on some of the relevant social and political conditions of immigration. Chapter 2 presents the understandings of justice through which the stories are viewed while Chapter 3 briefly introduces the seven immigrant women who were interviewed for the study. Two contrasting ideologies of motherhood are presented in Chapter 4 as theoretical backdrop to the discussion on parental involvement. This is followed by an exploration of how the official discourse of parental involvement fits within the broader context of social policy through the examination of a common underlying ideal parent norm across areas of policy related to family and women.

After introducing current perspectives on the dynamics of master and counter narratives, Chapter 5 looks into the significance of the tension observed within the stories of the women introduced in Chapter 3, and the signs of agency emerging from the coexistence of apparently contradictory narrative threads. In Chapter 6 the development of a sense of belonging in a new national context is illustrated through the stories shared by the seven women as they look back on their first interactions with their children's schools. In the analysis of these accounts, the details of what the process of acquiring a new sociocultural script involves are highlighted, as well as the key role of the community in finding spaces for agency in circumstances of vulnerability.

The significance of language resources and access to them is at the center of the next three chapters. In Chapter 7 some subtle and not-so-subtle ways in which exclusion is experienced in the formally inclusive spheres of US public schools are exposed by pointing to the paradoxical invisibility of language as a crucial symbolic resource, and illustrated in selected instances taken from the narratives of this group of women. While Chapter 8 centers on the consequences of the mediated quality of most interactions and how the power asymmetry of certain interactions can be accentuated by this factor, Chapter 9 introduces the notion of critical linguistic agency to illuminate how linguistic resources are accessed and shared. Chapters 9, 10 and 11 focus on the phenomenon of communal agency as embodied in the development and sharing of symbolic and material resources. In Chapter 10 immigration is explored as a gendered experience in which certain material resources such as physical mobility and documentation become crucial for independence. The notions of agency and structure which underlie all the chapters are at the center of the women's stories featured in Chapter 11. After the Conclusion, some final narratives presented by way of Epilogue illustrate the reach of educational motherwork beyond high school.

The excerpts from the interviews with Brenda, Luisa, Norma, Patricia, Sandra, Silvia and Susana included here appear in their original Spanish followed by a translation. This choice reflects a deeply held conviction that research conducted in multilingual contexts must be open about this process. The translations are provided as an aid to English-speaking readers but are not meant to replace the words of the interviewees; the analysis is based on the original. The names of all people and places have been changed to protect the confidentiality of the study participants.

# References

Chase, S. (2005). Narrative inquiry: Multiple lenses, approaches, voices. In N. Denzin & Y. Lincoln (Eds.), *The Sage handbook of qualitative research* (3rd ed., pp. 651–679). Thousand Oaks, CA: Sage.

Cibils, L. R. de (2011). *Immigrant women's narrative reconstruction of their interactions with their children's schools: A collective qualitative case study* (Doctoral Dissertation). New Mexico State University, Las Cruces.

González, N. (2005). *I am my language: Discourses of women and children in the borderlands*. Tucson, AZ: The University of Arizona Press.

## · 1 ·

# THE BIG PICTURE

## Immigration, Vulnerability and Marginalization

*All too often the freedom that Western women prize is won at the price of the enslavement of women elsewhere. To deny this fact is to deny the link between global capital and the local capitalist regime which governs our lives. When we remember that women are half of the human race, the poorest citizens on the planet performing approximately two-thirds of the world's work and earning about one tenth of the world's income and less than one-hundredth of its property, we face more directly the interconnectedness of race, class, and gender.* (hooks, 2000, p. 161)

The fundamental concern with social justice in the relationship of immigrant mothers with their children's schools at the basis of this book requires that we consider the broader context of the social conditions associated with immigration in the United States and the role of institutions in reproducing domination and oppression in the interactions of everyday life. This chapter provides an outline of some of the relevant transnational and national factors intervening in the phenomenon of immigration, explores it as a gendered experience, and exposes some of the crucial facets of the transition undergone by recent immigrant families of students entering the US school system.

## Immigration as a Social Outcome of Neoliberal Globalization

The data of population trends presented here pertain to a period relevant to the stories shared by the seven participants of a qualitative case study during three individual in-depth interviews which took place between 2008 and 2010 in a semirural area of a southwestern US border state. Worldwide, the percentage of people who were being displaced was increasing at a higher rate than world population, according to the figures in the report issued by the International Organization for Migration (IOM, 2005): "In 2005, there were 175 million international migrants in the world, that is, one out of every 35 persons in the world was an international migrant" (p. 379). These large population movements had their roots in neoliberal globalization, whose transnational economic consequences include the intensification of the rate of immigration from poor countries to rich ones, and a growth in part-time and contingency work (McLaren & Farahmandpur, 2001, p. 139). According to Falk (1994), among its inequitable socio-political outcomes, global capitalism contributed to create "a denationalized global elite that at the same time lacks any global civic sense of responsibility" (p. 135).

In the United States, the foreign-born Latin@ population continued to grow at an accelerated pace. Between July 2004 and July 2005, the increase in Latin@ population accounted for 49% of the total national population growth; almost 40% (500,000) of this increase was due to immigration (US Census Bureau, 2006). These figures, which only reflect one year's growth, offer a sense of the magnitude of the demographic changes occurring in US society at the time. They also contribute to underscore the need for an understanding of the processes that members of the immigrant Latin@ population go through as they interact with social institutions, such as schools, in their new environment.

## Extreme Vulnerability of Migrants: Globalization and the Feminization of Poverty

Bauman (2004) calls immigrants around the world the "casualties of rising vulnerability," and denounces the fact that displaced populations acquire the role of "deviant other" in governmental discourse as they become scapegoats used in the rhetoric of rationalization of the ravaging social evils politically generated by transnational neoliberal policies (Bauman, 2004, p. 56). In light of this description, to refer to parts of the immigrant population to the US as some of the most marginalized members of US society may well be an understatement at best. The gendered nature of these global phenomena has often been pointed out by critical feminist scholars.

In examining the need of the feminist movement to take a new direction which includes the struggle against economic injustice, hooks stresses the feminization of poverty among the global social problems to be addressed (2000, p. 109). Similarly, Schutte (2000) states, "The interests of transnational global capital hiding behind the purported neutrality of global consumption are not gender-neutral" (p. 61). In spelling out the workings of the global pauperization of women, hooks points to the interconnectedness of the privilege in some regions and the marginality in others. Further, hooks insists on the fact that the interlocking systems of domination derived from corporate interests and globalization are gendered and racialized. Within the social landscape of the US, hooks describes as "indentured slavery" the oppressive conditions created in part by the prison industry and the conservative immigration policies (p. 109).

In a clear illustration of globalization as a gendered process, Ong (2006) depicts the effects of neoliberalism on the lives of millions of migrant women across the globe. In her introduction to a series of ethnographic studies which shed light on the new versions of women slavery around the world, Ong (2006) expounds on how neoliberalism operates as a system of exception, which works selectively both to enforce privilege and to exclude, through "strategies that promote an economic logic in defining, evaluating, and protecting certain categories of subjects and not others" (p. 16). Although her research is set in East and Southeast Asia, it illuminates the vulnerability of migrant workers who are subject to economic exploitation and inhuman conditions, and are no longer protected as citizens of nation-states but instead fall under neoliberal exceptions within a globalized world.

## The Backdrop to Mexican Immigration to the US

Otero (2004) offers a political-economic context to the constant flow of migrants into the US from Mexico. One of several cycles of economic liberalism in Mexico started with the neoliberal restructuring, during the debt crisis in the 1980s, which involved the adoption of the conditions of international financial institutions for the restructuring of foreign debt by opening Mexico to the free markets, and dismantling all forms of protectionism, with the stated goal of "integrating Mexico more closely with the North American economy" (Otero, 2004, p. 9). If Mexico did not submit to the restructuring it would be left out from "the circuits of international finance (foreign loans and investment)" (Otero, 2004, p. 9). Mexico signed into NAFTA in 1994, joining the US and Canada through an agreement of economic collaboration. Mexico was seen by some analysts to have become part of the developed world by participating in this agreement, which may have been true for some sectors but for others it meant the extreme opposite (Otero, 2004, p. 10).

Within the framework of the North American Trade Act (NAFTA), and the unequal imposition of protectionist policies on either side of the US-Mexico border, Mexico has a deep dependency on trade with the United States for both its exports and imports. Exports to the US increased from 70% in the 1980s to a staggering 90%, and imports showed a marked rise (Otero, 2004, p. 11). Thus, as Otero stresses, Mexico's food sovereignty and its labor sovereignty may have been put at risk, challenged by the constant flow of workers who migrate to the United States in search of employment, given the job losses caused by the rural depletion (p. 11).

Arguably, trade agreements such as NAFTA are not the sole cause of poverty but they contributed to its intensification and to deepening its social consequences as millions of displaced workers are subject to exploitation and violence in extreme situations of vulnerability on both sides of the border (Bacon, 2004, p. 16). Bacon (2004) documents the dehumanizing consequences of NAFTA for workers, while at the same time, he underscores the power of collective organization through stories of social struggle on the border. The author explains that the title of his book, *The Children of NAFTA*, has several interrelated meanings: first, it refers to child labor brought about by the extreme poverty their families are steeped in; second, to the activists who have organized to resist its negative consequences; third, to the challenge of becoming involved, since "the inhabitants of all three countries [...] are now bound together by strong economic forces" so that, in a certain way, "we are all 'children of NAFTA'" (p. 16). This brings us back to the interconnectedness of privilege and marginalization, highlighted by bell hooks.

# Immigration and Marginalization in the United States: Racism and Xenophobia

In her research, Kristine Zentgraf (2002) describes the dire economic and so-cial conditions many working-class Salvadoran immigrant women encounter on their arrival in the US in terms which could apply to working-class immi-grants from different countries in Latin America:

> As a group, they are recruited to low-wage employment with few benefits and limited opportunities for economic mobility. Their poor working conditions and vulnera-bility to exploitation tend to be accentuated by limited access to legal status. Daily survival depends on the acquisition of at least the rudimentary elements of an unfa-miliar language and culture, which few of them possess on arrival. In addition, they periodically face hostile political climates [...] which include attacks on civil rights, scapegoating for social ills, and calls for restricting social services and for deportations [...]. (p. 625)

The anti-immigration sentiment is not a new phenomenon. Newcomers have historically been rejected and subjected to the symbolic violence of structural social exclusion (Bourdieu, 1991; De Vos & M. Suárez-Orozco, 1990; Shan-non & Escamilla, 1999; C. Suárez-Orozco, 2000, 2004). Tougher immigration policies tend to arrive hand in hand with renewed waves of xenophobic atti-tudes by which immigrants are perceived as having a negative socioeconom-ic impact for taking other people's jobs, depleting the social service system, contributing to the increase in crime and changing the face (and the sound) of society.

This nativistic rhetoric draws on the unfounded fears of the supposed economic drain caused by immigrants (M. Suárez-Orozco, 1990, p. 284). Anti-immigrant feelings, which usually rise when unemployment rates are higher, are often used by opportunistic politicians who adopt these misrep-resentations of immigrants as scapegoats in their own campaigns (C. Suárez-Orozco, 2000). One of the main underlying concerns which motivates "the anti-immigrant ethos" is "the fear of the cultural dilution of the country's Anglo-Saxon institutions and values" (p. 210). Zentgraf (2002) describes the impact of this hostile environment on immigrants as "heightening their sense of vulnerability and making them more reluctant to organize, change jobs, or access the social services to which they and their children are entitled" (p. 625). These attitudes are most likely also the product of a deep fear of deportation and its consequences.

The early roots of racism and xenophobia related to immigration policy are documented by Menchaca (1997) when she notes: "In the passage of the first Naturalization Act of 1790 our founding fathers declared that only free 'white' immigrants had the right to apply for citizenship" (p. 21). In more recent times, racism and xenophobia directed towards immigrants seem to remain untouched, within the context of a globalized economy, where "labor power is a unique commodity" (Cole, 2005). As Delgado-Gaitán and Trueba (1991) so eloquently expressed it over two decades ago, "they hire willing hands, but with the hands come bodies, and wives and children and extended families, and new languages and cultures" (p. 30). The same communities which benefit from an economic boost by opening their doors to immigrant populations who provide cheap labor have shown to be unprepared and/or unwilling to recognize the need to respond to this demographic transformation accordingly (Wortham, Murillo, & Hamann, 2002).

These issues were studied in a series of ethnographic studies focusing on the response of schools to the sociocultural phenomenon of the increased influx of Latin@ settlers arriving in regions of the United States not traditionally populated by Latin@s. Their findings, published in an edited collection, pointed to the widespread racism present in the host communities in its two manifestations: overt and covert (Wortham et al., 2002). Overt racism, on the one hand, is fed by stereotypical myths spread in the receiving community by powerful sectors such as the media, who misrepresent the newcomers through stories which focus on whether immigrants are documented or not, and create stereotypes of the unruly behavior of Latin@s, and their draining of the social services (Murillo, 2002; Villenas, 2002). As Houston and Pulido (2005) denounce, "a highly racialized picture has been created of an exploding mass of Latino parasites that burden communities and institutions: Latino immigrants are not constructed as workers, or members of the working class—they are 'illegals', and thus not deserving of consideration" (p. 325).

Covert racism or benevolent racism, on the other hand, is embodied in a paternalistically pro-immigration script which accepts the newcomers as workers, because they are hardworking and willing to take jobs no one else will, but not as whole human beings (Hamann, 2002, p. 79; Murillo, 2002, p. 225). In this neocolonialist view, society is portrayed as divided into givers and takers, where the traditional residents assume they know what is best for the newcomers, and tend to make decisions aimed towards assimilation. The latter form of racism is believed to be the most insidious and dangerous, since in refusing Latin@ immigrants any voice in the debate over policies which affect them directly, it denies them agency and, in so doing, it has dehumanizing effects (Hamann, 2002; Murillo, 2002).

## Immigration, Racism and Schooling

In terms of policy and practices, within a cultural deficit model, the arrival of Latin@s with their linguistic and cultural differences is constructed as a problem and a burden (Murillo, 2002; Nieto, 2004; M. Suárez-Orozco, 1990; Valencia, 1997; Valenzuela, 1999; Villenas, 2002). Since schools are the main actors in the debate as to whether cultural differences are to be celebrated through pluralism or erased through the assimilation of the newcomers, schools can be defined as "instruments of cultural policy" (Hamann, 2002, p. 68). The manifestation of structural racism in the inequitable situations for students whose home language is different from English is described by Giroux (1992) as follows:

> The language of schooling is implicated in forms of racism that attempt to silence the voices of subordinate groups whose primary language is not English and whose cultural capital is either marginalized or denigrated by the dominant culture of schooling. (p. 203)

In their chapter on education policy in Georgia, Beck and Allexsaht-Snider (2002) draw on Bourdieu's (1991) social theory to denounce official language initiatives as realizations of linguicism and instances of symbolic violence (p. 41). The *modus operandi* of structural linguicism, or discrimination based on language, is described by Skutnabb-Kangas and Phillipson (1995) as follows:

> Ethnicisim and linguicism socially construct the resources of powerless groups so that they become invisible or are seen as handicaps. In this way minority resources, among them their languages and cultures, become non-resources, hence cannot be converted to other resources or to positions of structural power. At the same time the resources of the dominant groups, among them their languages and cultures, are socially constructed so that they are seen as resources and can thus be converted into other resources or to positions of structural power. (pp. 105–106)

Symbolic violence is an insidious and covert form of domination, "an aspect of most forms of power which are deployed in social life," which are invisible and enjoy a certain degree of legitimacy (Bourdieu, 1991, p. 23). This power is particularly effective because "it presupposes certain forms of cognition or belief, in such a way that even those who benefit least from the exercise of power participate, to some extent, in their own subjection" (Bourdieu, 1991, p. 23).

Many newly arrived students and families begin their school experience highly motivated but often encounter barriers and disappointment in the way they are received (C. Suárez-Orozco, 2000, pp. 197, 220). As a direct consequence of the assimilationist environment on the family, parents may become somewhat alienated from their own children and find that the generation gap is rapidly intensified, since their children may adapt to the dominant culture and adopt the second language much faster. In their need to be accepted by their peers in their new context, children may even resist speaking their first language altogether if they perceive that it is not valued in the school culture (Delgado-Gaitán & Trueba, 1991; C. Suárez-Orozco & M. Suárez-Orozco, 2001).

In her ethnographic study, Cynthia Bejarano (2005) describes the predicament of Mexican immigrant students attending a borderland high school whose Latin@ classmates would label them "'ESL,' marking them according to their educational level, or would more offensively call them 'wetbacks'" (p. 172). Besides serving to illustrate the effects of hegemony and neocolonialism on Latin@ students, this use of ESL as a disparaging label speaks of the connection established between language classes (or ESL) and low level tracking in schools. In many cases, Latin@ immigrant students may find themselves placed into lower level tracks where class is devoted to filling out worksheets or to drill and rote exercises, instead of being an enriching learning environment where their talents are tapped and their backgrounds respected. Not surprisingly, these students may soon be discouraged, and find the school experience inadequate and even humiliating (Delgado-Gaitán & Trueba, 1991, pp. 121–124). Within the context of a critique of the racialized effects of globalization on education in general, and of high stakes testing specifically, McLaren and Jaramillo (2007) cite dropout data relevant to this study which are both alarming and outrageous: "Across ethnic groups, Latina/o have the highest high school dropout rate, nearly 28%, and for newly arrived immigrants, the dropout rate stands at 40%" (p. 104). These figures pertain to the time period alluded to in the interviews of the seven women whose experience is at the heart of this book.

# The Local Context of the Study

This broad national and transnational context of immigration and of some of its social consequences is provided as a backdrop to the stories and counter stories of parental involvement shared and analyzed here. The participants interviewed for the study at the center of this book are a group of immigrant women whose children attended public schools in several villages and a small town in a rural area of the Southwest of the United States, located approximately 80 miles away from the border with Mexico, and 40 miles from the closest city, Los Puentes. The school district in question serves approximately 1,500 students, through three elementary schools, a middle school and a high school. According to the student demographic data on the district's report card posted on its official web site, at the time of the interviews the student body is described as 90% Hispanic and 10% Caucasian; 50% of students are classified as English Language Learners, with 100% participating in the Free/Reduced Lunch program. These factors place all schools in the district in the High Poverty Schools category. This research site was chosen for the high influx of Mexican immigrant families and the rural context which contrasts with the site of a majority of comparable studies carried out in larger, more densely populated, urban areas.

The women who were interviewed for the study this book draws on have been directly affected by the social and economic global conditions outlined above, as the shifts undergone in their lives when migrating to the US from Mexico are part of the larger story of transnational displacement. The seven women are working mothers, whose occupations include seasonal agricultural jobs, both picking crops as well as doing grading in the processing plants; janitorial work, cleaning houses and offices; as well as caretaking, as children's nannies or in-home caregivers for elderly patients. The political and economic context bears heavily on the narratives of the participants as they reconstruct the development of strategies, resources and stances in the negotiations of their interactions with the schools. The focus of this book is on how within situations of vulnerability created by structural and institutional inequality associated with immigration there is a communal response characterized by resourcefulness and the development of agency, as told by the seven women in their stories of engagement in their children's education.

# References

Bacon, D. (2004). *The children of NAFTA: Labor wars on the U.S./Mexico border.* Berkeley, CA: University of California Press.

Bauman, Z. (2004). *Wasted lives: Modernity and its outcasts.* Cambridge and Malden, MA: Polity.

Beck, S., & Allexsaht-Snider, M. (2002). Recent language minority education policy in Georgia: Appropriation, assimilation, and Americanization. In S. Wortham, E. Murillo, & E. Hamann (Eds.), *Education in the new Latino diaspora: Policy and the politics of identity* (pp. 37–66). Westport, CT: Ablex.

Bejarano, C. (2005). *¿Qué onda?: Urban youth cultures and border identity.* Tucson, AZ: The University of Arizona Press.

Bourdieu, P. (1991). *Language and symbolic power* (G. Raymond & M. Adamson, Trans.). Cambridge, MA: Harvard University Press.

Cole, M. (2005). New labour, globalization and social justice: The role of education. In G. Fischman, P. McLaren, H. Sünker, & C. Lankshear (Eds.), *Critical theories, radical pedagogies, and global conflicts* (pp. 3–22). Lanham, MD: Rowman and Littlefield.

De Vos, G., & Suárez-Orozco, M. (1990). *Status inequality: The self in culture.* Newbury Park, CA: Sage.

Delgado-Gaitán, C., & Trueba, H. (1991). *Crossing cultural borders: Education for immigrant families in America.* New York, NY and London: Falmer Press.

Falk, R. (1994). The making of global citizenship. In B. van Steenbergen (Ed.), *The condition of citizenship* (pp. 127–140). London and Thousand Oaks, CA: Sage.

Giroux, H. (1992). Resisting difference: Cultural studies and the discourse of critical pedagogy. In L. Grossberg, C. Nelson, & P. Treichler (Eds.), *Cultural studies* (pp. 199–212). New York, NY: Routledge.

Hamann, E. (2002). ¿Un paso adelante? The politics of bilingual education, Latino student accommodation, and school district management in Southern Appalachia. In S. Wortham, E. Murillo, & E. Hamann (Eds.), *Education in the new Latino diaspora: Policy and the politics of identity* (pp. 67–97). Westport, CT: Ablex.

hooks, b. (2000). *Where we stand: Class matters.* New York, NY: Routledge.

Houston, D., & Pulido, L. (2005). The work of performativity: Staging social justice at the University of Southern California. In G. Fischman, P. McLaren, H. Sünker, & C. Lankshear (Eds.), *Critical theories, radical pedagogies, and global conflicts* (pp. 317–342). Lanham, MD: Rowman and Littlefield.

International Organization for Migration (IOM). (2005). *World migration 2005—Vol. 3. IOM World Migration Report Series.* Geneva: IOM. Retrieved July 15, 2007 from http://www.iom.int

McLaren, P., & Farahmandpur, R. (2001). Teaching against globalization and the new imperialism: Toward a revolutionary pedagogy. *Journal of Teacher Education, 52*(2), 136–150.

McLaren, P., & Jaramillo, N. (2007). *Pedagogy and praxis in the age of empire: Towards a new humanism.* Rotterdam: Sense.

Menchaca, M. (1997). Early racist discourses: The roots of deficit thinking. In R. Valencia (Ed.), *The evolution of deficit thinking: Educational thought and practice* (pp. 13–40). Washington, DC: RoutledgeFalmer.

Murillo, E. (2002). How does it feel to be a *problem?*: "Disciplining" the transnational subject in the American South. In S. Wortham, E. Murillo, & E. Hamann (Eds.), *Education in the new Latino diaspora: Policy and the politics of identity* (pp. 215–240). Westport, CT: Ablex.

Nieto, S. (2004). *Affirming diversity: The sociopolitical context of multicultural education.* Boston, MA: Pearson.

Ong, A. (2006). *Neoliberalism as exception: Mutations in citizenship and sovereignty.* Durham, NC: Duke University Press.

Otero, G. (Ed.). (2004). *Mexico in transition: Neoliberal globalism, the state and civil society.* London and New York, NY: Zed Books.

Schutte, O. (2000). Cultural alterity: Cross-cultural communication and feminist theory in North-South contexts. In U. Narayan & S. Harding (Eds.), *Decentering the center: Philosophy for a multicultural, postcolonial, and feminist world* (pp. 47–66). Bloomington, IN and Indianapolis, IN: Indiana University Press.

Shannon, S., & Escamilla, K. (1999). Mexican immigrants in U.S. schools: Targets of symbolic violence. *Education Policy, 13*(3), 347–370.

Skutnabb-Kangas, T., & Phillipson, R. (1995). Linguistic human rights, past and present. In T. Skutnabb-Kangas & R. Phillipson (Eds.), *Linguistic human rights: Overcoming linguistic discrimination* (pp. 71–110). Berlin and New York, NY: Mouton de Gruyter.

Suárez-Orozco, C. (2000). Identities under siege: Immigration, stress and social mirroring among the children of immigrants. In C. Robben & M. Suárez-Orozco (Eds.), *Cultures under siege: Collective violence and trauma* (pp. 194–226). New York, NY and Cambridge: Cambridge University Press.

Suárez-Orozco, C. (2004). Formulating identity in a globalized world. In M. Suárez-Orozco, & D. Baolian Qin-Hilliard (Eds.), *Globalization: Culture and education in the new millennium* (pp. 173–202). Berkeley: University of California Press.

Suárez-Orozco, C., & Suárez-Orozco, M. (2001). *Children of immigration.* Cambridge, MA: Harvard University Press.

Suárez-Orozco, M. (1990). Migration and education: United States-Europe comparisons. In G. De Vos & M. Suárez-Orozco (Eds.), *Status inequality: The self in culture* (pp. 265–287). Newbury Park, CA: Sage.

US Census Bureau. (2006). *Nation's population one-third minority.* Washington, DC: U.S. Department of Commerce. Retrieved May 16, 2008 from http://www.census.gov/PressRelease/www/releases/archives/population/006808.html

Valencia, R. (Ed.). (1997). *The evolution of deficit thinking: Educational thought and practice.* Washington, DC: Falmer Press.

Valenzuela, A. (1999). *Subtractive schooling: U.S.-Mexican youth and the politics of caring.* Albany, NY: State University of New York Press.

Villenas, S. (2002). Reinventing "educación" in new Latino communities: Pedagogies of change and continuity in North Carolina. In S. Wortham, E. Murillo, & E. Hamann

(Eds.), *Education in the new Latino diaspora: Policy and the politics of identity* (pp. 17–35). Westport, CT: Ablex.

Wortham, S., Murillo, E., & Hamann, E. (2002). *Education in the new Latino diaspora: Policy and the politics of identity*. Westport, CT: Ablex.

Zentgraf, K. (2002). Immigration and women's empowerment: Salvadorans in Los Angeles. *Gender & Society, 16*(5), 625–646.

## · 2 ·

# A SITUATED THEORY OF JUSTICE

## The Significance of Structure, Process and Agency

*According to this principle, justice requires social arrangements that permit all to participate as peers in social life. On the view of justice as participatory parity, overcoming injustice means dismantling institutionalized obstacles that prevent some people from participating on a par with others, as full partners in social interaction.* (Fraser, 2010, p. 60)

The lens adopted in the analysis and presentation of the stories of the seven immigrant women introduced in the next chapter draws on critical social theory, most prominently on critical feminist conceptualizations of social justice expounded by Young (1990, 1997) and Fraser (1997, 1998, 2003, 2010). From this perspective, for a theory of justice to have any transformative power or be effective in any significant way it must be contextualized and situated: "If the theory is truly universal and independent, presupposing no particular social situations, institutions or practices, then it is simply too abstract to be useful in evaluating actual situations and practices" (Young, 1990, p. 4). This approach requires, not only an analysis of the patterns and structures of production and reproduction of inequity, but also a focus on the processes that generate and sustain these patterns, perpetuating them. In other words, a situated view of justice takes into account the articulation of agency and structure as manifested in everyday social interactions and institutional practices (Wharton, 1991; Young, 1990).

# Young's Theory of Social Justice: The Five Faces of Oppression

Central to Young's (1990) critical theory of justice is its focus on the need to understand social processes as well as patterns. By focusing on the processes which produce and reproduce these regularities, this perspective avoids isolating individuals and their actions from institutional structures and large-scale patterns. Thus, instead of an abstraction "from the temporal flow of everyday interaction," this theory provides an articulation of structure and agency within a "temporal approach to social reality" (pp. 28, 30). Further, it points to a dynamic and relational conceptualization of power which has a structural basis and is reproduced through the interactions of many people who are not necessarily only those who hold most power or privilege.

At the core of her definition of social justice, Young (1990) places the absence of domination and oppression and insists on the need that they too be understood not only structurally, but also dynamically and relationally, as processes:

> By domination I mean structural or systemic phenomena which exclude people from participating in determining their actions or the conditions of their actions. Domination must be understood as structural because the constraints that people experience are usually the intended or unintended product of the actions of many people [...] The structured operation of domination whose resources the powerful draw upon must be understood as processes. (p. 31)

A crucial factor stressed here, which moves away from traditional theories of justice, is the need for the responsibility for behaviors which contribute to oppression to be separated from intentionality of institutions or people. According to Young, a model of justice which focuses on intention or consciousness is too narrow. For structural social change to be effective in interrupting cycles of exclusion and disadvantage will require "forward-looking remedies of institutions whose unconscious and unintended actions contribute to that disadvantage" (p. 151).

This understanding of justice includes the institutional conditions for self-development as well as for cooperation (p. 39). Oppression is defined as "the institutional constraint on self-development" and domination as "the institutional constraint on self-determination" (Young, 1990, p. 37). Young (1990) proposes that the structural aspect of oppression is materialized in what she has termed its five faces: exploitation, marginalization, powerlessness, cultural imperialism, and violence. These last two notions, namely, cultural imperialism and violence, carry special import for the seven women's narratives. Cultural imperialism creates the conditions for members of a group to undergo the paradoxical dual experience of invisibility while becoming simultaneously the deviant other (pp. 58–60). The conditions of injustice which characterize cultural imperialism are portrayed in these terms: "that the oppressed group's own experience and interpretation of social life finds little expression that touches the dominant culture, while that same culture imposes on the oppressed group its experience and interpretation of social life" (p. 60). Given that the dominant culture imposes its own perspectives as neutral and universal, this implies political and social exclusion of individuals and groups who fall outside of these naturalized norms.

Cultural imperialism goes hand in hand with segregation and marginalization, manifested in racist exclusion by which "the devaluation of the bodies of some groups still conditions everyday interactions among groups, despite our relative success at expelling such bodily evaluation from discursive consciousness" (p. 61). Young (1990) notes how the culturally oppressed have and do struggle to "take over definition of themselves and assert a positive sense of group difference," and adds that for justice to be actualized requires that a political space be made for such difference (p. 61).

Another relevant facet of oppression, drawn from this theory, is the notion of systemic violence which is directed against members of a group just for belonging to that group. According to Young (1990), the very threat of xenophobic irrational violence "deprives the oppressed of freedom and dignity, and needlessly expends their energy" (p. 62). The intersecting oppressive forces of cultural imperialism and violence are institutionalized and systemic, and may be encouraged or tolerated by institutions and daily practices. Therefore, there is a need for the study of the perspectives of members of oppressed groups on their experience of everyday interactions with institutions to open up spaces for self-definition.

The focus on oppression and domination in Young's theorization of justice becomes pivotal to the contextualization of immigrant women's stories because it takes into account cultural imperialism and xenophobia, and their latent violence, which are vital factors to bear in mind, given their impact on immigrant populations and their everyday experiences in their new contexts. In this study, as it was foreseen, the daily experiences of exclusion and invisibility of immigrant women in their relations with school officials challenge the official discourse of parental involvement defined in dominant cultural terms and adopted in education policy.

The inquiry into the narratives of a group of women's negotiation of social spaces also benefits from Young's temporal and situated approach to social reality, as each instance of interaction was studied with a view to an understanding of the process of power dynamics, and the articulation of structure and agency as it is realized in the flow of everyday life. Given its focus on social processes and interactions in different institutional contexts, Young's theory of social justice is particularly pertinent.

## Bourdieu and Foucault:
## Symbolic Violence and Normalization

Although the notions of normalization and symbolic violence are not explicitly part of the critical feminist theory of social justice, these concepts are embedded in the broader context of a critical feminist approach and are ultimately bound by its overarching focus and purpose. Closely connected to Young's theory, Bourdieu (1991) defines "symbolic violence" in contrast to overt violence as "a mechanism through which power is exercised and simultaneously disguised" (p. 23). Symbolic violence is an insidious and covert form of domination, and refers mostly to "an aspect of most forms of power which are deployed in social life," which is invisible and enjoys a certain degree of legitimacy (Bourdieu, 1991, p. 23). This power is particularly effective because "it presupposes certain forms of cognition or belief, in such a way that even those who benefit least from the exercise of power participate, to some extent, in their own subjection" (Bourdieu, 1991, p. 23).

Given the propensity of school agents—staff, teachers and officials—and their practices to be imbued in the dominant culture, and the likelihood of asymmetrical relationships to be established in such a context, the narratives of the interactions between the immigrant women and the schools refer to the types of sites where this form of domination is highly probable. One aspect of the home-school interface which was anticipated to manifest characteristics of symbolic violence was the more or less implicit but widespread implementation of institutional standards for the evaluation of parent involvement (Lareau & Weininger, 2003, p. 589).

The study was also informed by Foucault's (1984) theory of power and specifically his concept of normalization. Foucault (1984) describes the disciplinary systems governing institutions such as schools and how they operate to "normalize" behavior through punishment, in these words: "The perpetual penalty that traverses all points and supervises every instant in the disciplinary institutions compares, differentiates, hierarchizes, homogenizes, excludes. In short, it normalizes" (Foucault, 1984, p. 195). In social institutions, derived from the end of the classical age, he adds, "normalization becomes one of the great instruments of power" which "imposes homogeneity" and where "the nonconforming is punishable" (Foucault, 1984, pp. 194–196).

Within this theoretical framework, normalization may be seen as one of the processes by which cultural domination operates. In the context of this inquiry, it was anticipated to be found, for example, operating hand in hand with symbolic violence in the imposition by the school of its expectations for parents—which in the context of schools very often means mothers. These expectations may be implied, and not necessarily understood equally by both parts. Parents, or mothers, may be classified, explicitly or implicitly, according to whether they are seen as complying with these expectations or not. The punishment for working-class immigrant mothers, for example, if seen as non-compliant, may materialize in general attitudes of less deference, and in the response or lack thereof to requests or concerns related to their children's education or treatment.

## Fraser's Theory of Social Justice: Participation Parity as the Norm

At the most basic conceptual level, the inquiry at the center of this book rests on an understanding of social justice drawn from Fraser's (1997, 1998, 2003, 2010) work. This theorization of social justice which integrates both the claims of the politics of redistribution and the politics of recognition, requires a normative criterion. The norm suggested by Fraser (1998) to be applied to justice claims is participatory parity, defined as the possibility for groups and individuals to participate on a par with others in social interaction (p. 25). For the interaction of all members of society as peers to be possible, there are at least two prerequisites which correspond to each of the paradigms of justice, redistribution and recognition, based on both material and cultural parameters (p. 30).

The first requirement proposed by Fraser for participation parity to be feasible is the "objective" prerequisite, associated with the distribution of material resources which would guarantee independence and voice, as indispensable to participation. This precondition precludes "social arrangements that institutionalize deprivation, exploitation, and gross disparities in wealth, income and leisure time, thereby denying some people the means and opportunities to interact with others as peers" (Fraser, 1998, p. 31). The second prerequisite for participation parity is "intersubjective" and requires that all members of society are guaranteed "equal opportunity for social esteem" by means of "institutionalized cultural patterns of interpretation and evaluation" which "express equal respect for all participants" (Fraser, 1998, p. 31). Fraser (1998) further explains the second precondition for participation parity, or the "intersubjective" prerequisite, in the following terms:

> This condition precludes cultural patterns that systematically depreciate some categories of people and the qualities associated with them. Precluded, therefore, are institutionalized value schemata that deny some people the status of full partners in interaction—whether by burdening them with excessive ascribed "difference" from others or by failing to acknowledge their distinctiveness. (p. 31)

Thus this prerequisite addresses the same paradox of invisibility and deviance as exposed by Young in her definition of cultural domination. The two sets of conditions of participation parity, objective and intersubjective, correspond to the claims of both traditionally dissociated theories of justice, the theory of distributive justice, and the philosophy of recognition; the former, addressing inequities in the economic structure of society; the latter, focusing on the "culturally defined hierarchies of status" (Fraser, 1998, p. 32). The author synthesizes the operation of her theory of justice as follows: "Thus, a bivalent conception of justice oriented to the norm of participatory parity encompasses both redistribution and recognition, without reducing either one to the other" (p. 32).

By adopting parity of participation as the norm for justice claims, and its two preconditions, Fraser's theory not only integrates the two paradigms of justice (of redistribution and of recognition) but also avoids falling into the trap of psychologically-based concepts of misrecognition which ultimately may lead to "blame-the-victim" explanations of social inequity (p. 26). Fraser (1998) propounds her thesis by referring to institutional misrecognition as follows:

> It is rather to be denied the status of a full partner in social interaction and prevented from participating as a peer in social life as a consequence of institutionalized patterns of interpretation and evaluation that constitute one as comparatively unworthy of

respect or esteem. When such patterns of disrespect and disesteem are institutional-ized, for example in law, social welfare, medicine, public education, and/or the social practices and group mores that structure everyday interaction, they impede parity of participation, just as surely as do distributive inequities. (p. 26)

Thus, Fraser (1998) proposes that, when applying the norm of participation parity, overcoming institutionalized misrecognition becomes a matter of jus-tice in its interconnection with redistribution, since it refers to social relations and not individual psychology, and determines access to societal resources.

The stories shared throughout this book offer insights into moments of in-teraction which allow the contextualization and embodiment of some of these abstract concepts, through the analysis of institutional practices of schools as perceived and narrated by the group of immigrant mothers who defined their participation in these social interactions. These are examined against the norm of social justice proposed by Fraser of parity of participation, by which all adult members of society become full partners in societal interactions.

## The Matrix of Oppression in Critical, Black, and Chicana Feminisms

A critical feminist perspective focuses on intersectionality (Cho, Crenshaw, & McCall, 2013) and is founded on a commitment to the struggle against gender oppression as it interconnects with racism and class elitism. It views structures and practices as gendered and gendering, as well as marked by class and race, and focuses on understanding and dismantling the ways in which social ineq-uity is reproduced based on these categories of difference (Wharton, 1991). One of the central principles of a critical feminist approach is spelled out by Weiler (1988) in these terms: "A feminist theory that seeks social transfor-mation must take into account all forms of oppression and must actively resist them" (p. 64).

In her classic work, *Women Teaching for Change: Gender, Class and Power*, Weiler (1988) goes on to stress the need for the recognition of differences be-tween women, in an admission of the exclusivist generalizations of feminism which took as their norm the realities of white middle-class women:

Too often in studies of gender oppression, the effects of class and racial discrimina-tion and the structural nature of racism and classism are ignored. Instead, women are treated as a single group, with no further differences among themselves. But blindness to race and class leads to as much distortion of social reality as does blindness to the importance of gender. (p. 64)

Thus, Weiler draws attention to the concerns which should occupy critical feminist inquiry in these terms: "So in grounding ourselves and the objects of our research in gender we must not lose sight of the complex web of power and powerlessness resulting from our class and race positions as well" (p. 64).

Prominent theorists of Black feminism have proposed further elucidations of the interconnectedness among different forms of oppression. hooks (2000b) underscores the need to "take into consideration the ways interlocking systems of classism, racism, and sexism work to keep women exploited and oppressed" (p. 109); as an acknowledgement of this system of oppression is the "only hope of feminist liberation" which allows the creation of "a vision of social change" (p. 109). In the same vein, Collins (2000) refers to "intersectional paradigms" in which "race, class, gender, and sexuality constitute mutually constructing systems of oppression" (p. 228). In a statement which positions Black feminism within the larger paradigm of critical theory, Collins (2000) most clearly defines the "critical" aspect of feminism in her inclusive discourse:

> As critical social theory, Black feminist thought encompasses bodies of knowledge and sets of institutional practices that actively grapple with the central questions facing U.S. Black women as a group. Such theory recognizes that U.S. Black women constitute one group among many that are differently placed within situations of injustice. What makes critical social theory "critical" is its commitment to justice, for one's own group and for other groups. (p. 31)

Black feminist theory goes further in explaining how domination operates structurally through a "matrix of domination" which, according to Collins (2000), describes the "overall social organization within which intersecting oppressions originate, develop and are contained" (pp. 227–228). This domination takes place through social institutions such as "schools, housing, employment, government" among others (p. 228). Collins (2000), hooks (2000a, 2000b) and Hurtado (1996), from their distinctive standpoints, highlight the need to recognize the strategic centrality of class and race in feminist thought. Specifically, Hurtado (1996, 2000) refers to the significance of the struggle over the conditions of working-class women.

As a corollary to the matrix of domination theory, both Black and Chicana feminists have agreed in proposing that women of color occupy a position which may be defined as triple oppression in terms of race, class and gender (hooks, 2000a, p. 16; Hurtado, 1996, p. 46, 2000, p. 139; Lorde, 1995, p. 288). Black and Chicana feminist theorists concur as well in their rejection of a colonialist outlook which would dwell on powerlessness and victimization, and choose to emphasize instead "the joys of struggle" and "highlight the resistance" (Hurtado, 2000, p. 139). Further, given this matrix, it has been argued that women of color occupy a unique location from which to formulate a system of knowledge which may contribute to an understanding of issues relevant to and in solidarity with diverse historically marginalized groups.

## Author Contextualization: A View from Somewhere

Reflexivity about how a study is conducted, as an ongoing process during the inquiry, is a crucial component of critical feminist research (Riessman, 2008, pp. 191, 221). Reinharz and Chase (2003) refer to the centrality of reflection on social location and the relational aspect of feminist research in these terms, "What feminist researchers share, regardless of their status as insider or outsider in relation to interviewees, is a commitment to reflecting on the complexities of their own and participants' social locations and subjectivities" (p. 84).

A feminist epistemological approach embraces the notion of situated knowledges which, as Haraway (1988) argues, subverts the concepts of neutrality and objectivity by proposing that "the view from nowhere" be transformed into the view from somewhere which is embodied and situated (p. 590). Haraway (1988) notes that situated knowledges are the alternative both to relativism and to the totalizing claims of objectivity. The epistemological perspective of situated knowledges is adopted here within the broader antifoundational interpretivist paradigm and in congruence with the focus of this study, which centers on the narrative reconstruction by a group of immigrant women of their stances, resources and strategies developed in the process of negotiating their interactions with their children's schools.

The possibility of arriving at an unbiased truth, based on the objective observation of reality, in which observer and observed are separate and unrelated has been deeply questioned under the influence of postmodernism and its "emphasis on the social construction of social reality, fluid as opposed to fixed identities of the self, and, the partiality of all truths" (Guba & Lincoln, 2005, p. 204), and especially, by feminist epistemologists (Olesen, 2003). Harding (1993), for instance, in her definition of "strong objectivity," proposes investigating and making the relation between subject and object of knowledge explicit, instead of denying its existence (p. 63). This feminist epistemologist stresses the need to identify the values which shape science agendas, as a way of demystifying objectivity.

Along similar lines, in her argument for situated knowledges, Haraway (1988) notes that feminist research often privileges subjugated standpoints, not because they are "innocent" vantage points or unproblematic, "On the contrary, they are preferred because in principle they are least likely to allow denial of the critical and interpretive core of all knowledge" (p. 584). The collective, unfinished, and ongoing character of the process of developing (embodied) situated knowledges is emphasized thus:

> Situated knowledges are about communities, not about isolated individuals. The only way to find a larger vision is to be somewhere in particular. The science question in feminism is about objectivity as positioned rationality. Its images are not the products of escape and transcendence of limits (the view from above) but the joining of partial views and halting voices into a collective subject position that promises a vision of the means of ongoing finite embodiment, of living within limits and contradictions –of views from somewhere. (Haraway, 1988, p. 590)

Situated knowledges, Haraway (1988) continues, are as much an alternative to relativism ("the position from everywhere") as to the totalizing claims of objectivity (the single vision of authority, or "the position from nowhere"), which are similar in that "both deny the stakes in location, embodiment, and partial perspective" (p. 584). The author concludes: "Relativism and totalization are both 'god tricks' promising vision from everywhere and nowhere equally and fully, common myths in rhetorics surrounding Science" (Haraway, 1988, p. 584).

In embracing a critical feminist approach to research, I present here an account of how I situate myself within the study. The situations that draw me closer to the participants are those of my own cultural shock and first-hand experience of misunderstandings when interacting with the schools at the time I immigrated into the United States. At this stage, when I can make myself understood better and understand the system and the lingo better, I can say I am very grateful to the majority of hard-working and committed teachers who have devoted so much time to my children's education. But I am still a foreigner with a hard-to-pin-down accent. Although I am a privileged white bilingual Latina immigrant who has had enormous opportunities for education both in my country of origin and in the United States, to a xenophobe, I would probably be, first and foremost, an alien.

The daily experience of different individuals and groups of people in their interactions with institutions is likely to reflect wide variations which if carefully observed would probably present patterns closely correlated to their perceived social location—determined by race, class, gender, age, among other factors, and their intersections. Yet, as immigrants we often share some anecdotal measures of differential treatment based on sounding foreign, as evidenced in the questions an immigrant person is bound to be asked in public places by virtual strangers, "But where are you *really* from?", or "I perceive an *accent*, where is it from?" sometimes followed by "Are you planning to go back home?" As illustrated in these, some of the mildest and most innocuous instances, even after decades of having made her home in the US, a person may be subtly reminded on a regular basis of her perceived outsider status. If the answer to the first question happens to point somewhere south of the border, the geographic or cultural curiosity and interest in the exotic will probably not be pursued beyond the initial exchange.

I was born, raised and educated in Argentina during the infamous military dictatorships. My public school experience in elementary school, which in those days in my home country went from first to seventh grade, was one of racial and class segregation. Although the town in which I grew up in southern Patagonia was quite distant from the border with Chile, it had the feel of a border region, as much of the population had immigrated for work, and the nearest city was in Chile. Each one of the early grades in elementary school was divided into four sections, A, B, C, and D, which were closely correlated with class, race, national origin and relative economic standing of the families within the town. Although, in those days there were no extremely wealthy families in my hometown, the differences were clearly marked in school. For example, all the teachers' children were placed in section A, while coincidently all the newly immigrated children from the poor neighborhoods, who in extreme cases had no running water in their homes, would be placed in section D. The justification was one of meritocracy and academic levels but it did not take much close observation to recognize the systematic social segregation based on an ideology of class and racial superiority at work. In this context, I grew up as a white privileged child who attended section A and was keenly aware of these disparities.

When I immigrated into the United States as an adult, in the early 2000s, I found that surviving in a different country requires some relearning. Most obviously, for any immigrant from a non-English speaking country, there are language barriers to be overcome. I was raised bilingually, speaking English and Spanish at home. I also studied English since the age of four; I learned to read and write in English with a family friend in a small after-school class of bilingual children; also, I did four years of college in a teacher preparation program for teachers of English as a Foreign Language (EFL), and I hold an undergraduate degree in English-Spanish translation. English was not only part of my home life and my education but also of my professional experience, since most of my adult life in Argentina I worked either as an English-Spanish translator or as an instructor of EFL. Further, my family and I had already lived in the United States a few years earlier when I attended graduate school. Thus, in theory, language barriers should not have posed a major problem, except for the regional variations and specialized lingo.

As a mother of two young school-aged children, I did my homework before moving. As I lived in a relatively remote town in Patagonia, I was used to using Internet mostly as a source of current teaching materials and for research in general. So as soon as our move was confirmed, I researched the southwestern city of our destination, starting by the school districts. As an educator myself, and the daughter and granddaughter of teachers, education had always been in my family *"lo único valioso que les podemos dejar"* (the only valuable inheritance we can pass on). So, thinking ahead about my children's education was one of my highest priorities. I was excited at all the information I could find about specific schools. I studied school report cards, reported crime in the schools, parent surveys, and school academic standing as reflected in the test results—which it took me a while to interpret. Coming from so far away, this was all I had to go by. The city seemed to be marked by extreme contrasts. So I chose two elementary schools that seemed to be doing really well and, in fact, looked like the best public schools in the city. It also helped that they had appealing school web sites. I also found a map of the area of influence of each school. So I printed out all this information, and packed it in my suitcase.

Once in the States, we secured affordable housing at walking distance from one of the schools. It happened to be the only apartment complex in an otherwise upper-middle to upper class neighborhood. On the second day, we showed up at the school and went through the process of registering my children, filling out forms and more forms. It was mid-March, which coincided with the beginning of the school year for us in Argentina, but was closer to the end of the school year in the United States. Since then we have moved once more, and we have gone through the process of registration and negotiation of new situations over and over.

In spite of my privileged circumstances regarding education, language skills, and access to information, I did not find this process to be easy. I have since wondered what made my interactions with the schools at that time so hard, not only during registration but at every other unfamiliar situation: open house and parent-teacher conferences, among others. Some of my doubts centered on not knowing what questions to ask, who to ask, or even if I should ask, but also not knowing what to expect or what was expected of me, as a parent. Further, it was unsettling not to understand exactly the implications of the decisions being made about what classes my children were being placed in, or what their teachers were saying about their achievement. What did it all imply? Even when I thought I understood the words being spoken, I was not sure I had access to all the meaning. Then, again, when negotiating the process of filling out forms, when I first enrolled them in school: What significance did it have whether I checked "Anglo" or "Hispanic" in the slot for ethnicity? Did it make any difference what occupation I declared? However unsettling these circumstances were for me, since then I have wondered how much harder the experience must be for immigrant mothers who may not enjoy some of the privileges and resources I had, such as relatively easy access to information.

Several situations stand out as those where I felt powerless and confused as an immigrant mother who did not know yet that parents have a right to advocate for their children in school. Two weeks after we had arrived in the southwestern state, both my children, who at the time attended elementary school, were submitted to long testing sessions and came home in tears because they had no idea how they should know what to do in those tests. They were mostly unfamiliar with the way content was presented and the format of the tests. Shortly after that, during parent-teacher conference, I was informed that one of my children benefited from "much structure"; she was also described as being very "deliberate" in her answers. Although I am quite fluent in English, I wondered what connotation that might have in the school context and what exactly might the teacher have meant by those expressions.

My suspicions were confirmed when later I was also informed that my child was not being asked to do all the readings. My daughter had complained to me of being bored, since for weeks she was excluded from participating in any of the challenging activities with the rest of the class and, instead, would just be made to sit around and watch. This was a young child who had just switched hemispheres, languages, and cultures, and who was trying to adjust to her new school environment. After such a move, changes are abrupt. From one day to the next a child whose family immigrates needs to not only switch from their home language to English in school but also get used to the new non-verbal social codes; for instance, my children had to learn to do without the kisses and hugs from friends they were used to being greeted with at school every morning. In my experience, a few weeks after a child's arrival in a new country appears to be a bit too soon to label her as a slow learner.

Some time later I realized that during enrollment the first week in that city, in a moment of absent-mindedness, I had got two words mixed up when filling out school forms. In the blank for mother's occupation instead of "homemaker"—a new word I had recently picked up and which described my temporary situation—I had written "housekeeper". In a highly segregated school with a disproportionately high percentage of upper-middle-class white Anglo student population—as compared to the demographics of the city—this mix-up probably contributed to rendering us misfits. I often wonder if my daughter would have initially been labeled differently, and consequently placed in a higher track at that school, had I not got those words mixed up in her records.

A year later, when we moved to another state in the Southwest, another situation stands out as one of those where my status as an outsider was highlighted. Soon after our move, an acquaintance who had older children in the school system recommended that I request for my daughters to be tested in order to see if they qualified for services for gifted children. Although I was not sure I wanted my kids to be identified as such, I was told that if I did not want my children to be numbers, I should try and get them in that program, and that this would be especially beneficial in high school. I was not sure exactly how this might benefit them, but I went along with the friendly suggestion, and asked for my children to be tested at each of their schools.

At the middle school, the process went smoothly; at the elementary school, this was not the case. There I made this request to the teacher on my first visit, and then again at the next parent-teacher conference. My insistence was met with the following reason for not complying with my request: "I don't see it; she is bilingual, you know." I was not sure at that time what connection I should be making between being bilingual and not qualifying for a gifted program, but in her tone of voice I could tell it seemed quite obvious to the teacher. Since I had filled out a written request for my child to be tested, the teacher had to comply, but she waited until the very end of the school year to submit the request. Eventually, that summer, my daughter was tested and started participating in the advanced program the following year. The same child who had been labeled as slow two years before was now relabeled as gifted. I wonder now, should not "gifted and talented" be the label we give all our students so that we treat them and their parents accordingly?

Since then I have gained some experience and learned how the education system works. I have also made it one of my long-term goals to find out more about family-school relations, about the experience of immigrant mothers with diverse backgrounds, with a special focus on women who have had fewer opportunities to learn English and to participate in formal education. I am convinced that much can be done to facilitate these processes and initial interactions in the highly structured academic institutions which serve our children. I admit that mine are trivial anecdotes, almost frivolous, compared to the hardships some immigrants undergo. But I also realize that I can empathize with the deep anxiety recently arrived immigrant mothers may experience as they worry about their children's wellbeing—especially fearing that they will be underestimated in their abilities just for being foreign and, therefore, different. Further, I can identify with their moments of doubt, and of questioning the wisdom of the decision to immigrate, which is, paradoxically, usually made with one main goal in mind: the long-term wellbeing of our children.

# References

Bourdieu, P. (1991). *Language and symbolic power* (G. Raymond & M. Adamson, Trans.). Cambridge, MA: Harvard University Press.

Cho, S., Crenshaw, K., & McCall, L. (2013). Toward a field of intersectionality studies: Theory, applications, and praxis. *Signs*, 38(4), 785–810. Retrieved from http://www.jstor.org/stable/10.1086/669608 doi:1

Collins, P. H. (2000). *Black feminist thought: Knowledge, consciousness, and the politics of empowerment*. New York, NY: Routledge.

Foucault, M. (1984). *The Foucault reader*. (P. Rabinow, Ed.). New York, NY: Pantheon.

Fraser, N. (1997). *Justice interruptus*. New York, NY: Routledge.

Fraser, N. (1998). Social justice in the age of identity politics: Redistribution, recognition and participation. In G. Peterson (Ed.), *The Tanner lectures on human values* (Vol. 19, pp. 1–67). Salt Lake City, UT: Utah University Press.

Fraser, N. (2003). Social justice in the age of identity politics: Redistribution, recognition, and participation. In N. Fraser & A. Honneth (Eds.), *Redistribution or recognition? A political philosophical exchange* (pp. 7–109). New York, NY: Verso.

Fraser, N. (2010). *Scales of justice: Reimagining political space in a globalizing world*. New York, NY: Columbia University Press.

Guba, E., & Lincoln, Y. (2005). Paradigmatic controversies, contradictions and emerging confluences. In N. Denzin & Y. Lincoln (Eds.), *The Sage handbook of qualitative research* (3rd ed., pp. 191–215). Thousand Oaks, CA: Sage.

Haraway, D. (1988). Situated knowledges: The science question in feminism and the privilege of partial perspective. *Feminist Studies, 14*(3), 575–599.

hooks, b. (2000a). *Feminist theory: From margin to center*. Cambridge, MA: South End Press.

hooks, b. (2000b). *Where we stand: Class matters*. New York, NY: Routledge.

Hurtado, A. (1996). *The color of privilege: Three blasphemies on race and feminism*. Ann Arbor, MI: The University of Michigan Press.

Hurtado, A. (2000). Sitios y lenguas: Chicanas theorize feminisms. In U. Narayan & S. Harding (Eds.), *Decentering the center: Philosophy for a multicultural, postcolonial, and feminist world* (pp. 128–155). Bloomington, IN and Indianapolis, IN: Indiana University Press.

Lareau, A., & Weininger, E. (2003). Cultural capital in educational research: A critical assessment. *Theory and Society, 32*, 567–606.

Lorde, A. (1995). Age, race, class, and sex: Women redefining difference. In B. Guy-Sheftall (Ed.), *Words of fire: An anthology of African-American feminist thought* (pp. 284–291). New York, NY: The New Press.

Olesen, V. (2003) Feminisms and qualitative research at and into the millennium. In N. Denzin & Y. Lincoln (Eds.), *The landscape of qualitative research: Theories and issues* (2nd ed., pp. 332–397). Thousand Oaks, CA: Sage.

Reinharz, S., & Chase, S. (2003). Interviewing women. In J. Holstein & J. Gubrium (Eds.), *Inside interviewing: New lenses and concerns* (pp. 73–90). Thousand Oaks, CA: Sage.

Riessman, C. K. (2008). *Narrative methods for the human sciences*. Thousand Oaks, CA: Sage.

Weiler, K. (1988). *Women teaching for change: Gender, class and power*. South Hadley, MA: Bergin & Garvey.

Wharton, A. (1991). Structure and agency in socialist-feminist thought. *Gender & Society, 5*(3), 373–389.

Young, I. (1990). *Justice and the politics of difference*. Princeton, NJ: Princeton University Press.

Young, I. (1997). *Intersecting voices: Dilemmas of gender, political philosophy, and policy*. Princeton, NJ: Princeton University Press.

# · 3 ·

# SEVEN WOMEN

## Seven Stories

*From its beginnings, feminist scholarship has been concerned with recovering what has been lost, with telling stories. In fact, feminist scholarship has been largely defined by its political stance—its attempt to know the world differently, to recover what has been hidden and lost, in order to contribute to the building of a more just world for women and men.* (Middleton & Weiler, 1999, p. 4)

Before starting this journey into the issues surrounding parental involvement, its definitions and its interpretations as they relate to the reality of Latina immigrant women, it is important to introduce the seven protagonists of this book: Norma, Sandra, Luisa, Patricia, Silvia, Susana, and Brenda. The reader will become familiar with each of their stories which breathe life to this book and create a space for critical reflection on the meaning of parental involvement. Each one of the sketches of these seven immigrant women intends to capture some of the salient moments in their narratives, which we will explore in more detail later as we set them side by side the official discourse and the ideology behind it.

## Norma—*Acababa de llegar y no conocía muy bien el sistema aquí.* (I had just arrived and didn't know the system here very well.)

Norma is in her late forties, a divorced single mother of three: two grown-up sons, Maximiliano and Carlos, and a daughter, Verónica, who was seven at the time of our first interview. Twelve years earlier, when Norma arrived in the United States with her now ex-husband, her sons were six and eight. Thus, she can now compare her daughter's current experience in school with that of her sons, and reflect on how things have changed for her since then.

In the early days, Norma recalls, she worried constantly because she was not able to help her sons with homework, and she was uncertain of how they were progressing in school. At the time, she also experienced some instances of serious miscommunication, adding to this anxiety. To begin with, as a rule, when she first arrived Norma was explicitly discouraged from visiting the school. Throughout the first year, she received notes saying that scheduling for parent-teacher conferences was underway but that she did not need to attend because her children were doing well. As she did not understand how the system worked, she followed what seemed to be clear instructions without second thoughts. To her dismay, at the end of that school year, his teacher recommended that Carlos, her younger son, be held back in first grade. This suggestion to retain him came as a surprise to Norma, not only because she was unaware of any difficulties—given the constant notes informing her that she could disregard parent-teacher conferences—but even more so because when Carlos started first grade in the United States he could already read in Spanish. Norma shares the details of her situation at the time.

> Mi hijo menor, cuando yo me lo traje, leía en español. Leía … Era como noviembre u octubre y la escuela ya había empezado. Estaba en primer grado y ya sabía leer. Juntaba palabras y palabras. Pero cuando terminó el año, la maestra me sugirió dejarlo y yo acepté, porque me dijo que no sabía nada de inglés y todo era en inglés. Pues, se le había hecho un poquito más difícil porque a los niños de primer año en ese tiempo les habían empezado a enseñar de "kínder" algunas palabras, para las letras y todo eso. Entonces, él no tenía esas bases que necesitaba para leer como los demás. Pero ya sabía leer en español.

> My younger son, when I brought him here, could read in Spanish. He could read. He had just … it was November or October, and school had started already. He was in first grade and he could read already. He joined words and words. But when the school year ended, the teacher suggested that they held him back, and I accepted, because she said he didn't know any English, and it was all in English. Well, he had

found it a bit difficult, because by the time the other children got to first grade they would have already started learning some words in kindergarten, learning the letters and all that. So, he didn't have the same basis he needed to read, as everybody else. But he could already read in Spanish.

In the midst of all this uncertainty, without understanding how education in the US worked, and especially how much of a say parents actually had, Norma had to make vital decisions about her children's schooling. After all these years, Carlos still resents the fact that she followed the teacher's recommendation. He is convinced that he would have managed and done well had he been given the opportunity to pass instead of being held back in first grade. Now Norma also seems to regret her decision.

Y fíjese que eso fue algo que a él lo marcó. A mí me dieron la opción de dejarlo o pasarlo. Pero la maestra me dijo que era lo mejor. Pues, yo no sé … Acababa de llegar y no conocía muy bien el sistema aquí. Y se me hizo mejor que se quedara. Pero él sí, siempre me dijo que por qué lo había dejado, y que él hubiera ido en el grado, que él hubiera aprendido, si yo le hubiera dado la oportunidad, y así.

And, see, that was something that marked him. They gave me the option to put him back or to promote him. But the teacher said that it was better that way. But, I don't know … I had just arrived, and didn't know the system here very well. So I thought it was better for him to be held back. But he always asked me, why I had had him held back, and that he would have passed, and he would've learned, if I had given him the opportunity, and so on.

As she compares the school's decision in each of her sons' cases their first year in the US, Norma wonders. While her younger son was held back, her older son was promoted to the next grade level even though he was not fluent in English yet. According to Norma, the teacher's attitude made all the difference. Whereas Maximiliano's teacher acknowledged his progress and his effort while making allowances for the time it takes to acquire a second language, Carlos's teacher only compared him with his English-speaking first grade classmates.

Y yo digo que tienen que ver mucho los maestros. Porque la maestra del niño de tercero, el que vino a tercero, de ocho años, me motivó y me dijo: "El niño no sabe inglés, todavía es muy poco el tiempo para que lo aprenda, pero se esfuerza. Está luchando por aprender, asique yo quiero que sí vaya a cuarto."

And I say that teachers have a lot to do with it. Because my other kid's teacher, the third grade teacher, of my eight-year-old who came to third, encouraged me and said:

"The child doesn't know English; it's been a very short time for him to learn it, but he is making an effort. He is working hard in his struggle to learn, so I do want him to move on to fourth grade."

Norma recognizes significant changes from those first years, both in the schools, and in how she relates to them in the present. Nowadays, within her group of friends, Norma takes on an informal leadership role, and it is she who urges them to attend school meetings so as to take an active part in the decisions. Yet, she is aware of some of the barriers that still discourage Spanish-speaking mothers like herself from participating more. In spite of her critique, Norma is pleased with many aspects of her daughter's schooling. Most of all, she is delighted that Verónica can take advantage of the bilingual program and study both in English and Spanish, as she recognizes the benefits for herself and for her daughter. Verónica is developing her bilingual and biliteracy skills, while this time around, Norma does not feel as excluded from her child's schooling, partly because she can help with her Spanish homework, and also because she feels more confident as, in her own words, she can now communicate in English "a little better".

Norma mentions the effort she put into learning English, through her work with English-speaking employers. Also, she contrasts her own experience—her many years doing housework for English-speaking families; her recent painting jobs; and earlier serving as a caretaker for an elderly lady— to the narrow experience of the women who have stayed at home instead, and have not learned English. Although Norma's efforts were commendable in pushing herself and going out of her way to learn English, it is worth noting that in her assessment of the reason for other women not learning English a significant factor is left out. Many immigrant women who do work outside of the home, often have jobs which do not require learning English and offer limited opportunities to learn—such as the seasonal agricultural jobs, either picking crops in the field or selecting and grading in the processing plants. This was a common situation for most of the women who shared their stories.

### Sandra—*Ahí fue donde yo me orienté más, donde aprendí; se me abrieron los ojos.*
(That is where I found my way, where I learned; my eyes were opened.)

Sandra is in her mid-forties and has two children; her 12-year-old son is in sixth grade, and her nine-year-old daughter is in fourth. When Sandra moved

to the States, she was married and her children were ages five and three; she
has since divorced. At first, their family moved in with Sandra's brother-in-
law and his wife. The situation became tense, and after some time, to escape
domestic violence, Sandra left and went to a shelter with her children. She
feared for their safety, since her husband had once taken their daughter away
to Mexico, without her knowledge. As her husband's violence towards her
continued to escalate, once she recovered her child, moved out, Sandra credits the shelter for survivors of domestic abuse for the guidance and support she
found to be able to sustain herself and her children in these terms: "*Ahí fue
donde yo me orienté más, donde aprendí; se me abrieron los ojos.*" (That is where I
found my way, where I learned; my eyes were opened.)

Before leaving the shelter, with the counselor's guidance, Sandra was able
to set tangible goals for herself, which helped her regain her confidence and
start over, alone, in a new country. Months later, when a Head Start[1] counselor asked her about her goals, Sandra pulled out the same list she had drawn
up during her stay at the shelter. Within a year of that first meeting with the
Head Start counselor, she was congratulated for being the first parent in the
group to have achieved all her goals: finding a job, starting to learn English,
getting a car, and helping her children to do well. With the help of social
workers and her friend Norma, whom she met at the shelter, Sandra and her
children moved to the rural area where they now live. Years later, also, with
assistance from the shelter, she obtained a divorce, once she found out that,
legally, the school staff would not be able to stop her husband from taking her
children out of school if he ever tried. For safety reasons, she keeps her current address from anyone who might be in touch with her ex-husband. That
is why, Sandra explains, although she finished high school in Mexico, she has
not contacted her hometown to retrieve her diploma, and has resumed her
education here.

At the time of our first interview, Sandra was employed part-time, doing housekeeping in several homes and offices. Two years later, due to the
economic downturn, she temporarily lost two of her jobs, so she had to take
up a part-time job at an agricultural processing plant, and supplemented her
income by making and selling crafts. Her goal is to continue studying English and, ultimately, complete the GED (General Education Development)
program to obtain a high-school equivalent diploma, and to improve her job
opportunities. One of her employers has mentioned that, once she becomes
more proficient in English, he could hire her as an administrative assistant for
his office, since in Mexico she used to work as a clerk in a bank.

Sandra stands out from the group, and has adopted a leadership role in her community similar to Norma's. For instance, as she is concerned about the low attendance rate at parent meetings at her children's schools, she is proactively trying to help reverse this trend. Recently, at the end of a meeting at her son's middle school, besides volunteering to make reminder calls and persuade other parents to attend, Sandra urged the administrators to schedule their next meeting before the group broke up, since she believes that one of the problems may be the need for advance notice. Sandra proudly describes how she spoke up to make it happen.

> Ve, entonces, la próxima junta, la tenemos el 19 de marzo. Ay, hasta casi yo fui. ¡Puse la fecha! Como se fueron todos, le digo: "¿Qué pasó? No dijeron la fecha de cuándo tenemos la próxima junta." Y ahí va la directora y el otro señor y dicen: "Oh, sí, cierto, la fecha." Y ya estuvimos decidiendo: "¿Qué día está bien?" "No," decía ella "No, no, este día está bien." Entonces, ya establecieron que el 19 de marzo es la junta, antes de que tengan los niños el examen. Antes de esas fechas y ya. Asique, nos entregaron las hojitas con nombres de padres. Y una semana antes empezamos a hablarles a los papás, para recordarles que el 19 había junta de padres.

> You see, then, the next meeting is on March 19. And, it was me, almost. I set the date! As they had all left, I said: "What happened? You didn't say the date for the next meeting." So then the principal and the other man said: "Oh, right, the date." So, there we were deciding: "What day would work?" "No," she said. "No, no, this day would work." So, there they scheduled the next meeting for March 19, before the children have their exams. Before that date, and that was that. So, they gave us the lists of parents. And we started calling the parents a week in advance, to remind them that on the 19th there is a parents meeting.

Sandra is committed to contributing her ideas when she is given a chance, and seems very excited to see some of her suggestions being adopted. Adding to a common thread in these stories, Sandra stresses how helpful everyone at the school has been to her, as a rule. Yet, she also points out the difficulties faced by Spanish-speaking parents at some of the meetings, especially when no language resources are provided.

**Luisa—*Como hasta ahorita, ellos me están ayudando siempre en la escuela. Nunca me han dicho así feo. No, no, nunca.*** (Even right now, they are always helping me at the school. They have never spoken to me in a mean way. No, no; never.)

Luisa is in her late forties and has been in the United States for 13 years. She has two sons, Manuel and Jesús, who were 13 and seven when their family migrated. Luisa is a widow; her husband died soon after Manuel graduated from high school. Even though both her sons are grown up now, over the years Luisa has kept close ties to the schools in her area, since she has served as a caregiver to many in her extended family and her community, and still does. On weekdays, she babysits Norma's daughter, Verónica, who goes to the same elementary school Jesús attended. She picks her up after school, participates in most of their special events, and even helps out whenever there is a community cleanup organized by the school, as she lives just down the street. Her connections go even further. When Luisa first arrived, she worked for several years as a nanny for a family whose three children have all grown up to be teachers; one of them now works at that same elementary school in her neighborhood.

At the time of our first interview, Luisa is also taking care of members of her extended family. She supports her son Jesús and his wife by babysitting their one-year-old son, so that they can both attend community college. She is still in touch with the high school also because of her teenage nephew, Raúl, who came from Mexico for school and was initially staying with her. Although he has since moved out, the school still keeps contacting her when there is a problem, since she is his only adult relative living in the area. Luisa repeatedly refers to her nephew's problems as we discuss her relationship with the schools in the area.

> Luisa: Y ya le digo, ahorita están mandando cartas y me hablan que Raúl no está aquí en la escuela, y me hablan en inglés.
> Lilian: ¿Y ellos saben que él no está aquí?
> Luisa: Y yo ya les hablé y les dije que él ya no vive aquí conmigo, por eso dicen: "Necesitas venir a hablar porque quieren tener una junta contigo. Raúl no puede vivir solo con un amiguito; él no es mayor de edad. Tiene que estar como responsable tú o tu hermana. Y ya le digo, como hasta ahorita, ellos me están ayudando, siempre en la escuela. Nunca me han dicho así feo. No, no, nunca. Nunca me han dicho eso, siempre me hablan, cuando me hablan que él no está en la escuela, les entiendo que Raúl no está en la escuela y que sí está en la casa.

Luisa: And as I said, now they are sending me letters and they call me saying that Raúl is not here at school, and they speak to me in English.
Lilian: And do they know he is not here?
Luisa: I have already called them, and explained that he doesn't live here with me anymore, that is why they say: "You need to come and talk, because they want to meet with you. Raúl can't live alone with a friend; he is not of age. You or your sister must be responsible." And, right up to now, they are helping me in the school, as always. Well, they have never spoken to me in a mean way. No, no, never. They have never said that. They always call me. When they call me to tell me that Raúl is not at school, I understand that he is not at school, and [that they're asking] if he is home.

Due to his absenteeism, Raúl is in trouble, and Luisa is evidently deeply upset by how serious this whole situation has become. Even though her nephew is no longer in her charge, she does not complain about the school contacting her, and instead finds words to praise the staff for their helpfulness at all times, as she tries to work things out.

Porque él se vino con la prima, y ahí se fue con el amigo. Y allá vive con un amigo, como si él fuera adulto y todo. Pero, como ya le digo, las cartas y las llamadas me las hacen a mí. Y ahorita nada menos tengo que ir a una junta porque dicen que si él tiene muchas faltas, que van a ver, que lo van a meter como a un programa para investigar a ver por qué está faltando. Y que le pueden quitar su licencia también, porque a lo mejor anda no más manejando y fuera de la escuela. Y, luego, dicen que van a investigar eso y luego van a investigar si el problema es de los papás. Y, pues, ahorita y con todo eso, ellos me ayudan.

Because he came with his cousin and then he went with a friend. And there he is living with a friend, as if he were an adult and all. But, as I was telling you, they still send me the letters and they call me. And, in fact, now I have to attend a meeting because they say that if he has many absences, they will have to see, that they may place him in a program to find out and see why he has been skipping school. Also, that they may take away his driver's license, because he may just be driving and staying out of school. And, then, they say they are going to investigate that and then they are going to investigate if there is a problem with the parents. And, well, now they help me with all that.

This is a complicated problem for Luisa, who was caught in the middle, feeling rather powerless. She is concerned about Raúl, since he has been in more trouble than her sons ever were. By the last interview, she was glad to share that her nephew had graduated from high school and had moved back home to Mexico with his parents.

In the midst of her explanation of how she was contacted by the school time and again on account of her nephew, she intersperses comments of how helpful the school staff has been all along. She refers to how they have never been unpleasant to her or used harsh words, and instead explain the situation with her nephew very clearly and give her some recommendation.

Most importantly, she is grateful for how they always try to find someone who can explain things to her directly in Spanish or someone who can interpret for her. Over the years, one of her most intense struggles has been with communication; in her own words, *"batallaba y batallaba"* (I struggled and struggled). Luisa would like to attend English classes if she could but she can hardly ever participate in the adult ESL and GED programs in her area, which are only offered during the summertime, overlapping with most opportunities for seasonal agricultural work, which is one of her main sources of income.

## Patricia—*Yo sí quiero que aprendan los dos idiomas y a escribir en los dos idiomas.*
## (I do want them to learn both languages and to write in both languages.)

Patricia is in her early thirties and has lived in the States, with her family, for nine years. When describing her background, Patricia shares how she started working at an early age. She helped her father with agricultural work, at a time when it was tougher than it is today. As the eldest of her siblings, she was the one who worked the most. In those days, she reminisces, what is now done with tractors her family used to do with oxen and by hand. As a child, she would walk behind the animals as they plowed, sowing the corn from a small bucket. Patricia has worked all her life; she does not recall any time in her life when she did not work.

When they first arrived from Mexico, she and her husband lived in a neighboring western state for six years, where they both worked in a meat-packing plant. Patricia recalls working all through her first pregnancy. After they moved to the Southwest, she worked in the fields for a year. Her husband is a long-distance truck driver and is often out of town, so Patricia is the one who attends to any business related to the school. Although she first comments on how now she cannot go out to work because she has several children, she later explains that she actually does have a home-based job. She provides daycare to several children under a state-subsidized program for low-income families.

Lilian: Y cuénteme, en su familia, ¿quién es la persona que se comunica con la escuela?

Patricia: Pues, siempre si hay algún problema, siempre yo soy la que estoy aquí en casa. Pues mi esposo siempre trabaja, ya llega tarde y yo, pues, ya con tanto niño ya no puedo trabajar. Entonces, como quiera, pues es trabajo, el cuidar aquí niños de otros. Estoy en el trabajo de "childcare" en ese programa y yo soy "babysitter." Y el estado paga a uno también si las mamás de los niños califican; como a mí me paga el estado.

Lilian: And tell me, in your family, who's the person who communicates with the school?

Patricia: Well, always, if there's a problem, I'm the one who's always home. Because my husband is always working, and arrives late and I, well, with so many kids, I can't work anymore. Then, anyway, it is work, taking care of other people's kids. I work in childcare, in that program, and I am a babysitter. And the state pays you also, if the mothers of the children qualify; the state pays me.

Even if her husband does not recognize it as a real job—as she comments jokingly—she is proud of the fact that the extra income she earns has made a difference to them, and they have recently been able to finish paying off their house.

Bueno, a mí también me da para ayudar en la casa, con los gastos. Porque ya para una familia como la de nosotros, ya se necesita traer mucho dinero a la casa. Y antes estábamos pagando esta casa, pero ya no. Hace como unos tres meses o dos meses que la acabamos de pagar.

Well, it also allows me to help out in the house, with expenses. Because for a family like ours, you need to bring a lot of money home. And we were paying for the house, but not anymore. It's been now three or two months since we finished paying for it.

At the time of the first interview, Patricia had four children: three sons, ages nine, five and one; and a three-year-old daughter. When they moved to the rural town where they now live, her eldest son, Alex, had already completed first grade; he is now in fourth grade, and his five-year-old brother, Pedro, is in kindergarten. Patricia sent both of them to Head Start and would also like to enroll her daughter, Cris. Since their income has recently increased, she suspects they might have just surpassed the minimum income requirement, as she is aware that most families with two adults working year round tend not to qualify.

Patricia is satisfied with her children's schooling, and comments: "*Se portan bien [con nosotros]; siempre me han tocado buenos, buenos maestros con los niños*" (They treat us well; I have always had good, good teachers for my children). Her eldest son, Alex, the fourth-grader, is an avid reader; his teacher has told her that he is at the top of his class in reading and that she has high hopes for his future. Patricia is also pleased with how her five-year-old son, Pedro, is doing in his bilingual kindergarten program. His teacher expects him to be reading by the end of the school year. Alex was also in a bilingual class until third grade, and was recently exited from the program. Even though she was never asked to choose whether she wanted her children to be in the bilingual program, Patricia values the opportunity for them to maintain their home language and become biliterate. Some mothers, she comments, complain because they do not want their children to be placed in a bilingual class but this is not her case: "*En mi ver mío, yo sí quiero que aprendan los dos idiomas y a escribir en los dos idiomas*" (In my view, I do want them to learn both languages and to write in both languages.). Although Patricia shares her overall positive stance with most of the women in this group, parts of her narrative raise some questions as to the methods used in some important decision-making processes when Spanish-speaking immigrant mothers and their children are involved, especially those related to issues which can have long-term consequences in a child's schooling.

## Susana and Silvia—*Para mí, un apoyo muy grande es cuando nos ponen a alguien que nos interprete lo que nos están diciendo los maestros.*
(To me, it's a great help when they assign someone to interpret what the teachers are saying.)

Susana and Silvia are sisters. Susana is in her late thirties and has lived in the United States for 12 years. She is married and has four children: two daughters ages 13 and four, and two sons who are 12, and almost two, at the time of the first interview. For two years and until recently, Susana also took care of one of her young nieces, the daughter of one of her sisters. At first, Susana refers to her niece as her own child. A few months after she arrived, Susana started doing agricultural work. She did so every year after that, in the harvest season, until she gave birth to her youngest daughter. By then, what she would make per day would barely be enough to cover daycare expenses for her children, so it was no longer worthwhile. To make ends meet, Susana regularly prepares and sells tamales, either to order, or in the offices in her small rural town.

Susana's extended family figures prominently in her life. They came to the United States from Mexico following family stage migration (Hondagneu-Sotelo, 1994). Her father immigrated first, her mother followed, and the chil-

dren were brought later, in successive phases. Once her father had left, Susana's mother was the main provider in their household. When news that he
had fallen ill reached them, Susana's mother decided to travel to the United
States in search of her husband, whom they had not heard from in several
years. Susana and her siblings stayed in Mexico, until they were sent for, in
stages. From that time on, as the eldest sibling, Susana became the main caregiver in the family.

When she arrived in the United States, Susana had an 11-month-old
baby of her own and was expecting her second child. At first, her mother
was the spokesperson for the family who communicated with the schools on
a regular basis. But two years after their arrival, when her mother returned to
Mexico, Susana took over this responsibility. From then on, she took care of
five of her siblings who were in the US and were all in school at the time: her
older brother was in high school, her middle brother and sister were in middle
school, and her two youngest sisters attended elementary school. Thus, much
like Norma, Susana is able to compare her past and present experiences.

> Lilian: En su familia ¿quién es la persona que generalmente se comunica con la es-
> cuela?
> Susana: Bueno, ahorita soy yo. Antes, era mi mamá. Mi mamá era la que iba a las
> conferencias. De vez en cuando, verdad, porque verdaderamente ella nada más duró
> como dos años con nosotros y se regresó a México y me dejó a mí con todos. Asique
> yo era la que iba a las conferencias de mis hermanos.
> Lilian: Tenía hermanos más chiquitos…
> Susana: Mis hermanas, sí. No estaban todos tan chiquitos, pero de todas maneras
> necesitaban de alguien que los cuidara.

> Lilian: In your family, who is the person who generally communicates with the
> school?
> Susana: Well, now it's me. Before, it was my mom. My mom was the one who used
> to attend the conferences. Once in a while, right, because truly she only was here for
> about two years with us, and she returned to Mexico and left me in charge. So, I was
> the one who went to my siblings' conferences.
> Lilian: So, you had little siblings…
> Susana: My sisters, yes. Not all of them were that little, but they still needed someone
> to take care of them.

Silvia is one of Susana's younger sisters, who is in her early thirties, and has
lived in the United States now for eight years. She is married and has two
children in elementary school; at the time of our first interview, her 10-year-
old son, Juan Manuel, was in fourth grade and her six-year-old daughter, Sa-

rina, was in first grade. Following Susana's recommendation, she sent both her children to Head Start, so that they would be prepared for school and, especially with her younger child, so that it would free her to work. Silvia does seasonal agricultural work, and her husband is a carpenter.

When Silvia discusses their family's story, she focuses on the figure of their mother, whom she considers a powerful role model. Silvia credits much of her own well-being and that of her siblings to the sacrifices she made for them over the years. Their close-knit family has adapted to their new environment and kept together through all the adjustments. Silvia compares their lifestyle in the United States to that left behind in Mexico. Even as they moved from one rural setting to another, there were many changes involved, especially in the modes of communication and in their transportation needs. Before migrating, in Mexico, their extended family all lived at walking distance from one another and hardly needed a car. Even though they now live further apart, they still keep in touch constantly. For instance, during one of our conversations, Silvia received several phone calls from her siblings with updates on their youngest sister, who was in the hospital about to have her first baby. Silvia describes how her life has changed, as she shares details of her past lifestyle in rural Mexico with her close-knit extended family.

> Como nosotros en el rancho, pues, casi vivíamos así: mi abuela, mis tías, nosotros, así cerca. Pues, ya corría uno, caminando: "Ve con la tía, dile que esto." Y, pues, iba uno corriendo o caminando. Sí, pues, estaba así alrededor; así es en los ranchitos, los ranchos, adonde vive casi pura familia y otra familia así, sí. Casi carros no usábamos, pero, caminando. Sí, estaban más cerca las casas.

> On the farm we used to live like that: my grandmother, my aunts, and us, like that, close to each other. So one used to run or walk over: "Go tell your aunt this." And one would run there or walk. Yes, because it was all close by, that is how it is in the farms where those who live around you are mostly family. We almost used no cars, but walked. Yes, our houses were closer.

In mentioning not needing a car in their rural home in Mexico, Silvia touches on an issue common among many immigrant women, that is, the new need for independent physical mobility (Hirsch, 2003; Hondagneu-Sotelo, 1994; Menjívar, 2000).

## Brenda—*M'hija, mira, no faltes, estudia; el trabajo adonde andamos nosotros es duro.*
## (Honey, look, don't skip class, study; the line of work we are in is tough.)

Brenda is in her early fifties, and has lived in the United States with her family for 15 years. During the harvest, she and her husband both work in the fields picking onions and chilies, as well as in agricultural processing plants, grading and sorting produce. At the peak of the season, she often endures long hours under strenuous work conditions, only stopping briefly for breaks. With the overtime earned during those months, her family manages to save up for the rest of the year when there is no work.

Brenda has three daughters; at the time of our first interview, Sara, the eldest, was 19 and had graduated from high school two years earlier; Luz, 17, was a senior in high school; and Adriana, 12, was in sixth grade. Her experience with each one of them in school was quite different, Brenda reflects. Of her three daughters, Sara was who gave her most reasons for concern. One of the most trying times was in high school when she started skipping class, Brenda reminisces. When she found out, Brenda made sure that Sara thought about her long-term prospects, by reminding her why school mattered based on her own life experience. She could not just stop attending school, just as her parents could not just stop showing up for work. Most importantly, Brenda focused on the sobering facts and the hardships associated with her own and her husband's line of work:

> Pues, el día que falten, ni modo porque uno no tiene ni modo de dejar de trabajar, ¿verdad? Pues, uno también sí habla con ellas: "Y, m'hija, mira, no faltes, estudia; el trabajo adonde andamos nosotros es duro," les digo. "Échele ganas, m'hija, estudie. Usted no las siga a sus amigas, [cuando dicen] 'que vamos para acá y que vamos para allá'."

> Well, the day they skip school, no way, because there's no way I can stop working, right? Well, one also speaks to them, "And, honey, look, don't skip class, study, the line of work we are in is tough," I tell them. "Give it your all, honey, study. Don't follow your friends, [when they say,] 'let's go here and let's go there'."

These *consejos* (words of wisdom and advice) embody one of the facets of Brenda's advocacy for her children. After stressing the value of schooling, the importance of studying and graduating from high school, she underscores, as well, how hard it is for her husband and herself to make a living.

As is the case with most mothers in this group, when we first approached the subject of her interactions with the schools and how she is treated by school personnel, Brenda has only praises for them. She emphasizes how friendly everyone is, how helpful the school secretaries are with information, and, especially, finding someone to interpret for her if necessary. Yet, Brenda's narrative is not free of tensions. One particularly stressful incident comes up repeatedly, when she had to intervene on behalf of her youngest daughter, Adriana, to advocate for her at the middle school. Brenda offers some of the most nuanced accounts of the learning process she has undergone as part of a community in which resources are developed in order to be shared.

## Note

1.  Head Start is a US federally funded preschool program for low-income families.

## References

Hirsch, J. (2003). *A courtship after marriage: Sexuality and love in Mexican transnational families*. Berkeley, CA: University of California Press.

Hondagneu-Sotelo, P. (1994). *Gendered transitions: Mexican experiences of immigration*. Berkeley, CA: University of California Press.

Menjívar, C. (2000). *Fragmented ties: Salvadoran immigrant networks in America*. Berkeley, CA: University of California Press.

Middleton, S., & Weiler, K. (1999). Introduction. In K. Weiler & S. Middleton (Eds.), *Telling women's lives: Narrative inquiries in the history of women's education* (pp. 1–6). Philadelphia, PA: Open University Press.

# · PART II ·

# NARRATIVES AND COUNTER NARRATIVES OF PARENTAL INVOLVEMENT

# · 4 ·

# THE DISCOURSE OF PARENTAL INVOLVEMENT AND THE IDEOLOGIES OF MOTHERHOOD

*American public policy has shown a strong preference for educating mothers instead of pro-*
*viding resources—such as publicly funded child care, generous cash assistance and universal*
*health care—to help all caregivers do the work of looking after those who cannot care for*
*themselves.* (Vandenberg-Daves, 2014, p. 281)

The concept of discourse in its interrelatedness with power and language becomes central to the exploration presented here of the views of a group of immigrant women in a border community on how they have developed stances,
resources and strategies to interact with other social agents within the educational system. The relation of power and knowledge underlies those processes
by which cultural imperialism operates within our institutions of education
through dominant discourses. Thus, Foucault's theory of power and knowledge becomes relevant to our specific focus on instances of interaction between institutional agents and social actors. In their official discourse, schools
generally predicate the importance of the participation of parents and family
in the education community. Yet, because of issues of power derived from
social roles and social standing, not all parents may make full use of the official channels for their views to be known by the schools. Furthermore, there
often is a conflict between home culture and school culture—i.e. mainstream
culture. The values expressed in policies and practices may be "complicit with

the oppression of some students' home cultures and other social identities" (Gee, 2012, p. 110).

Within post-structural theory, "discourse" is a central concept which is pivotal in establishing the link between power and knowledge production in society. This centrality is expressed by Foucault (1977) as follows: "…in any society, there are manifold relations of power which permeate, characterize and constitute the social body, and these relations of power cannot themselves be established, consolidated nor implemented without the production, accumulation, circulation and functioning of a discourse" (S. Foss, K. Foss, & Trapp, 1985; Foucault, 1977, p. 93). At issue is the circularity of this system of power which is self-perpetuating since what is accepted as "truth" is validated by the discourses it produces and sustains (Foss et al., 1985, p. 205; Foucault, 1977, p. 93).

In the same vein, Gee (2012) makes the distinction between merely discourse and Discourse with a capital "D" to refer to the relation of language and power, and describes the application of this notion in the contexts of US schools. While some Discourses, such as school-based Discourses, can put some members of society at an advantage they can also contribute to placing others at a disadvantage through exclusion (Gee, 2012, p. 191). "Discourse" does not refer to words only but to "social and political practices with material effects" (Boler & Zembylas, 2003, p. 120). Discourses are, then, considered ideological in that they contribute to determining the centrality or marginalization of groups of people through the establishment of hierarchies of certain beliefs and values above others and the consequent distribution of social power (Gee, 2012, p. 159). Kincheloe (2005) highlights the intricate connections between discourse and power relations manifested in rules which govern institutions and behavior, for instance, those establishing "who can speak and who must listen" (p. 122). To illustrate the workings of these power relations he stresses the fact that in research often "power operates to privilege the data coming from particular academic or political-economic locales" (Kincheloe, 2005, p. 148).

## The Official Discourse of Parental Involvement: An Exclusionary Narrative

Parental involvement has become part of the official discourse of schools in the United States, as it is explicitly included in federal, state and local education policy (Hurtig & Dyrness, 2011). Most interactions between families and schools have been defined within this discourse, which establishes the institutional standards for acceptable parent behavior and expectations of parent responsibility. In the process of becoming officially sanctioned, the discourse of parental involvement has contributed to reinforcing, updating and extending the reach of the social construct of the ideal parent, which permeates social policy, by reifying it in the context of education.

In the last decades, not only has this discourse developed into a set of narrower definitions by the schools of the specific roles assigned to parents but it has also contributed to a shift from the schools to the families of the greatest bulk of the responsibility for quality education for all (Nakagawa, 2000). Under US federal law, local educational agencies receive funding for certain programs if they comply with parental involvement regulations. At the local level, these stipulations translate into compacts between families and schools, which are tied to Title I funds destined to support remedial literacy programs in schools serving low-income families. These social contracts have been deemed to establish an unequal partnership as they tend to be lopsided towards the responsibilities of parents (Nakagawa, 2000).

These policies also prescribe the types of access to school staff and the communication channels available to families, mainly in the form of conferences to discuss student achievement; thus they "minimize and control the ways that parents may interact with teachers", and tend to leave "parents with no organized outlet for challenging the school" or to express their concerns (Nakagawa, 2000, p. 460). What counts as parental involvement is unilaterally defined by the school and limited to those behaviors and attitudes which reflect strict alignment with school decisions and approaches. As Olivos (2006) notes, "In the public school setting it is clearly understood that if parents are to be involved in school-related matters, then they should always support, not question; follow, not lead; and trust, not doubt" (p. 18).

The official discourse of parental involvement has long been found to have exclusionary effects (De Carvalho, 2001; Nakagawa, 2000; Torres & Hurtado-Vivas, 2011). For decades, a constant flow of studies have questioned the adequacy of the mainstream approach to family-school relations and its cultural relevance to African American and Latin@ parents, to working-class mothers especially, and to immigrant mothers in particular (Dantas & Manyak, 2010; Delgado-Gaitán, 1994a, 1994b; Fine, 1993; Hurtig & Dyrness, 2011; López, 2001; Luttrell, 1997; Olivos, 2006; Olivos, Jimenez-Castellanos, & Ochoa, 2011; C. Suárez-Orozco, M. Suárez-Orozco, & Todorova, 2008; Valdés, 1996). The research points to links between the dominant discourse of parent involvement and a deficit view of families from underserved communities which results in lowered expectations for their children. Although at the federal level some of the language has shifted to include engagement and two-way communication (Mapp & Kuttner, 2014), it remains to be seen if these changes will have any lasting effects on the day-to-day experiences of all parents.

## "Parents" Equals "Mothers" in Social Policy Discourse

The focus of this chapter may well raise the following question: Why should a discussion about policies and institutional practices affecting families in their relations with schools and other institutions center on mothers only? This approach does not seek to deny the significance of other relationships, neither that there are fathers and other family members or guardians who are engaged in their children's upbringing and education, nor that there is an on-going effort for their involvement. Rather, the object is to underscore the existence and far-reaching effects of social and institutional expectations, reflected in different areas of social policy, which are directed mainly at mothers, and differentially affect historically marginalized women (Anthias & Yuval-Davis, 1983; Collins, 1999; Kawash, 2011; Schroedel & Fiber, 2001).

For instance, in the context of US schooling, when parental involvement is invoked, as a rule, it is tacitly understood that the parent expected to be most actively engaged in a child's education by default is the mother (González, 2005, p. 42; Hurtig & Dyrness, 2011; Kernan, 2012). The following example illustrates for how long this has been informally recognized to be the case. At a conference entitled "A New Understanding of Parental Involvement: Family-Work-School," Nancy R. Hoit acknowledged this fact in so many words, "We've learned that too frequently we say 'families and children' when we really mean mothers and children" (Cookson, Ferguson, & Townsend-Butterworth, 1997, p. 27). In this statement, it seems fair to assume that Hoit is referring to the official language used by policymakers, since at the time she was serving as Family Policy Consultant and Advisor to the Vice President of the United States.

Despite the gender-neutral terminology of "families" and "parents" or "parenting", in official discourse(s), "parents" often means "mothers" (Reay, 1998a). Thus, "by using the term 'parents' to refer implicitly to mothers, parent involvement programs and policies legitimize a paternalistic relationship between school systems and families" (Hurtig & Dyrness, 2011, p. 532). In this light, it then becomes clear how at the basis of the prevailing normative assumptions of institutional policies and practices concerning families and parenting lies the dominant ideology of motherhood which inspires and sustains them.

## The Dominant Ideology of Motherhood: Intensive Mothering and the Good Mother Myth

The Western master narrative of the good mother has been studied as a powerful myth which seeps into our everyday life and influences not only how we speak about mothers but even how we think about our own experiences (Andrews, 2004; Pope, Quinn, & Wyer, 1990). The binary quality of this cultural paradigm of motherhood, which comprises both the idolized perfect all-nurturing mother and its counterpart, the demonized monstrous mother, is most eloquently portrayed by Pope et al. (1990), "In its essentials, this patriarchal story of mothering is of a woman, entirely nurturant and provident, whose shadow side—potential or realized—is entirely wicked and withholding" (p. 441). This idealization of the role of the mother places an unrealistic burden on women with expectations of selflessness, availability and undivided devotion to childrearing (Thurer, 1994). In other words, this ideal carries in it the potential for societal judgment and blame of individual mothers.

The myth of the good mother operates as a societal yardstick against which mothers are constantly measured; when they are found to be missing the mark, they are subject to mother-blaming and, even more intensely, to self-blame (Hattery, 2008, p. 194; Kawash, 2011, p. 988; Pope et al., 1990; Thurer, 1994, p. 300). In contemporary US society, the good mother myth has reemerged in the ideology of intensive mothering defined by Hays (1996) as "the contemporary cultural model of socially appropriate mothering" which "is a gendered model that advises mothers to expend a tremendous amount of time, energy, and money in raising their children" (p. x). Hays (1996) points to the stark contrast existing between, on the one hand, the societal expectations for mothers to devote themselves entirely and selflessly to childrearing and, on the other, the parallel phenomena and realities of women's work responsibilities outside of the home as well as the culture of self-interest and gain that dominate society. These tensions constitute what Hays (1996) calls the "cultural contradictions of contemporary motherhood" (p. x).

The ideology of intensive mothering remains firmly entrenched in US society, despite much resistance to it, and "contemporary mothers, simply by living in this culture, are exposed to this dominant form of motherhood ideology" (Hattery, 2008, p. 198). The tenacity of the grip this myth has on our collective mind is described as creating "a world in which cultural expectations of mothering speak with a stronger voice than does the actual individual experience of mothering" in such a way that in shaping our stories they influence "not only what is heard but also what can be understood" (Pope et al., 1990, p. 445).

The debate on motherhood saw a shift for some decades, as it lost impetus in some arenas; by and large set aside, away from the center, by academia in general, and by feminist academics in particular—with some remarkable exceptions—it was taken up as the focus of investigation by popular literature and various mothers' movements (Kawash, 2011). Two clear trends emerged in the popular press: one, exposing and resisting intensive mothering; the other, unquestioningly contributing to its perpetuation through its recommendations for good mothering. In the first category, two separate books authored by journalists, Warner (2005) and Schulte (2014), do not only add to the popular literature on motherhood but also contribute to the continued exploration of the myth of the good mother as they update its portrayal. A mere glimpse at the titles of these works (*Perfect Madness: Motherhood in the Age of Anxiety* and *Overwhelmed: Work, Love, and Play When No One Has the Time*) affords us a sense of the perceived intensity of the demands still bestowed on the exacting role of the mother as constructed in mainstream present-day US society.

In the second category of popular literature on motherhood, publications with recommendations for good parenting have increased exponentially, as women are bombarded in a myriad of forums with expert (and non-expert) advice. One of the main contributions that these publications make to the perpetuation of the good mother myth is that they continue to accentuate the individual character of the responsibility of mothers. The consequences of this exclusive focus on individual mothers rather than on the reigning structural social conditions impacting motherhood are exemplified by this portrayal of the work-family balance debate:

This attention to individual behavior diverts attention away from the role that social structure plays in balancing, and weaving work and family. As long as issues of mothering and balancing and weaving work and family are defined as individual issues and women's issues [,] then those in positions of power in the society will not have to address the structural constraints, such as the lack of high quality, affordable childcare, responsible family leave policies [...]. (Hattery, 2008, p. 197)

This individual approach serves as a distraction and systematically prevents public attention from being focused on underlying social concerns and root causes of many women's circumstances. Whereas the bulk of the demands continue to be placed on individual women, the structural issues remain unacknowledged and unaddressed in any significant way to have a lasting social impact. The case Thurer (1994) made over two decades ago for exposing the myths of motherhood as an important step towards social transformation maintains its relevance today:

By unmasking the myths of motherhood, we can enlarge the possibility for taking control—through education, public policy, psychotherapy, even moral preachment—to achieve the climate we desire. In such a family climate, there would be personal sacrifice for a common good, but it would not be mother doing all of the sacrificing. [...] At the societal level, child rearing would not be dismissed as an individual mother's problem, but one in which nurturance and the well-being of all children are a transcendent public priority. This society would accept changes in family structure as inevitable (and not necessarily bad) and would devise for them new forms of public and private support. I hope for a society that will tolerate and encourage a diversity of mothering styles and cohabiting groups. (pp. 300–301)

Historically, the same ambiguity which characterizes the mother myth has marked the deep distrust of women as decision-makers even when concerning their own reproduction or their child-caring responsibilities. As highlighted in this chapter's epigraph, public policy tends to mirror the mainstream focus on a perceived social need to educate mothers rather than support them in meaningful ways to be able to carry out their work (Vandenberg-Daves, 2014).

In order to further contextualize the discussion on societal expectations for parents in their relations with institutions such as schools, it is necessary to recognize the extent to which the myth of the good mother permeates social interactions, practices, policies, and institutional life. An acknowledgement of these parallels across contexts can contribute to shed light on how this widespread and far-reaching web of assumptions and social expectations influences policies and behaviors across spheres and contributes to the societal control of mothers. The much needed shift from superficial and fragmented solutions to structural changes in social policy and institutional practices affecting families, parents, and women in particular would require such an interdisciplinary effort. As a small step in this direction, the remainder of this chapter analyzes the close connection between the dominant ideology of motherhood and the dominant conceptualization of parenting, that is, the ideal parent norm. In order to illustrate the analogies existing in these different issues and across disciplines, selected examples are drawn mainly from the literature on the official discourses of parental involvement in education, of family-work balance and of reproduction. Finally, an alternative ideology of motherhood, drawn from Collins's Black feminist theory, is presented within a critical feminist framework, as the basis of one of the strands of the analyses in this study in particular and, more broadly, for the insights it offers for the development of policies and practices against the grain.

## The Ideal Parent Norm in Social Policy

The dominant ideology of motherhood is reconstructed, reinforced and perpetuated in the ideal parent norm, the conceptualization of parenting found at the center of most social policy pertaining family issues. Researchers in different areas of social science who have focused on the discourse of social policy and the institutional practices concerning families, parents, and women in particular have reached similar conclusions. Across disciplines and issues, such as parental involvement in education, family-work balance, and reproduction, a constant emerges of an ideal social norm for parents. This norm is seen to underlie policies which affect women directly, define institutional expectations for them, and have a disparate impact on historically marginalized women. At the basis of the ideal parent norm lies the deeply ingrained dominant ideology of motherhood in its various iterations. The official discourse of parental involvement fits into this larger ideological context.

Work-family balance and reproduction are two areas of policy in which the ideal parent norm has been explored as part of the mainstream discourse. The public debate on the balance between work and family illustrates the significance of inquiring into how parenting is conceptualized in social policy. In her in-depth analysis of the discourse of the work-family policy debate, Sperling (2013) stresses the need to contest the mainstream ideal parent norm which "valorizes a time-intensive, parent-centric, and maternal-dependent model of childrearing that demands more resources than ever before from those individuals carrying the biological, legal, and/or cultural label of 'parent'" (p. 49). Sperling proposes that the solutions put forward in academic circles as well as in the popular press intended to alleviate the conflict at hand—such as efforts to add flexibility to the workplace or to encourage further involvement of fathers in parenting—remain ineffective because they do not question the underlying assumptions.

> Making it easier for working mothers to be Ideal Parents does not challenge the overburdened and self-sacrificial model of childrearing that imagines women at its center, parenting intensively, without meaningful options for delegation whatever the cost to their individual selves. (p. 49)

Thus, the solutions being advanced not only mirror the ideal parent norm but further contribute to its perpetuation. Instead of critically examining this unreachable standard based on "Non-Delegation, Maternal Bias, and Exhaustive Care", these proposals merely introduce plans to develop further ways of supporting those who are following this idealized form of parenting (i.e. intensive mothering) and are attempting to meet its high bar (p. 49).

Regulation of reproduction constitutes another forceful example of the ideal parent norm at work. Population policies and the regulation of reproduction are examined by Collins (1999) in the intersections of race, ethnicity, class, and citizenship status through the lens of motherhood ideology. Collins underscores the need to understand how crucial the ideas about motherhood are "to constructing both the citizenship rights of diverse groups of women and American social policy" (p. 118). The resulting analysis constitutes a glaring example of the prevalence of the ideal parent norm (i.e. ideal mother norm) across wide areas of social policy. Collins (1999) observes that, "Some women emerge as more worthy 'mothers of the nation' than others"; women in different social locations are perceived as occupying different categories in their potential role as mothers for the purpose of policy-making, ranging from "desirable" to "invisible", through "capable of becoming fit" and "unfit" (p. 119). At the far end of this spectrum stand undocumented Latina immigrants, who are often employed as caretakers by more privileged groups to carry out the job of social motherhood. Whereas they are considered suitable "mothers for hire", they remain invisible for all policy and planning purposes; they are regarded as existing "outside the national family" and, therefore, "as employable mothers, undocumented Latinas remain virtually invisible" (Collins, 1999, pp. 126–127). If any attention is paid to immigrant women in this context, it is to blame them within the anti-immigration discourse, as burdens to the economy and the welfare system, while they are often simultaneously being exploited. In spite of this, Collins insists, differential social locations, such as race, ethnicity, class or citizenship status, should not be taken as the basis of social determinism, instead it is often the case that "these categories constrain choices and may foster women's agency in ways that can be quite unintended" (Collins, 1999, p. 120). This is precisely the case with the seven women on whose stories we focus.

## Ideal Parents vis-à-vis Real Mothers in the Literature on Parental Involvement

The good mother myth—in its iterations of intensive mothering and of the ideal parent norm—manifests itself in the context of education barely disguised under the mantle of the discourse of parent involvement. Critical educational researchers and feminist scholars who have focused on parental involvement in the United States have pointed out the inconsistencies between the official discourse and the experience of exclusion of those who do not meet the standard of the ideal parent. Comparable studies conducted throughout the past decades in the UK have found striking similarities. As we have seen, the standards which comprise the official discourse of parental involvement are crystalized in policy specifically addressing the family-school relationship, but they also include implicit expectations commonly shared by teachers such as being "active, involved, assertive, informed, and educated advocates for their children" (Lareau & Weininger, 2003, p. 589). These teachers' expectations for parents to be actively engaged in their children's education have some outward signs that may not be easily achieved by all parents, such as being able and willing to "question the school" (Suárez-Orozco et al., 2008, p. 76).

These expectations tend to reflect middle-class approaches to parenting (Gewirtz, Dickson, Power, Halpin, & Whitty, 2005). As was noted above with reference to the broader context of social expectations and the discourse of public policy, in the context of family-school relations the focus tends to center on the individual responsibility of mothers. Often "individual mothers are blamed, and they in turn blame themselves for the institutional failure of schools to educate disadvantaged children" (Luttrell, 1997, p. 112). Focusing on the individual responsibility of mothers shifts the attention from the schools and encourages "'blame-the-victim' explanations of differential educational outcomes" (Gewirtz, Ball, & Bowe, 1994, p. 3).

Two authors, Annette Lareau (together with several co-authors) in the US, and Diane Reay in the UK, carried out a series of comparable studies, which have become iconic for the field of parental involvement research on each side of the Atlantic, examining home-school relations through an adaptation and expansion of Bourdieu's framework to study social reproduction in schooling. They consider the impact of social class on home-school relations by comparing the interactions of groups of middle-class parents to those of working-class parents, within the context of different schools—a comparison which was possible given the high level of segregation across class lines present in the schools observed in each case. These studies pointed to the workings of social reproduction in schools, as they illustrated how social class advantage is maintained and how everyday practices in home-school relationships tend to perpetuate inequity. On the one hand, middle-class mothers find themselves empowered not only by financial resources, educational knowledge, and information on schooling, but mainly by a sense of confidence and entitlement; on the other hand, working-class mothers often feel (or are made to feel) incompetent, and are often rebuffed when expressing their concerns to school agents (Lareau, 2011; Lareau & McNamara Horvat, 1999; Lareau & Weininger, 2003; Reay, 1998a, 1998b, 2004).

According to the patterns observed, instead of adopting an assertive attitude as many middle-class mothers are found to do in similar situations, working-class mothers' interactions are characterized by distrust and constraint (Lareau & Weininger, 2003; Luttrell, 1997; Weininger & Lareau, 2003). In these studies, poor and working-class mothers often resort to deference, instead of insisting on their requests and, consequently, are perceived as passive and disinterested by the school. Weininger and Lareau (2003) examine the transcripts of parent-teacher conferences comparing those of poor, working-class and middle-class parents. In most cases, the parents were mostly mothers, or, in the few cases where both parents were present, mothers took on the most active role. Patterns were found not only in the strategies employed by both groups, but in the teachers' responses to them. The amount and quality of information obtained by the different groups of parents, as well as the roles of authority were markedly contrasting and followed clear class divisions, privileging the middle-class parents. Teachers were observed to control the conversation in conferences with poor and working-class parents, whose role was mostly reactive; while with middle-class parents often the roles were reversed, and teachers became passive listeners (p. 386). Similarly, in her earlier work, Lareau (1987) found that the advantages of cultural capital for the middle-class mothers in her study rested on the type of information they accessed; on the type of communication with teachers, which tended to center on academic talk, as contrasted with that of poor or working-class mothers, which was anecdotic or related to behavior; and even on their informal exchanges, which differed in quantity and in quality from that of working-class mothers in the study.

Weininger and Lareau's (2003) findings on "the tendency of working-class and poor parents to rely on teachers for evaluations" coincides with Reay's (1998a) observations of the higher propensity of working-class mothers to define teachers as the experts, which ended up "undermining a conflicting feeling that their children were being treated unfairly" (pp. 388, 59). Underlying this trend, Reay (1998a) observes a contrasting pattern of middle-class mothers who attributed the cause of any educational problems "to deficits in schooling", while working-class mothers expressed certainty "that educational difficulties were due to failings in the individual rather than the system" (p. 58).

These studies also coincided in noting how often the middle-class mothers' strategies of intervention to impact their children's schooling in some desired way—for example, moving their child into a higher track—were effective because they were legitimized by the schools, whereas the strategies employed by the working-class mothers were often rejected by professionals as inappropriate, considered too passive, too aggressive or overemotional (Lareau, 2011; Lareau & McNamara Horvat, 1999; Lareau & Weininger, 2003). In her feminist qualitative study, Reay (1998a, 1998b) applies and expands Bourdieu's theory to conclude that middle-class mothers work to replicate habitus, while working-class mothers' harder job is to transform habitus, since the actions of the former are sustained by school practice while those of the latter are undermined by it.

Along the same lines, several other studies carried out in the UK found that working-class and immigrant parents question the official concept of parental involvement, since often the policies and practices which are put forward in the name of inclusion are perceived and experienced as intensifying their exclusion (Blackledge, 2001; Gewirtz, 2006; Gewirtz et al., 1994). In the context of a larger research project which focused on the implementation of a governmental initiative in the UK intended to overcome disadvantages in schooling through parent education, Gewirtz (2006) notes how working-class parents interviewed for her study question the limited view of these programs and suggest that "it was the teachers not the parents who needed educating about how better to relate to others" (p. 73). In her conclusions, Gewirtz (2006) underscores the need for contextualization in the development of equitable educational policies and practices (p. 80).

Similarly, Blackledge (2001) and Gewirtz et al. (1994) found that recent immigrant parents who speak languages other than English may not benefit from their cultural capital, because of the high levels of proficiency in English required to meet school expectations. Blackledge's (2001) study focuses on home-school relations of Bangladeshi immigrant women, and the dynamics and structures of power associated with the school and home languages and literacies. The author points to the different ways in which Bangladeshi women were marginalized both in their communication with their children's school, and their attempts to support their children's literacy processes, since literacy learning was equated with English proficiency. The school practices—defined in terms of "symbolic domination"—reflected the notion that immigrant women have the "wrong sort of capital" (Blackledge, 2001, p. 345).

In their longitudinal study of immigrant students in the US, Suárez-Orozco et al. (2008) found similar attitudes from the schools towards immigrant parents. The teachers they interviewed considered showing up at the school often and helping their children with homework to be the two pillars of parental involvement. Most teachers voiced negative assessments of immigrant parents they knew, because they did not see them enough. In the teachers' eyes, this group of parents did not seem to be interested in their children's education. Instead, they suggested, they were mostly concerned with day-to-day life as they settled in their new context, and not with their children's progress. As the authors state, "overall teachers' assessments of immigrant parents were often patronizing at best and hostile at worst" (Suárez-Orozco et al., 2008, p. 77). Similar patterns of variation in parent-school interactions along the lines of social class, race, language and national origin continue to be observed in the educational literature (Olivos, 2006; Olivos et al., 2011).

## Historical Social Control of Women: Individual Blame for Structural Conditions

Throughout Western history, mothers have been held to high standards of parenting, and thus have been subject to harsh public evaluation; they have been demonized just as vehemently as they have been idolized. As described above, these high and sometimes unspoken social expectations derive from a gendered ideology of parenting—and a heteronormative one at that—which is mostly individual-oriented rather than centered on the extended family or the community, holds mothers and fathers to different standards, and results in mothers being expected to single-handedly carry out most of the practical parenting tasks in and out of the home (Berry, 1993; Hattery, 2008; Schulte, 2014).

This binary norm contributes to the historical pattern of social control of mothers, since: "Through it all, she has rarely been consulted. She is an object, not a subject" (Thurer, 1994, p. 299). Within public policy, conceptualizations of motherhood have often been devised with specific agendas in mind to establish sharp distinctions between "good" and "bad" mothers. This demarcation tends to also fall "along the lines of other categories of identity, especially racial or ethnic identity and socio-economic status, thus further solidifying the oppression and state control of all women who are members of these marginalized groups" (DiQuinzio, 2006, p. 61).

Public policy discourse often tends to have the effect of disempowering marginalized women as it is designed to "protect women and children from themselves" (DiQuinzio & Meagher, 2005, p. 2). It also often creates a "double bind" for the same population. Rooted in dualistic Western philosophy, public policy is often based on the concept of abstract individualism, which involves the attributes of autonomy and rationality, considered prerequisites to citizenship. At the same time, within this dualistic philosophy, the standard of "good mothering" based on "essential motherhood" contributes to define womanhood in terms of emotionality and caring, and operates to virtually exclude women—especially from historically marginalized populations, and often in this context defined as and equated to the role of mothers—from participation in the public sphere, given their purported lack of the prerequisite of abstract individualism (DiQuinzio & Meagher 2005, p. 3). In a perspective derived from essential motherhood, "claims about mothers and motherhood in the dominant discourse of individualism easily slip into or become claims about all women" (DiQuinzio, 2006, p. 61). As Young (1990) proposes, the ideal of impartiality of the civic public, based on a unified and homogenous citizenship, normalizes privilege, and creates a dichotomy between "universal and particular, public and private, reason and passion" (p. 97). Historically, the association of the general interest with an impartial point of view associated with reason in opposition to the body and the affective, has served to exclude whole groups of people, especially women and ethnic groups, defined by difference and their association to these traits (p. 97).

Social practices in two spheres serve as striking examples of social control of women. Historically, reproduction is one area in which women living in poverty have experienced some of the most egregiously violent forms of social control, especially through forced sterilization. In the 1960s in response to the rise in the number of women on welfare "medical doctors started to make decisions regarding poor women's bodies and economic situations. Women were often coerced into signing consent forms for sterilization or they did not know what was going on" (Jackson, 2014, p. 327).

Another one of the consequences of the paternalistic control of women involves policy language on women's issues concerning their responsibility towards their children, by which this alone is prioritized with complete disregard for the woman's wellbeing. In some instances, through an exclusive focus on the child's wellbeing, these policies virtually pit one against the other. One extreme instance of this can be observed in the impact of the preponderance of a punitive approach (versus a public health approach) to the complex issue of drug addiction in pregnant women living in poverty. Besides being seen as monsters, pregnant addicts are often prevented from seeking treatment in public health care institutions given their fear of the legal repercussions for them and their children, which in many cases may involve the removal of their child at birth (Schroedel & Fiber, 2001; Young, 1997). These punitive measures tend to reflect institutional sexism, classism and racism, as historically they have disproportionally been imposed on poor black women (Young, 1997, pp. 77–79). An examination of patterns in the regulation of these extreme situations allows us to bring to the forefront the glaring absence of any consideration for structural issues which contribute to these dire circumstances in the first place.

This social control of women can be understood as derived from the discourse of traditional family values, which perpetuates the gendered public/private dichotomy and defines full citizenship in limited terms of independence (Fraser, 1989; Young, 1997). Public policy often assumes the moral superiority of the two-parent household, and virtually punishes single parents, especially those who live in poverty, who are predominantly mothers, based on the stigma of dependency of the "deviant mother" (Young, 1997). Young proposes that, in order to recognize the need for support while respecting people's different experiences, it is crucial to unpack the two meanings of independence.

The first is autonomy: within the bounds of justice, to be able to make choices about one's life and to act on those choices without having to obey others, meet their conditions, or fear their threats and punishments. The second is self-sufficiency: not needing help or support from anyone in meeting one's needs and carrying out one's life plans. (pp. 125–126)

Nowadays, as independence is mostly understood as self-sufficiency, "having a well-paid secure job" is the main social contribution which is socially valued (Young, 1997, p. 126). Caretaking, for instance, carried out mainly by women as unpaid and unprofitable work is not considered a social contribution or a sign of independence. Thus, as autonomy is granted to individuals based on their self-sufficiency, commonsense and social policy discourse punishes individual women and blames their poverty on their failure without consideration of the structural restrictions of the employment market or of the lack of support for needs and social contributions which go unrecognized (Jackson, 2014; Young, 1997, p. 131). Households dependent on welfare are considered "failed families" and are subjected to close state oversight (Fraser, 1989; Young, 1997). "Too many single mothers fall in this category, and contemporary rhetoric and policy proposals seem determined to deprive them further of their autonomy" (Young, 1997).

Single mothers living in poverty are marginalized further through the loss of autonomy and thus denied full social citizenship. They are considered deviant from the normalized ideals for women for failing to meet them on several grounds, while the same system that punishes them contributes to create some of the social traps responsible for these situations in the first place. These dilemmas include the following set of circumstances, among others: first and foremost, their households do not match the male bread-winning model of the traditional family, and are therefore considered "broken homes"; second, since there are not enough options for affordable childcare, some single mothers living in poverty may not be able to hold full-time jobs or earn anywhere near living wages; third, if they do, their wages may also disqualify them based on maximum income requirements for such childcare services; and, fourth, paradoxically, a society whose collective mind is permeated by the ideology of intensive mothering frowns upon women who are not full-time caretakers of younger children but also punishes the dependency of those who cannot provide for their children if they are (Fraser, 1989; Jackson, 2014; Young, 1997).

In this way, the cultural and ideological demands of motherhood are disconnected from the structural realities of single women living in poverty. The urgent call for "feminist ethics in general, and the ethics of care in particular," made by Iris Young (1997) in the late 1990s is still relevant today, or even more so (p. 83). Young insisted on the imperative "to apply its insights to the pressing social policy issues of justice" and towards "interpreting the reasons for welfare and publicly funded social services very differently from the dominant interpretation in the United States" (p. 83). There is a pressing need to recognize the institutional structures and complex power relations at play which result in the predicament many mothers living in poverty face. This would require rethinking the stigma associated with certain forms of assistance which "are regarded as handouts," as compared to entitlements for those who are seen as having earned them, such as social security or unemployment benefits (Young, 1997, p. 83).

## Intersectionality and Structural Issues

When the discussion of motherhood ideologies takes into account intersectionality by the addition of other social locations besides gender—such as race, class, national origin, citizenship status—further inequalities and contradictions in societal expectations for women emerge (Anthias & Yuval-Davis, 1983; Collins, 1999). In her historical survey of the conceptualizations of motherhood, Thurer (1994) reflects on how the apparently new dilemmas of the exacting expectations for women in the second half of the 20th century were only new issues to white middle-class women.

> Women in the 1970s absorbed the baby and the bathwater, that is, the baby and the contemporary inflated ideology of good mothering (relentless tenderness, total availability, and so on). Given permission (in theory, anyway) to "have it all" –children and careers—these young American mothers attempted to become superwomen. Facing formidable problems—no federally backed maternity leave, day care, or hospitalization for childbirth [...]; a job market that discriminates against women and makes no concessions for the needs of mothers and children—they stumbled. *Had they consulted women of color and immigrant women, many of whom had been struggling all along, they might have been forewarned.* (p. 266, Italics added)

Even though focus on women in the workplace in the popular press suggests otherwise, women's employment outside of the home is not a new phenomenon, since there is a long history of women working in factories and farming (Guerrina, 2014, p. 469). "Women of color have always worked" (Hondagneu-Sotelo & Avila, 2003, p. 319). There were women who had been juggling the often conflicting demands on working mothers long before these surfaced as part of the public debate. Yet, work patterns for women and issues of the balance of work inside and outside the home only gained widespread attention when white middle-class women went into the workforce (Berry, 1993, p. 149). These facts point to the historical invisibility of marginalized women whose interests, for the most part absent from the focus of public attention, are hardly ever adopted as the main vantage point for policymaking.

This invisibility is not a new phenomenon either. Anthias and Yuval-Davis (1983) remind us that, for centuries, invisibility in history was a distinct form of oppression for women in general, and that once women were taken into account, no effort was made to shed light on the differentiated struggles along class and ethnicity lines (p. 71). Even within early socialist feminist writings, the oppression persisted in that their analyses often ignored underprivileged migrant and ethnic groups, whose mere existence and issues remained unacknowledged (Anthias & Yuval Davis, 1983, p. 71; hooks, 2000, p. 19). Consistent with this relentless invisibility of differences among women, the public debate on reform concerning issues of social motherhood such as maternity leave and workplace day-care arrangements tend to be centered on the needs of white middle-class women (Collins, 1999, p. 122). The same applies to the social demands surrounding education and schooling. As becomes clear from different mothers movements, "the group 'mothers' is not a monolithic group with a single, unified set of perspectives, interests, and concerns" (DiQuinzio, 2006, p. 60; Hondagneu-Sotelo & Avila, 2003). The issues raised by the mainstream mothers movements mostly represent the interest of white, middle-class women. DiQuinzio (2006) points to the contrast between the concerns of different groups in these terms:

> In the U.S., for example, there are motherhood-based groups led by women of color, especially African-American women. These groups, however, tend to focus on different issues than those raised by groups like MOTHERS [...] they are particularly concerned with poverty, welfare reform, public schooling, and the effects of violence, especially gun violence, in predominantly African-American communities. (p. 56)

Since most social arrangements are made with the interest of white middle-class mothers in mind, what remains invisible is how the nature of these social provisions affects the everyday life of women differently depending on their social location.

Attention to the structural conditions underlying these social debates requires that intersectionality matters be placed in the forefront. A long-standing dilemma stems from the need to assert the equality of women and their agency while maintaining a focus on the specific needs of women, as well as the differences among them (DiQuinzio & Meagher, 2005, p. 3). Even when feminist writings started broadening their scope to include historically marginalized groups of women, a new pitfall appeared in the risk of creating stereotypes by not taking into account the internal differences within groups (Zavella, 1991). Specifically, research centered on Latinas often fails to recognize, for example, the distinction between US-born Latinas of Mexican descent and Mexican-born immigrant women living in the US (Segura, 2007). In studies on employment, for instance, this leads to a common misguided assumption that all groups will share patterns of motherhood/work (Segura, 2007, p. 372). In educational research there is a similar tendency to conflate the stories of quite disparate groups of women under the broad umbrella of Latinas.

To address these oversights, and to ensure that attention is paid to significant commonalities and differences, Zavella (1991) advocates for an analysis which starts out by recognizing "the historically specific structural conditions constraining women's experiences" (p. 74). This does not imply an abandonment of the centrality of specific women's experiences. Instead, Zavella urges that our research have "the structure in which women's experiences are framed become the primary analytical locus" (p. 74). Such focus on historical contextualization and attention to the intersections of social locations would foster the emergence and examination of both the commonalities as well as of a clear differentiation within groups. This would not only help reverse stereotypes reproduced by dominant discourses but may open up the possibility of finding affinities across groups who may not all share an identical background, but may have in common certain social locations (Young, 2002; Zavella, 1991). This group "assertion of specificity and difference towards a wider public" is proposed as the basis of solidarity in political agency for justice against structural inequity (Young, 2002, p. 103).

## The Need for Diverse Cultural Stories of Motherhood

This deepening awareness of the structural consequences of the historical invisibility of intersectionality points to a compelling need for different cultural stories of mothering to be allowed to emerge so that it may inform relevant aspects of public policy. Pope et al. (1990) eloquently refer to this need in these words:

> In critiquing the ideology of mothering, we see the limitations and dangers of one particular cultural story. We see, too, the limitations in privileging a version that re-

ifies and overburdens the mother's role, omitting the influential nurturing and shaping effects of other women in women's lives. Finally, it is not the story, or a story,
that must be told, and crucially, must be heard. It is the stories: stories of mothering,
of daughtering, of history, of this minute, stories of all classes and cultures, stories of
experience and possibility. (p. 446)

Those stories which are left out from the mainstream discourse emerge from
a different context and thus reflect a different ideology of motherhood altogether. Collins (1994) calls attention to the fact that often feminist theories
of motherhood suffer from the same decontextualization common in most
Western social thinking (p. 45). In not taking into account race and class,
Collins argues, these theories of motherhood leave out the contexts of mothering that contribute to shape it. Thus, this decontextualization leads to misguided assumptions.

The central assumption in this decontextualized view is that the "struggle for individual autonomy" against "male domination in the political economy and the household" remains the pivotal issue (Collins, 1994, p. 46).
Another set of assumptions follows, namely: first, a marked separation between public and private spheres, i.e. the strict demarcation of the economic and political as separate from the noneconomic and apolitical family
and household; second, public and private spheres are gender-segregated,
and this gives way to work and family as sex-segregated institutions, based
on sharply distinguished gender roles; third, the public/private dichotomy
translates into gender roles within the family, with the corresponding divi-
sion of labor into the male bread-winner role and the female labor of nurturing and mothering; fourth, the central human undertaking consists of
striving for individual autonomy from the oppressions of patriarchy and/or
society (Collins, 1994, p. 46).

When the experience of women of color becomes the center of theorization, Collins (1994) argues, this framework and all its assumptions are rendered inapplicable, since its notions of motherhood do not fit the context and
the experiences of Latina, African-American, Asian-American, or Native
American women. Although gender oppression remains an issue, "For women
of color, the subjective experience of mothering/motherhood is inextricably
linked to the sociocultural concern of racial ethnic communities" (Collins,
1994, p. 47).

# Motherwork: A Critical Ideology of Motherhood

Collins (1994) proposes the concept of motherwork as an alternative both to the mainstream ideology of motherhood as well as to feminist theories of motherhood which leave out considerations of race and class. With the notion of motherwork Collins introduces a contextualized framework which is critical of the sharp dichotomies present in previous feminist theorization.

> I use the term "motherwork" to soften the existing dichotomies in feminist theorizing about motherhood that posit rigid distinctions between private and public, family and work, the individual and the collective, identity as individual autonomy and identity growing from the collective self-determination of one's group. Racial ethnic women's mothering and work experiences occur at the boundaries demarking these dualities. (Collins, 1994, pp. 47–48)

One of the pronounced shifts in this redefinition of the central issues of motherhood is that survival is no longer taken for granted. In contextualizing this difference, Collins (1994) states that whereas "physical survival is assumed for children who are white and middle-class" this is not the case for most children of women of color, given the fact that "approximately one-third of Hispanic children and one-half of African-American children who survive infancy live in poverty" (p. 49). The struggle for survival of the community and the survival of children emerge as central issues. Therefore, in motherwork, the experience of mothering is intricately connected to the wider political and economic social structures.

> Specifying the contours of racial ethnic women's motherwork promises to point the way toward richer feminist theorizing about motherhood. Themes of survival, power, and identity form the bedrock and reveal how racial ethnic women in the United States encounter and fashion motherwork. That is to understand the importance of working for the physical survival of children and community, the dialectical nature of power and powerlessness in structuring mothering patterns, and the significance of self-definition in constructing individual and collective racial identity is to grasp the three core themes characterizing the experiences of Native American, African-American, Hispanic and Asian-American women. (Collins, 1994, p. 49)

When race and class are taken into account, at the center of the work carried out by racial ethnic women, the themes which emerge are the survival, power and identity of the community as well as of the individual (Collins, 1994,

2000). Thus, the ideology of motherwork in its community-oriented focus on survival and empowerment differs fundamentally from the mainstream ideology of motherhood centered on the individual or the nuclear family. In its focus on community survival, motherwork includes helping children develop a strong identity in the face of racism and the oppressive assimilative forces they encounter in their daily social interactions outside of the home (Collins, 1994; Delgado Bernal, 2006; Cibils, 2011).

Further, motherwork includes the figure of the othermother who contributes to taking care of children in the extended family and other members of the community (Collins, 2000). This is the case in African American as well as in Latin@ communities. Mothering has long been a communal experience and a valued resource for Latina mothers, within a less individualistic social organization. In it the extended family has a central role, and "Reliance on grandmothers and comadres for shared mothering is well established in Latina culture, and it is a practice that signifies a more collectivist shared approach to mothering in contrast to a more individualistic, Anglo American approach" (Hondagneu-Sotelo & Avila, 2003, pp. 327–328). Segura and Pierce (1993) refer to this as "the practice of non-exclusive mothering," which is described as one aspect of familism in Latin@ communities which is based on the value of *confianza* (trust derived from close relationships). The significance of this value is explained in these terms, "Trust that resides solely within Chicana/o families serves as an important strategy for cultural survival and resistance in the face of racism and other forms of domination by creating ties within and across kin networks" (Segura & Pierce, 1993, pp. 73–75). The support of the community in child-rearing is central to the well-being of families and children, and contrasts with the individualistic approach to motherhood in nuclear family-centered communities.

> Extensive interaction across kin networks also enhance the opportunities for relatives other than the mother to become involved in child rearing and providing child care as well as emotional support. In times of crisis, members of the extended family provide physical and affective care for children and emotional and economic support for the parents. (Segura & Pierce, 1993, p. 75)

Since its labor extends the nurturing function beyond the scope of the needs of the immediate family to include the survival of the community, the notion of motherwork challenges the dichotomies of work and family, and male and female roles as concerning the respective separate spheres of public and private.

The locus of conflict lies outside the household, as women and their families engage in collective effort to create and maintain family life in the face of forces that undermine family integrity. But this "reproductive labor" or "motherwork" goes beyond ensuring the survival of one's own biological children or those of one's family. This type of motherwork recognizes that individual survival, empowerment, and identity require group survival, empowerment, and identity. (Collins, 1994, p. 47)

These conclusions apply to the Latina women whose stories are at the heart of this book. First, the dichotomy of family and work does not stand, since these two spheres are closely interconnected in the experience of working-class Latina immigrants (Segura, 2007). Second, the experience of mothering/motherhood goes beyond the individual and nuclear families, and extends to the whole community. Third, physical survival is not taken for granted, as it is in middle-class views of mothers, but is instead at the center of motherhood, as illustrated in the stories of the seven women who shared with us their stories of engagement with their children's education. Motherwork was found to be the common thread in their counter stories.

# References

Andrews, M. (2004). Opening to the original contributions: Counter-narratives and the power to oppose. In M. Bamberg & M. Andrews (Eds.), *Considering counter-narratives: Narrating, resisting, making sense* (pp. 1–6). Amsterdam/Philadelphia: John Benjamins.

Anthias, F., & Yuval-Davis, N. (1983). Contextualizing feminism: Gender, ethnic and class divisions. *Feminist Review, 15*, 62–75.

Berry, M. (1993). *The politics of parenthood: Child care, women's rights, and the myth of the good mother*. New York, NY: Penguin.

Blackledge, A. (2001). The wrong sort of capital? Bangladeshi women and their children's schooling in Birmingham, UK. *The International Journal of Bilingualism, 5*(3), 345–362.

Boler, M., & Zembylas, M. (2003). Discomforting truths: The emotional terrain of understanding difference. In P. Trifonas (Ed.), *Pedagogies of difference: Rethinking education for social change* (pp. 110–136). New York, NY and London: RoutledgeFalmer.

Cibils, L. R. de (2011). *Immigrant women's narrative reconstruction of their interactions with their children's schools: A collective qualitative case study* (Doctoral Dissertation). New Mexico State University, Las Cruces.

Collins, P. H. (1994). Shifting the center: Race, class, and feminist theorizing about motherhood. In E. N. Glenn, G. Chang, & L. R. Forcey (Eds.), *Mothering: Ideology, experience, and agency* (pp. 45–65). New York, NY: Routledge.

Collins, P. H. (1999). Producing the mothers of the nation: Race, class and contemporary US population policies. In N. Yuval-Davis (Ed.), *Women, citizens and difference* (pp. 118–129). London: Zed Books.

Cookson, P., Ferguson, S., & Townsend-Butterworth, D. (Eds.). (1997). *A new understanding of parent involvement: Family-work-school.* Darby, PA: Diane Publishing.

Dantas, M. L., & Manyak, P. (Eds.). (2010). *Home-school connections in a multicultural society: Learning from and with culturally and linguistically diverse families.* New York, NY: Routledge.

De Carvalho, M. E. (2001). *Rethinking family-school relations: A critique of parental involvement in schooling.* Mahwah, NJ: Lawrence Erlbaum Associates.

Delgado Bernal, D. (2006). Learning and living pedagogies of the home. In D. Delgado Bernal, A. Elenes, F. Godinez, & S. Villenas (Eds.), *Chicana/Latina education in everyday life: Feminista perspectives on pedagogy and epistemology* (pp. 113–132). Albany, NY: State University of New York Press.

Delgado-Gaitán, C. (1994a). *Empowerment in Carpintería: A five-year study of family, school, and community relationships.* Report No. 49. Baltimore, MD: Center for Research on Effective Schooling for Disadvantaged Students, The Johns Hopkins University.

Delgado-Gaitán, C. (1994b). Spanish-speaking families' involvement in schools. In C. Fagnano & B. Werber (Eds.), *School, family, and community interaction: A view from the firing lines* (pp. 85–96). Boulder, CO: Westview Press.

DiQuinzio, P. (2006). The politics of the mothers' movement in the United States: Possibilities and pitfalls. *Journal of the Association for Research on Mothering, 8*(1–2), 55–71.

DiQuinzio, P., & Meagher, S. (2005). Introduction: Women and children first. In S. Meagher & P. DiQuinzio (Eds.), *Women and children first: Feminism, rhetoric, and public policy* (pp. 1–13). Albany, NY: State University of New York Press.

Foss, S., Foss, K., & Trapp, R. (1985). *Contemporary perspectives on rhetoric.* Prospect Heights, IL: Waveland Press.

Foucault, M. (1977). *Power/Knowledge: Selected interviews and other writings 1972–1977.* (C. Gordon, Ed.; C. Gordon, L. Marshall, J. Mepham, & K. Soper, Trans.). New York, NY: Pantheon.

Fraser, N. (1989). *Unruly practices: Power, discourse, and gender in contemporary social theory.* Minneapolis, MN: University of Minnesota Press.

Gee, J. (2012). *Social linguistics and literacies: Ideology in discourses* (4th ed.). London and New York, NY: Routledge.

Gewirtz, S. (2006). Towards a contextualized analysis of social justice in education. *Educational Philosophy and Theory, 38*(1), 69–81.

Gewirtz, S., Ball, S., & Bowe, R. (1994). Parents, privilege and the education market place. *Research Papers in Education, 9*(1), 3–29.

Gewirtz, S., Dickson, M., Power, S., Halpin, D., & Whitty, G. (2005). The deployment of social capital theory in educational policy and provision: The case of Education Action Zones in England. *British Educational Research Journal, 31*(6), 651–673.

González, N. (2005). *I am my language: Discourses of women and children in the borderlands.* Tucson, AZ: The University of Arizona Press.

Guerrina, R. (2014). Working mothers: Performing economic and gender ideologies. In A. O'Reilly (Ed.), *Mothers, mothering and motherhood: Across cultural differences* (pp. 467–485). Bradford, ON: Demeter Press.

Hattery, A. (2008). Intensive motherhood ideology: Shaping the ways we balance and weave work and family into the 21st century and beyond. In J. Nathanson & L. C. Tuley (Eds.), *Mother knows best: Talking back to the "experts"* (pp. 192–202). Toronto, ON: Demeter Press.

Hays, S. (1996). *The cultural contradictions of motherhood.* New Haven, CT and London: Yale University Press.

Hondagneu-Sotelo, P., & Avila, E. (2003). "I'm here, but I'm there": The meanings of Latina transnational motherhood. In P. Hondagneu-Sotelo (Ed.), *Gender and U.S. immigration: Contemporary trends* (pp. 317–340). Berkeley, CA: University of California Press.

hooks, b. (2000). *Feminist theory: From margin to center.* Cambridge, MA: South End Press.

Hurtig, J., & Dyrness, A. (2011). Parents as critical educators and ethnographers of schooling. In B. A. U. Levinson & M. Pollock (Eds.), *A companion to the anthropology of education* (pp. 530–546). Oxford, UK: Wiley-Blackwell.

Jackson, H. (2014). Mothering in poverty. In A. O'Reilly (Ed.), *Mothers, mothering and motherhood: Across cultural differences* (pp. 323–339). Bradford, ON: Demeter Press.

Kawash, S. (2011). New directions in motherhood studies. *Signs: Journal of Women in Culture and Society, 36*(4), 968–1003

Kernan, M. (2012). *Parental involvement in early learning: A review of research, policy and good practice.* The Hague: Bernard van Leer Foundation.

Kincheloe, J. (2005). *Critical constructivism primer.* New York, NY: Peter Lang.

Lareau, A. (1987). Social class differences in family-school relationships: The importance of cultural capital. *Sociology of Education, 60,* 73–85.

Lareau, A. (2011). *Unequal childhoods: Class, race, and family life* (2nd ed.). Berkeley, CA: University of California Press.

Lareau, A., & McNamara Horvat, E. (1999). Moments of social inclusion and exclusion: Race, class and cultural capital in family-school relationships. *Sociology of Education, 72*(1), 37–53.

Lareau, A., & Weininger, E. (2003). Cultural capital in educational research: A critical assessment. *Theory and Society, 32,* 567–606.

López, G. (2001). The value of hard work: Lessons on parent involvement from an (Im)migrant household. *Harvard Education Review, 71*(3), 416–438.

Luttrell, W. (1997). *Schoolsmart and motherwise: Working-class women's identity and schooling.* New York, NY and London: Routledge.

Mapp, K.L., & Kuttner, P.J. (2014). Partners in education: A dual capacity-building framework for family-school partnerships. U.S. Department of Education, Washington, DC, and Southwest Educational Development (SEDL), Austin, TX. Retrieved from http://www2.ed.gov/documents/family-community/partners-education.pdf

Nakagawa, K. (2000). Unthreading the ties that bind: Questioning the discourse of parent involvement. *Educational Policy, 14*(4), 443–472.

Olivos, E. (2006). *The power of parents: A critical perspective of bicultural parent involvement in public schools.* New York, NY: Peter Lang.

Olivos, E., Jimenez-Castellanos, O., & Ochoa, A. (Eds.). (2011). *Bicultural parent engagement: Advocacy and empowerment.* New York, NY: Teachers College Press.

Pope, D., Quinn, N., & Wyer, M. (Eds.). (1990). Editorial. The ideology of mothering: Disruption and reproduction of patriarchy. *Signs, 15*(30), 441–447.

Reay, D. (1998a). *Class work: Mother's involvement in their children's primary schooling.* London: UCL Press.

Reay, D. (1998b). Cultural reproduction: Mothers' involvement in their children's primary schooling. In M. Grenfell & D. James (Eds.), *Bourdieu and education: Acts of practical theory* (pp. 55–71). New York, NY: RoutledgeFalmer.

Reay, D. (2004). Gendering Bourdieu's concept of capitals? Emotional capital, women and social class. In L. Adkins & B. Skeggs (Eds.), *Feminism after Bourdieu* (pp. 57–74). Oxford and Malden, MA: Blackwell.

Schroedel, J. R., & Fiber, P. (2001). Punitive versus public health oriented responses to drug use by pregnant women. *Yale Journal of Health Policy, Law, and Ethics, 1*(1), 217–236.

Schulte, B. (2014). *Overwhelmed: Work, love, and play when no one has the time.* New York, NY: Sarah Crichton Books, Farrar, Straus and Giroux.

Segura, D. (2007). Working at motherhood: Chicana and Mexican immigrant mothers and employment. In D. Segura & P. Zavella (Eds.), *Women and migration in the U.S.-Mexico borderlands: A reader* (pp. 368–387). Durham, NC: Duke University Press.

Segura, D., & Pierce, J. (1993). Chicana/o family structure and gender personality: Chodorow, familism, and psychoanalytic sociology revisited. *Signs: Journal of Women in Culture and Society, 19*(1), 62–91.

Sperling, J. (2013). Reframing the work-family conflict debate by rejecting the Ideal Parent norm. *Journal of Gender, Social Policy & the Law, 22*(1), 47–90.

Suárez-Orozco, C., Suárez-Orozco, M., & Todorova, I. (2008). *Learning a new land: Immigrant students in American society.* Cambridge, MA: Belknap Press of Harvard University Press.

Thurer, S. (1994). *The myths of motherhood: How culture reinvents the good mother.* New York, NY: Penguin.

Torres, M. N., & Hurtado-Vivas, R. (2011). Playing fair with Latino parents as parents, not teachers: Beyond family literacy as assisting homework. *Journal of Latinos and Education, 10*(3), 223–244. doi:10.1080/15348431.2011.581108

Valdés, G. (1996). *Con respeto: Bridging the distances between culturally diverse families and schools—An ethnographic portrait.* New York, NY and London: Teachers College Press.

Vandenberg-Daves, J. (2014). *Modern motherhood: An American history.* New Brunswick, NJ: Rutgers University Press.

Warner, J. (2005). *Perfect madness: Motherhood in the age of anxiety.* New York, NY: Riverhead Books, Penguin.

Weininger, E., & Lareau, A. (2003). Translating Bourdieu into the American context: The question of social class and family-school relations. *Poetics, 31*, 375–402.

Young, I. (1990). *Justice and the politics of difference.* Princeton, NJ: Princeton University Press.

Young, I. (1997). *Intersecting voices: Dilemmas of gender, political philosophy, and policy.* Princeton, NJ: Princeton University Press.

Young, I. (2002). *Inclusion and democracy.* New York, NY: Oxford University Press.

Zavella, P. (1991). Reflections on diversity among Chicanas. *Frontiers, 12*(2), 73–85.

# POLYPHONY

## Master and Counter Stories

*What we learned, instead is [...] that critical stories are always and at once in tension with dominant stories neither fully oppositional nor untouched.* (Torre et al., 2001, p. 151)

Critical researchers who do narrative inquiry, especially feminist critical scholars interested in women's personal stories, have often focused on counter narratives, those which go against the grain of master narratives, and have posed questions such as, "Under what conditions do women develop 'counternarratives' as they narrate their lives?" (Chase, 2005, p. 655). In the last decades, this line of research has tended to shift away from solely identifying the clear-cut distinction between the established master narratives and their counter narratives, and has started to focus on exposing the subtleties of power dynamics manifested in the internal tensions within an individual's story. The prior expectation of unequivocally finding a sharp separation between the counter and master stories is now called into question. Instead, closer observation of the collaborative process of an interview is now seen to reveal the coexistence of master and counter narratives in the participant's story in an oscillation between complicity and countering (Bamberg, 2004, p. 353). A study by Andrews (2004) illustrates this apparent inner conflict within a narrative through the analysis of the stories of individuals' early memories of their mother and their interpretation of their mother's long-term influence on their lives. Andrews observes the tensions within each story as it alternately comes close to the master narrative to embrace the mother myth, and then distances itself from it and resists it. This juxtaposition is highlighted in the analysis by the use of contrasting pairs of verbs, such as reveal/challenge; reproduce/evaluate; mirroring/challenging; and dipping in and out (Andrews, 2004, pp. 8–11).

In the current less deterministic view of the relation between master and counter narratives, the different strands within a person's account and the fluctuation between them are understood as pointing to the significance of agency, and as shedding light on the individual's positioning process (Bamberg, 2004, p. 366). Thus, the study of those stories which run counter to the master narratives holds the promise of helping elucidate the intricacies of power relations as they manifest themselves in the language of daily interactions and institutional practices, the social micro processes of everyday life (Norton, 2013; Young, 1990). Given their role in opening a window into the articulation of agency and structure, a better understanding of counter stories and how they emerge in the discursive process may help "make headway in designing alternative strategies to public, institutionalized power relations, resulting in more egalitarian reciprocity" (Bamberg, 2004, p. 353). Ultimately and cumulatively, these insights may contribute to practical approaches to the transformation of the underlying structural power imbalance of institutions.

This chapter explores how both the master narrative of parental involvement and the counter narratives coexist in the stories of the seven Mexican immigrant women introduced in Chapter 3. As proposed earlier, the official discourse of parental involvement constitutes the institutionalized educational adaptation of the ideology of the "good mother" and its contemporary version of "intensive mothering". This master narrative, as we have seen, also fits into a larger historical pattern within social policy which, by means of the ideal parent norm, contributes to the social control of mothers and, by extension, and its essentializing thrust, to the social control of all women, especially women of historically marginalized groups. In contrast, by viewing motherhood through an intersectional lens, the ideology of motherwork provides a perspective from which to examine social policy and parental involvement against the grain. In our study, the ideology of motherwork was found to underlie the counter story which emerges from the narrated experiences of this group of Mexican immigrant mothers. Despite the marked contrast between these ideologies, in the women's stories these appear intricately intertwined, so that the master and counter narratives emerge distinctly and yet closely combined, reflecting both antithetical ideologies of motherhood in their inner tension. The oscillation between these narrative strands, from instances of alignment with the official discourse to instances of resistance and countering, creates a narrative counterpoint or polyphony (Bakhtin, 1984, 1986).

Analyzed within a critical reevaluation of the definition of parental involvement, these instances of apparent contradictory coexistence of complicit and oppositional discursive strands shed light on the subtle articulation of structure and agency as manifested in home-school relations. These may be seen as pointing to some of those "openings of possibility" that Greene (1995) continues to inspire us to access through our social imagination (p. 5) in these terms:

> If power is not conceived as a superstructure, if there are discontinuities as the institutions and discourses concerned mesh with one another, then we cannot see any individual simply as an object totally conditioned by the whole. There are gaps, and these potentially open spaces may be identified as spaces for thought [...]. (pp. 189–190)

The rest of this chapter is devoted to presenting instances of the different narrative strands which appear tightly interlocked in the women's accounts but are separated here for analytical purposes.

## Counter Narratives of Maternal Involvement: Educational Motherwork

Several of the immigrant mothers' stories reflect aspects of their engagement in their children's education and moments of interaction which emerge as instances of educational motherwork (Cibils, 2011; Collins, 1994; Wilson Cooper, 2007). This ideology of motherhood, characterized by the women's agency within a context of vulnerability, manifests itself in various ways in the narratives, for instance: in *consejos* (words of wisdom) shared with their children; in descriptions of the type of information about the new sociocultural script that participants would provide to a newly arrived mother; in references to the direct support of their children's education beyond high school; and, most notably, in detailed depictions of occasions when they stepped in as advocates for their children in difficult circumstances. Some of these accounts of advocacy referred to moments of direct intervention of the women in defense of their children in situations of injustice. In these cases, the persistence and proactive roles required by the women in order to obtain any results reflected similar patterns of interaction to those documented in previous educational studies which have pointed to the existence of differential access in schools, with marked variation across race and class lines.

The following are selected instances of counter narratives in the seven women's stories. Each one illustrates different combinations of the factors which contribute to define them as counter narratives. They embody these women's views of involvement on their own terms; that is, narratives that go against the grain. As such, these counter stories are able to transform the narratives that society has assigned to them based on the standards of the official discourse of parental involvement.

## Luisa—*Quiero que mi hijo se enfoque no más en el estudio.* (I only want my son to focus on his studies.)

Both Luisa's sons were athletes in high school, and also enjoyed weight training, which was required of students participating in sports. Although she had always supported both her sons' participation in sports, Luisa started worrying when her older son's grades were dropping in his last year, and feared that he might not graduate. Since she believed too much was at stake, this time around Luisa took the initiative to go and speak to the principal. There was, in Luisa's view, only one solution that would be effective in motivating her son to do better in school: Manuel should be banned from participating in sports and weights training, until his grades went up.

> Lilian: ¿Tuvo alguna vez que ir como a negociar alguna situación, algo así?
> Luisa: Sí, a negociar, pero no a favor de… yo no quería, o sea yo, por ejemplo, yo decía: "No, no, no. Si él tiene malos grados, no le deje hacer pesas. No me lo deje jugar." No era que yo era "Ah, sí, que déjelo jugar." No, no, no. Yo lo que quería era que sacaran buenos grados primero (*stressed*). Y luego, después, el juego. Está bien, yo sé que son jóvenes y que quieren jugar y que necesitan juego. Pero yo no quería así: "No, mire, déjelo jugar y verá que le prometo que para la otra él hace bien": No. Primero… Yo, a mi hijo el grande, con el más chiquito yo no batallé mucho, pero con mi hijo el grande yo tuve que quitarle que hiciera pesas, tuve que sacarlo de deportes, tuve que sacarlo de ayudar en la oficina… allí estar cuando la gente llega y pregunta … Yo le dije: "No quiero que mi hijo haga eso; no quiero deportes, no quiero pesas. Quiero que mi hijo se enfoque no más en el estudio. Cuando él levante los grados, hasta donde tiene… las clases más importantes que son para graduarse (*stress on 'más'*), entonces. Pero mientras él no esté bien, verdad, que, en sus grados, no."

Lilian: And did you ever have to go and negotiate in any situation, something like that?

Luisa: Yes, to negotiate, but never in favor of... I didn't want to... So, for example, I would say, "No, no, no. If he has bad grades, don't let him do weight-lifting. Don't let him play." I wasn't one to say, "Oh, yes, let him play." No, no, no. What I wanted was that he get good grades first (*stressed*). And then, after that, sports. It's ok, I know they're young and that they want to play, and that they need sports. But I didn't want to be like, "Look, let him play and you'll see, I promise that next time he'll be doing well." No. First... With my older son, I, with my younger son I didn't struggle so much, but with the oldest, I had to make him quit weight-lifting, I had to pull him out of sports, I had to pull him out from helping in the office—being there for when people come up to the front desk to ask questions. I told him, "I don't want my son to do that; I don't want sports, I don't want weights. I only want my son to focus on his studies. When he raises his grades, once he has... in the most important classes for graduation (*stress on "most"*), only then. But while his grades are not good, then no."

From Luisa's perspective, her duty was to make sure her sons were doing well in school. Luisa underscores the fact that she would never speak on their behalf to condone a situation she did not approve of, or to protect their participation in their favorite activities, to the detriment of their academic progress. Luisa also requested that Manuel be relieved from any other duties that were not relevant to graduation, until he got his grades up, such as helping at the front desk as a student aide. Luisa recalls how she spoke to her son and said that if he had to repeat a year in school, he would have wasted a whole year of his life.

Lilian: Y ¿con quién habló?

Luisa: Pues, también con las secretarias, incluso, ellas tenían que entrar conmigo al cuarto de... a hablar con el principal.

Lilian: Ah, ¿directamente tenía que ir... con el director?

Luisa: Sí, con el director ... directamente: "No quiero que mi hijo juegue; no quiero que mi hijo haga pesas. Quiero que saque sus clases primero".

Lilian: ¿Y qué dijo él?

Luisa: No, estaba bien.

Lilian: ¿Sí? ¿Estaba de acuerdo?

Luisa: Estaba de acuerdo. Decía: "Sí, está bien, que él saque primero sus ... que levante sus grados", porque llegaba a bajar. Y decía yo, si no se gradúa a tiempo... ahí está otro año más. Yo a ellos siempre les he dicho que si no se gradúan o si reprueban el año, es un año tirado a la basura. Es un año perdido. ¿Verdad? (*ahh, heavy sigh, like complaining, as of a burden*) Porque, mira, me levanté temprano todos los días y mira y voy a volver a hacerlo. Eso, no. Y cuando tuve que hablar así siempre me ayudaron esas personas, pues, las secretarias son las que hablan español.

Lilian: ¿Y funcionó bien esto, anduvo el quitarle…? ¿Después pudo volver a sus actividades?

Luisa: Volver, sí. No, sí, en cuanto… Él sabía que era algo que yo nunca le iba a decir: "Pues, ándale, pues, déjame hablar para que juegues…" No. Él sabía: "Si tú tienes buenos grados y tú los levantas, si tú no me das problemas, y no me están llamando de la escuela eso… tú vas a poder hacer todo. Pero primero, los grados." Y, sí. Sí funcionó, para mí, sí funcionó, el que… Y las mujeres que siempre me ayudaron para poderme comunicar.

Lilian: And who did you talk to?

Luisa: Well, even with the secretaries, also. They had to come in with me to the room…. to speak to the principal.

Lilian: Oh, so you had to go straight to the principal?

Luisa: Yes, straight to the principal, "I don't want my son to play; I don't want my son to do weight-lifting. I want him to do well in his classes first."

Lilian: And what did he say?

Luisa: He agreed. He said, "Yes, that's good, that he first gets his grades up," because they were dropping. And I would say, if he didn't graduate on time, that's another year. I've always told them that if they don't graduate or if they fail one year, it's a year that they've thrown in the trash. It's a lost year. Right? (*ahh, heavy sigh, like complaining, as of a burden*) Because, look, I got up early every day and look, I have to do it all over again. No way. And when I've had to go and speak like that, I've always received help from those people, the secretaries, who speak Spanish.

Lilian: And did that work? Taking away . . . [privileges]? Was he able to go back to his activities later?

Luisa: Return? Yes. As soon as… He knew that something I was never going to say to him, was, "Go ahead; let me talk to them so that you can play…" No. He knew, "If you have good grades and you raise them, if you don't cause any trouble, and they aren't calling me from the school… you will be able to do everything again. But first, your grades." And yes, it worked, to me, it worked, that… And the women, who always helped me to communicate.

In her interview with the principal, Luisa presented a direct and clear request: "*No quiero que mi hijo juegue; no quiero que mi hijo haga pesas. Quiero que saque sus clases primero*". (I don't want my son to play; I don't want my son to do weight training. I want him to do well in his classes first.) With the principal's support, Luisa's system worked. Manuel raised his grades and was able to participate in sports again. Both her sons graduated from high school. Later, Luisa explains at length how this was her system of discipline in many other areas, so as to help them with their priorities. In this case, graduation was to be first and foremost on their list.

Luisa: Y, pues, en la escuela, ya le digo, todo siempre batallé, así… pero, pues, con las muchachas, esas señoras, ellas me ayudaban. Pero también tenían que dejar su trabajo por venir a la junta, conmigo y con el director. Y a veces hasta con maestras.
Lilian: Y ¿siempre podían o…?
Luisa: Sí, sí, dejaban como a estas… como se llama… a las secretarias, ellas … los niños tienen, los muchachos tienen una clase de ayudar en la oficina. Entonces, cuando la secretaria entraba conmigo a la junta, dejaba de encargados a los muchachos. Para mí, lo que hice trabajó bien. Trabajó porque están bien; salieron bien de la escuela; los recuerdan bien, como buenos muchachos. Como, a Manuel, al más grande, lo recuerdan que siempre fue de chistes, de bromas. Hasta los maestros, con bromas. Pero se acostumbraron tanto a él, porque eran bromas no pesadas, verdad, y también con respeto. Pero, siempre bien, así. Y al menos, mis reglas funcionaron.

Luisa: And, well, in the school, as I said, I always struggled like that… but, well, with the young ladies, those women, they helped me. But they also had to leave their work to come to the meeting, with me and the principal. And sometimes even with teachers.
Lilian: And, were they always able to or…?
Luisa: Yes, yes, they left in charge these… what are they called… secretaries, they… they have kids, who help in the office as a class. So, when the secretary came in with me to the meeting, she left these kids in charge. To me, what I did worked well. Because they are doing well; they finished school well; they remember them well, as good kids. For instance, Manuel, the older one, they remember as the one who was always full of jokes, kidding. Even with teachers, he had jokes. But they got used to him, because they weren't bad practical jokes, right, it was with respect. But always good, like that. And, at least, my rules worked.

Luisa is very proud of her sons and recognizes that she played an important part in their successful graduation. However, Luisa's modesty and gratefulness is evident in how she reconstructs the sequence of events leading to her son's accomplishment of his goals. In Luisa's narrative on how she worked with the school to support both her sons towards graduation, there are two threads that are interwoven throughout her story. On the one hand, there is the theme of her strategic intervention on behalf of her children's success in school. On the other, there is the theme of gratefulness for all the help she received from *"las mujeres que siempre me ayudaron para poderme comunicar"* (the women who always helped me to communicate).

Never once does Luisa fail to recognize the support she has received all along. Her story is one of vulnerability and agency, but also of community, solidarity and shared resources. It is at these points in Luisa's narrative of her interactions with the schools where the boundary between "them" and "us" seems to be blurred, and there is a sense of communal agency, which here includes the helpful staff at the schools.

## Advocacy in the Face of Racism

**Brenda—*Es que para que miren también las maestras, que uno mira por sus hijos.***
**(It's for the teachers to see that one is looking out for one's children.)**

As Chicana and Black feminist scholars have established, the role of women of color in raising their children is very different from that of white mothers in the United States. Women of color are faced with the dilemma of the need to both advocate for them and to protect them from the hostility of racism and other forms of oppression, while making sure they become self-sufficient and independent at the same time (Collins, 2000; Delgado Bernal, 2006; Villenas, 2002). The fundamental role of the home in educating Latin@ children is eloquently described by Hurtig and Dyrness (2011), as it emerges from critical studies which challenge the dominant deficit views.

> Latino homes shift from being sites of deficit in need of professional intervention to spaces of critique, engagement, and personal and collective transformation. Education in the home becomes visible as not only different from school learning, but as critical to the struggle for personal integrity and cultural survival. (p. 536)

Young (1990) proposes that there is a need for privileged groups to recognize their participation and responsibility even when unintentional in the perpetuation of racism in order for this form of oppression to be interrupted. The role of schools in this process is clear in that, "differential privilege of members of different racial groups is perpetuated in part by the process of schooling [...] many if not most teachers unconsciously behave differently towards Blacks or Latinos than they behave toward whites" (p. 154).

Some of the episodes related to advocacy shared by the women involved direct interventions in defense of their children. Within the larger theoretical context, these stories can be contemplated as instances which allow us a glimpse into the articulation of agency and structure. On these occasions, the participants were proactive in defense of their children against unjust situations where they were being treated as the "deviant other" (Young, 1990). One of the incidents in Brenda's account presents the sharpest contrast with her own overall positive assessment of her interactions with the schools. In this case, Brenda recalls a time when she had to go to the school to speak to a teacher who was accusing her youngest daughter of stealing her pens. Brenda hesitates before explicitly suggesting that the underlying problem is racism. There are some teachers who treat children differently because they are Mexican, Brenda says. In two different interviews, Brenda spontaneously recounts the details of this unsettling event and of how she intervened.

> A veces, como con sus maestras también ... Yo creo que a veces las maestras son... ummm ... bueno, por no decir *(pause)* racistas, a veces hacen menos a los mexicanos y a veces se les cargan más. Y una vez a mi hija, la más chiquita, Adriana, una maestra ... la empezó como a recriminar que le había agarrado los lápices. Y ya me dijo mi hija: "Mami, la maestra dice que yo le agarré este lapicero" dijo "pero, ¿te acuerdas que los compré en el Walmart?" Y todavía ella tenía más en un paquetito. Le dije: "M'hija, llévele otro." Le dije: "Aquí está otro." Dijo: "No, Mami. Yo no le voy a llevar si no va a creer que sí se lo agarré." Y luego, bueno, pues así quedó. Y luego, ya, no, pues, que en otra ocasión, que la maestra le dijo a otra niña, dijo: "Se me están perdiendo los lapiceros, de estos." Dijo: "A mí se me hace que Adriana los está agarrando." La niña le platicó a Adriana y entonces ya vino y me volvió a decir: "Mami, la maestra cree que le estoy agarrando los lapiceros."

> Well, sometimes with their teachers also... I think that sometimes the teachers are... uhm... well, not to say *(pause)* racists, they sometimes put Mexicans down and sometimes they blame them more. Once a teacher started blaming my youngest daughter, Adriana, of taking her pencils. And my daughter told me, "Mom, the teacher says that I took this pencil" she said, "but, remember that I bought them at Walmart?" And she still had some left in a packet. I said, "Honey, just take her another one." I said, "Here's another one." She said, "No, Mom, I won't give it to her, if not she'll think that I did take them." So, well, that was it. And then, well, on another occasion, the teacher told another girl, "My pencils are getting lost, these." And she continued, "I think it's Adriana who's taking them." The girl told Adriana, and she came to me and said, "Mom, the teacher thinks I'm taking her pencils."

As on other occasions, Sara, Brenda's eldest daughter, stepped in as a mediator, and offered to make and appointment and accompany her mother to the school in order to clear her sister's name from false accusations. Brenda is aware of the significance of being able to count on her daughters' language and advocacy skills in circumstances like these, as is evident from her reference to how, *"Ellas saben hablar, se saben defender, ¿verdad?"* (They know how to speak, they know how to defend themselves, you know.)

Brenda was determined to advocate for her daughter and must have been visibly upset, because her husband advised her to stay calm, and not to "say bad things". But she insisted that she was only going to stand up for her daughter and to put an end to the accusations against her, and the rumors the teacher appeared to be spreading about Adriana among her classmates.

> Y luego dice mi esposo: "No le vayas a decir cosas feas." "Ya sé" *(she whispers)* "No, no más hablar bien," le digo, "porque yo sé que si voy en son de guerra, pues, guerra va a tener con mi hija, ¿verdad?" Y le digo: "Voy no más a decirle que mi hija no es," verdad. Y sí, nos puso una cita, ahí la secretaria. Y ahí vamos otro día. Y luego dijo mi hija: "Pues, yo voy con usted por si no habla español."

> And my husband said, "Don't go and say bad things to her!" "I know" *(she whispers)* "No, I'm just going to talk in good terms," I said, "because I know that if I declare war, well, war is what my daughter is going to have, right?" And I said, "I'm just going to tell her that it wasn't my daughter," right? And the secretary made an appointment for us. And there we went another day. And then my daughter said, "Well, I'll come with you, in case she doesn't speak Spanish."

Even if she was outraged at the unfairness of the whole situation, Brenda was aware that she should be polite and present her case respectfully because otherwise the teacher might ultimately take it out on her daughter.

> Pues, bueno, ya nos fuimos, y no sí, ya... Pues, yo creo la maestra ya estaba avisada. Y luego, ya entramos, y luego ya nos dijo: "Oh, que querían hablar conmigo". Le dijo Sara: "Yes" y luego ya pues ellas... ahí Sara le explicó, verdad, que ... a lo que íbamos, que ella le decía a Adriana que le estaba agarrando los lapiceros y, pues, que nosotros estábamos seguras que no, porque nosotras mismas se los habíamos comprado en el Walmart.

> So, well, there we went, and well... I think that the teacher was put on notice. And then, we came in, and she said, "Oh, so you wanted to speak to me." And Sara said, "Yes (in English)" and then they just... There Sara explained to her, right, why we had come, because she was saying that Adriana was taking her pencils, and, well, that we were sure that she wasn't, because we had bought them for her at Walmart ourselves.

When Brenda received an apology from the teacher, through Sara's mediation, she made the teacher know that Adriana's name needed to be cleared, because the damage had already been done, and the consequences of this incident would probably live on. Other students would continue to suspect Adriana for any missing supplies.

> Y luego, no, ella ahí se disculpó. Y, luego, ya le dijo que me dijera a mí, que "I'm sorry..." que ella no lo había hecho por hacerla sentir mal o esto y lo otro. Le dije yo: "Pero, dile que las demás niñas están ya creyendo que ella sí se los agarra."

And then, well, she apologized. And she told my daughter to tell me, "I'm sorry" and that she hadn't done this to make her feel bad, and this and that. But I told my daughter, "Tell her that the other girls already believe that she is the one who's taking them."

In Brenda's recountal, it becomes clear that if she had not intervened, her daughter would have continued to be blamed. Instead, that same day, the teacher changed her tone and even recognized that Adriana was a strong student, a smart child who was doing well in school. Brenda points out that teachers sometimes need to be made aware that parents are paying attention and looking out for their children.

Le dije: "Pues, yo estoy segura que no, porque los lápices que ella dice que usted dijo que le habían agarrado," le digo, "ella los compró en el Walmart cuando ella iba a entrar a la escuela." Le dije: "Pues, yo sé, yo sé lo que le compro y yo sé que esos yo se los compré." "Oh, no" dijo, y ya ahí se disculpó. Dijo, ya empezó: "Que mira que…" Le empezó a enseñar en la computadora a Sara, a la más grande, dijo: "Mira, Adriana va bien, y que es una niña muy inteligente" y quién-sabe-qué y quién-sabe-cuánto… Y luego, pues, ya pasó todo eso ¿verdad? Y, luego le preguntó mi hija: "¿Y cómo se ha portado tu maestra?" "No, Amá," dijo "vieras cómo cambió" (aspirate whispering). Le digo, es que para que miren también las maestras, que uno mira por sus hijos, verdad. Porque si la dejo así, pues ahí la maestra se la… Y como dice ella "A mí me da vergüenza con mis compañeros, que crean que yo soy así y que robo."

I said, "And I'm sure it wasn't her, because the pencils that she says you had said they had taken," I said, "she bought at Walmart before starting school." I told her, "Well, I know, I know what I buy her and I know that I bought her those." "Oh, no," she said, and there she apologized. She said, and there she started, "And look… see that…" And she stated to show the computer to Sara, my eldest daughter, and said, "Look, Adriana is doing well, and she is a smart girl" and so on and so forth. And then, well, all of this was over, right? Later my daughter asked her, "And how has your teacher been behaving?" "No, Mom," she said, "you should see how she's changed" (whispering, in an aspirate way, for emphasis). And I say, it's for the teachers to see that one is looking out for one's children, right. Because if I let it go, the teacher would… and as she says, "I'm embarrassed in front of my classmates, that they think that I'm like that, and that I steal."

Brenda describes her satisfaction with the results of having intervened in a timely manner in an effort to set things right, and repeatedly points out the fact that from that day on the teacher's attitude toward Adriana was completely transformed.

In her role as an advocate for her child, Brenda created a counter narrative of maternal involvement and educational motherwork at different levels. First, Brenda's intervention in the situation, speaking up in defense of her child, contributed to change the story in the classroom. As is often the case, marginalized groups and individuals do not have an opportunity to tell their own story and instead it is being told for them by members of dominant groups. Brenda stood up and changed the narrative; by doing so she transformed the way her child was being portrayed (and therefore treated) in her classroom. Second, Brenda stood up and spoke in defense of her child and in doing so contributed to define maternal involvement on her own terms. As Brenda commented later, by speaking up she was making sure that the teachers knew that we—Latina immigrant mothers—are paying attention. Third, in this case, Brenda's counter narrative substituted the narrative derived from motherwork, in its focus on survival, identity and empowerment of ethnic communities (Collins, 1994) for the dominant assessment of parents according to a cultural deficit model underlying the official discourse of parental involvement. This instance of maternal involvement illustrates the transformative power of counter narratives. Brenda's story is also an example of how agency may be developed from situations of vulnerability.

## "Consejos" (Advice)

**Brenda—*A la [maestra] más malita, váyasela ganando, poco a poquito. Ya sabemos la clave.***
(The meanest [teacher], win her over. Little by little. We already know the key [to winning teachers over].)

Latina mothers often use *consejos* (advice) as a way of transmitting their wisdom to their children. Delgado-Gaitán (1994) considers these words of wisdom from parents to be advocacy tools; thus, she points to this as a pivotal concept in understanding Latin@ parent involvement as it plays an important role in the process of empowerment (p. 313). It has been noted that in their "counter story of involvement" immigrant parents' *consejos* often center on hard work as a fundamental value (López, 2001).

Even from the outrageous situation of having to defend her daughter from her teacher's wrongful accusations of theft, Brenda drew the moral that her daughters needed to behave well, work hard and be exemplary students, so as to win over their teachers, especially the meanest ones. Although Brenda was aware of the fact that some teachers on some occasions treated her daughters unfairly—and she would not let it go by without speaking up against it—she believed that the way for her daughters to win that battle was to respond by being well-behaved and hard-working. That was the key, according to Brenda. *"Váyasela ganando"* (win her over) is Brenda's motto.

> Brenda: Aha, y entonces, pues, que esas niñas ya algo que se les pierda le van a echar la culpa a ella. Y no, pues, que eso iba a hablar con todos los alumnos. Le dije después: "Pero, m'hija, ¿qué les dijo la maestra a los niños?" "Ah, Mami, ahora habló con todos, dijo que se le estaban perdiendo los lapiceros pero que ella creía que era una niña, pero que no iba a decir quién, dijo, pero que no era verdad, porque ella ya había encontrado sus lapiceros."
>
> Lilian: Pero, ¿si no hubiera ido usted?
>
> Brenda: Si no hubiéramos ido, entonces, sí eso hubiera quedado. Y, pues también como dice ella: "Como que Mami, como que ella quiere más a los gringos, pues, que a los mexicanos" *(lowering the volume, as if this were the "unspeakable")*. "Ah, m'hija, no le tome en cuenta eso" le dije "usted poco a poquito váyasela ganando, m'hija. Váyasela ganando." Y ella notaba que le ponía las calificaciones más bajas… *(stressed, rise-fall)*
>
> Lilian: Tanto…
>
> Brenda: Sí *(stressed by lengthening)*, así. Y, luego, "No," le dije, "m'hija. Váyasela ganando, m'hija, váyasela ganando." Y luego: "Usted no platique en la clase, usted no haga esto…" Y le empecé a dar consejos. No, mire, ahora, ya re-tebien, re-tebien que le da bien ya las calificaciones y todo…
>
> Brenda: Aha, and then, next time those girls lose something, they're going to blame her. And, she said she would talk to all the students. But I asked her later: "What did the teacher tell the kids?" "Oh, Mom, now she spoke to everybody, and said that she had been losing her pencils, and that she had thought it had been a girl, who she wasn't going to name, but that it wasn't true, because now she had found her pencils."
>
> Lilian: But, what if you hadn't gone?
>
> Brenda: If we hadn't gone, then, that would have stuck. And, also it's as she says, "Mom, it's as if she likes 'gringos' more than Mexicans" *(lowering the voice to a whisper, as if mentioning "the unspeakable")*. "Oh, forget about it," I said, "little by little, just start winning her over, honey. Just win her over gradually." And she noticed that she gave her lower grades.
>
> Lilian: That bad!
>
> Brenda: Yes, it was so. And, then, "no, I said, honey, just win her over, win her over." And then, "Don't talk in class, don't do this or that…" And I started giving her advice. No, look, now it's really good, she even gives her fair grades and all.

Adriana had suspected that while she was being accused of stealing, her grades were also dropping, as the teacher was biased against her. As soon as the whole situation was cleared, she shared with her mom how the teacher had changed towards her, and even her grades were higher.

After this episode, Adriana's teacher had started treating her with greater respect, had announced her mistake to the class, and had started grading her more fairly. Brenda does not dismiss her daughter's suspicion of favoritism for *"gringos"* but Brenda's advice implies that she believes that even a racist teacher can change, and can be "won over". Also, Brenda recognizes that having stepped in to defend her daughter in the face of injustice and racism had made a difference. In analyzing this narrative strand, some prosodic markers are quite noticeable. At several points in her description of her daughter's situation, specifically when naming racism and discrimination, Brenda lowers her voice to a whisper. These prosodic markers have been described in the literature as signaling *the unspeakable* (Riessman, 2008). This same change in tone of voice was detected in Sandra's story (Chapter 11). In both cases, these prosodic markers point to moments of agency in situations of extreme vulnerability.

Later, Brenda recalls a similar incident they had gone through with another one of her daughters. Luz, Brenda's middle daughter, had also had a situation in which she believed her teacher did not like her and was not being fair to her. As Brenda explains how, some years back, this teacher had apparently lost some of her daughter's work, and did not believe her, she shares with us the advice she had given to Luz: "Do the work again. Don't answer back. Do all that she tells you to do."

> Lilian: Sí, pero tenía que ella mostrar…
> Brenda: Luego le dije: "Váyase ganando la maestra." Le digo: "Usted no sea respondona con ella. Usted haga todo lo que la maestra le dice." "Ay, Mami, es que también no me cae bien esa maestra." "No, m'hija. Le tiene que caer bien. Aguántese. Al cabo y es una temporada no más. No más una temporada. Todavía fuera su mamá, que me tuviera que aguantar todo el tiempo…"
> Lilian: *(laughs)*
> Brenda: Y, sí, ya cambia de maestra y ya. También, la granjeó mi hija… a la maestra. La maestra terminó regalándole unos zapatos. Llegó bien contenta, eh *(laughs)*. Llegó bien contenta: "Mami, la maestra que no me quería me regaló unos zapatos." Terminó ganándosela. Sí, pues, como yo le dije. "Ya ve, m'hija." Y ese es el temor de mi hija la chiquita, de Adriana, que como cada año cambian… Dijo: "Ay, mami, sabe cómo me vayan a tocar ahora las maestras…" "No se apure, m'hija. Ya sabemos la clave…" Digo: "Váyase ganándose… a la más malita, váyasela ganando. Poco a poquito."
> Lilian: … despacito.
> Brenda: Sí, despacito. Sí le digo: "No más no platique en la clase; haga lo mejor que pueda su trabajo; entréguelo a tiempo," le digo "y no platique ni juegue ahí en la clase, m'hija." Y así es como se las van ganando.

Lilian: Ya la experiencia…
Brenda: La experiencia, sí. Se ríen ellas porque yo les digo: "Ya sabemos la clave." *(laughs)*

Lilian: Yes, but she had to show her…
Brenda: I told her later, "Win her over." I said, "Don't answer back. Do all that she tells you to do." "Oh, Mom, but it's that I don't like that teacher either." "No, honey, you need to like her. Put up with it. In the end, it's just temporary. Just one year. At least it's not your mom that you have to put up with all the time!"
Lilian: *(laughs)*
Brenda: And, yes, she'll soon have a new teacher, and that's it. She also won her over, my daughter won the teacher over. The teacher ended up giving her some shoes. She arrived really happy one day, "Mom, the teacher who didn't like me gave me some shoes." She ended up winning her over. Yes, well, as I said to her, "You see!" And that's Adriana's fear, as they change every year, "Oh, Mom, I wonder what kind of teachers I'm going to get now!" "Don't worry, dear. Now we know the key." I say, "Win her over… the meanest one, win her over. Little by little."
Lilian: …slowly.
Brenda: Yes, slowly. Yes, I tell her, "Just don't talk in class; do your work as best as you can; hand it in on time," I say. "And don't talk or play in class, honey. And that's how you win them over."
Lilian: With experience already…
Brenda: Experience, yes. They laugh because I tell them, "We already know the key." *(laughs)*

Brenda insists on what she calls "the key": winning the teachers over through good behavior and diligence. Then, she expounds on the definition in these terms: "'Just don't talk in class; do your work as best as you can; hand it in on time', I say. 'And don't talk or play in class, honey, and that's how you win them over.'"

## Keeping Attendance Records Straight

**Brenda—*¡Mira lo que dice en este papel! Me van a llevar a corte o me van a meter a la cárcel porque tú faltas.***
(Look at what this paper says! They're taking me to court or sending me to jail because you are skipping class.)

At a certain point during her eldest daughter's high school days, Brenda suddenly became aware that attendance records were much more important than she had understood. One day she was shocked to receive an official letter in the mail warning her that Sara had too many absences and that this could have serious consequences for her parents. Brenda confronted her with this information, and asked her why she had so many absences. Sara had been arriving a few minutes late to class, and was being counted as absent. Brenda decided to go and speak to the principal about it, and got her daughter's attendance record cleared.

Lilian: Cuénteme, me decía que una vez la llamaron, le mandaron decir que su hija no estaba en la escuela.
Brenda: Sí, pues, me hablaban… y me decían: "Sara no vino a la clase de fulano" "¿Cómo que no fue? No, pues, sí fue," le digo, "De aquí sí fue." "Y no", dijo "pues, no vino a la clase de fulano". Y ¿adónde las vamos a buscar? Uno, pues, no sabe. No tenían, no les teníamos ni celular ni nada. Pues esperé que llegara ella y hablar con ella. El año pasado, fue cuando ya de cuántas… tres veces que llegaran tarde a una clase, ya les contaba una falta. Y esas otras tres llegadas tarde, es otro día de falta. Entonces sí fue cuando me llegó una carta que me iban a llevar a corte, que porque mi hija estaba faltando mucho, que quién sabe. Le digo: "¿Cómo que estás faltando mucho? ¡Hija!" Le digo, "¡mira lo que dice en este papel! Que me van a llevar a corte o me van a meter a la cárcel porque tú faltas…" "Mamá no falto…" "¿Cómo que no faltas?" "No falto." "¿Ni llegas tarde?" "No llego tarde, Mamá, yo no sé por qué, a veces, con dos minutos que llegue tarde a una clase, ya no me la cuentan." "¡Ah, no!" le dije "¡Yo voy a ir a hablar con el principal!" Y fui y ya le dije. La saqué de donde estaba en su clase: "Ven, vamos a hablar con él." Y no, dijo que había sido un error de las secretarias y quien-sabe-qué, que él iba a hablar y que iba a arreglar eso. Yo ya mirando un papel escrito: "Te vamos a llevar a corte, que puedo ser arrestada, que quién-sabe-qué." Pues ya eso ya como que asusta. Sí saqué una cita con el principal y sí fuimos a hablar y: "No," dijo "pues, yo eso lo arreglo. Eso es error de las de ahí de enfrente." "Ah," le digo "pues uno también se asusta ¡que tengan más cuidado!"

Lilian: Tell me, you were saying that once they called you, to let you know your daughter wasn't in school.
Brenda: Yes, well, they'd call me and say, "Sara didn't come to so-&-so's class." "How come she didn't attend? She did go," I said, "She left from here." "But no," they said, "she didn't come to so-&-so's class." Well, wait 'till she came back, and where is one going to look for her… one doesn't know. We hadn't got cell phones for them, they didn't have cell phones either. So I'd wait for her to arrive and speak to her. Last year it was when what was it? With three times they were late to class, they received an absence. And after three more tardies, it was counted as another absence. Then it was that I received a letter, saying that they would take me to court, that because my daughter was missing too much school, and who-knows-what else. I said, "How come you are missing too much? Daughter!" I said, "Look at what this paper says! That they're taking me to court or that they're sending me to jail because you are cutting class." "Mom, I'm not skipping." "How come?" "I'm not skipping." "And you're not

late?" "I'm not late, Mom. I don't know why, sometimes when you arrive even two minutes late to a class, they don't count it." "Oh, no!" I said, "I'm going to go and speak to the principal!" And I went, and I told him. I pulled her out from her class, "Let's go and speak to him." And no, he said it had been a mistake of the secretaries, and who-knows-what, that he was going to speak to them, and fix it all. And I was already looking at this paper, "We're going to take you to court, you can be arrested, and who-knows-what." Well, that is scary. So I made an appointment with the principal and we went to speak and, "No," he said, "I'll fix it. It's just a mistake of whoever is at the front desk." "Oh," I said. "Well, one also gets scared. They should be more careful!"

Once Brenda found out what serious consequences attendance problems could entail, she made sure to keep an eye on this herself. Brenda learned that attendance records were available at the school and that she could request them whenever she wished or whenever she could. So, Brenda made a habit of picking up attendance records for her daughter Sara, once a week, to prevent her from getting in trouble again for absences.

Lilian: Entonces, ¿le parece que usted cambió también en su manera de relacionarse con la escuela? Por ejemplo, ¿usted siente como que puede ir si tiene alguna consulta o pregunta?
Brenda: Sí, ya, también cuando quiero saber cómo van de sus grados, voy y pido la hoja de sus grados y voy y pido la lista de asistencia. Aha, porque ahí también en la lista de asistencia, ahí también le ponen cuándo llega tarde, cuándo faltó y las clases que estuvo durante el semestre. Y eso es lo que yo también hago. Siempre, los viernes digo: "Vengo por la lista de asistencia de Luz," y me dan la hoja. Y ahí me explican: "Esto significa que llegó tarde, esto significa que no estuvo en clase," y así. Y ya yo hablo con ella. Cuando ella mira que está mal esa lista, entonces ya hablamos con el principal. Si llega unos cinco minutos, tres minutos más tarde a esa clase, ya se la ponen que no asistió. Y, entonces, ella tiene que llevar esa lista y decirle a la maestra: "Maestra, yo sí estuve, pero llegué dos, tres minutos tarde." Entonces la maestra ya le pone ahí y ya le rectifican su asistencia.
Lilian: Tiene que estar pendiente.
Brenda: Sí. Sí, pues, eso también les cuenta a ellas. Y si le van poniendo tarde y si le van poniendo que falta y que falta y que falta, pues, entonces van a bajar sus grados. Y si ella no ha faltado.
Lilian: Entonces tiene que estar pendiente.
Brenda: Sí. De la lista de asistencia también.

Lilian: So, do you think you changed in the way you relate to the school? For example, do you feel you can go if you have a question or have to consult something?
Brenda: Yes, also, if I want to know how their grades are, I go and ask for the grades report and I go and ask for the attendance record. Aha, because there, in the attend-

ance record they also record when they arrive late, when they've missed and the classes she has been to during the semester. And that is what I also do. On Fridays, I always say, "I'm here to pick up the attendance record for Luz," and they give me the paper and there they explain: "This means she was late, this means that she wasn't in class," and so on. So then I go and talk to her. When she notices that the record is wrong, then we go and talk to the principal, and the principal … If she arrives five minutes, three minutes late to the class, they already count her absent. So, then, she has to show this record to the teacher and explain to her, "I was there, but I was two or three minutes late." Then, the teacher changes that and they correct her record…
Lilian: So you have to be paying attention.
Brenda: Yes, yes, because that also counts. If they keep counting her tardy, or they count her absent over and over, well, then her grades are going to drop. And if she hasn't been absent…
Lilian: So you have to pay attention.
Brenda: Yes, to the attendance record too.

That is how, after receiving a letter with an official warning, Brenda took it upon herself to make sure that her children were not absent and that their attendance records were kept accurately. Especially when her eldest daughter was in school, Brenda paid close attention to her records, both for attendance and grades. Since she learned this could be corrected, later Brenda would let her daughters know if they seemed to have been counted absent by mistake. Through an official warning, Brenda had become aware of how serious an issue attendance could become but also that she could intervene as an advocate for her children.

## Advocacy and Persistence

### Sandra—*Yo estoy aquí porque quiero ayudar a mi hijo.* (I am here because I want to help my son.)

In response to a question about some occasion when she had visited the school in order to find a solution to some problem, Sandra shared her experience of an instance when she became an advocate for her son. When a difficult situation with her son's fourth grade teacher intensified, she had to work it out with the principal directly. The main problem was that the teacher conducted class in an authoritarian style and this deeply affected Sandra's young son, as he felt intimidated and bullied by him. It took some insistence and perseverance on Sandra's part but eventually she managed to have this situation resolved.

En cuarto me tocó un maestro también bilingüe pero era un maestro muy autoritario, muy dominante, muy controlador y le afectó en su carácter a él. Le afectó. Entonces yo fui a la escuela, al segundo día yo fui a la escuela y le dije: "Cámbiemelo, porque el niño no está a gusto con ese maestro." Entonces, dijo: "No, ¿sabe qué? Espérese, déle tiempo al maestro; acaba de llegar; no lo conocemos. Déle tiempo."

In fourth we had a teacher, also bilingual, but who was a very authoritarian teacher, very domineering, and controlling, and it affected his temper. It affected him. So I went to the school, on the second day, and I said, "Let him switch, because the child is not happy with that teacher." So, she said, "No, you know what? Wait; give him time; this teacher has just arrived; we don't know him. Give him time."

At first, Sandra gave the teacher the benefit of the doubt, and thought that her son was probably not used to having a male teacher, so that was why he might not feel at ease. She even thought that one of the reasons why her son felt so intimidated may have had to do with the fact that he had no father figure at home. But, as the days went by, she noticed that her son was becoming more and more aggressive and she insisted on her son's need to switch teachers.

Lilian: Usted me contó sobre cuando trató de cambiar de maestro. Cuando decidió ir ¿con quién habló? ¿Cómo hizo la primera vez que usted fue?
Sandra: En cuanto el niño me dijo, el segundo día: "Sabes qué, ese maestro no me gusta, grita mucho, grita mucho. Y no me gusta."
Lilian: El segundo día, ya sabía.
Sandra: Sí, él dijo eso. Entonces, le dije: "Sabes qué, espérate." "No," dijo: "Habla. Haz algo, porque no me gusta." Le dije, "¿Cómo que no te gusta? ¿El primer día? Hay que probarlo." Y yo dije: "Es un maestro mano dura; él siempre tuvo maestras, entonces," dije, "sintió el cambio. Y como en la casa no hay la imagen paterna, a lo mejor es que está desesperado." Entonces, pedí cita con la principal inmediatamente. Hablé con la secretaria, y le dije: "Sabes qué, necesito hablar con la principal." Entonces fui y le dije: "Mire, ¿qué posibilidades hay de que me cambie al niño?" Y dijo: "No". "No", dijo, "porque no conocemos al maestro, están empezando; vamos a darle tiempo. Deme tiempo para que los dos se conozcan y se adapten. ¿Ok?" Entonces, se va uno directo al principal. Entonces, ahí lo que sucedió fue que la segunda vez… ah, me dio una entrevista, nos entrevistamos otra vez, con el maestro, la principal y yo.

Lilian: You told me about the time you tried to switch teachers. When you decided to go, who did you speak to? How did you do the first time you went?
Sandra: As soon as my son told me, on the second day, "You know what, I don't like that teacher; he yells a lot, he yells a lot. And I don't like him."
Lilian: He already knew on the second day.

Sandra: Yes, he said that. So, I said, "You know what, wait a bit." "No," he said, "Go and talk; do something, because I don't like him." I said, "How come you don't like him? On the first day? You need to give it a try." So I thought, "He's a heavy-handed teacher, and he's always had women teachers, so," I thought, "He's felt the change. And as at home there is no father figure, maybe he's despairing." So, I asked to meet with the principal immediately. I spoke to the secretary, and said, "You know what, I need to speak to the principal." So I went and told her, "Look, is there a possibility of allowing my son to switch classes?" And she said, "No." "No," she said, "because we don't know the teacher, they're just starting; let's give it time. Give me time, so that they get to know each other and adapt. Ok?" So, I go straight to the principal. So, there what happened was that the second time, oh, she gave me an appointment, we met again, with the teacher, the principal, and I.

Sandra retells in detail the process she went through to finally manage to get the principal to pay attention to her, and take her request seriously. The principal first asked Sandra to be patient and explained how she was supporting this teacher who was new to the school, and had recently come from a larger city.

Although the principal did not immediately meet Sandra's request, she eventually called a meeting with the teacher, due to Sandra's insistence. At this meeting with the principal and the teacher, they agreed to give the situation some time, to see if it improved. The teacher tried to explain the whole situation away by blaming the child for being afraid of him. According to the teacher, Sandra's son would always cry in response to any of his questions, and that was probably because he had always only been placed in classrooms with female teachers.

By the end of the meeting Sandra and the teacher had agreed to work together. Showing her good will, she agreed to wait and see if her son adapted. But Sandra did not see any improvement; on the contrary, her son's behavior got increasingly aggressive and the tensions rose at home. Sandra went back to the principal.

Entonces, duró quince días y ya le estaba afectando al niño en su carácter. Ya no tenía deseos de ir a la escuela, ya se quería morir. Y yo estaba batallando mucho con él. El estaba enojado conmigo porque yo no estaba haciendo nada por él. (*"yo" and "él" are stressed*) El dijo: "Es que tú no estás haciendo nada por mí." Entonces, volví a ir a la escuela y le dije: "Sabe qué, necesito que me lo cambien. (*stressing each word by slowing down*) Está muy agresivo el niño, está violento. Es más, yo ya no puedo alzar la voz, ya," le dije. "Yo no tengo problema; yo soy una mamá, nada más vivo para mis hijos, yo no les doy mal ejemplo a mis hijos, o sea, nada, de ningún aspecto," le dije. "Entonces, no tiene mi niño por qué estar así. Y ha cambiado. Y el problema está aquí en la escuela." Sí, o sea, gracias a Dios, yo vivo, trato de vivir bien. Entonces dijo: "Bueno, le vamos a atender su petición porque usted ya había venido."

So, 15 days went by and it was already affecting my son's temper. He didn't want to go to school, he wanted to die. And I was struggling a lot with him. He was mad at me because I wasn't doing anything for him. *("I" and "him" are stressed)* He said, "You aren't doing anything for me." So, I went back to the school and said, "You know what, I need you to change him. *(stressing each word by slowing down)* He is being very aggressive, he's getting violent. What's more, I can't raise my voice anymore," I said. "I don't have a problem; I am a mom, I only live for my kids; I don't give them a bad example, that is, nothing, in any way," I said. "So there's no reason for my child to be like this. And he has changed. And the problem is here in the school." So, thanks to God, I live, and try and live well. So she said, "Ok, we will heed your request because you had already come in before."

As the principal did not listen to Sandra the first two times she made her request, and the situation with her son's teacher was worsening, Sandra insisted. She went to the principal once more. Her son's behavior was deteriorating, and he was becoming more and more aggressive. He was so distressed that he had even begged his mother to please do something about this situation. After some weeks, Sandra's son grew so despondent he did not want to go back to school. Emphasizing the depth of his misery through the use of hyperbole, Sandra goes as far as to say "he wanted to die".

Entonces, dijo: "Mire, le voy a atender su petición, no más porque usted ya había venido. No más porque usted vino. ¿Sí?" Entonces, perdimos las relaciones diplomáticas, el maestro y yo; dejó de saludarme. Pero dije, "Es más importante la salud mental de mi hijo." El niño sí mejoró calificaciones, sí, y él siempre ha traído buenas calificaciones. Pero ya su deseo de no ir a la escuela, su agresividad y todo eso ocasionó muchos problemas en nuestra casa, ¿ve? Entonces, ya ese maestro venía de La Vía, estaba acostumbrado a tratar a niños "gangueros", a niños rebeldes. O sea, uno sabe. Mi niño no era contestón, no. Él era calmado. Pero él estaba completamente agresivo. Entonces, fue cuando atendieron mi petición de cambiarlo; hasta entonces, que ya vieron los resultados más. O sea que yo le dije: "Que yo no aguanto más... o..."

So, she said, "Look, I'm going to heed your request, only because you'd already come in. Only because you came before, ok?" So, we weren't on speaking terms, the teacher and I; he stopped saying "Hi" to me. But I thought, "My son's mental health is more important to me." My son's grades improved, and yes, he always gets good grades. But his not wanting to go to school, his aggression, and all that, created many problems here at home, you see? So, that teacher had come from La Vía and he was used to working with kids who were in gangs, rebellious kids. So, one knows. My son was not one to answer back, no. He was calm. But he had turned completely aggressive.

So, that's when they met my request to switch him; once they saw the consequences more clearly. That is, that I said, "I can't put up with this any longer… or…"

The principal finally heeded her request, but only after Sandra had visited her office several times. As a last resort, Sandra had asked the principal directly if she was going to move her son to a different class or, if not, where else could she go or who else should she talk to who would deal with this situation. By this, she implied that, if necessary, she would appeal to someone further up in the institutional hierarchy; she was willing to bring this up with the school district officials, if it came to that. By then, Sandra insisted, her son did not even want to attend school anymore, and was very scared of the teacher. In the meanwhile, Sandra had asked the opinion of other women who had children in the same class as his son. One other mother, who happened to be a school employee, had managed to have her son moved to another class with another teacher sooner than Sandra.

Sandra: Le dije: "¡Dígame! Dígame si lo va a cambiar o ¿adónde tengo que ir?" (stressing her words in a determined, firm, almost defiant tone of voice) "Ya, adónde tengo que ir para que atiendan mi petición." Entonces, ya fue cuando ella atendió. Pienso que sí tardó más de los 15 días, porque no recuerdo bien cuándo me llegó el primer reporte de calificaciones…"Asique quizá que tardó mes, mes y medio. Como a los dos meses. Sí, el primer bimestre. Asique como a los 15 días recibo yo la calificación y ya le digo, "Mira, mejor te hubiera dejado ahí." Pero no lo hubiera soportado. No, no, su carácter no lo aguantaba ya. No, no. Fue mejor así, por su salud mental.
Lilian: Quién sabe, a la larga.
Sandra: No, no, no, deja de ir a la escuela (in a whisper). Yo sé que él tiene carácter… algo hubiera pasado. No, no puede uno imaginarse las consecuencias. Y ese maestro ya no está aquí. Nada más duró dos años y ya no está. ¿Qué me enseña a mí? Que él sí podría tener buena técnica pero, el alzar la voz a los niños: tenía un vozarrón, pero con tantito que lo alzara. No, no!

Sandra: I said to her, "Tell me! Tell me if you are going to move him, or where do I need to go?" (stressing her words in a determined, firm, almost defiant tone of voice). "Where do I need to go, then, for my request to be met?" So, that was when she listened. I think it took her more than 15 days, because I don't remember when I received the first report card. So maybe it took about a month, a month and a half. About two months into the year. Yes, the first nine weeks. So about 15 days later I got his grades, and I said "Look, maybe I should have left you there." But he wouldn't have put up with it. No, no, his temper, it was hard to take. No, no, it was better for his mental health.
Lilian: Who knows, in the long run.

Sandra: No, no, no, he would've quit school (*in a whisper*). He has a strong character... something would have happened. No, one can't imagine the consequences. And that teacher isn't here anymore. He only lasted two years and he's not here anymore. What does that show me? Maybe he did have good methods but, raising his voice at the kids: he had such a deep loud voice, just by raising it a bit. ¡No, no!

Ultimately, Sandra was proved right, since that teacher lasted only two years in their school. According to her, that teacher would raise his voice and constantly harass his students.

One factor worth noting in this case is one which coincides with findings in previous studies. Since Sandra was able to compare here own situation with that of another mother, who was a school employee and whose request was met faster, her experience signals the existence of privileged access by some parents to important decision-making processes, not available to all parents unless they insist. In spite of the resistance she initially encountered at the school to make any changes, Sandra did not tolerate the postponement of a decision, and only through her insistence did she manage to be heard. It was her concern for her son's wellbeing that had motivated her to intervene in the first place, to protect him. In this incident, Sandra acted as an advocate for her son, who was being treated aggressively, even bullied, by a teacher.

## Brenda— *Yo pienso que los desayunos que están dando, eso sí es muy bueno y es ayuda para nosotros.*
(I think that the breakfast they offer, that is very good and it helps us.)

Both Brenda and Susana mention the fact that children receive breakfast and lunch as one of the positive aspects of their children's schooling. Brenda offers this response to a question about her suggestions for a program to help immigrant mothers. She refers to existing programs in the schools in this area, which offer free breakfast and lunch to all their students because they qualify for it based on the income level of their student body.

Lilian: Si la escuela de sus hijas estuviera tratando de organizar un programa para ayudar a la relación con las mamás inmigrantes y le pidieran su opinión, basándose en su propia experiencia ¿qué sugeriría que haga la escuela para ayudar a las mamás cuando llegan?
Brenda: ¿La escuela? ¿Para las mamás? Pues, en primer lugar, yo pienso que los desayunos que están dando, eso sí es muy bueno y es ayuda para nosotros. Porque a veces sale uno a trabajar temprano y para dejarles almuerzo listo. Es muy grande ayuda lo que están haciendo en las escuelas. Luego que no no más les dan almuerzo, almuerzo y comida, ¿verdad? Ese programa es muy bueno. Y, pues, aquí, bueno, a nosotros no nos

cobran nada. En otras partes, tengo entendido que sí pagan algo. Pero aquí en Greenfields, no. También, por ejemplo, para el día del "turkey" les dicen a los niños que lleven dos o tres latas de comida. Y también allí miran los ingresos que tiene uno y si está muy bajo de ingresos, ahí le dan a uno la comida para ese día, hasta el "turkey" le dan y le dan comida embotada y eso. Eso también es muy buena ayuda. Como hay personas que de veras no les alcanza, no tienen para comer ese día, verdad, para su pavo y todo eso, y ya. Pues ya ve, las criaturas, es lo que anhelan, tener un día especial también, así, verdad. Y, pues, yo pienso que eso es muy bueno que hagan en la escuela.

Lilian: If your daughters' school were trying to organize a program to help the relationship with immigrant mothers and they asked your opinion, based on your experience, what would you suggest that the school should do to help the mothers when they arrive?
Brenda: The school? For the moms? Well, first, I think that the breakfast they offer, that is very good and it helps us. Because sometimes one leaves very early for work and to leave breakfast ready… It is a great help what they're doing in the schools. Then, it isn't only breakfast, they give them breakfast and lunch, right? That program is very good. And, well, here they don't charge us anything. In other places, I understand that they do pay something. But here, in Greenfields, they don't. Also, for example, for turkey day, they ask the children to bring two or three cans of food. And they also check and see your income level and if it is very low, they give you food for that day, they even give you a turkey and preserves and that. That is also good help. As there are people who can't make ends meet, they don't have enough to eat on that day, for the turkey and all that. And, you know, the kids, it's what they crave for, to have a special day too, like that, you know. And, well, I think that it is very good of the school to do that.

Similarly, when Susana is asked what information she would share with a newcomer that she would need to know about the schools in the United States, she first mentions the free breakfast and lunch programs as one of the differences between schooling here and in Mexico. The second point she makes is that children must be ready on time, so as not to miss the school bus. This is also different, she comments, because if they arrive late, in this country, they will not be admitted unless they are signed in by a parent.

Lilian: Si usted estuviera hablando con una amiga suya de México y que piensa venir aquí a Estados Unidos. ¿Qué le contaría usted si ella le pregunta su experiencia con las escuelas? ¿Qué es lo que tiene que esperar? ¿Cómo se las arregló? ¿Qué necesita saber ella? Basado en su experiencia.
Susana: Que fuera diferente. ¡Ay! (sighs) Que no se preocupen por la comida porque llegando a la escuela les dan desayuno (laughs). No tiene muy mucho que preocuparse por porque vayan desayunaditos porque ahí en la escuela llegando, lo primero que hacen, desayunar. Aha. Así es que, allá en México, pues, no… allá tienen que ir de-

sayunaditos y llevar lonche. Aha, y aquí es una ventaja. Aha, bueno, también, tener los niños a tiempo tempranito, listos tempranito para que no se les pase el camión. De lo contrario tiene que llevarlos hasta la escuela. Uhm. Y allá en México es diferente porque, pues, los niños se van caminando. Es que no importa la hora. Aquí si el niño ya llega tarde, pues, tiene que ir a firmar, para que se lo dejen entrar.

Lilian: If you were speaking with a friend from Mexico who is thinking of coming to the US. What would you tell her if she asks you about your experience with the schools? What should she expect? How did you manage? What does she need to know, based on your experience?
Susana: Something different. (sighs) Oh, that she doesn't need to worry about food because when they get to school, they give them breakfast. She doesn't need to worry about giving them breakfast, because at the school as soon as they arrive, the first thing they do is have breakfast. Aha. So, in Mexico, well no, over there they need to have breakfast at home and bring their lunch with them. Aha, here that's an advantage. Well, also, have the children ready early, so that they don't miss the bus. Or else she will have to take them to school. Over there, in Mexico it is different because, well, children walk to school. The time doesn't matter so much. Here, if the child arrives late, well, you have to sign so that they let him in.

Under the dominant discourse of parental involvement, the fact that the women mention free food as one of the first advantages of schooling would be viewed as a lack of real concern with their children's schooling and academic progress. In the eyes of some educators, they would be seen as more concerned with their day-to-day life than with their children's education (Suárez-Orozco et al., 2008, p. 77). If, instead, the schools were to try and understand these women's circumstances in the light of the ideology of "motherwork", the verdict would be very different. As Collins (1994) maintains, whereas "physical survival is assumed for children who are white and middle-class" this is not the case for most children of women of color, given the fact that "approximately one-third of Hispanic children and one-half of African-American children who survive infancy live in poverty" (p. 49). In this light, the concern with their children receiving a meal before school would be considered a sign of involvement and educational motherwork.

What these examples of counter narratives of maternal involvement have in common with each other is the underlying ideology of motherwork (Collins, 1994). The communal resources developed and shared by the participants as well as the instances of advocacy for their children all come together under the notion of motherwork. Further, the counter narratives are observed to have a transformative power. What the transformation involves and at what level it occurs varies in each case. As was analyzed above, these counter narratives coexist in the participants' accounts with instances of complete alignment with the official discourse, which would be a reflection of the ideology of intensive mothering (Hays, 1996). The instances of ventriloquation discussed below underscore this contrast, given that this double voicing has been analyzed to signal the existence of conflicting perspectives in the social world (Wortham, 2001, p. 66). Further, in the thematic analysis (with some elements of dialogic/performance analysis) of the polyphony in the texts, the coexistence of contrasting narrative threads in the seven women's stories was observed as going hand in hand with the possibility for immigrant mothers of exercising transformative agency in their interactions with the schools from within (Riessman, 2008).

## Narratives of Parental Involvement: School Expectations

These are the women's stories which align with the mainstream discourse of parental involvement either directly, through their understanding of the school's expectations and by voicing their appreciation of them, or indirectly through references to their own behavior which corresponds with them. Every one of the women interviewed was not only able to enumerate the school's expectations but they also expressed their agreement with them, and shared different ways in which these expectations weighed on their attitudes and actions. For example, in many instances they demonstrated a keen awareness of their children's development of literacy; they expressed their concerns about being able to help them or not with homework; or they referred to their active participation in school events.

**Susana—*Yo creo que sí [las expectativas] están claras y son muy buenas.***
(I think that they [the expectations] are clear and they are good.)

In their individual interviews the participants responded with unwavering certainty as to what schools expect from parents (or mothers). They also unanimously expressed their approval of these expectations. In most cases, they interspersed comments on these expectations in their responses to questions on how they participated in the schools, as part of their own views on what mothers were supposed to do.

In response to the direct question about of school expectations for parents, Susana draws up a specific list, which seems to echo exactly the words she has heard from the school. Among the expectations Susana understands the school has for her as a mother, she enumerates supporting her children's learning, ensuring they get a good night's sleep, making sure they do their homework, providing a quiet environment for them to do their homework and making sure they read before going to bed. Some of the items on this list closely resemble the recommendations principals usually offer parents on the day before schools start an intensive period of testing.

> Lilian: ¿Usted qué piensa? ¿Qué esperan las escuelas de las madres? ¿Son claras estas expectativas que tienen las escuelas de la mamás?
> Susana: ¿Qué esperan las escuelas de los papás? Pues, que los apoyemos, que cuidemos que no se desvelen, que duerman bien, que llegan a tiempo a la escuela, que hagan sus tareas, que tengan un lugar tranquilo dónde hacer sus tareas, que estemos atentos con ellos, que cuidemos que tienen que leer antes de irse a dormir, cosa difícil.

> Lilian: What do schools expect from mothers, in your opinion? Are the expectations schools have of mothers clear?
> Susana: What do schools expect of parents? Well, that we support them; that we make sure they don't stay up; that they sleep well; that they arrive to school on time; that they do their homework; that they have a quiet place to do their homework; that we pay attention to them; that we make sure they read before going to bed—which is hard.

Homework came up frequently in the women's narratives. Most times they mentioned their concerns about not being able to help their children with it because it was in English, and how they found someone to help them, often a relative. In some cases, especially if their children were in a bilingual program, they expressed their satisfaction with being able to help with their Spanish homework. Other expectations Susana mentions here are punctuality and making sure children get enough sleep. A phrase Susana uses sums up her view of what schools expect of parents. Susana mentions paying attention to one's children ("*que estemos atentos*"), an idea which was repeated by other participants, such as Luisa, in terms of "*estar pendiente*". This phrase highlights the awareness of one's children's needs, and stresses the continuity and constancy of this attention. In another context, Brenda uses a similar expression to refer to the need for teachers to be aware that mothers are looking out for their children ("*que uno mira por sus hijos*").

After listing the expectations the school has for parents, Susana explains where she finds out what these are. She also stresses the fact that they are clear, that she agrees with them, and that she considers them to be good expectations.

> Lilian: ¿Y qué opina usted de estas expectativas que tiene la escuela?
> Susana: Pues, son muy buenas. Yo creo que sí están claras y son muy buenas. Aparte, tengo una niña que apenas entró a primero y ya sabe leer.

> Lilian: And what do you think of these expectations the school has?
> Susana: Well, that they are good. I think that they are clear and they are good. Also, I have a daughter that has just started first grade and she already knows how to read.

Susana ends this section of the interview with a comment on her daughter's progress. This seems to be a confirmation for her of the results of doing things right. The fact that her daughter, who has just started first grade, is already reading is related in this story to these expectations, or maybe to this agreement between both parties, home and school. As her daughter's example shows, what is being done jointly by school and parents is working.

## Silvia—*Así como ellos nos apoyan a nosotros, a ellos también les gusta que uno, como padre, apoye también a la escuela.* (Just as they support us, they also want one, as a parent, to support the school.)

Silvia explains how she was invited to participate in conferences and meetings from the very beginning, and she adds that the school is very interested in the parents' support. As is the case with Susana, Silvia's words reflect her familiarity with the school's parental involvement policies. Silvia emphasizes how from the very beginning, when her children started school, she liked to attend all meetings called by the school, and how she still does. In a comment that shows her own agreement with school policies, she offers her own opinion of how important it is for children to know that they have their parents' support.

> Lilian: ¿La invitaron al principio a participar a usted en esas entrevistas individuales con los padres y la maestra, o la mamá y la maestra?
> Silvia: Sí, desde un principio, cuando uno va a la escuela aquí, a ellos les interesa mucho el apoyo; saber del apoyo de los padres para con los hijos, que apoyemos a los hijos. Entonces de un principio a mí me gustó, empezar a ir a las juntas de las escuelas

de mis niños, porque eso es muy importante y también porque los niños saben que reciben el apoyo. Saben que sus papás también los están apoyando.

Lilian: Did they invite you at the beginning to participate in these individual interviews between parents and teacher, or the mother and the teacher?

Silvia: Yes, from the very beginning, when one goes to the school here, they are very interested in our support; they want to know that parents support their children, that we support our children. So, from the very beginning I liked to go to the meetings at my kids' schools, because that is very important, and because the children know that they have our support. They know that their parents also support them.

Once again, when asked directly about the school's expectations for parents, Silvia discusses the importance of supporting the school, and supporting one's children. At this point, Silvia's tone of voice changes abruptly, and becomes louder and sterner, as she stresses her words as if adopting the role of the school representatives—teachers or officials—in requesting the support of parents.

Lilian: ¿Qué es lo que la escuela espera de las mamás? ¿Cuáles son estas expectativas que tiene la escuela hacia usted? ¿Cómo las ve usted?

Silvia: Pues, lo que a ellos les interesa es que en cada junta o en cada reunión que se haga, así como ellos nos apoyan a nosotros, a ellos también les gusta que uno, como padre, apoye también a la escuela. Porque es muy importante, también, que los papás apoyemos las decisiones que toma la escuela sobre lo que van a hacer. Es muy importante que también los papás apoyen a la escuela adonde va su hijo, o su hija. *(louder and sterner tone of voice)*

Lilian: What does the school expect from mothers? What are those expectations the school has of you? What do you think of them?

Silvia: Well, what they care about is that, at every meeting that is held, just as they support us, they also want one, as a parent, to support the school. Because it is very important, also, that as parents we support the decisions the school makes about what they are going to do. It is very important also that parents support the school that their son or daughter attends. *(louder and sterner tone of voice)*

In a similar context, the same prosodic marker, this change in tone of voice, is observed in another interviewee's story. Patricia explains that she attends festivals where her children participate in musical performances, such as a Christmas show, and she underlines the importance of watching her children take part in these activities as well as when they are honored at award ceremonies, because it makes them feel proud. In reference to attending both the award ceremonies and the performances, Patricia emphasizes the fact that she attends for her children to be happy and feel supported. At the end of this segment, Patricia's tone of voice also changes abruptly and becomes louder and sounds more serious.

> Lilian: ¿Le ha pasado con los dos?
> Patricia: Con el más grande más. El más chiquito sólo he ido como a juntas y como en navidad que les hicieron ... les hacen un festival donde pasan ellos a cantar y todo eso. Pues sí, va uno a verlos cantar, a oírlos ahí *(voice becomes tender)*. Sí, y... pues, son bonitas también para uno, porque ya pues, ya mira uno lo que ellos hacen y ellos, pues, yo pienso que hasta se sienten más contentos y cantan con más ganas ahí *(laughs)*.
> Lilian: ¡Cómo no! Que los vea uno...
> Patricia: Sí, que los está uno mirando, y ya se sienten contentos.
> Lilian: Sí.
> Patricia: Y hasta llegan contentos a la casa... "¡Sí, me viste? ¿Sí, me viste?" *(high pitched, and said fast, imitating the child's excitement)* "Sí, pues, sí te miré, ahí." Y ahí. Yo pienso que es bonito, también poder ir uno a todo, verdad, pues es responsabilidad de nosotros, de los padres, asistir. *[Voice is serious, and loud, as if reflecting an administrator's or a teacher's formal voice. Marked contrast in tone on the last phrase.]*
>
> Lilian: Has this happened with both, with the older one more maybe?
> Patricia: With the older one more. For the youngest I have only gone to like conferences and like for Christmas they had... they organized a festival for them, where they go up to sing and all that. Well yes, one goes to watch them sing, to listen to them. *(voice becomes tender)*. Yes, and ... well, it's nice for one also, because, well, one sees what they do, and they, well, I think that they even feel happier and they sing with more enthusiasm there *(laughs)*.
> Lilian: Of course! That you can see them...
> Patricia: Yes, that one is watching them and they feel happy.
> Lilian: Yes.
> Patricia: And they even come back home happy, "Did you see me? Did you see me? *(High-pitched, and said very fast imitating the child's excitement)*. "Yes, I saw you there." And so. I think that it's nice, also for one to be able to go to everything, right, because it's our responsibility, of the parents, to attend. *[Voice is serious, and loud, as if reflecting an administrator's or a teacher's formal voice. Marked contrast in tone on the last phrase.]*

In these comparable individual accounts, both Luisa and Patricia not only use language which reflects the official discourse of parental involvement in much the same way but its contrast with the rest of their narration is identically highlighted by a marked shift in their tone of voice to mirror that of a person in authority. In both cases, the participants seem to be appropriating the voice of a school official to state the responsibility parents have of attending all school events. Within the narrative analysis, these examples point to how dialogic/performance analysis and attention to prosodic features may contribute to underscore the thematic meanings and to signal distinctive narrative threads (Riessman, 2008). These are instances of official discourse ventriloquation, a phenomenon which will be discussed in further detail below.

In response to a final open question, Silvia comments on how satisfied she is with her children's school. At the same time, she stresses the importance of two aspects of family-school relations. The first one is parent-to-parent sharing of information; the second one, attending meetings both so as to find out how kids are doing, and also for children to perceive their parents' support so that they do not slack off in school. In conclusion, according to Silvia, ultimately, all of this support matters in view of how it will contribute to the children's bright future.

> Lilian: ¿Hay algo que usted quiera agregar, comentar alguna cosa sobre su interacción con la escuela o sobre la escuela con usted o sobre la comunicación, algo que no se me haya ocurrido a mí?
> Silvia: No, sí, pues, no más que estoy a gusto con la escuela adonde van mis hijos y, pues, que si algún padre escucha algo, pues, en las escuelas, pues, debemos de avisar, y de también ir a las juntas para aprender lo que nuestros hijos están haciendo y que ellos también se sientan apoyados por sus papás, verdad, para que a ellos no les dé flojera ir a la escuela sino seguir adelante y tengan un buen futuro en adelante.

> Lilian: Is there anything you would like to add, comment on anything about your interactions with the school, or the school's interactions with you, or about communication? Anything that I might not have thought about?
> Silvia: Well, yes, just that I am happy with the school where my children attend and, well, if any parent hears something, in the schools, well, we must let others know, and also go to meetings to learn about what our children are doing and also for them to feel supported by their parents, right, so that they don't feel like slacking off in school, but continue and progress and have a good future ahead of them.

Silvia's final reflection summarizes her deep interest in her children's education. In her comments, Silvia embraces the school expectations as valuable and as a way of working towards her children's progress. However, she does not limit this work to the individual but instead adds the community as a resource and an important aspect of communication with the schools. The fact that in her conclusion Silvia mentions the need for parents to share information among those issues worth highlighting is significant, since in so doing she signals her communal perspective on home-school interactions.

# Awareness and Encouragement of Literacy Development

Many common assumptions about immigrant parents, examined in the literature (see Chapter 4) are debunked in the following examples. Given the deficit thinking often directed to low-income, immigrant and Latin@ homes, the following accounts spontaneously shared by the participants in this study are illuminating as they stand in stark contrast with those negative assessments of parental attitudes which tend to dominate home-school relations.

### Silvia—*Ya lee mucho. Ya agarra su libro y ya lee sola. Y lee rápido. Bien rápido.*
(She takes her book and she already reads on her own. And she reads fast. Very fast.)

Silvia speaks with pride of how her first-grader, Sarina, takes a book and reads it on her own and very fast. Silvia is also aware of her children's differences and points out how her son, Juan Manuel, is not as interested in reading. She comments on the fact that he still does well in school, because he does his work, and he also does read at school, when he needs to. Later, Silvia makes a point of adding as a reason that her son does well in school the fact that he is very respectful and well behaved—which in Spanish is often referred to as being "educado", or having "buena educación", an idiomatic expression which implies courtesy and politeness, even though, quite tellingly, translates literally into being "educated" or having a "good education". At another point in her narrative, Silvia compares both her children's experiences and wonders whether what made a difference might have been that her daughter had been placed in a bilingual program, and thus had benefited from the fact that she first learned how to read in her home language.

> Lilian: ¿Y la niña de primero es la que lee tanto?
> Silvia: Uy, sí. Ya lee mucho. Ya agarra su libro y ya lee sola. Y lee rápido. Bien rápido. Y le digo: "¿Ya acabaste?" "Ya," dice "ya acabé." Y al otro no le gusta nada. La lectura no le gusta. No más en la escuela. En la escuela sí lee porque lo ponen. Pero ya llegando a la casa, ya que se olviden de lectura porque él no. No. Pero de todos modos, como hace las cosas bien en la escuela y todo, pues, es un niño que va avanzado, porque lo que hace lo hace bien y lo hace bien en la escuela. Luego lo que pasa es que muy respetuoso, él no crea que anda peleando ni jugando ni.... No, no, no. Muy respetuoso él ahí, aha, en la escuela, pero sí, ya.
> Lilian: ¡Qué orgullo! ¿No?
> Silvia: El papá, orgulloso está, según él.

Lilian: And, it's the first-grader who reads so much?

Silvia: Oh, yes. She reads a lot already. She takes her book and she already reads on her own. And she reads fast. Very fast. And I ask her, "You're done already?" "Yes," she says, "I'm done." And the other one doesn't like it at all. He doesn't like reading. Only at school. At school he reads because they make him.

But when he gets home, you can forget reading, because he won't read. No. But anyway, as he does well at school and all, well, he's a child who is advanced, because what he does, he does it well and he does it well at school. Also, the thing is that he is very respectful; he won't get into fights or start playing or… No, no, no. He is very respectful over there, at school, and yes.

Lilian: How proud [you must be]!

Silvia: His dad is proud, according to him.

Silvia shares her detailed observations about her daughter's early childhood development and literacy. She mentions how Sarina was very active and could already write her name at an early age. In this way, Silvia stresses the fact that her daughter was already highly motivated before entering Head Start, and was curious and learned alone. She recounts how, at a very early age, Sarina was aware of the concepts of print, and on her own would copy the letters from books. In her account, Silvia not only demonstrates a keen interest in the stages in her child's development of literacy but also a profound awareness of the process. Hers is an example of a mother who is paying close attention to her child's development and is proud of her progress.

Silvia: Antes de que entrara a Head Start, ella ya sabía los colores, los números, ya sabía reconocer… como cuando reconocen la lectura, cómo mover un libro. Ella sabía todo eso. Entonces, ella desde que ella entró ahi, ella tuvo el avance muy grande. Sí, pero porque ella era bien activa; ella de chiquita agarraba los colores y agarraba todo, todo agarraba.

Lilian: Ah, ya estaba muy motivada.

Silvia: Su nombre, ella cuando entró ella ya sabía su nombre, también.

Lilian: Oh, de chiquita.

Silvia: De chiquita, sí, es que ella solita se ponía y miraba los libros y ella se ponía a copiar las letras, aunque no sabía qué dijera, pues, ella de todos modos copiaba.

Silvia: Before she started Head Start, she knew the colors, the numbers, she could recognize… in reading, how to turn [the pages of] a book. She knew all that. So, when she started there, she made great progress. Yes, because she was very active; from an early age she would get hold of colored pencils, and she would grab everything, everything.

Lilian: Oh, so she was motivated already.

Silvia: Her name, when she started, she also knew her name already.

Lilian: Oh, since she was little.

Silvia: Since she was little, yes. On her own, she would sit down and look at books, and she would start copying the letters, even if she didn't know what it said, well, she would copy them anyway.

Following this account of how her daughter had been an active learner from an early age, Silvia shares with excitement a current example of Sarina's literacy development. Silvia narrates how, on her own, her daughter wrote a story book, illustrated it and took it to school to show it to her teacher. At this point in her story, Silvia explains how when Sarina told her she had written and illustrated her own story book, she reminded her that she needed to sign it, as authors do.

Y ahora, el otro día, dijo qué: ¡Que había armado un cuento! Se puso a escribir y digo, ¿esta qué está haciendo? Estaba escribiendo. Y escribe y escribió un cuento y luego le puso los dibujos que iban en el cuento. Según ella, dibujó los dibujos que iban en el cuento. Y digo, "ay, hija pues ¿qué estás haciendo?" "Es que ya me inventé un cuento." Y le digo: "Ahora, no más falta firmarlo. Porque para un cuento tiene que llevar la firma del que lo hizo." Y luego, le digo: "Ándale, pues. ¿Y dónde lo vas a firmar?" Y le puso, hasta le puso firma y lo firmó. "No, si mañana lo llevo a la escuela y le digo a mi 'teacher'": "Mire "teacher" ya armé un cuento, fírmemelo." Ella es así, así es ella. Y ella se arma sus cuentos, se arma sus palabras. Ella armaba palabras sola, ve, cuando estaba en "kínder", ella armaba palabras. Solita.

And now, the other day, she said what: That she had made a story book! She started writing and I said, what's she doing? She was writing. And she writes and she wrote a story and then she made the drawings that went in the story. According to her, she drew the drawings that went in the story. And I asked her, "What are you doing?" "I've already invented a story." And I told her, "Now you only need to sign it, because a story needs to have the signature of the one who made it." And then I said, "So, then, where are you going to sign it?" And she did, she signed it. "And tomorrow I'll take it to school and I'll tell my teacher: 'Look teacher, I've already made a story book, would you sing it for me?" She is like that; that is how she is. She makes her story books, she builds words. She would put words together, you see, when she was in kindergarten, she built words, on her own.

Silvia's awareness and encouragement of her daughter's progress are clear from this reported conversation. Silvia does not only ask Sarina about her work, but she also encourages her to sign it, and in so doing, to claim ownership of her work. Then her daughter feels the need to show it to her teacher, and get it signed by her. In this story, there is no reference to direct communication between the mother and the school, and there may be no knowledge on the part of the teacher of the mother's awareness, support and encouragement of her daughter's progress, or of her engagement in her learning process. The mother in this story also gives all the credit to her child, for her curiosity and active learning.

## Patricia—*Él sabe leer rapidito en inglés. ¡Sí! ¡Creo [que] lee por minuto más de cien palabras!*
(He can read really fast in English. Yes, I think he reads more than a hundred words per minute!)

Patricia recounts how her eldest son has participated in a bilingual program, and recently exited it, and is now in a monolingual English class. He has excelled in school, and especially in his reading skills. Patricia explains at great length how much her fourth-grader enjoys reading and devours all the books he brings home.

> Patricia: Sí, él aprendió y sabía mucho, él mucho, mucho inglés. (*All in this low drop… as if asserting a very important fact*). Y allá no recuerdo si le dieron clases de español, pero sabía. Y, como quiera, sabía español también. Y cuando llegó aquí, a él lo pusieron en clases de bilingüe… como en tercer grado. Ya cuando iba a entrar a cuarto, lo sacaron. Dijeron: "él ya no necesita." Ya le dan puro inglés a él. Dijeron: "El está listo para salir de bilingüe."
> Lilian: ¿Pero aprendió a leer y escribir los dos?
> Patricia: Sí sabe, sí sabe, sí sabe leer español y en inglés también. En español, pues, como no tiene mucha práctica, no, no mucho lee en español. Porque ahorita casi siempre todo… como es la pura clase de inglés, les dan puros libros en inglés, y pues, libros grandes. (*laughs*) Pero libros grandes (*stress, with rise-fall intonation on "grandes"*) pero puro inglés y él sabe leer rapidito en inglés. ¡Sí! ¡Creo lee por minuto más de cien palabras!
> Lilian: ¡Qué bien!
> Patricia: Sí, es bueno para leer. (*very serious, recognizing and stressing its significance*) En inglés.
> Lilian: Es muy lector…
> Patricia: Oh, ¡le gusta mucho leer a él!

> Patricia: Yes, he learned and he knew a lot, he knew a lot, a lot of English. And there I don't remember if they taught him Spanish, but he knew. And, anyway, he knew Spanish also. And when he got here, they placed him in bilingual classes… in third grade. When he was going to start fourth grade, they pulled him out. They said, "He doesn't need it anymore." He is doing just English now. They said, "He is ready to exit [the] bilingual [program]."
> Lilian: But he learned how to read and write both?
> Patricia: Yes, he knows, yes he does, he does know how to read Spanish, and in English too. In Spanish, well, as he doesn't have that much practice, no, he doesn't read

so much in Spanish. Because now almost everything… as he only has English classes, they only give them books in English, and well, big books *(laughs)*. But big books, *(stress, with rise-fall intonation on "big")* but only in English. And he can read really fast in English. Yes, I think he reads more than a hundred words per minute!
Lilian: That's great!
Patricia: Yes, he's very good at reading *(pauses – very serious, recognizing and stressing its significance)* in English.
Lilian: He is a good reader.
Patricia: Oh, he enjoys reading very much!

In her comments, Patricia manifests a detailed understanding of the program used by the school to encourage reading in their students. She is not only amazed at the length of the books her son gets through in just a couple of days but at the speed he reads as well. Also, she is aware of the fact that the school keeps record of the amount of words each child can read per minute, and that her son is doing well.

Lilian: Me decía usted que traía los libros, ¿no?
Patricia: Sí. Trae libros y… y se pone a leer él y cuando ya acaba de libro, lo llevan y lo pasan por la computadora y les hacen preguntas. Y van ganando puntos. Si se sabe todo lo que le preguntaron, le dan … no recuerdo, son diferentes libros. A veces, que unos traen tres puntos, pero los que traen tres puntos están bien gruesos. *(sing-song – rise-fall; laughs)*
Lilian: Y es un plan de lectura, ¿no?
Patricia: Sí. Y hay otros, son historias. Son como historias en los libros, son cuentos. Pero hay veces que trae unos bien *(bieeen, stressing by extending the word)* gruesos. Y le digo: "¡Todo eso vas a leer?" "Sí, como en unos tres días lo acabo," dice. *(Imitating the child's tone, and gesture, as if shrugging it off.)* Y llega y hay veces que ahí está leyendo, leyendo, leyendo, ¡ y no se aburre!

Lilian: You said he brings books home, right?
Patricia: Yes. He brings books and he settles down to read and when he finishes a book, they take him and he gets on the computer and they ask him questions. And they go earning points. If he knows all the answers, they give him… I don't remember; there are different books. Some have three dots, and those are really thick. *(rise-fall; laughs)*
Lilian: So, it's a reading plan, right?
Patricia: Yes. And there are other ones that are stories. They are like books of stories. But sometimes he brings some really thick ones *(stressing "really" by extending the word)*. And I ask him, "Are you going to read all that?" "Yes, I'll finish it in about three days," he says. *(Imitating the child's tone, and gesture, as if shrugging it off.)* And he gets home and sometimes there he is reading, reading, and reading, and he doesn't get bored!

Patricia comments on how she hears her son when he reads aloud and plays the parts of the characters, with different tones of voice and how he expresses different emotions through modulation of the voice in his reading. Although she admits she does not understand everything he is saying, the excitement in her voice while she speaks about her son's passion for reading reveals Patricia's pride in her son's literacy skills.

Lilian. ¿Está en cuarto grado, no?
Patricia: Sí, en cuarto grado. Pero sí le gusta a él.
Lilian: Bastante lee, eh.
Patricia: Sí, le gusta leer. Le gusta mucho leer. Yo pienso que son por las historias que vienen en los libros. Y… y ya… ya como empiezan, ya no quieren dejar, están emocionados con la historia. Y hay veces que lo oigo yo leer y…y… como que le da el son de lo que pasa, si está asustado… (*shows suspense, lowering her voice, imitating her son*), si está contento así como que habla recio, cuando se sorprenden así, sí le cambia la voz, como que…
Lilian: Ah, ¡sí le gusta!
Patricia:… como está emocionado por lo que está pasando y… Sí, sí lo oigo yo. Yo no lo entiendo mucho lo que dice pero… (*chuckles*)… lo oigo cómo de repente cambia la voz, como asustado (*lowering voice*) o de repente como así… diferentes (*higher pitch, very excited telling me about her son's reading skills*) … de repente de lo que diga ahí. Así, pero no…
Lilian: Disfruta mucho la lectura.
Patricia: Sí. Sí le gusta… sí le gusta mucho leer. Y está… le digo: "Pues, está bien que te guste", porque así aprenden ellos más palabras, leyendo, si no saben, ahí aprenden más y…y… (*highlighting "leyendo"; stress made through the use of pause: "así aprenden más palabras//leyendo// si no saben// allí aprenden más*) tienen más práctica en leer rápido. Ve que hay niños que no saben leer rápido.
Lilian: No…
Patricia: Muy muy lento. Pues, hay de todo, verdad. Hay niños que son buenos para leer y niños que son muy lentos para leer.

Lilian: So, he's in fourth grade, right?
Patricia: yes, in 4th grade. But, yes, he likes that.
Lilian: He reads quite a bit.
Patricia: Yes, he likes reading. He likes reading a lot. I think it must be because of the stories that come in the books. And once they've started, they don't want to leave, they're excited with the story. And sometimes I hear him read and… and… it's like he give it the tone of what is happening, if scared, (*shows suspense, lowering her voice, imitating her son*), if happy, he speaks fast, when they are surprised, also, he makes different voices, like…
Lilian: Oh, ¡he really likes it!

Patricia: ... he gets excited with what's going on and... Yes, yes, I hear him. I don't understand much of what he's saying but ... *(chuckles)*... I can hear him how all of a sudden he changes his voice, as if he were scared *(lowering voice)*, or suddenly like that... different depending on what it says there. Like that, well...
Lilian: So, he enjoys reading a lot.
Patricia: Yes, he likes it. He likes reading a lot. And it's... I tell him, "Well, it's good that you like it," because that's how they learn more words, reading, if they don't know them, there they learn more and... *(highlighting "leyendo'; stress made through the use of pause: "así aprenden más palabras//leyendo// si no saben// allí aprenden más)* he gets more practice reading fast. You know that there are kids who can't read fast.
Lilian: They don't ...
Patricia: Very, very slowly. Well, there's a mix, right. There are kids who are very good at reading and kids who are very slow readers.

Finally, Patricia elaborates on the virtues of reading for children, because of how it helps them expand their vocabulary. Patricia is highly aware of her son's abilities and of their significance. Patricia's tone of voice and the details which she offers of her son's reading signal her deep interest in his literacy skills and his progress in school.

## Active Participation in the Schools

As a single mother, after her divorce from an abusive husband, Norma is very aware of the need to fend for herself and not depend on anyone. Norma is proud of her efforts and of their results. She expresses her excitement now that she is able to help in her daughter's school, because she has learned English and she can communicate better with everyone.

Norma: Ahora, me invitaron en la escuela a enseñarles folklore. Y ahora, el 2 de mayo va a haber, van a tener una presentación ahí en la escuela. Y sí acepté porque ahora puedo entenderles, a los niños que no hablan español y puedo decirles más o menos cómo.
Lilian: Entonces, ¿usted sabe danzas folclóricas?
Norma: Sí, un poquito... un poquito, pero lo poquito que sé me gusta compartirlo con ellos...
Lilian: ¿En el aula de su hija? ¿O es para toda la escuela?
Norma: Nada más... Aquí les ponen el folclore... Todos participan... pero el folclore es nada más cuarto y quinto, los niños de esos dos grados. Y mi hija está en primer grado...
Lilian: Ah, es chiquita.
Norma: Sí. *(laughs)*
Lilian: Ya va a llegar... *(laughs)*

Norma: Ya va a llegar … *(laughs)* Y estoy bien orgullosa. Cuando llegué aquí yo decía: "¿Por qué no nací aquí para saber el idioma, para poderme mover y todo? Y ahora digo: "Qué bueno que soy mexicana y me gusta mi cultura, y mi gente, cómo nos esforzamos, cómo venimos a trabajar, para un futuro para nuestros hijos y luchamos." Es como doble esfuerzo, porque, por el idioma, como doble esfuerzo.

Norma: Now they've invited me to the school to teach them folklore. And now, on May 2 there is, they are going to put on a performance there at the school. And yes I accepted because now I can understand them, the kids who don't speak Spanish, and I can tell them more or less how.
Lilian: So then, you know folkloric dance?
Norma: Yes, a little… a little, but the little I know I like to share it with them…
Lilian: With your daughter's class? Or is it for the whole school?
Norma: Only… Here they offer folklore classes… They all participate… but folkloric dancing is only for fourth and fifth, for the kids in those two grades. And my daughter is in first grade…
Lilian: Oh, she's little.
Norma: Yes *(laughs)*.
Lilian: She'll soon get there… *(laughs)*
Norma: She'll get there… *(laughs)* And I am very proud. When I first arrived here I used to think, "Why wasn't I born here, to know the language, to know how to manage and all?" And now I say, "How good that I'm Mexican and I love my culture and my people, how we strive, how we come to work, for a future for our kids and we are fighters." It's like double the effort, because of the language, like double the effort.

Norma describes how at first she despaired when she did not understand anything of what was being said to her. She admits that at first, in her frustration, she sometimes felt so bad, that she even wished she had been born in the US, so that she could speak and understand English. However, as she explains, this was only a sign of the anxiety she experienced when she had first arrived, since she says that she is very proud of her Mexican culture, and has been asked to teach Mexican folkloric dance at her daughter's elementary school as an extracurricular activity. Norma stresses the fact that she is very proud of belonging to a hard-working people who make sacrifices for their children's' future. And, she adds, this effort is double after moving to the US because of the language. So, she is glad she can share these expressions of her culture with others.

# Official Discourse Appropriation: Ventriloquation

On some occasions the women seemed to unwaveringly side with the school in referring to the lack of parental involvement. These instances would point to their seeming identification with the school's expectations of involvement, especially noticeable in words reflecting the assessment of parents derived from the official discourse, which often adopts a cultural deficit perspective. The interviewees used expressions such as "negligence" and "not responding" to refer to the attitudes of immigrant parents and their perceived lack of involvement. In each of these cases, a parallel phenomenon was observed: the meaning of these words was highlighted by a marked change in the tone of voice, as if the speaker was impersonating some authority figure. These appear as extreme cases of appropriation of the official discourse and are examples of a phenomenon called ventriloquation (Bakhtin, 1981; Riessman, 2008, pp. 118–119; Wortham, 2001). Several interpretations of these occurrences are possible within the thematic analysis of the women's narratives. But a closer look at the concept of ventriloquation is required first in an effort to understand its implications.

Ventriloquation has been described as a phenomenon by which narrators adopt the voices of others in their own words and may thus express multiple and conflicting perspectives almost simultaneously (Wortham, 2001, pp. 66–67). According to Bakhtin (1984), in these instances of voice appropriation, "Someone else's words introduced into our own speech inevitably assume a new (our own) interpretation and become subject to our evaluation of them; that is, they become double-voiced" (p. 195). This type of double-voicing can also be described as "internally polemical discourse", which highlights the inner tensions created by the apparently contradictory narrative strands (Bakhtin, 1984, p. 196). Thus, in the case of the women's narratives, their words are found to be alternately aligned with the master story and then departing from it to resist it. As Wortham (2001) explains, often this juxtaposition of voices tends to reflect some type of conflict present in the complex social world in which they originate.

The findings of two studies which have observed similar tensions in their participants' narratives exemplify the current more complex view of the power dynamics involved in the construction of counter stories. In both inquiries, the researchers call attention to the significance of understanding double-voicing as manifestations of those larger societal power issues, and as a means of gaining insight into them. Riessman's (2008) analysis of the instances of ventriloquation in the dialogue of teenage girls drawn from Brown's study is relevant here. The participants in that study appropriated dominant voices in derogatory expressions that indirectly were demeaning to themselves. In Brown's study, the recognition of ventriloquation served to understand how "girls appropriated the dominant cultures' denigration of feminity, on the one hand, and struggled against it on the other" (Riessman, 2008, p. 118). This apparent contradiction, or inner textual conflict, illuminates the positioning of the narrators with respect to dominant discourses. Although, on the surface, the teenage girls were using voices that devalued themselves, in a subtle way, they may be seen as appropriating power through the use of that language: "Among and between these working- and middle-class girls, resistant, frustrated voices disrupt the regulatory fictions of realized feminity, revisioning both who they are and who they might become" (Brown, 1998, p. 154).

Similarly, a superficial reading of the stories of the seven immigrant women at the center of this book would render the instances of ventriloquation simply as an internalization of the dominant discourse and a mere reflection of the fact that they are subjected to the assimilatitionist forces of their current environment. Yet, Riessman's (2008) interpretation of the appropriation of power through ventriloquation points to a different explanation. Subtly, by appropriating the discourse of the school authorities—as marked through prosody, with a noticeable change in tone of voice—the participants may be indirectly identifying with those in power, and thus deriving a sense of inclusion. This appropriation of the official discourse may contribute to create in the participants a sense of belonging and loyalty to the institutions in which they occupy an ambivalent position. At the same time, in blurring the them/us distinction, the instances of ventriloquation throw into sharper relief those counter stories offered by the same participants. Bakhtin's (1984) description of the different manifestations of this appropriation helps elucidate this phenomenon further.

> Our practical everyday speech is full of other people's words: with some of them we completely merge our own voice, forgetting whose they are; others, which we take as authoritative, we use to reinforce our own words; still others, finally, we populate with our own aspirations, alien or hostile to them. (p. 195)

Even more pertinent to our findings, the conclusions drawn in another study focusing on counter narratives shed new light on how the inner tensions of a story may be interpreted. In an action research study conducted with participants in a college program at a high security prison for women, while the researchers had anticipated that the women's counter stories would unambiguously stand out in clear-cut contrast to the master story, they were surprised to observe instead the "co-mingling of counter and dominant discourses" (Torre et al., 2001, p. 148).

The harsh and self-deprecatory language used by the interviewees—inmates in a high-security prison participating in a college program—to refer to their former selves directly reproduces the dominant discourse and its images of women prisoners, as well as of poor women and of women of color. The researchers later reflected on their initial expectations and on their "naïve sense that counter stories from women in prison would sit somehow untainted, untouched and in clean opposition to dominant discourses" (p. 151). Based on their original assumptions, one early reaction was to read these as expressions of internalized self-loathing. But a closer look at the inmates' stories uncovered much subtler dynamics at work. This echoing of the master narrative showed the participants' understanding of their need to embrace the images of themselves as commonly portrayed in the dominant discourse, as a first step towards gaining access to the public dialogue. This allowed them an entry, a discursive bridge, as it were, in order to find then the necessary space to claim agency through their own stories.

> In other words, if a self-narrative begins with a statement of remorse, then a critical voice, a social critique, and perhaps most subversive in the prison context, a claim to personal agency, may be smuggled in. In the absence of remorse, no such hearing is permitted. What we initially understood as redemption stories are not just narrative techniques, sequences used by the women as a way to make sense of a major life transition [...] nor are they an internalized expression of self-hatred. Rather they are strategic and sincere points of entry into a hostile public conversation, paving the way for an expression of their power to think, speak and act as fully engaged citizens. (Torre et al., 2001, p. 160)

Although there are major differences with the focus of our study, the conclusion reached by the research team in the study done at the women's prison, "that critical stories are always (and at once) in tension with dominant stories, neither fully oppositional nor untouched," coincides with our interpretation of the internal tensions observed in our participants' stories (Torre et al., 2001, p. 151). When the seven immigrant women interviewed for our study tell their stories, they both reproduce and subtly subvert the official discourse of parental involvement and its underlying master narrative, that is, the predominant ideology of motherhood, centered on the myth of the good mother. To be able to tell their counter stories, they first need to place themselves within the master narrative. This coexistence of contrasting narrative strands helps understand how immigrant mothers struggle to exercise transformative agency from within by claiming access through positioning strategies in managing their interactions with the schools. This chapter concludes with an analysis of some of the most salient examples of ventriloquation in the women's narratives, followed by a note on counter narratives.

### Norma—*Me dice que hay mucha ... como es... negligencia de los padres para asistir a esas juntas.*
(She says that there is a lot of ... what is it ... negligence—*spoken louder, in an authoritative tone*—on the part of the parents, in not attending those meetings.)

Norma, who has explained all the ways in which she has always been involved in her children's schooling and in many aspects of their education, seems to be echoing the school's verdict when referring to the attitude parents display when not attending meetings. Norma includes herself in this, but then gives an explanation of why she actually cannot always attend. Her change in tone of voice and the way she stressed the word "negligence" serve as a prosodic signal to indicate impersonation or official discourse ventriloquation.

Sí, o a veces cuando tengo el tiempo, que digo, me voy a dar el tiempo cuando manden la nota así voy a ir, toca una cita al doctor, o... algo así *(laughs)*... Sí se me ha hecho muy difícil. Y la encargada de las reuniones, ella es mi amiga, y me dice que hay mucha... como es... negligencia *(spoken louder, in an authoritive tone)* de los padres para asistir a esas juntas y ver qué está pasando y todo eso, sí. Sí, pero es un problema también. Cómo le digo cuando uno se dedica a su casa y a sus hijos, es más fácil. Pero cuando uno tiene que salir, trabajar, aparte cumplir con las citas a los doctores, que ir a arreglar este papel o este otro... Se toma uno el tiempo para hacer eso.

Yes, or sometimes when I have time, I say, I am going to make time when they send the note so that I go, and then I have a doctor's appointment, or... something like that *(laughs)*...Yes, it's been very hard. And the person in charge of these meetings, she's my friend, and she says that there is a lot of... what is it... negligence *(spoken louder, in an authoritative tone)* on the part of the parents, in not attending those meetings to find out what's going on and all that, yes. Yes, but it's a problem too. As I say, when one only takes care of the home and one's kids, it's easier. But when one has to go out, work, and also keep doctor's appointments, and take care of this or that paper... One uses that time to do all that.

In the same vein, Norma continues to use deprecatory terms to describe her own attitude. Thus, she uses the term *"cómodo"*, which in this context may mean "convenient", but may also connote laziness, or imply choosing the easy way out of something. She uses this term to refer to the fact that she sometimes waits for the note that is sent to parents after a meeting with a summary of what had been discussed and decided, which arrives usually in both English and Spanish.

> Sí, yo comentaba con una amiga eso, que teníamos que ir a las reuniones, saber qué está pasando y todo eso. Y luego, otra parte cómoda también, es que después le mandan una nota también, qué se dijo, qué se acordó, y todo eso. (*laughs*) Y ya se la mandan a uno español, entonces, ya dice uno: "Bueno, me espero a la nota."

> Yes, I was talking with a friend about that, that we should go to the meetings, find out what's going on and all that. And then, another thing that is convenient is that afterwards they send a note also, about what was said, what was agreed, and all that. (*laughs*). And they send it to you in Spanish, so, one says, "Well, I'll wait for the note."

Here Norma completes this narrative segment by describing how, in her words, "my people, Hispanics" may be making excuses for not learning English. These views clearly reflect mainstream stereotypes and sweeping generalizations about Spanish-speaking immigrants.

> Yo por una parte también pienso, por mi parte, en mi gente, los hispanos, que a veces venimos y decimos: "Yo no puedo ir a la escuela a aprender inglés, porque yo trabajo mucho. Yo no puedo aprender inglés porque ya estoy grande y ya no se me pega." Y, no, no hay excusa. Debemos de poner nuestra mente a trabajar a cualquier edad, ¿verdad? Y hacer el tiempito.

> I also think about my people, Hispanics, that we sometimes come and say, "I can't go to school and learn English, because I work a lot. I can't learn English because I'm too old, and it doesn't stick." And, there is no excuse. We need to put our minds to work at any age, right? And make the time.

These sternly critical comments contradict Norma's own account of her attitudes and her experience as a single immigrant mother who has made every effort to learn English. Through her own learning experience, Norma is probably aware of the fact that acquiring an additional language takes many years of instruction and opportunities to interact, especially to reach a point where it is possible to understand the specific topics dealt with at school and to be able to actively participate in a public discussion. As Norton (2013) explains, in many cases, immigrant women often have much fewer chances than men of developing the language of the new country through real life interactions given the types of job opportunities they encounter.

> It is in the public world that language learners have the opportunity to interact with members of the target language community, but it is the public world that is not easily accessible to immigrant women […] even when such access is granted, the nature of the work available to immigrant women provides few opportunities for social interaction. (p. 52)

These occasions in which the women adopt a judgmental self-deprecatory attitude, mirroring the deficit aspect of the mainstream discourse of parental involvement—the master narrative—are the most striking examples of ventriloquation which stand out in the women's stories, although not the only ones.

## Luisa—*La gente no responde.*
## (People don't engage.)

Luisa, for example, explains that a very useful program existed for a while for newcomer parents after school, which helped them with all types of issues. In the following excerpt Luisa explains in detail how useful this program was, giving specific examples of all the services that were offered to parents.

> Si me preguntaran a mí en la escuela: ¿qué podremos hacer para la gente que llega? Ya lo han hecho. Había, ya no sé, pero antes tenían un programa que era como después de la escuela. Cuando ellos salían a las 3, había algo que duraba hasta las 5. Y, si alguien que llegó, como mi amiga, o mi hermana, o algo, pues tiene que ir. Había como un programa donde puede ir y hablar: "Mire, pues yo acabo de llegar…" Y ahí le decían, verdad: "Mire, vamos a hacer esto y como ya está empezado el año, vamos a ayudarle con los niños en esto. Y usted también le puede ayudar en la tarea. Pero si usted no puede, usted puede venir a la escuela."

> If they asked me at school: What could we do for the people who arrive? They've done it already. I don't know about now, but before there used to have a program that was after school. When they left at 3, there was something that lasted until 5. And someone who's just arrived, like a friend, or my sister, or someone, well, they had to go. There was a program where they could go and say, "Look, well, I've just arrived." And they'd tell you, "Look, we're going to do this and as the school year has already started, we'll help you with your children in this. And you can also help with homework. But if you can't, you can come over to the school."

Further, Luisa proposes that if something were to be done to help immigrant parents when they have just arrived, they should restore that same program because it was so useful. She goes on to suggest that this program left immigrant parents without excuses for failing to show up at the school. In this comment, Luisa anticipates a moment, later in her account, were she expresses a full-blown critique of uninvolved parents. This is a clear illustration of ventriloquation of the official discourse, as Luisa takes on the voice of the school representatives, in a clear instance of double-voicing.

> Antes había ese programa, yo no sé ahora. Y luego, como para que se relacionen un poco, para que no dejen a los niños solos ahí no más, que los papás puedan venir. Que no estén así con que: "Oh, no, ¿a qué voy si ni les entiendo?" O "¿A qué voy? Pues como soy mexicana ni si quiera…" No, eso no. Era de que: "Sí venga, participe con su niña, con su niño. Nosotros aquí estamos para ayudarle." Todo eso había. Yo no sé ahora. Pero, si se tratara de hacer algo así en la escuela, yo creo que volvieran a hacer lo mismo: "Aquí estamos. Nosotros le podemos ayudar a que le ayude a su niña o a su niño a hacer tarea, o venga y pregunte. Nosotros le podemos ayudar si necesita llevar otro niño para la otra escuela. Venga y tráigame los papeles, yo se los lleno."

> Before there used to be this program, now I don't know. Then, so that they'd relate a bit, so that they didn't only drop off the kids, so that the parents could come. So that they wouldn't say, "Oh, no, what am I going to go for if I don't understand them?" Or, "What am I going to go for? As I'm Mexican, I can't even…" No, not that. It was, "Yes, come, participate with your daughter or your son. We are here to help you." There was all of that. I don't know about now. But, if they tried to do something like that in the school, I think they should do the same thing, "Here we are. We can help you help your daughter or your son to do their homework, or come and ask us. We can help you if you need to enroll your other child to the other school. Come and bring all your papers, I'll fill them out for you."

Luisa does not spare any details about this program through which the school helped immigrant parents in many different ways, such as: by answering their questions; helping them with doctor's appointments or to fill out forms; or offering them guidance with their children's homework. It seemed to have been well organized and to have filled a pressing need for support of newcomers. According to her account, Luisa seems to have benefited from it soon after having arrived in the US.

> Luisa: Todo eso había antes, pero ahora, yo no sé si habrá. Lo que haría la escuela, pues, yo pienso que haría lo mismo que antes con ese programa que trataban de ayudar a todos, no no más a mí, a mucha gente le pasó. Si tenían otros niños, por ejemplo, le decían: "Si va a llevar a otro niño a la otra escuela y… necesita llenar papeles," o algo

así, "Tráigame, yo le ayudo." Y así. Y yo pienso que ahora, pues, también lo podrían hacer igual. Lo harían así, diciendo, "Tráigame," o "Yo la llevo," o "Yo le puedo decir dónde puede ir a vacunarlo." Porque vio que tienen que ir a vacunarlos primero. "Yo le puedo decir dónde," o "Yo la puedo llevar." Todo eso había aquí.
Lilian: ¿Cuando usted vino? ¿O…?
Luisa: Sí, cuando yo vine. Pues, al poquito tiempo… empezaron a hablarnos y a decirnos: "Si necesita ayuda, si necesita esto." Y luego ya se hizo ese programa y, pues, ya fue mejor.

Luisa: There used to be all of that, but now, I don't know. What the school would do, then, I think is do the same as before, with that program that tried to help everyone, not just me, it happened to many people. If they had other kids, for example, they'd say, "If you are going to take another child to another school and you need to fill out paperwork," or something like that, "bring them to me, and I'll help you." And so on. And I think that now, they could do it the same way. They'd do it like that, and say, "Bring it by," or "I'll take you there," or "I can tell you where you can take him to get the shots." Because you know they have to get their shots first. "I can tell you where," or "I can take you." There used to be all of that here.
Lilian: When you arrived, or…?
Luisa: Yes, when I arrived. Well, a bit later they started to talk to us and tell us, "If you need help, if you need this." And then they started that program, and, well, it was better.

According to Luisa's account, this program was cut because there was not enough participation on the part of the parents. Luisa then expands on this, and quotes a teacher as saying that there is no response from parents, who do not engage and only worry about their children when it is too late and they have failed.

Lilian: Asique ese programa le fue bueno. ¿Y estuvo mientras usted tenía los niños en la escuela? ¿Siempre estuvo ese programa?
Luisa: No, no, lo quitaron. Y, porque había mucha gente que no participaba en las juntas, no estaba atento a que el niño no iba a la escuela.

Lilian: So you found that program to be good. And was it there while you had your kids in school? Was this program always there?
Luisa: No, no, they canceled it. Well, because there were many people who did not participate in the meetings, who were not paying attention to their children's school attendance.

The extended context is included here for its relevance as it shows how Luisa regrets the disappearance of a program that she seems to have valued highly and that she deemed helpful for herself and other parents. This sets the backdrop to the opinion she voices which clearly echoes the views held by teachers and other school staff. Luisa explains that the responsibility for the program's demise lies with the parents, because of their lack of interest. However, ironically, she has just expressed her own interest and participation, as a parent, in the program. Then Luisa goes on to explain how it is because of parents' lack of participation that the program disappeared.

> Lilian: Me dijo del programa ese que desapareció porque no iba la gente…
> Luisa: Porque la gente no iba. Sabe, que mucha gente no va a las juntas, no está al pendiente si los niños faltan o así. Y ellos, como que, dicen: "No, la gente no responde." Uno de los maestros dice: "La gente cuando reacciona es cuando el niño está reprobado." Cuando: "Ah ¿por qué? ¿Cómo? ¿Cómo? O ¿por qué tanta falta, si el venía a la escuela? Pero es que no saben que ellos no estaban aquí." Es por eso que ellos… Y desapareció ese programa.

> Lilian: You told me about that program that disappeared because people didn't show up…
> Luisa: Because people didn't attend, many. You know, many people don't go to the meetings, they are not paying attention to whether the children are skipping school, or so. And they say, "No, people don't respond." One of the teachers says, "People react when the child is failing." Then, "Oh, why? How? How is it? Why so many absences if the child came to school? It's that they didn't know that they weren't here." That's why they… And the program disappeared.

Luisa goes on to stress how much teachers do to make sure children are in school, for instance, through home visits. As an example, she refers to the three siblings she used to babysit, who are now grownups and have all become teachers. Luisa notes how they go out of their way to follow up with those children who have been absent. The following anecdote shows Luisa's identification with the school, and her acknowledgement of how hard teachers work on behalf of the children. In her words there is an evident identification with the teachers' point of view.

> Ya no sé si estén al pendiente de eso. Pero yo he visto, ese señor que le digo que era mi patrón, bueno… el maestro de Verónica es hijo de él. Entonces, una vez estábamos allá limpiando chiles y él fue. Mario se llama. Y estaba diciendo que habían ido a buscar a unos niños allá, allá como para el río, que vivían muy adentro y que esos niños no estaban viniendo a la escuela. Y me preguntó por unos que viven aquí… Y ellos siempre están al pendiente. Sé que todavía están al pendiente de los niños, de que vayan a la escuela, vienen y los buscan. Como…. unos que viven aquí, se apellidan igual que yo, pero no… pero yo casi no ni… no hablo con nadie, y me preguntó a mí: "Oiga, ¿los niños Hernández?" Y en eso sí sé que están al pendiente de los niños. No

sé del programa, de los papás o… Porque sabe que en aquél tiempo si alguien no podía o no asistía, así que le mandaban una nota que tenía que venir esto y lo otro. ¡Ellos venían! Y Mario, ese maestro, se me hace que todavía viene. Porque le digo que él estaba preguntando por esos niños que tenían una semana que no iban y otros de por ahí afuera, del río. Y él siempre está así al pendiente, yo creo; él es todavía el que… Y antes, pues, él no estaba todavía de maestro, cuando yo trabajaba con ellos; él estudió en la universidad. Pero, ya le digo, ya cuando … Mi patrón tiene dos hijos o tres, ahí de maestros. Son Delia, Nancy y Mario. Los tres son maestros. Es más, todos los hijos de él son maestros, pero los demás, tres más, están en otras partes.

I don't know if now they are focusing on that. But I have seen, you know this man that I mentioned was my boss, well, Veronica's teacher is his son. So, once we were cleaning chilies and he came. His name is Mario. And he was saying that they had gone to look for one of the kids over there, going towards the river, they lived very far in, and that those kids weren't attending school. And he asked me about some who live around here. And they are always watching out. I know they are still watching out for the children, to make sure they come to school, they come and look for them. Like… some who live here close by, they have the same last name as me, but no… but I hardly… I hardly speak to anyone, and he asked me, "Listen, what about the Hernández kids?" And in that they are watching out for the kids. I don't know about the program for parents or… Because you know that in those days if someone couldn't or didn't attend, they sent them a note saying they had to come, this-and-that, they would come! And Mario, that teacher, I believe stills comes to visit. Because, as I said, he was asking after those kids who hadn't attended for a week and some other ones from further away, by the river. And he always is concerned, I believe; he is still the one… And before, well, he wasn't a teacher yet, when he worked with them; he went to college. But, as I said, once he… My boss has two children, or three, who are teachers here. They are Delia, Nancy, and Mario. The three are teachers. Actually, all his children are teachers, but the rest, three more, are in other places.

Luisa ends this account of this program, and her voicing of a teacher's explanation for its disappearance as lack of parental involvement, with a note on the children she helped raise. Luisa speaks with pride about all the children who she took care of, who have all become teachers. There is a striking internal contradiction in the contrast between the official discourse adopted here by Luisa and her own story of a single mother who cares deeply about her children's education, and who has gone out of her way to support them.

## A Word on Counter Narratives

The seven women's stories and the counter narratives at the heart of them contribute to an anti-deficit perspective by offering analytical tools to be able to read the official discourse of parental involvement against the grain. Thus it is important to restate the ways in which the contrasting strands in these stories function as counter narratives.

First, they are counter narratives because they portray the active involvement and deep interest the participants have in their children's education. Thus, these narratives counter the general view of immigrant parents as uninvolved, which has been widely documented in the literature. Second, these are counter narratives because the participants tell their own story of involvement, on their own terms. Third, these are counter narratives because—especially in the cases of advocacy and of *consejos*—the participants' actions contributed to change the narrative in their children's classrooms. In some cases, they led to change the definition of who their child was in their classroom (and therefore how the child was treated), and who they—both the mother and the child—were in the eyes of the teacher, or the administrators. Fourth, some are counter narratives of maternal involvement because they refer to instances of educational motherwork when the participants intervened as advocates of their children in situation of inequity, because, as Collins (1994) so eloquently states, "For women of color, the subjective experience of mothering/ motherhood is inextricably linked to the sociocultural concern of racial ethnic communities" and is a matter of survival and identity (p. 47). Fifth, these are counter narratives because the participants relate the challenges experienced and the efforts made to overcome these difficulties in order to support their children in their educational process. In sum, the seven women's stories present counter narratives of maternal involvement and educational motherwork in accounts characterized by both vulnerability and agency.

# References

Andrews, M. (2004). Opening to the original contributions: Counter-narratives and the power to oppose. In M. Bamberg & M. Andrews (Eds.), *Considering counter-narratives: Narrating, resisting, making sense* (pp. 1–6). Amsterdam/Philadelphia: John Benjamins.

Bakhtin, M. (1981). *The dialogic imagination: Four essays* (C. Emerson & M. Holquist, Trans.). Austin, TX: University of Texas Press. (Original work published 1935).

Bakhtin, M. (1984). *Problems of Dostoevsky's poetics* (C. Emerson, Ed. & Trans.). Minneapolis, MN: University of Minnesota Press.

Bakhtin, M. (1986). *Speech genres and other late essays* (C. Emerson & M. Holquist, Eds.; V. McGee, Trans.). Austin, TX: University of Texas Press.

Bamberg, M. (2004). Considering counter narratives. In M. Bamberg & M. Andrews (Eds.), *Considering counter-narratives: Narrating, resisting, making sense* (pp. 351–371). Philadelphia, PA: John Benjamins.

Brown, L. (1998). *Raising their voices: The politics of girls' anger.* Cambridge, MA: Harvard University Press.

Chase, S. (2005). Narrative inquiry: Multiple lenses, approaches, voices. In N. Denzin & Y. Lincoln (Eds.), *The Sage handbook of qualitative research* (3rd ed., pp. 651–679). Thousand Oaks, CA: Sage.

Collins, P. H. (1994). Shifting the center: Race, class, and feminist theorizing about motherhood. In E. N. Glenn, G. Chang, & L. R. Forcey (Eds.), *Mothering: Ideology, experience, and agency* (pp. 45–65). New York, NY: Routledge.

Collins, P. H. (2000). *Black feminist thought: Knowledge, consciousness, and the politics of empowerment.* New York, NY: Routledge.

Delgado Bernal, D. (2006). Learning and living pedagogies of the home. In D. Delgado Bernal, A. Elenes, F. Godinez, & S. Villenas (Eds.), *Chicana/Latina education in everyday life: Feminista perspectives on pedagogy and epistemology* (pp. 113–132). Albany, NY: State University of New York Press.

Delgado-Gaitán, C. (1994). "Consejos": The power of cultural narratives. *Anthropology & Education Quarterly, 25*(3), 298–316.

Greene, M. (1995). *Releasing the imagination: Essays on education, the arts, and social change.* San Francisco, CA: Jossey-Bass, Wiley.

Hays, S. (1996). *The cultural contradictions of motherhood.* New Haven, CT and London: Yale University Press.

Hurtig, J., & Dyrness, A. (2011). Parents as critical educators and ethnographers of schooling. In B. A. U. Levinson & M. Pollock (Eds.), *A companion to the anthropology of education* (pp. 530–546). Oxford, UK: Wiley-Blackwell.

López, G. (2001). The value of hard work: Lessons on parent involvement from an (Im)migrant household. *Harvard Education Review, 71*(3), 416–438.

Norton, B. (2013). *Identity and language learning: Extending the conversation* (2nd ed.). Tonawanda, NY: Multilingual Matters.

Riessman, C. K. (2008). *Narrative methods for the human sciences.* Thousand Oaks, CA: Sage.

Suárez-Orozco, C., Suárez-Orozco, M., & Todorova, I. (2008). *Learning a new land: Immigrant students in American society.* Cambridge, MA: Belknap Press of Harvard University Press.

Torre, M. E., Fine, M., Boudin, K., Bowen, I., Clark, J., Hylton, D., … Upegui, D. (2001). A space for co-constructing counter stories under surveillance. *International Journal of Critical Psychology, 4,* 149–166.

Villenas, S. (2002). Reinventing "educación" in new Latino communities: Pedagogies of change and continuity in North Carolina. In S. Wortham, E. Murillo, & E. Hamann (Eds.), *Education in the new Latino diaspora: Policy and the politics of identity* (pp. 17–35). Westport, CT: Ablex.

Wilson Cooper, C. (2007). School choice as "motherwork": Valuing African–American women's educational advocacy and resistance. *International Journal of Qualitative Studies in Education, 20*(5), 491–512.

Wortham, S. (2001). *Narratives in action: A strategy for research and analysis.* New York, NY: Teachers College Press.

Young, I. (1990). *Justice and the politics of difference.* Princeton, NJ: Princeton University Press.

· P A R T   I I I ·

# FORMAL INCLUSION/
# INFORMAL EXCLUSION

## · 6 ·

# BELONGING AND
# THE NEW CULTURAL SCRIPT

*[...] the more experienced immigrant women offered newly arrived immigrant women a general orientation to living in the US: where to shop, how to enroll children in school, where to obtain emergency medical services, and how to obtain in-home child care or paid domestic work.* (Hondagneu-Sotelo, 1994, p. 116)

In its basic meaning, belonging may be associated with "feeling 'at home,'" and with "a sense of rootedness in a socio-geographic site or be constructed as an intensely imagined affiliation with a distant locale where self-realization can occur" (Yuval-Davis, 2011, pp. 10–11). As such, it is often defined by contrast. The members of a community draw a sense of belonging from their shared sociocultural scripts, which are taken for granted, normalized. In the face of the displacement created by migration, the boundaries and requirements of belonging may need rethinking beyond these naturalized assumptions.

In a broader sense, the concept of belonging can be understood in relation to three analytical levels or facets: social locations; identification and emotional attachment; and ethical and political values (Yuval-Davis, 2006, p. 199). These levels of belonging make for a dynamic process in which a complex set of power relations are at play. Massey's (1994) exploration of the interplay of place, space, time, power and social relations may contribute to a less fixed and more fluid understanding of belonging.

> The view, then, is of space-time as a configuration of social relations within which the specifically spatial may be conceived of as an inherently dynamic simultaneity. Moreover, since social relations are inevitably and everywhere imbued with power and meaning and symbolism, this view of the spatial is as an ever-shifting social geometry of power and signification. (p. 3)

In their intersectional approach to belonging within the context of immigration, Anthias (2006) and Yuval-Davis (2006), point to the power differentials which determine hierarchies in social structures and practices, and contribute to the definitions of "them" and "us". Given these power asymmetries, and in order to subvert the borders of inclusion and exclusion in normative social relations, there is a need to shift away from a focus on cultural initiation and refocus on the preconditions of quality of life. Thus, moving away from an ideology of assimilationism requires redirecting our attention from judgment of the newcomers' cultural predispositions to an assessment of the mechanisms that society establishes through its normative narratives and structures (Anthias, 2006, p. 20).

## Immigration: Trauma and Opportunity/ Vulnerability and Agency

Immigration has been described as one of the most stressful events and highly disruptive transitions in life, especially when the individual is not able to cope in usual ways, or when the stakes of adapting to the new situation are high. The psychological processes involved in adapting to the displacement and dislocation experienced by an immigrant are described as "cultural mourning" since they are comparable to mourning for the loss of a loved one (Ainslie, 1998, pp. 287, 297). Someone who leaves his or her country does in fact undergo separation and relative loss of all that is familiar, including contexts and relationships (Ainslie, 1998, p. 287; C. Suárez-Orozco, 2000, p. 195; C. Suárez-Orozco et al., 2008, p. 30). In the case of undocumented immigrants, who are often exposed to the elements or to violence, the physical dangers of the actual crossing of the border may further contribute to this traumatic experience. Among border crossers, often women are considered to be at higher risk of robbery, physical abuse, and even murder (C. Suárez-Orozco, 2000, pp. 195–196).

Yet, immigration scholars remind us that immigrants are usually neither victims nor heroes in their life stories; instead, they are participants in social relations marked by power differentials (Gabaccia & Leach, 2004). Leach and Gabaccia (2004) point out that "immigrants, like other humans, make their own lives but rarely under conditions of their own choosing, and often in struggle with people—teachers, parents, employers, rulers—who can mobilize much more power than they can" (p. 198). This relative vulnerability, however, does not automatically prevent immigrants from being actors and subjects in their own lives. Thus, vulnerability is not to be equated with powerlessness, or a lack of agency, but instead often, for those immersed in situations of unequal power, this same vulnerability is at the center of the drive for action in solidarity (Collins, 1999, p. 120; Keet, Zinn & Porteus, 2009, p. 115).

The notion of displacement is a given in the lives of the seven women interviewed for this study since they have all relocated after migrating across national borders, thus its impact on their redefinitions of self and community becomes pivotal. Whereas their lives have vulnerability at their center, this same vulnerability fosters solidarity and communal agency. Belonging is viewed here as a dynamic concept, as it involves the transformation of individual and collective perceptions and practices through time and in relation to geographical and social space(s).

# A New Sociocultural Script: Relearning the Ropes

A person who emigrates leaves behind familiar places, people and possessions. Foremost among the many losses is a familiar cultural script, with its inherent understanding of how social roles are carried out. Norton (2013) describes this form of everyday competence people exercise in their home country in these terms: "the adequate functioning of an individual assumes a common-sense knowledge of the organizational forms which determine how the society works" (p. 82). This type of knowledge helps give meaning to most people's everyday life and renders a sense of basic safety and predictability as members of a community. It is usually taken for granted as an "effortless proficiency" by those who have never moved away from their region or country of origin (C. Suárez-Orozco, 2000, p. 195; C. Suárez-Orozco & M. Suárez-Orozco, 2001, p. 90). As Yuval-Davis (2011) best expresses it, "Belonging tends to be naturalized and to be part of everyday practices" (p. 10). Immigration causes a disjuncture between this assumed everyday knowledge and the way the new context functions which contributes to underscore a person's differences, including social, cultural and ethnic differences in the new environment (Norton, 2013, p. 82).

Immigration affects the role of parents directly, as a result of this loss of a familiar sociocultural script; when faced with new challenges, they may no longer feel the same confidence in guiding their children. In the wake of their displacement, part of the parents' experience may seem to have become irrelevant. Immigration "undermines this function by removing the 'map of experience' necessary to competently escort the children in the new culture," thus, the process of crossing borders renders immigrant parents "less able to provide guidance in negotiating the currents of a complex society" (C. Suárez-Orozco & M. Suárez-Orozco, 2001, p. 90). Moreover, in many contexts, immigrant parents and their children find themselves forced into a reversal of roles.

## The Dual Frame of Reference Reformulated Through Communal Agency

Recent immigrants are often described as using a dual frame of reference, as they tend to assess their experience by comparing and contrasting most situations in the new context with how these would play out in their country of origin (M. Suárez-Orozco, 1990; Zentgraf, 2002). This double lens appears explicitly in the interviewees' stories, as the seven women relate their first experiences in the US, moving narratively back and forth between the familiar and the unfamiliar, between how-it-was-back-home and how-it-is-here—or more precisely, how they perceived "here" when they first arrived.

However, the double reference framework is far from unproblematic, since its unnuanced application may contribute to essentializing the migrant experience. In her study of the Italian diaspora in London, Fortier (2000) proposes "scrutinizing the social dynamics of rootings and routings in the construction" of a specific immigrant identity, to avoid the overemphasis on hybridity and difference "without any sense of continuity" (p. 17). Thus, she sets out to "uncover the constitutive potency of 'betweenness' in the formation of a [. . .] migrant belonging" (p. 16). Further, she points out that although many have "suggested that diaspora compels us to examine how 'there' is rearticulated 'here'," this argument may neglect "the ways in which a number of diasporic populations or individuals negotiate new forms outside of this two-way geography" (p. 16). Comparably, Yuval-Davis (2011) explores a dynamic conceptualization of belonging against the static hegemonic construct.

> People can "belong" in many different ways and to many different objects of attachment. These can vary from a particular person to the whole of humanity, in a concrete or abstract way, by self or other identification, in a stable, contested or transient way. Even in its most stable "primordial" forms, however, belonging is always a dynamic process, not a reified fixity—the latter is only a naturalized construction of a particular hegemonic form of power relations. (p. 12)

The added subtlety of this approach allows us to take into account agency in the development of a sense of belonging, as well as pointing out its articulation with structure in the social microprocesses of everyday life. It is in this light that the stories of the women in this study are explored here.

## First Interactions with the Schools

### Brenda—*Todo se le hace difícil y da como más vergüenza.* (Everything seems difficult and one feels more embarrassed.)

The excerpts from the interviews presented below capture the level of anxiety which may be experienced by a person who has just arrived in the US when visiting a school for the first time. Brenda, for instance, underscores the difference in how she feels about her interactions now and what it was like at first. She refers to an upcoming parent-teacher conference where she now knows exactly what to expect. The comfort she derives from this knowledge and its contrast with the apprehension she used to experience at an earlier stage in anticipation of any such event point to the learning process she has undergone.

> Lilian: ¿Usted ve que cambió un poco su relación con la escuela desde las primeras veces, de cuando recién llegó, a ahora como se relaciona usted con la escuela? ¿Le parece que usted ya cambió su manera de relacionarse, o que la escuela cambió algo? Brenda: Pues, sí, porque, pues cuando recién empieza, pues, no sabe uno. Todo se le hace difícil y da como más vergüenza. Y ahora no, pues, ya va viviendo eso, va pasando y ahora ya sabe uno a lo que va. Pues, sí, ya va uno a lo que le van a decir, "Su hija de este modo y de este otro; estudia o no estudia," o así, ¿verdad? Y al principio, no, pues, es que, "Ay, no, y ¿cómo lo voy a hacer? Y ¿cuál será su maestra? Y ¿adónde voy a ir?" Pues, uno no sabe, verdad. Y ya, pues, uno va viviendo y va pasando eso. Ya va sabiendo: "Tengo que ir a tantos; si tiene a tantos maestros, a todos los salones voy a ir."

Lilian: Do you see that your relation with the school has changed a bit since the first times, from when you first arrived up to now, the way you relate to the school? Do you think that you changed the way you relate to the school, or that the school changed something?

Brenda: Well, yes, because when one first starts, well, one doesn't know. Everything seems difficult and one feels more embarrassed. And now, well, one goes living through those things, time goes by and now one knows what one is going for. Well, yes, you already have an idea of what sort of thing they are going to tell you, "Your daughter is doing this or that…" And, "she studies" or "she doesn't study" or something like that, right? And, at the beginning, no. Well, it's like, "Oh, no, and how am I going to do this? And, I wonder which one is her teacher? And, where am I going to go?" Well, one doesn't know, right? And now, well, you have lived and gone through all that, and you begin to know: "I have to go to so many; if she has this many teachers, I will go to all the classrooms."

Brenda's words bring about a sense of immediacy to her perceptions of her loss of a cultural script. She refers to how a person feels in these initial encounters in the new context: *"no sabe uno"* (one doesn't know), *"todo se le hace difícil"* (everything seems difficult), *"da como más vergüenza"* (one feels more embarrassed). Beyond describing the general experience, Brenda shares how this uncertainty plays out in the newcomer's mind through a number of questions. Her first-person account serves as a vivid illustration of the circumstances depicted in the following passage in *Learning a New Land*:

Immigrant parents face a daunting set of tasks—finding work, making a home, enrolling their children in new schools, grasping the new cultural rules of engagement, learning English, and establishing new social ties. Moves of any kind are considered by social scientists to be among the most stressful of events, but the stakes are higher and the process all the more challenging when a change of country is involved. (C. Suárez-Orozco et al., 2008, p. 70)

## Susana—*Como que uno no encaja a veces, como que está de más en ese lugar.*
## (It's as if one doesn't fit in, as if one is unwanted/out of place there.)

When Susana and her family first moved to the United States from Mexico, she was left in charge of her siblings for long periods of time. In the following excerpt, she responds directly to a question about how she felt in her first interactions with the schools.

Lilian: Al principio, cuando usted se relacionaba con la gente de la escuela—los maestros, la secretaria, la directora ¿Cómo se sentía usted? ¿Cómo era el trato?
Susana: Siempre han sido buenos. Han sido amables, han sido muy amables. Pero, sí, ellos hablando puro inglés, y uno puro español, y decía: "Pues, quién sabe qué dirán." Y uno no más se quedaba viendo. Pues, ay, ¿cómo le digo? Como que uno no encaja a veces, como que está de más en ese lugar, así…

Lilian: At first, when you related with the people at the schools—the teachers, secretary, principal. How did you feel? How did they treat you?
Susana: They have always been good. They have been kind. They have been very kind. But, yes, they spoke only English and one only spoke Spanish, and I'd say, "Who knows what they're saying." And one would just stand there staring. Well, how could I put this? It's as if one doesn't fit in, and is in the way or out of place.

Susana describes the situation of lack of communication in the expression "*y uno no más se quedaba viendo*" (and one would just stand there staring). This leads to a direct comment on not belonging and feeling out of place, "*como que uno no encaja a veces, como que está de más en ese lugar.*" (It's as if one doesn't fit in, and is unwanted/out of place there.) Susana notes how kind and helpful everyone in the schools has been to her; and yet there is still this perception of not belonging. Thus, in her account, Susana appears to indicate that she is not set out to criticize the school staff or lay blame on any person for this experience. What she offers is a description of how she feels in a given context. In this situation, what triggers that sense of exclusion is the issue of language, which Susana mentions immediately before describing her feelings of not belonging and being out of place.

In the same vein, Silvia, Susana's younger sister, who arrived later from Mexico, and also has children in school, attributes the struggle that a person goes through at first to what she refers to in these terms, "*…a veces cuando uno llega y no conoce, verdad, las raíces de aquí, que viene siendo el inglés*" (…sometimes when one arrives and doesn't know the roots from here, that is to say, English). This expression in which Silvia refers to English as "the roots from here" goes to the heart of those deep feelings of not belonging mentioned repeatedly. Silvia illustrates this point as she explains how "it was a bit complicated" as "one struggles a bit" at first.

Lilian: Cuénteme sobre la primera vez que visitó la escuela ¿Cómo fue su experiencia? ¿Con quién habló? ¿Qué pasó?
Silvia: Bueno, la primera vez que yo tuve que ir a la escuela, pues, fue para conocer a los maestros de mi niño, que fue mi primer niño y fue ahí cuando yo empecé. Pero sí fue un poquito complicado porque a veces cuando uno llega y no conoce, verdad, las

raíces de aquí, que viene siendo el inglés, pues, uno batalla un poquito porque de aquí a que se familiariza con los padres de los amigos de los hijos de uno... Es difícil porque a veces uno no sabe ni lo que están diciendo. Pero ya, ya después se va uno acoplando, verdad, junto con ellos al sistema en el que estamos.

Lilian: Tell me about the first time that you visited the school. What was your experience like? Who did you speak to? What happened?
Silvia: Well, the first time I had to go to the school was to meet my son's teachers, because he was my first child, and that was when I started. But, yes, it was a bit complicated because sometimes when one arrives and doesn't know the roots from here, that is to say, English, well, one struggles a bit because, until one gets acquainted with the other kids' parents... It is difficult because sometimes one doesn't even know what they are saying. But then, one starts adjusting, with them, and getting used to the system we are in.

In other parts of their accounts, it becomes evident that they are now well integrated in their community, and that here they are mainly referring to how they felt in their first interactions with the schools. As is the case with Silvia, the same women who express the early uncertainty of not belonging, have since made friends, have been proactive in relating with other parents, and have learned to navigate the school system. In the long run, Silvia reflects, "*se va uno acoplando*" (you go adjusting).

## Susana—*Hay muchos papeles que firmar cuando uno mete un niño a la escuela.*
## (There are a lot of papers to sign, when one puts [enrolls] a child in school.)

Among many other aspects of schooling, the bureaucracy surrounding the process of enrolling a child may be new to an immigrant mother. For instance, in their country of origin some parents or guardians may only need to show a child's ID or birth certificate, and they may not be the ones in charge of filling out the forms, which are often taken care of by school staff instead.

Susana and Sandra each describe first-time enrollment as an overwhelming process, given the amount of paperwork involved. Susana, who has been in the United States the longest, admits that it is not as difficult now, and that this process has become easier with time. With her long pauses and hesitation about comparing her earlier days with her experience now, Susana seems to be avoiding any negative comments as she hesitates as to whether or not to mention what these changes might be. Since this is one of the first interviews, Susana may not yet feel "*en confianza*" (trust derived from closeness and familiarity). Her hesitation seems to imply that she perceives the school staff as being more helpful nowadays.

> Lilian: ¿Cómo se las arregló usted, al principio, para llevarlos a la escuela, anotarlos y todo eso?
> Susana: Pues, hay que firmar muchos papeles. Hay muchos papeles que firmar cuando uno mete un niño a la escuela. No, que le traen a uno una buena pila de papeles. Todos hay que firmarlos, hay que leerlos, hay que … no sé. Uno piensa a veces que es muy difícil, pero a la vez no es tanto. No, sobre todo ahorita que … pues, son como más … más … Es más fácil. Es todo más … no sé. A mí no se me dificultó mucho. Sobre todo porque … porque no sé … Estaba, estaba no más el papeleo que hay que llenar y todo. Más bien a los que se les dificulta es a ellos, a los niños, por el idioma, que si vienen de allá. Yo tuve la suerte con los niños que todos empezaron la escuela aquí, porque estaban chiquititos. La más chiquita tenía, cuando llegó aquí, tenía 11 meses y el otro niño, pues, ya nació aquí. Así es que, pues, empezaron desde chiquitos aquí.

> Lilian: How did you manage, at the beginning, to take them to school, enroll them and all that?
> Susana: Well, there are a lot of papers to sign, when one puts (enrolls) a child in school. They do bring you a huge pile of papers. You have to sign them all. You have to read them, I don't know. One sometimes thinks it is difficult, but at the same time it isn't that hard. Especially, not so much now … because, they are more … more … It is easier. It is all … I don't know. It wasn't that difficult for me. Especially because I don't know … There was just all the paperwork that you need to fill out and all. They are the ones who have a hard time, the children, because of the language, if they are coming from over there. I was lucky with my children because they all started school here, because they were very young. My youngest daughter, when she arrived, was 11 months old and the other boy, well, was born here already. So, they started here since they were little.

For her part, Sandra points out that the whole process of enrollment is completely different here from how it is in Mexico. The number of forms that need to be filled out here makes it harder and requires asking many questions. She also compares her experience at the school in a larger city where she first arrived with that in the rural area where she lives now, where it was much easier because most people are bilingual and friendlier. Even though she refers to having had to spend a whole morning filling out forms all over again when she moved, her direct quotes reflect the time taken by the school staff to explain to her the purpose of each form, in other words, their helpfulness.

> Cuando llegamos aquí, pues, "¿Por dónde empezar?" Bueno, vamos a la escuela. Las personas que nos asistieron aquí eran personas que sí hablaban español. Es lo que tiene aquí, en este pueblo, que la mayoría habla inglés y español. Asique no fue mucho, o sea, el batallar. Pero en Puentes, la mayoría habla inglés, al principio se ve uno

que, ah pues, "¿Cómo le hago? ¿Por dónde empiezo" Pero ya al llegar aquí, llegamos a inscribir a los niños y, "Llena papeles, esto, y firma, y esto es por esto…". Entonces, es un papelero, se lleva uno toda la mañana a veces, el inscribir a los niños. Pero la persona hablaba español, por eso no fue tan difícil y nos tocó personas muy amables, serviciales. O sea que al verlos llegar, a uno lo apoyan, "No, mira haz esto y esto." Por eso no fue tan difícil. Esa es la ventaja. Al principio, como en Puentes, era más cohibido, porque, pues, no entiende uno, ¿verdad? Sí, fue un poquito, no difícil, pero sí se enfrenta uno con eso. Y ya lo inscribí al niño allá y después avisé que nos veníamos para acá. Y volver a hacer lo mismo acá.

When we arrived here, well, "Where do we begin?" Well, let's go to the school. The people who helped us here where people who did speak Spanish. It is what happens here, in this town, that most people speak English and Spanish. So it wasn't so much, I mean, the struggle. But in Puentes, most people speak English, and at first one feels like, "Oh my, how do I do this? Where should I start?" But once we arrived here, we went to enroll the children, and, "Fill out papers, this, and sign, and this is for this…" So it is a pile of papers, it sometimes takes you all morning, enrolling the children. But the person spoke Spanish, so that's why it wasn't so hard and they were very friendly and helpful people. I mean, that when they see you arrive, they support you. "No, look, do this and this." That is why it wasn't so hard. That is the advantage. At the beginning, as in Puentes, it was more inhibiting, because, well, one doesn't understand, right? Yes, it was a bit, not difficult, but one does face that. And I enrolled my son over there and I let them know that we were moving here. And had to do it all over again here.

Immediately after mentioning the amount of paperwork required of her, however, Sandra adds that she understands and considers the whole process to be important, and that it is for the good of both children and parents. So, "one adapts," she comments. Nowadays, if the school sends any papers home with her children, and if they are in English, she asks for an appointment at the school with someone who can explain to her what each paper is for. In this detail, as in many other aspects of her interactions with the schools, Sandra shares how she now exercises her agency and determination to figure out how the system works, and to actively find answers and solutions to her problems.

Lilian: Y ¿aparte del idioma, hay alguna otra cosa como que tenía que resolver ahí que es diferente?
Sandra: Sí, tanto papelerío, eso es diferente. Sí, todavía en estas fechas que entró mi niño a la "middle school", ay, a llenar papeles y si me mandaron papeles en inglés, pues, ahí voy a la escuela: "Oiga, es que esto no lo entiendo" … y a pedir la entrevista con el consejero o la secretaria. "Pues, llamen a la secretaria." Y lo mismo he hecho ya, desde un principio. "Este, ¿qué quiere decir?" "No, pues…" le explican, ¿ve? Entonces, eso es lo que dificulta mucho: tanto papel. Que lo de seguridad del niño, que… sí, ¿me entiende? Muchas cosas. Pero uno entiende que es por el bien de los

niños, que tienen cuidado y atención para los niños. Entonces, ahí se queda uno, a llenar papeles y a preguntar lo que no entiende.

Lilian: And, apart from the language, is there any other thing that you had to solve there that was different?

Sandra: Yes, so much paperwork, that is different. Yes, still up until now that my son started middle school, oh, to fill out papers and if they sent me papers in English, there I go to the school: "Listen, I don't understand this," and I go and ask for an interview with the counselor or the secretary. "Call the secretary." And I have done the same already, from the very beginning. "This one, what does it mean?" "No, well…" and they explain it to you, see? So, that is what makes it so difficult, so much paperwork. What with, my son's security, and then… right, do you understand? Many things. But one understands that it is for the children's wellbeing, that they take care and pay attention to the kids. So one stays there to fill out the papers and to ask whatever one doesn't understand.

In this context, Sandra also draws a connection between learning how to interact with the schools and learning the ropes of the health care system, just as Brenda does. She compares the process of enrolling her children in the school with all the paperwork and the need to ask for explanations at the time she received medical attention during her pregnancy.

Siempre y aprende una desde que está una embarazada. Que va a una parte a llenar papeles y papeles y papeles y que le explican. Entonces, es totalmente diferente que en México. Es muy diferente. Pero, bueno, uno se adapta… se adapta. Y entiende uno que es por el bien tanto del padre como de los niños. Que a veces por un lado y por otro hay gente irresponsable, verdad, que no atiende la importancia de la educación de los niños, que faltan a cada rato y cosas así. Entonces, todo eso uno va viendo, que es por el bien de ellos.

Always and one learns from the time that one is pregnant: that you go to one place to fill out papers and papers and papers, and that they explain. So, it is completely different from Mexico. It is very different. But, well, one adapts… one adapts. And one understands that it is for both the parent's and the child's good. That sometimes, here and there, there are people who are irresponsible, right, that do not pay attention to the importance of education for their children, that skip school all the time and so on. Then, you start seeing, that all this is for the children's good.

These various pieces of information gained through experience, when linked together, make up the larger puzzle that immigrant women are building for themselves, proactively developing their new sociocultural script.

## Brenda—*No la dejaría sola, sabiendo lo que yo sufrí ... porque aquí no es igual.*
(I would not leave her alone, knowing what I suffered... because here it is not the same.)

In her response to a question about what she would share with a newly arrived immigrant friend, Brenda chooses certain situations and settings that she would show her how to negotiate first. This detailed list offers some insight into the social practices which may need to be relearned and are perceived as priorities.

> Lilian: Imagínese que está conversando con una amiga que piensa venir a EEUU y le pregunta sobre su experiencia, cómo se las arregló, lo que más necesita saber y qué tiene que hacer cuando llega para ir a las escuelas ¿Qué le diría usted de su experiencia o sobre qué es lo que tiene que hacer o sobre qué es lo más importante?
>
> Brenda: Cómo si llegara queriendo echar sus niños a la escuela. Ah, pues, yo le diría que sí se viniera, que los niños aquí tienen, por decir así, casi un doble futuro, porque, pues, ya sus niños iban a saber el inglés. Y luego, pues, yo le diría que sí se viniera y que yo le ayudaría. Le diría cómo y adónde ir a inscribirlos a la escuela y cómo empezar a conocer la escuela. La llevaría a que conociera la oficina y luego la llevaría para adelante si quería visitar a los maestros de sus niños, verdad. También, le mostraría cómo hacer para ir a recoger un niño cuando tuviera una cita y estuviera enfermo, verdad.

> Lilian: Imagine that you are talking with a friend who is thinking of moving to the US and asks you about your experience, how you managed, what she needs to know, and what she needs to do when she arrives, to go to the schools. What would you tell her about your experience, or about what she needs to do, or about what is most important?
>
> Brenda: If she arrived wanting to put her children in school. Oh, well, I would tell her to come, that children have, so to speak, a double future, because her children would already get to learn English. And then, well, I would tell her to go ahead and come, and that I would help her. I would tell her how and where to go and enroll them in school, and how to start to get to know the school. I would take her to get to know the office and then I would take her if she wanted to meet her children's teachers, right? Also, I would show her how to do in order to go and pick up a child, when the child has an appointment and was sick, right?

This list suggests how overwhelming the whole process can be, if not mediated by someone who shares the experience of having immigrated. It is not only about language, it is about the specific ways in which tasks and interactions are carried out. Not all schools around the world are organized the same way or function the same way as they do in the US. To begin with, they may not even be physically comparable. Nor are parents in all countries expected to behave in the same way when they relate to their children's schools. Thus, there are assumptions of knowledge about schooling and about how things are done that not all parents or guardians may share because they may have had a very different schooling experience as students and, maybe, as parents.

First, Brenda mentions the benefits of children being able to learn both English and Spanish and so, indirectly, she expresses her satisfaction with the opportunity children have of attending a bilingual program. She then draws a detailed list of the essential information a mother would need to know in order to go about enrolling her children, meeting the teachers, and the daily business of picking up her children from school when they have an appointment or if they are sick. Finally, Brenda adds to this information the need to show a woman who has just arrived the basics of how to go about going to the doctor or making an appointment for the first time, or even going to the grocery store. Here she stresses the fact that she would need to explain all this to her because "it is not the same here".

> Pues, la llevaría a ella, yo pienso. Yo no la dejaría sola porque, sabiendo lo que yo sufrí, la ayuda que yo necesitaba y, pues, así como me ayudaron a mí ¿yo por qué no ayudarla a ella, verdad? Tanto, para ir a la tienda como para ir al doctor, porque aquí no es igual. En México, pues, no más llega usted a un doctor y va y ahí lo atienden. Pero, aquí no. Pues, aquí necesita uno hacer la cita. Y la llevaría también y le ayudaría a hacer su cita, a llevarla al doctor, a que conociera Greenfields.

> Well, I would take her, I believe. I would not leave her alone, because, knowing how I suffered, the help I needed and, well, in the same way they helped me, why wouldn't I help her, right? To go to the store as well as to go to the doctor, because here it isn't the same. In Mexico, well, you just get to the doctor's, and you go and you get seen to right there on the spot. But here, no. Here one needs to make an appointment. And I would also take her and help her to make her appointment, to take her to the doctor, and to get to know Greenfields. [the rural village where Brenda lives]

In passing, Brenda shares how much a person goes through in their first interactions with schools and other institutions. Yet, her comments on how much suffering she endured are followed by a reference to the help she received, and to how, in turn, she is committed to helping others in a similar situation.

The awareness of the difference a helping hand makes in a person's early experiences is the basis of Brenda's solidarity. As she reminisces about her own vulnerability in her early days, Brenda offers a vivid illustration of how exposed a person feels when they have just arrived. She shares the image of a person trying to pay in a store when they are not yet familiar with the local currency. Just as a child would do in a similar situation, the person needs to extend a handful of cash for the cashier to count it for her.

> Lilian: ¿Había otra cosa que le diría a su amiga?
> Brenda: No, pues, que se viniera que yo la ayudaba [...] porque uno cuando llega aquí ni el dinero conoce. ¿Verdad que no? No lo conoce y, pues, uno no más apronta el puño: "Pues, ahí, agarre," porque uno no lo conoce. Y, no, pues, le ayudaría a ella en lo que ella necesitara. Sí, porque yo ya sé lo que se sufre cuando uno llega sin ... a ciegas, como luego dicen, verdad, sí. Sí la ayudaría y la apoyaría en todo eso.

> Lilian: Was there anything else you would tell your friend?
> Brenda: Well no, just to come, that I would help her. [...] because when one arrives here, one isn't even familiar with the money, right? One doesn't know it and one just holds out one's hand, "There, take it," because one doesn't know it. And, well I would help her in whatever she needed. Yes, because I know what one suffers when one arrives without ... in the dark, as they say, right? I would help her and support her in all of that.

Brenda reiterates her commitment to helping a newcomer, because she knows what it is like to arrive without understanding anything and "being in the dark" (or more literally, "being blind when one arrives").

Each one of these aspects of everyday experience, which usually go unnoticed, become part of a complex learning process which is taking place at many different levels and on many different fronts simultaneously in the life of a newly arrived immigrant woman. On each first interaction with an institution in the new country, there is a whole new process to be understood and actively learned, starting from the basics, in order to be able to function in society.

## Knowing, Belonging and Agency

**Brenda—*Porque yo ya sé lo que se sufre cuando uno llega sin ...
a ciegas.***
(Because I know what one suffers when one arrives without ...
in the dark.)

Although now, as a rule, Brenda can navigate the social and institutional contexts of the school, her experiences still oscillate between being an outsider and an insider. This ambiguity matches her perceptions of being someone who, on some occasions, seems to be defined by lack of knowledge and, on others, as being the person who goes out of her way to help others by sharing information.

On the one hand, at very specific points Brenda has the perception of herself as not knowing, not being able to participate, and not fully belonging. The isolation is experienced, for instance, at a particular informative session or in a decision-making process at the school. In sharp contrast to her general attitude of strong support of her children's education, Brenda expresses her frustration with this one issue. Although Brenda attends all meetings, and comments on those who do not, because she considers it very important, she even ends up suggesting that there may be no point in being present at some of the school events, if she ends up getting nothing out of them. What is the use of going, she wonders, if it makes no difference, if she cannot understand what is being said or cannot speak English in order to participate? "Y, *pues, así es como uno se va dando cuenta, porque si se sale como entró, pues, entonces, ni para qué fuimos, verdad.*" (So, well, that is how one starts realizing that if one leaves just as one arrived, then, what did we go for, right?). Brenda's reflection points to the significance of language resources and the difference their availability makes.

On the other hand, Brenda sees herself as someone whose knowledge can help other mothers navigate the school system. Brenda expresses the importance of sharing her understanding of the details of how business is carried out, and what is expected of mothers in the context of schools in this area. She is aware of the fact that by sharing her knowledge she can ameliorate the difficulties facing a newly arrived immigrant mother. Brenda considers her knowledge and know-how significant, since it can prevent someone who needs to learn the ropes of how to relate to her children's school from experiencing the uncertainty she had to go through. The idea of knowing is associated with Brenda's role as an agent, to how she can help someone in need. In her case, knowledge is a resource that she has developed in order to negotiate the new situations, and that as she shares it has become a community resource. Thus, Brenda offers one of the clearest examples of the workings of communal agency.

# References

Ainslie, R. (1998). Cultural mourning, immigration, and engagement: Vignettes from the Mexican experience. In M. Suárez-Orozco (Ed.), *Crossings: Mexican immigration in interdisciplinary perspectives* (pp. 283–305). Cambridge, MA: Harvard University Press.

Anthias, F. (2006). Belonging in a globalising and unequal world: Rethinking translocation. In N. Yuval-Davis, K. Kannabiran, & U. Vieten (Eds.), *The situated politics of belonging* (pp. 17–31). London: Sage.

Collins, P. H. (1999). Producing the mothers of the nation: Race, class and contemporary US population policies. In N. Yuval-Davis (Ed.), *Women, citizens and difference* (pp. 118–129). London: Zed Books.

Fortier, A. (2000). *Migrant belongings: Memory, space, identity.* Oxford and New York, NY: Berg.

Gabaccia, D., & Leach, C. (Eds.). (2004). *Immigrant life in the U.S.: Multi-disciplinary perspectives.* London and New York, NY: Routledge.

Hondagneu-Sotelo, P. (1994). *Gendered transitions: Mexican experiences of immigration.* Berkeley, CA: University of California Press.

Keet, A., Zinn, D., & Porteus, K. (2009). Mutual vulnerability: A key principle in a humanising pedagogy in post-conflict societies. *Perspectives in Education, 27*(2), 109–119.

Leach, C., & Gabaccia, D. (2004). An afterword: The work and the wonder in studying immigrant life across the disciplines. In D. Gabaccia & C. Leach (Eds.), *Immigrant life in the U.S.: Multi-disciplinary perspectives* (pp. 191–200). New York, NY: Routledge.

Massey, D. (1994). *Space, place, and gender.* Minneapolis, MN: University of Minnesota Press.

Norton, B. (2013). *Identity and language learning: Extending the conversation* (2nd ed.). Tonawanda, NY: Multilingual Matters.

Suárez-Orozco, C. (2000). Identities under siege: Immigration, stress and social mirroring among the children of immigrants. In C. Robben & M. Suárez-Orozco (Eds.), *Cultures under siege: Collective violence and trauma* (pp. 194–226). New York, NY and Cambridge: Cambridge University Press.

Suárez-Orozco, C., & Suárez-Orozco, M. (2001). *Children of immigration.* Cambridge, MA: Harvard University Press.

Suárez-Orozco, C., Suárez-Orozco, M., & Todorova, I. (2008). *Learning a new land: Immigrant students in American society.* Cambridge, MA: Belknap Press of Harvard University Press.

Suárez-Orozco, M. (1990). Migration and education: United States-Europe comparisons. In G. De Vos & M. Suárez-Orozco (Eds.), *Status inequality: The self in culture* (pp. 265–287). Newbury Park, CA: Sage.

Yuval-Davis, N. (2006). Belonging and the politics of belonging. *Patterns of Prejudice, 40*(3), 197–214.

Yuval-Davis, N. (2011). *The politics of belonging: Intersectional contestations.* Thousand Oaks, CA: Sage.

Zentgraf, K. (2002). Immigration and women's empowerment: Salvadorans in Los Angeles. *Gender & Society, 16*(5), 625–646.

# · 7 ·

# LINGUISTIC RESOURCES

## Centrality, Contingency and Invisibility

*[. . .] power is neither monolithic nor invariant; it is not simply something that can be physically possessed, but a relation which always implies social exchange on a particular set of terms. By extension, it is a relation that is constantly being renegotiated as symbolic and material resources in a society change their value. [...] power does not operate only at the macro level of powerful institutions such as the legal system, the education system and the social welfare system, but also at the micro level of everyday social encounters between people with differential access to symbolic and material resources—encounters that are invariably produced within language.* (Norton, 2013, p. 47)

This chapter intends to lay bare the workings of exclusion from the formally inclusive spheres of US public schools by pointing to the paradoxical invisibility of language as a crucial symbolic resource. Some such instances of exclusion taken from the narratives of the women interviewed illustrate this point. It is important to bear in mind that the context of these interviews, the area served by these schools in the rural Southwest, may otherwise appear to be one of the friendliest environments to Spanish-speaking immigrant parents in the US. It is, therefore, necessary to expose this jarring contrast between the general sense of a highly welcoming context and the repeated moments of exclusion and invisibility highlighted by each one of the women who shared their stories, which may otherwise continue to go unnoticed. It is within this context that Young's conceptualization of justice becomes relevant, both for its insistence on responsibility of people and institutions being kept separate from intentionality, and for its view of institutionalized power relations such as domination as processes produced and reproduced by the actions of people who may not necessarily be powerful themselves, and may even be well intentioned.

## Formal Inclusion/Informal Exclusion

Contrary to assumptions of open access and freedom for all to participate in social institutions on an equal basis, in the liberal model of democracy it is often the case that there are forms of informal exclusion which contribute to perpetuate systemic social inequities in the public sphere. In revisiting Habermas's concept of public sphere, Fraser (1997) argues that underlying unequal social relations do not disappear in spite of the outward "bracketing of social inequalities in deliberation," which consists of acting as if they did not exist (p. 78). There is enough reason to remain skeptical, as these inequalities reflect deeper power dynamics, which do not vanish just by ignoring them.

> We should question whether it is possible even in principle for interlocutors to deliberate *as if* they were social peers in specially designated discursive arenas, when these discursive arenas are situated in a larger societal context that is pervaded by structural relations of dominance and subordination. (Fraser, 1997, p. 79, Italics in the original)

In a public deliberative forum, which is inherently inclusive in name, there are implicit expectations of discursive and cultural styles, which function as markers of status inequality. There are certain "expectations about norms of articulateness and dispassionateness" which are culturally specific, and serve to work in favor of the socially privileged and exclude participants who, by virtue of their social location may "feel intimidated by the implicit requirements of public speaking", and whose claims tend to be dismissed mainly on the basis of communication style (Young, 2002, pp. 38–39). These hidden requirements for participation contribute to establishing different degrees of privilege and marginalization of individuals and groups, which mirror the inequalities governing larger structures of society, as the speech styles which are considered acceptable in public forums tend to be a reflection of social privilege (Fraser, 1997, p. 79; Young, 2002, p. 39). Thus, Fraser urges critical theorists to pay attention to "informal impediments to participatory parity that can persist even after everyone is formally and legally licensed to participate" (p. 78).

In the same vein, Charmaz (2005) questions the applicability of the concept of "negotiation" to refer to social interactions in situations of power asymmetry. She notes that the term implies not only the existence of an understanding of the institutional structures and how they function but also that both parties have "sufficient power to make their voices heard, if not to affect outcomes" (p. 526). To be part of a negotiation, you first need to be sitting at the same table. Fraser (1997) proposes that "one task for critical theory is to render visible the ways in which societal inequality infects formally inclusive existing public spheres and taints discursive interaction within them" (p. 80). In other words, even when invitations to participate exist outwardly, there may be unspoken rules or assumed conditions which exclude some from enjoying the freedom to participate.

## Brenda—*Me daba vergüenza opinar.*
## (I was too embarrassed to give my opinion.)

One of the first signs of the still uneven playing field is the recurrent theme in the seven women's stories of feeling embarrassed or ashamed to speak up in public, especially in open forums where people were expected to give their opinion. When discussing parents meetings, Brenda says she paid attention and tried to find out what was going on; she would just listen but never speak. She refers to the meetings in the past but to feeling embarrassed to express her opinion in the present.

> Lilian: Entonces, cuénteme sobre alguna de estas reuniones. ¿Iba a las reuniones de los papás?
> Brenda: De los papás, sí.
> Lilian: La conferencia, o …
> Brenda: Sí, también, pero en las reuniones, pues, allí yo … me daba a veces vergüenza opinar o algo. Pues, yo no más iba y escuchaba y ya. Me da pena. Me enteraba, verdad, de lo que se trataba la conferencia, porque también, hablaba una inglés y la otra interpretaba el español.

> Lilian: So, tell me, about some of those meetings. Did you go to parents meetings?
> Brenda: For parents, yes.
> Lilian: To conferences, or…
> Brenda: Yes, also, but at the meetings, there I… I was too embarrassed to give my opinion or something. So, I just went and listened and that was it. I feel embarrassed. I would find out, right, about what the conference was about, because also one spoke English and the other one interpreted into Spanish.

Like Brenda, Susana mentions she is too inhibited to speak up at general meetings, she just listens silently, and sees what she can get out of it. She would rather let the next person offer their opinion.

> Lilian: ¿Y le parece que es fácil participar si uno va a las reuniones, a dar su opinión y participar de las decisiones y todo?
> Susana: Uno a veces va y no más oye.
> Lilian: Ah, sí. ¿Por qué?
> Susana: Mmm… A veces por pena, a veces porque dice uno, "no, pues, que opine el que sigue". Yo oigo, y callo y a ver qué se me pega.
> Lilian: Habíamos hablado de cómo había cambiado todo… y si le parecía que había sido que había sido algo que hizo la escuela o algo que usted cambió también, cómo ve la escuela y todo. ¿Le parece que usted también cambió?
> Susana: Ah, pues, y yo también, porque antes a veces como que decía: "Ay estoy tan cansada de ir. No, mejor no voy." Y ahora como que ya sí me intereso más por las cosas que, de estar presente en cada junta, en cada entrevista. Digo: "Es importante."

> Lilian: And do you think it's easy to participate if one attends these meetings, to give your opinion and take part in the decisions and all?
> Susana: One sometimes goes and just listens.
> Lilian: Yes, and why?
> Susana: Mmm… Sometimes because of embarrassment, sometimes because one says, "No, so, let the next one give their opinion." I listen and stay quiet, and see what sticks.
> Lilian: We had spoken about how everything had changed… and if you thought that it had been something the school did or that you also changed, how you see the school and all. Do you think you also changed?
> Susana: Oh, well, I also did, because before sometimes I would say, "Oh, I'm so tired of going. No, I'd rather not go." And now it's like I am more interested in these things, in attending each meeting, each conference. I say, "It's important."

Earlier Susana explains she was referring to whole-school informative meetings, not parent-teacher conferences, and offers some reasons why parents are not always able to attend. Finally, she admits that she currently attends more systematically, as she now is more aware of the importance of showing up. Yet, in these large group meetings she still remains silent.

## Invisibility: The Role of Language and Power

The notion of power embraced here coincides with Norton's (2013) definition, inspired in Foucault's work, and refers to "the socially constructed relations among individuals, institutions and communities through which symbolic and material resources in a society are produced, distributed and validated" (p. 47). Norton's view of power as dynamic and relational operating at the macro and micro social levels as well as the role assigned to language as a crucial symbolic resource are especially relevant to the stories presented here and to the experience of the seven immigrant women.

Many events are organized by districts, schools and teachers in the name of parental involvement with the expectation that all parents will receive important information or participate in the school's decisions, according to the official discourse. Thus, they are deemed important both by the schools and by the parents. Yet, in these same events, the participation of a whole group of parents, namely immigrant mothers, is limited due to an inadequate provision or complete absence of translation. This often appears to be seen by school personnel as a need that can easily be met with spur-of-the-moment solutions.

In the seven women's narratives, many such situations emerged in which language resources were left to contingency. At some meetings intended to inform parents about the school's direction, or some aspect of student performance, whole presentations took place before someone mentioned that most attendants had not understood a word. In these cases, evidently, those organizing the meetings had not foreseen the need for interpretation, even when the demographic information of their school should be eloquent enough to point to it. On other occasions, the administrators and staff in charge of the events may have been under the impression that language issues had been solved, since someone had been assigned to interpret. Yet, often the participants perceived that there was much more being said than was translated. At most meetings, the process of deciding who would act as interpreter was left to each parent to resolve.

From the perspective of the Spanish-speaking women in the study, these situations amounted to being left out, as they ended up with a sense of not having understood enough of what had been discussed. In many cases, the frustration was so deep that participants felt as if their presence did not count, and that it would have been the same to have not attended. Some admitted having given up attending these meetings after having the experience of not understanding most of what was going on, and feeling it was not much use being present. At every such meeting organized for parents in the name of parental involvement where, at the same time, paradoxically, active participation is implicitly denied to a whole group of parents, their full sense of belonging is in fact being compromised.

It seems worth reiterating here that the schools in question belong to a district which, at the time of the interviews, reported that nearly 90% of students are Latin@ (Hispanic), and almost 50% of students were classified as English Language Learners. Even a higher percentage of parents would be likely to need language services to communicate with the schools on a daily basis, given the fact that students are often exited from bilingual programs once they acquire fluency in English for social purposes. Although the official data does not state this, it may be inferred from this information that most parents in this school are Spanish-speaking, and many mostly monolingual. In the group of participants in this study, for instance, at least three children in different families have been exited from bilingual programs, and thus are probably not counted as ELLs, whereas their mothers require interpreters to communicate with monolingual English speakers.

Therefore, it is not surprising that translation and the availability of interpreters or translators, in all the interactions in which their interlocutors do not speak Spanish, emerges in the women's stories as the most significant resource on which most communication pivots. Even though language may seem to be an obvious factor in these exchanges and not worthy of notice, it is this same matter-of-fact quality which renders it invisible, and therefore in need of having a light shone on it. From the perspective of the seven women who shared their experiences with us, language resources for parents play a much more central role in the schools' functioning and communication than they seem to be attributed. There appears to be a marked disconnect between the idea of an informative meeting for parents of children in this district and the absolute lack of foresight to provide interpreters, again, given the available demographic information. Ironically, in this context the invisibility of such a crucial resource becomes conspicuous.

The fact that most relationships and most interactions in this context require a competent interpreter and most written communications need to be adequately translated does not seem to be on the list of urgent priorities for those in charge of making decisions, in other words, for those who have the power to make a difference. In this region of the country, where it may be reasonable to expect that there will always be some bilingual person at hand, the availability of language resources seems to be assumed as an issue that can be easily resolved. Thus, it is often left to chance and improvised solutions. For the women who were interviewed this topic comes up first as the main reason for concern and the main focus of their energy. Translation is a central resource to an immigrant mother who needs to interact with the schools. As was the case with all the interviewees, immigrant women often provide their own interpreters/translators or make sure they find someone in the school or in the community to help them at the time they need to communicate with the schools.

The significance attached to this resource by interviewees, its potential impact on the effectiveness of communication, and the demographic data contrast starkly with how the availability of such a critical resource appears to be subject to contingency. Given that the need for translation is made invisible, in turn, this invisibility of a resource that plays such a central role in the participants' experience renders them invisible as well. As Anzaldúa's (1987) powerful exclamation, *"I am my language,"* reminds us, a person's language is tantamount to a person's identity (p. 59). In thrusting their language into invisibility, schools may inadvertently be contributing to strengthen the outsider status of immigrant mothers. Besides being intricately related to a person's identity, and an invaluable symbolic resource, language is crucial as a means to accessing most other material and symbolic resources in the new environment:

> [...] it is through language that a person negotiates a sense of self within and across different sites at different points in time, and it is through language that a person gains access to—or is denied access to—powerful social networks that give learners the opportunity to speak. (Norton, 2013, p. 45)

Iris Young (1990) analyzes how in our daily interactions, these social micro processes contribute to perpetuate structural inequity. As these narratives illustrate, power operates structurally "as a function of dynamic processes of interaction within regulated cultural and decision-making situations" where "many widely dispersed persons are agents of power without 'having' it, or even being privileged" (Young, 1990, p. 33). Ignoring difference in the name of equality entails oppression in the form of assimilation (Young, 1990). Given the assimilative forces which underlie such situations of institutional interaction, the immigrant women in this study were found to be at a disadvantage. Assimilation operated through the apparent neutrality and universality of the form assumed in informative and decision-making meetings where cultural and linguistic differences were not acknowledged. Thus these may be regarded as examples of how "blindness to difference perpetuates cultural imperialism by allowing norms expressing the point of view and experience of privileged groups to appear neutral and universal" (Young, 1990, p. 165). In her definition of the five faces of oppression, Young (1990) includes cultural imperialism. This form of inequity is characterized by the assumption, on the one hand, of the dominant culture as both neutral and universal, and on the other, of the non-dominant culture(s) as deviant, while simultaneously—and paradoxically—being rendered invisible (pp. 59–60). In the seven women's cases, their narratives offer an illustration of the at times subtle and at other times blatantly evident effects of cultural imperialism in the context of the schooling of immigrant children and of home-school relations, when the parents are working-class Spanish-speaking immigrants.

### Sandra—¿A qué voy a perder el tiempo si no voy a entender? (What am I going to waste my time for, if I am not going to understand?)

After her detailed description of a recent informative meeting for parents held by the principal at her son's middle school, Sandra says she is frustrated in so many words, and adds that she often feels as if she is not being taken into account. She attends these events because she cares and wants to hear their reports on how the school is doing, and their plans for the children. But, even when an interpreter has been assigned, much goes untranslated, and it is very hard to follow.

> Lilian: Y cuénteme, dijo que en una junta, o que a veces uno batalla en las juntas en la "middle school". No en la conferencia con los maestros, no, las otras reuniones. Cuénteme.
> Sandra: "Middle school", es la primera que hemos tenido. Como el niño acaba de entrar ahí. Entonces, la principal está aprendiendo español. Dijo que estaba aprendiendo. Entonces, había mucha gente que habla puro inglés. Entonces, se dedica a hablarlos. Estos, los puntos, los desarrolló muy bien. Pero había momentos en que no paraba para que el otro explicara en español. Y había como tres o cuatro personas que hablaban español, que no entendemos en inglés. Entonces, pues, le digo, se siente uno… es más aburrido. Se aburre uno porque está uno en un lugar donde no lo están tomando en cuenta. Entonces, si se distrae uno, si poquito entiende, entonces, ya no trata de entenderlo, ¿por qué? porque no le están poniendo también a usted la atención. Uno está ahí porque le interesa saber el desarrollo, qué planes tiene la escuela, cuál es la perspectiva que quieren para nuestros hijos, qué está bien y qué está mal, cosas que están sucediendo en la escuela, sí, ¿me entiende?

> Lilian: So, tell me, you said that at a meeting, or that sometimes… one struggles… at the meetings at the middle school… not those with the teacher, not the conference, no, the other ones. Tell me about it.
> Sandra: Middle school… it is the first meeting we have had. As my son has just started there. Then, the principal is learning Spanish. She said she is learning. Then,

there were many people there who only speak English. Then, she got down to talk about them. These, the points she made, she presented them very well. But there were times when she did not stop for the other person to explain in Spanish. And there were about three or four of us there who speak Spanish, and don't understand English. So, well, I tell you, one feels... it is boring. One gets bored because one is somewhere where they are not... as if they are not taking you into account. Then, if one gets distracted, if you understand very little, then, you stop trying to understand. Why? Because they are not paying attention to you, either. One is there because one is interested in finding out about the development, what plans the school has, what perspectives they want for our children, what is going well and what isn't, about things that are going on at the school, do you see what I mean?

Later Sandra notes that she is not alone in her frustration, and refers to the pointlessness of participating, and to a certain degree of hopelessness that she and other parents sometimes feel. She wonders what the use of attending these meetings is, anyway, if they will walk away without getting anything out of them, without having understood a thing. This conclusion stands out in her story, as it contrasts sharply with Sandra's steadfast commitment to participating in every event that is organized at her children's schools, and her insistence on the need for more parents to attend school meetings.

Y la "middle school" es la etapa de los niños... sí, bien tremenda, usted sabe, enton-ces... Eso fue la falla única que noté, que en cuanto podía el intérprete nos decía lo que estaban diciendo. ¿Sí? Pero se pierde. Está hablando ella allá y este acá, entonces, se pierde. Perdón... no podía él estar oyendo y estarnos interpretando, entonces, ahí se perdió un poco. Entonces, esperemos, estoy esperando la próxima junta, a ver cómo se desarrolla. Y, si no, a veces uno con el que habla español decirle, platique, o algo, sí, porque es incómodo y para no perder el interés de asistir a las juntas. Sabe qué, por eso, muchas veces, es mínimo, mínimo, el número de padres que va a las juntas. Yo pienso que ha de ser una de las causas: que si no entienden, pues: "Ahí, me daré cuenta con los niños a ver qué pasa." Pero no es falta de interés en sí, sino que lo genera el que no entiende uno: "¿A qué voy a perder el tiempo si no voy a entender?"

And middle school is a stage for children... right, that is terrible, you know, then... That was the only problem I noticed, that whenever he could, the interpreter told us what she was saying, right? But some gets lost. She is speaking over there and he is over here, then, he got lost. Sorry... He couldn't be listening over there and inter-preting to us, we missed a bit. So, let's hope, I am waiting for the next meeting, to see... to see what happens. And, if not, sometimes one wishes to tell the person who is speaking Spanish tell him "Speak", or something, because it is awkward, and so as not to lose interest in attending the meetings. You know what, that is why, many times, the number of parents who attend meetings is very low, very low. I think this must be one of the reasons: that if they don't understand, then: "There, I'll find out through the kids to see what happens." But it isn't a lack of interest, but what comes from not understanding: "What am I going to waste my time for if I am not going to understand?"

From Sandra's account it becomes clear that sometimes, even when there is someone who has been assigned to interpret, after a meeting that was meant to be informative, people in the audience can still leave frustrated and feeling left out, because of language issues. There is a subtle detail in Sandra's description of the situation with the interpreter when some of what the principal says is missed, as the interpreter gets lost, which contributes to this feeling of being left out. Sandra suggests that there is some physical distance between the two groups, saying "what she is saying over here" and "he is interpreting for us over there". The spatial distribution described could be brushed aside as a matter of organization. As teachers understand well, though, when there is a choice, how we set up a room reflects how we envision the dynamics of a group. As it is hard to deny after Foucault, space and physical distribution can be analyzed in terms of power dynamics. Thus, in the context of the stories of the immigrant women, the apparent detail of this physical distance or separation may be interpreted as signaling the existence of boundaries between insiders/outsiders, or at least, as contributing to this perception.

Sandra's words are significant because of the manifest tension between her deep interest in her children's academic progress and general well-being, her concern for her son and children in his age group, on one hand, and her feeling of being left out and not taken into account by the school at times like these, on the other. Again, in stark contrast to her overall attitude, she even confesses that her efforts to attend, dropping everything she is doing for a meeting, sometimes seem in vain.

Lilian: ¿Era la directora la que estaba hablando?
Sandra: A veces. Sí, en ese tipo de juntas ahí, que citan a los padres, es la directora la que da. Y como ella acaba de llegar aquí, estaba exponiendo su plan de trabajo, lo que quiere hacer, qué fondos para la escuela, y eso. Sí, eran cosas importantes. A ver, la próxima junta de padres que tengan, a ver cómo se desarrolla. Pero, yo digo, tiene muy poca asistencia de padres, es nada. Es un 1% de padres de la escuela que van. Lo mismo…Y en otras escuelas, las otras chiquitas, van, suponga, un 30%, ya un poquito más. Ya es más. ¿Por qué? Porque es la época de trabajo y los padres trabajan todos en la mañana o en la tarde. Y no sé, acá sí, en las otras escuelas procuran traducir lo que está diciendo el director o el maestro de ceremonias. Procuran traducir en la Monte Verde [one of the elementary schools], sí, en la otra, también, entonces sí. Sí, es muy

frustrante, o sea, tener uno el interés de saber y no entender lo que están diciendo. Y le dedica uno el tiempo, para uno todo por ir, para que se salga, pues sí, ¿qué?

Lilian: Was it the principal who was speaking?
Sandra: Sometimes. Yes, in that type of meetings there, where they call parents, it is the principal who presents. And as she has just arrived here, she was presenting her work plan, what she wants to do, what funds for the school, and that. Yes, they were important things. Let's see, next meeting that they have for parents, let's see how it unfolds. But I say, attendance of parents is very low, it's nothing. It is one per cent of parent of the school who go. The same... and in other schools, the little ones, let's say, about 30% attends, a bit more. It is a bit more already. Why? Because it's the season for work and parents are all working morning and afternoon. And I don't know, here yes, in the other schools they try to translate what the principal or the speaker is saying. They try to translate at Monte Verde [one of the elementary schools], yes, at the other one too, then yes. Yes, it is very frustrating, that is, to be interested and want to know and not to understand what they are saying. And one devotes the time, stops everything to go, to leave, well yes, saying "what?"

Sandra speaks at length about how she cares about her community and other mothers in her same situation. Both from her own account of her interest and active participation in recruiting parents for school meetings, and from the narratives of the other participants in the study, Sandra has emerged as a leader. So, in a way, it would seem that Sandra's frustration is voiced for a whole group, even for those parents who may not show up, because of this sense of pointlessness. Not only does Sandra reiterate this appraisal on two other occasions, but four other participants echo it too, all in separate interviews: Brenda, Susana, Silvia, and Norma. Susana refers to this situation as *"quedarse a medias"* (to be left half empty or with half answers, literally, to be left halfway). Similarly, Silvia calls it *"quedarse en cero"* (to be left with nothing or empty). Susana repeats the same idea of how pointless it is to attend if one will not be able to understand. It is worth noting that all along these participants have insisted on the centrality of attending meetings. These are the same women who often in their suggestions for other mothers, the newcomers, underscore the need to get to know their children's teachers, visit on the first day, and attend all conferences and meetings.

# Interpretation as an Afterthought

**Silvia—*Ella hablaba y hablaba puro inglés, sin preguntar quiénes de las mamás no sabían inglés.***
(She talked and talked, only in English, without asking who among the mothers didn't speak English.)

Silvia refers to an episode that had occurred the year before at a parents meeting held by her son's teacher to which all parents were invited so as to receive specific information for their children's class. The teacher in this situation had not foreseen the need for interpretation, and the meeting was almost done when one Spanish-speaking woman asked another mother in the group, who was bilingual, to intercede for those who did not understand. The teacher then apologized for not having asked beforehand if anyone needed interpretation.

> Ah, sí, bueno, en una ocasión, verdad, que llegamos y fue en un grupo de…. cuando se juntan… no no-más una mamá, si no muchas mamás y platican de lo que es bueno para los niños de ese salón, de esa aula. Entonces, pues esa maestra hablaba y hablaba y hablaba puro inglés y los que sabíamos español no podíamos contestar, porque estábamos ahí oyendo *(louder)*, pues no sabíamos de lo que hablaban. Si no que, bueno, ya hasta el último ya casi para terminarse la junta, una de las mamás, también que no sabía inglés, luego le preguntó a otra mamá que sabía inglés, que le preguntara a la maestra si podía darnos una clase especial de lo que estaba hablando, para las mamás que no sabíamos inglés. Y ahí fue adonde ella pidió disculpas porque ella hablaba y hablaba puro inglés, sin preguntar quiénes de las mamás no sabían inglés y sí fue una experiencia que tuvimos ahí.

> Oh, well, yes, on one occasion, right, when we arrived… it was in a group of… when we get together, not just one mom, but many mothers, and they talk about what is good for the children in that room, that classroom. So, well, that teacher kept on, and on, and on speaking only in English, and those of us who didn't know weren't able to answer, because we were there listening *(louder)*, but we didn't know what she was talking about. So then, well, at the very end, when the meeting was about to finish, one of the moms who doesn't know English either, asked one of the moms who does know English if she could ask the teacher to hold a special class about what she was talking, for those moms who didn't know English. And that was when she apologized because she talked and talked, only in English, without asking who among the mothers didn't speak English. And that was an experience we had there.

This situation had occurred relatively recently, Silvia comments. After describing the context as an informative meeting called by the teacher for the parents in her own class, Silvia explains that the situation was solved, near the end of the meeting, by a bilingual mother who was asked to summarize what the teacher had said during the whole meeting. Her son's teacher was not aware of how many of her students' mothers or who among them were Spanish-speakers and would have needed interpretation. This instance illustrates the invisibility of linguistic resources and, transitively, the invisibility of the people who would need to make use of them.

Lilian ¿En qué grado estaba el niño? ¿Más o menos?

Silvia: Pues, él estaba … no eso fue el año pasado. Estaba en tercero; él está en cuarto ahora, y estaba en tercero. Pero fue una de las que me tocó, porque casi siempre tenía el apoyo de otra maestra que sabía español. Pero sí fue una de las que pasamos.

Lilian: Y esta ¿que tipo de reunión era? ¿Era como… la maestra invita a todos los padres de su aula nada más?

Silvia: Aha (rising intonation). Sí, porque tienen cada quien, cada maestra invita a los papás de sus alumnos,

Lilian: ¿Como el "open house"? ¿O no?

Silvia: Ah, no, no más sé que fue para platicar de los avances que necesitaban poner, para que los niños estuvieran más a gusto en las aulas y cosas así, detalles del salón… Aha, y cuando les iban a enseñar que en la computadora y todo eso, si estaba bien para los niños y todo eso, fue en una ocasión de esas.

Lilian: Y finalmente ¿cómo resolvieron? ¿Tuvieron otra reunión, o…?

Silvia: No, al final, ella puso a una de las mamás y esa mamá estaba explicándonos lo que ella había dicho, pero en frente de ella, sí… sí.

Lilian: What grade was your son in, more or less?

Silvia: Well, he was… no, this was last year. He was in third; he is in fourth now, and he was in third. But it was one that we went through, because almost always I had the support of another teacher who knew Spanish. But, yes, this was one of the things we went through.

Lilian: And this, what type of meeting was it? Was it like when the teacher invites all of the parents in her classroom only?

Silvia: Aha, Yes, because each one has, each teacher invites the parents of their students.

Lilian: Like an open house? Or not?

Silvia: Oh, no, I only know it was to talk about the changes they needed to implement for the kids' wellbeing in their classrooms, and details of the classroom… Yeah, and when she was going to start teaching the children on the computers, and if it was ok for the children, and so on. It was one of those occasions.

Lilian: And finally, how was this solved? Did you have another meeting, or…?

Silvia: No, in the end, she assigned one of the moms, and that mom was explaining to us what she had said, but in front of her, yes.

A significant factor that places this episode in perspective is that Silvia shares this experience just after she mentions how much help she usually receives, especially at parent-teacher conferences where, if the teacher is not bilingual, Silvia asks her child to in turn ask the teacher if someone can interpret. Silvia stresses the fact that, *"es lo que me gusta de la escuela de mis niños"* (it's what I like about my children's school), that they offer her this type of support. This comment intensifies the contrast between Silvia's general positive stance towards the school, and this recent experience in her child's classroom.

### Brenda—*Uno, que no sabe inglés, no más pela los ojillos.* (So, if you don't know English, you just keep your eyes peeled.)

For her part, Brenda often mentions how she finds herself spending most of her time at parents meetings looking around trying to weigh her options as to who might be the best person to ask for a translation or a summary of what went on, once the meeting is over. Brenda comments that most of these informative meetings are usually held completely in English.

> Es que a veces, sí hay conferencias y, pues, uno, nada más está pelando los ojos porque no sabe ... Oh, pues, sí, cuando hay reuniones así que por ejemplo que los maestros tienen algo para los niños, como hacer un trabajo o si nos gusta cómo van ellos en sus calificaciones y todo eso, verdad, entonces, nos llaman a conferencia y como es puro inglés, esas sí las conferencias a veces sí son puro inglés, y pues uno no más que no sabe inglés que no más pela los ojillos. Pero ya ... ya cuando se acaba la conferencia, como mi hija ya conoce más o menos allí el personal, verdad, ella me dice: "Mira, mami, aquella señora habla español." Y ya voy con ella y le explico: "Pues, como se habló puro inglés, yo no, pues, no supe de lo que se trató." Y luego, ya me dice: "Ok." Luego, "Vente, vamos para explicarte." Y ya allí, pues, en palabras más cortas me explica lo que se trató la conferencia. Sí, ya me pregunta ella: "¿Tú qué opinarías en respecto a esto?" Y ya yo le digo, más o menos, lo que yo pienso, verdad. Y, pues, así es como uno se va dando cuenta, porque si se sale como entró, pues, entonces, ni para qué fuimos, verdad.

> It's that sometimes yes, there are meetings and well, one, just is there with one's eyes wide open because one doesn't know... Oh, well, yes, when there are meetings like that for example when the teachers have something for the kids, like a project for them to complete, or to see if we like how they are doing with their grades and all that, right, then, they call us to a meeting and as it is all in English, those yes are sometimes all in English, so one who doesn't know English just keeps one's eyes peeled, but once the meeting is over, as my daughter more or less knows already the staff, right, she tells me, "Look, Mommy, that lady speaks Spanish." So I go with that person and I explain, well, as only English was spoken, I wasn't... able to find out

what it was about." And then she says, "Ok, then, come on and I'll explain it all to you." And then, well, in short, she explains what the conference was about. And she asks me, "What do you think about this? And I tell her, more or less, what I think, right? And, so, that is how you start realizing, because if you leave the same as you arrived, well, then, why did we even go, right?

Again, her final comment about having left "the same as you arrived," reflects the perception that it did not seem to make a difference whether she attended or not, which was shared by a majority of the participants. This situation was regarded as one of the most significant underlying reasons most Spanish-speaking parents do not always attend informative meetings, since an improvised hurried summary at the end of the meeting is all they may hope for.

## Luisa—*Había muchas mamás que no entendíamos.* (There were many of us, moms, who didn't understand.)

Luisa is the participant who most fervently expresses her gratitude for the help she received at the schools attended by her children some years ago, by her nephew more recently, and currently by the child she babysits. In her narration Luisa pours out her warm gratefulness and never spares praises for teachers, educational assistants, secretaries, and everyone who has helped her throughout the years. Luisa often refers to each person by name, and describes the specific type of help she has received from them. Yet, when asked to share her story of some specific interaction with the schools, Luisa recounts a series of three very different episodes that are linked by one significant element they have in common: the frustration of being unable to communicate during a crisis or to participate in some decision-making process deemed important.

The three incidents Luisa refers to are all moments of intense anxiety for her. In the first case, she receives a call from the school letting her know that her teenage son is not at school. For Luisa, who had recently lost her husband, this was probably a situation where she felt the lack of a relevant cultural script most intensely, as she did not know what was expected of her when her son skipped school. In the second case, her son has suffered an accident, and was sent to the hospital. When she returns to the school, he cannot act as interpreter, as it seems he usually does, because he is in shock and under the effects of strong medication; this is probably a new situation for Luisa. At the time, she is mostly concerned about being unable to secure the homework her son will need to complete so as not to fall behind during his convalescence.

In the third case, communication problems arise at an informative meeting organized at the school in preparation for her older son's graduation. This was an emotionally charged time for Luisa, because she was recently widowed. In her vivid account of the event, she conveys her frustration for not being able to understand what was being discussed, and not knowing what they would have to do in preparation for graduation.

> Luisa: Y para mí fue muy difícil, fue muy difícil. Cuando se iba a graduar, también fue difícil para mí, porque tenía que ir a las juntas de que se iban a graduar, de que se iban a comprar eso... su capa, de este. Y la junta era en un comedor donde había muchas mamás que no entendíamos y nadie... Porque el hombre estaba allá diciendo lo que tenían que hacer y cómo caminar y con quién iban a caminar y que comprar el libro y el anillo y que no-sé-qué-tanto. Y nosotros cuando más oíamos, pero no entendíamos...
>
> Lilian: ¿Quién era? ¿Un maestro u otra persona?
>
> Luisa: Era otra persona y un maestro, también, y el director y el que les iba a enseñar qué iban a hacer y todo. Pues, muchas personas. Y nos preguntábamos: "Oye, sí, ¿qué dijo?" "Que dijo que ya se iban a graduar y pero que no le entendí." Y así. Pero así fue, como le digo. Sí hemos batallado; batallamos bastante. Bastante cuando ellos estuvieron en la escuela, mucho. Pero pues, ya, mire, ya terminamos y ya tenemos todos esos recuerdos con Norma...

> Luisa: And for me it was very difficult, it was very difficult. When he was about to graduate, it was also difficult for me, because I had to go to the meetings about their graduation, about what they were going to buy, their gown, and this and that. And the meeting took place in a cafeteria where there were many of us, moms, who didn't understand and nobody... Because the man was over there speaking about what they had to do, and how to walk, and who they were going to walk with, and about buying the book and the ring, and I don't know what else. And we just heard, but we couldn't understand...
>
> Lilian: Who was it? A teacher or somebody else?
>
> Luisa: It was another person, and a teacher, too, and the principal, and the person who was going to show them what they had to do and all. So, many people. And we asked each other, "Listen, yes, what did he say?" "He said that they are about to graduate, but I didn't understand." And so on. So that's how it was, as I say. We have struggled; we struggled quite a bit. Quite a bit while they were in school, a lot. But look, now we are done and now we have all those memories, Norma and I..."

In this episode, there are signs of confusion, not only about what is being said but as to who is who. As Luisa narrates her impressions of this meeting, there seems to be a blurring of the distinction between the roles of the company representatives selling graduation paraphernalia and their sales pitch and that of the school officials sharing information about the graduation ceremony. In

Luisa's story, it seems that buying all of these products is part and parcel of the preparation for her son's graduation ceremony.

In this narrative trilogy, Luisa relates events interconnected by the fact that in all three she had found the challenge of communicating with the school staff overwhelming, since it added to the anxiety of each situation. She sums up her experiences referring to these struggles in the plural, "we struggled quite a bit while they were in school," and closes her narration in a lighter tone by commenting on how now these experiences have become memories she and her close friend Norma can share.

## Norma—*La mayor parte de la reunión es en inglés y una que otra cosa les traducen.*
(Most of the meeting is in English and they translate a thing or two for them.)

When asked about attending PTO (parent-teacher organization) meetings, Norma first points out that most parents who are members of the board are English-speaking, so that meetings are held mostly in English, as they must find it easier to do so.

> Lilian: ¿Y tiene usted amigas que van a la reunión de la organización de padres, o no?
> Norma: No, la verdad, no. Pero una vez, y a lo mejor por eso no van también, porque si dicen que la mayor parte de la reunión es en inglés y una y que otra cosa les traducen. Entonces, también por eso se desaniman. Mucho del desánimo, también, en parte, es el idioma. Es el idioma, sí.
> Lilian: No está en los dos idiomas, la reunión.
> Norma: No, no está. Porque aunque hay personas ahí que sí hablan español, pero la mayoría hablan inglés. Porque, yo no sé por qué, pero en la mesa directiva como le llamamos nosotros, son más los americanos que participan. Entonces, a la hora de las reuniones, como es más los que hablan puro inglés, entonces se les hace más fácil hacerla en inglés. Sí, yo comentaba con una amiga eso, que teníamos que ir a las reuniones, saber qué está pasando y todo eso. Y luego, otra parte cómoda también, es que después le mandan una nota también, qué se dijo, qué se acordó, y todo eso. Y ya se la mandan a uno español, entonces, ya dice uno, bueno, me espero a la nota.

> Lilian: And do you have friends who attend those PTO meetings or not?
> Norma: No, the truth is, that no. But once… and maybe that is why they don't go either, because they say that most of the meeting is in English and they translate a thing or two. And so, that is also why they get discouraged. Much of the disappointment is the language. It's language, yes.
> Lilian: It's not in both languages, the meeting?

> Norma: No, it isn't; because although there are people there who speak Spanish, most speak English. Because, I don't know why, but on the board—as we call it— there are more Americans. Then, when there are meetings, as there are more people who speak only English, then it is easier for them to have them in English. Yes, I was commenting on that with a friend, that we had to attend meetings, to find out what is going on and all that. And then, there is also some convenience too, in that afterwards they send you the note, with what was said, what was agreed on, and all that. And they send it in Spanish, so then, one says, well, I'll wait for the note.

Once again, there is reference to some sort of effort to offer some interpretation at these meetings, but it is perceived as limited. It would seem as though there is on the part of the organizers of these meetings the intention to bridge this gap, but there may not be an awareness of the perception of inadequacy of the effort, or the incompleteness of the resulting communication. Again, the idea that language may be the main reason why Spanish-speaking parents may feel excluded from some types of meetings appears prominent in Norma's account.

The absence of interpretation is discouraging to many parents who would have to make an enormous effort to attend meetings in the first place, so that frequently this becomes a factor contributing in their decision to stay away. When judged through the lens of the official discourse of parental involvement without considering the context or any of the factors discussed above, the seven women in this study would probably be labeled uninvolved. It is such uncritical practices, based on a one-sided definition of what it means to be a parent engaged in a child's education, which contribute to perpetuate deficit thinking, and to the prevalence of stereotypical views of working-class Spanish-speaking immigrant mothers.

# References

Anzaldúa, G. (1987). *Borderlands/La frontera: The new mestiza*. San Francisco, CA: aunt lute books.

Charmaz, K. (2005). Grounded theory in the 21st century: Applications for advancing social justice studies. In N. Denzin & Y. Lincoln (Eds.), *The Sage handbook of qualitative research* (3rd ed., pp. 507–535). Thousand Oaks, CA: Sage.

Fraser, N. (1997). *Justice interruptus*. New York, NY: Routledge.

Norton, B. (2013). *Identity and language learning: Extending the conversation* (2nd ed.). Tonawanda, NY: Multilingual Matters.

Young, I. (1990). *Justice and the politics of difference*. Princeton, NJ: Princeton University Press.

Young, I. (2002). *Inclusion and democracy*. New York, NY: Oxford University Press.

# · 8 ·

# MEDIATED INTERACTIONS

## Translation, Interpretation and Power Asymmetry

*But in parent-teacher conferences these multiparty exchanges were even more complex than the kinds of interpreter-mediated interactions [...]. In these encounters, interpreters were multiply positioned. They were children whose social, linguistic, moral, and academic trajectories were being evaluated by their parents and teachers; they were both the objects of those evaluations and the vehicles for transmitting them.* (Orellana, 2009, p. 78)

The women who shared their stories were aware of the fact that the quality of the communication and ultimately the outcome of their interactions depended heavily on how it was being translated and, thus, on who was assigned to act as interpreter on each occasion. In a community where a large percentage of the population is considered bilingual to a certain degree, it is often the case that the intricacies of the highly demanding tasks of translating and interpreting and the sophistication of the skills required may be underestimated and the work of translation undervalued. In this chapter, in most cases, the term translation is used in its broader meaning which includes both writing and speech, while interpretation refers only to oral communication across languages.

Every translation is an act of interpretation, in the general sense of the word. How accurately the messages are conveyed in both directions, how much information is provided and how much is left out will depend on many factors, beyond the interpreter's diligence and willingness to be of help. Evidently, first among these lies the translator's skills in both languages; but being bilingual does not necessarily imply a capacity to adequately serve as an interpreter. An awareness of the subtleties involved in word choice, connotation, and register, and especially a lack thereof, may gravely impact a translation. Familiarity with the topics and depth of understanding of the matters discussed come in a close second. The final rendering and its tone will also be affected by the intention of the interpreter and their social role in that context. The process of translating requires a nuanced understanding and precision in communicating different perspectives and expectations. Thus, as it is the case in any social interaction, the positions an interpreter adopts and transmits will be impacted directly by their overall stances towards the issues at stake, as well as by how closely the results of this interaction may affect him or her, or the individual, group or institution they may represent.

The invisibility of translation and the marginality of the role of the interpreter and the translator in society, in spite of their consequential function, have been documented in different contexts (Valdés, 2010; Venuti, 1995). In the lives of the seven women who shared their stories, interpreters act as invisible mediators of most interactions with the schools and other institutions. In their narratives it becomes evident that, especially when the situation at hand is perceived as a serious one, each woman makes sure to find someone who they consider to be the most reliable person and someone she trusts deeply. Given the power issues involved, language skills are not the only factor in deciding who to bring along; other factors carry weight, such as, experience, assertiveness, an understanding of the situation, and above all, closeness to the person being represented, on whose behalf he or she will be speaking.

## Who Acts as Interpreter or Translator?

As suggested in the seven women's stories, there is more energy devoted to finding linguistic resources than might be imagined. This may mean seeking an interpreter at or after a meeting, or finding a translator to read a letter and help understand what, if anything, needs to be done. Who serves in this capacity and how this is decided varies in each case. Immigrant women often provide their own interpreters or translators—neighbors, children, bosses— but often the need is met by whoever is available and willing to interpret—a secretary, a teacher, a student, or another parent. Most participants mention specific members of the school staff who are willing to help either by speaking Spanish, by interpreting, or by finding someone else who is able to interpret for them, especially when communicating with school officials.

As a response to the question about how she went about interacting with the schools at first, what helped her the most in those initial stages, and what she would say about it to a friend who has just arrived, Brenda starts out by referring to her own efforts and agency.

Lilian: Y ¿qué le contaría de cómo se las arregló usted? ¿Cómo hizo usted? ¿Qué fue lo que más la ayudó a usted para arreglárselas al principio?
Brenda: Pues, para arreglármelas yo tenía que hacer amistades, verdad. Para poder preguntar algo en la escuela, verdad. Pues, yo llegaba a la oficina y lo primero que preguntaba si hablaban español porque era del modo que yo podía comunicarme. Y ya si no … si no hablaban español, pues, ellas mismas buscaban una persona que hablara español, para poderme comunicar yo con ellas. Y pues así, poco a poco, una va aprendiendo y pues para seguir adelante con sus problemas. Porque a veces sí dice uno: "Ay, pues, si no me hubiera venido, yo no estuviera batallando así," ¿verdad? Pero con la ayuda de Dios también, Dios no nos deja y salimos adelante … con amistades y pues uno se basa también en personas que … que han estado aquí, verdad, ya llevan tiempo aquí, verdad. Y son las que también le van diciendo a uno cómo. En esa parte yo sí ayudaría a una amiga que viniera de allá, sí.

Lilian: And, what would you tell them about how you managed? How did you do it? What was it that helped you the most to manage at the beginning?
Brenda: Well, to manage I had to make friends, right. To be able to ask about something at school, right? Well, I arrived in the office and the first thing I would ask was if they spoke Spanish, because that was the way I could communicate. And then, if not … if they didn't speak Spanish, they would find someone themselves who spoke Spanish, so that I could communicate with them. And so, little by little, one goes learning and to go ahead and handle one's problems. Because sometimes one does say, "Oh, well, if I hadn't come I wouldn't be struggling like this," right? But with God's help, also, God doesn't leave us and we go ahead … with friends and one also relies on people who … who have been here, right, longer, right? And they are the ones that go telling you how to [do things]. So, in this, I would help a friend who came from over there, yes.

The helpfulness Brenda found when she arrived was common in all the women's stories, as they referred to teachers and secretaries who either spoke Spanish or would find someone to interpret for them. However there is one exception in this respect among the participants' narratives. After describing how difficult it was for her, when she first arrived with her siblings, Susana explains how once they learned English, her brothers acted as interpreters. Further, she comments that it is easier nowadays because there are more teachers and members of the school staff who are bilingual. In the context of her description of these changes, Susana mentions in passing that there are some teachers who speak Spanish but do not like to, and choose not to, so she takes her own children to interpret for her. In how she decides who will interpret for her, Susana is also an exception in that she shares how she purposefully brings with her the child whom the meeting is about. This stands in contrast to most participants' preference to have an adult interpret for them.

> Lilian: Si se acuerda la primera visita que hizo a la escuela. ¿Cómo fue su experiencia? ¿Con quién habló y qué pasó?
> Susana: En ese entonces, mis hermanos ya estaban grandes cuando llegaron aquí, y no hablaban inglés. Entonces, a veces era difícil la traducción, porque si el maestro hablaba puro inglés, y uno puro español y los niños, pues, apenas estaban empezando, pues era un poco difícil, a veces encontrar a un traductor.
> Lilian: ¿No había en esa época?
> Susana: Casi no. Se batallaba a veces ahí, a puras señas y…
> Lilian: ¿Cómo hacía? ¿Iba alguien con usted a veces, o…?
> Susana: A veces, ya después, sí, me hice una amiga americana (laughs) que hablaba los dos idiomas, y ahí ya…
> Lilian: ¿La acompañaba?
> Susana: Sí, y luego está eso, que tengo hermanos muy inteligentes que aprendieron rápido, aprendieron rápido a hablar el inglés más o menos. Siempre procuraba llevarme al que iba a la junta, por el que me tocaba ir, del niño que correspondía. Y así, ya. Ya lo usaba como intérprete.
> Lilian: Y ellos mismos interpretaban.
> Susana: Ellos mismos, como ahora los maestros hablan los dos idiomas, por lo regular. Pero hay uno que otro que no quiere. Que lo habla pero no lo quiere hablar, el español. Pero siempre llevo a mis niños. "Es que yo no quiero ir a ninguna junta, Mami," dicen. "Es que tienes que ir", le digo, "si no ¿cómo voy a saber qué me dicen?" Que uno a veces, póngale que uno entiende algo, verdad, pero hay cosas que a veces se le atoran a uno.

> Lilian: If you remember your first visit to the school, how was your experience? Who did you speak with? And, what happened?
> Susana: In those days, my brothers were big kids when they arrived, and they didn't speak English. So, sometimes translation was difficult, because if the teacher spoke only English, and one spoke only Spanish and the kids, well, they were barely starting, well, it was a bit difficult to find a translator.
> Lilian: Weren't there any in those days?
> Susana: Almost none. We would struggle sometimes, just with gestures and…
> Lilian: What did you do? Did someone come with you sometimes, or…?

Susana: Sometimes, later, yes, I made friends with an American woman who spoke both languages. And, so then...
Lilian: And she went with you?
Susana: Yes, and later, the thing is that I have very smart siblings who learned fast, they soon learned how to speak English, more or less. I would always try and take with me the one whose conference this was about. And so, they would act as interpreters.
Lilian: And they would interpret?
Susana: Themselves, as now teachers speak both languages, as a rule. But there are a few who don't want to, who can speak it, but don't want to speak Spanish. But I always take my kids. "I don't want to go to a meeting, Mom," they say. "But you have to come," I say. "If not, how am I going to know what they are telling me?" It's that sometimes one, say one understands a bit, right, but sometimes one gets stuck on something.

A factor that may also impact the situation is the difference among school levels. According to several of the women, at the elementary school parents seem to find it easier to communicate and language resources are more readily available than at the middle school or the high school. In Susana's account of her own participation in parents meetings, it becomes clear that, in her current interactions, there is a difference between the middle school and the elementary school, where the number of parents attending school functions is also larger. Sandra, Susana and Luisa refer to how much easier it is at the "little schools" ("*las chiquitas*" or "*la escuela chiquita*"), as the elementary schools are referred to, since they seem to make a greater effort to provide interpreters.

## Interpretation and Power Asymmetry

Linguistic mediation contributes to add an extra layer of asymmetry to institutional interactions which already are, inherently, asymmetrical in power (Drew & Heritage, 1992; Valdés, 2010). Besides, "adult immigrants are frequently subject to discrimination, which has a significant impact on social interactions," (Norton, 2013, p. 78). The situations considered below are examples of how the determination of who acts as interpreter or translator and how this is decided may have long-term consequences.

## Brenda's Boss

*"Ella era contratista y ella nos ayudó mucho."*
(She was a contractor, and she helped us a lot.)

Brenda recalls that the first person who acted as interpreter and translator for her was her boss at the time. The context of this conversation was Brenda's reference to how many more opportunities there were to be able to manage and make ends meet in the United States. In her experience, there were many more possibilities in the US to settle down, to buy your own house and even to pay medical bills. She contrasted the availability of credit and payment plans in the US to her experience in Mexico at the time her family moved away, where cash down was the only possibility. The follow-up prompt focused on resources.

The issue of language and the need for an interpreter arose as Brenda referred to the fact that although there are many opportunities in the US, there is still much groundwork to be done by being proactive, asking, and finding out. Brenda explains that in her early interactions with different institutions, she counted on the help of a contractor. Miriam Carrasco was the person who employed her and her husband to work in the fields; so, she was their boss and at the same time she used to translate for Brenda and help her fill out forms. Although they no longer work for her, sometimes Brenda still relies on her former boss for guidance and translation.

> Brenda: Pues, todo, todo tiene que saber uno y preguntar y cómo. Como para una cuenta en el hospital, cómo me pueden ayudar, dónde, y todo eso, ¿verdad? Pues, está difícil para uno también, pues, como no sabe el inglés. A veces, tiene uno que llevar intérprete, o decirles ahí que si alguien puede interpretarlo.
> Lilian: ¿A quién llevaba usted antes?
> Brenda: A una amiga, pues, la que me hacía el favor. Antes trabajábamos con una señora, se llama Miriam Carrasco. Ella era contratista y ella nos ayudó mucho, sí, mucho nos ayudó, nos daba el trabajo.
> Lilian: ¿Y le ayudaba como intérprete?
> Brenda: Sí, me ayudaba también. A veces, así, papeles de la escuela y ya iba y se los llevaba a ella que me los leyera. Como de esos, cuando mandan la aplicación para la comida, ella me ayudaba y me los llenaba, no más. Me interpretaba lo que decía ahí y yo le contestaba y me los llenaba. Ella también me ayudó mucho. Hasta la fecha todavía, cuando surge algo, un problema que traigo, "¡Ay! Pues, fíjese que tengo este problema, pues, ¿cómo lo puedo hacer?" Y luego me dice, "Pues, no, pues, mire, que vamos a hacerle de este modo y de este otro." Ella sí me ayuda mucho. La conocí cuando recién llegamos. Ella es muy buena persona, ella y su esposo, son muy, muy

serviciales. Y, pues, ella es ciudadana de aquí. Ella es nacida aquí. No más su esposo, no, pero yo creo también por eso, ella es muy buena mujer. Como que entiende. Y siempre nos anda preguntando: "¿Cómo está? ¿No necesita nada?" "No, pues, estamos bien." Sí.

Lilian: ¿Ya no trabaja para ella?

Brenda: No, ella se salió y ella se puso a cuidar niños de estos que tiene el gobierno, de esos. Ya no quizo andar en el "field", también.

Brenda: Well, everything, everything, one has to know and ask, and how. For instance, for an account at the hospital [to apply for credit], how they can help me, where, and all that, right? Well, it is hard also because one doesn't know English. Sometimes, one has to take an interpreter, or ask them there if someone can interpret.

Lilian: And who would you take before?

Brenda: A friend, one that would do me that favor. Before we used to work for a lady, Miriam Carrasco was her name. She was a contractor, and she helped us a lot. Yes, she helped us a lot. She gave us work.

Lilian: And she helped you by interpreting?

Brenda: Yes, she also helped me. Sometimes, when papers came from the school I would just go and take them for her to read them to me. Like those they send for the application for food, she would help me and fill them out. She would interpret what they said to me, and I would answer the questions, and she would fill them out. She also helped me a lot. Up until now, when anything comes up, a problem I have, "Oh, see I have this problem, so, what can I do?" And she says, "Well, now look, we are going to do it this way and the other." She helps me a lot. I met her when we had just arrived. She is a very good person. She and her husband are very helpful. And, well she is a citizen. She was born here. Only her husband isn't, but I think that is why she is such a good women. She understands. And she is always asking us, "How are you? Do you need anything?" "Oh, no, we are fine."

Lilian: And you don't work for her anymore?

Brenda: No, she quit, and now she takes care of children, those that the government has. Also, she didn't want to be in the fields any more.

The context of the second reference to Miriam Carrasco was an explanation of Brenda's strategy to find interpreters during and after a school meeting. The next prompt came right after Brenda referred to how she did to find help. The question turns to written communication from the school.

Lilian: Y ¿cómo fue al principio con los papeles y eso, cuando le llegaba un papel? Siempre tuvo a alguien que le ayudara, me dijo ¿no?

Brenda: Sí, como la hermana, esta, Miriam Carrasco, ella sí siempre, como ella fue nuestra contratista, desde que llegamos, con ella trabajamos. Y ella siempre me ofrecía su ayuda. Me decía: "En algo que usted necesite interpretación, pues, no más dígame." Y me llegaban papeles, así como los de la comida o papeles que tenía que llenar como para el "Medicaid" y esas cosas y ella me ayudaba a llenarlos. Siempre estaba ahí, continuamente con ella. Y sí, ella me ayudaba y me llenaba los papeles. Y ya, yo los regresaba y todo. Pues, cuando las mías todavía estaban en la escuela chiquita, todavía no sabían cómo llenarme un papel, verdad. Y ella sí me ayudó mucho. Por eso, así como otras personas me ayudaron, yo sí ayudaría a otra persona que necesitara ayuda.

Lilian: And, how was it at the beginning with the paperwork and that, when a paper arrived? You've always had someone to help you, you had told me, right?
Brenda: Yes, like sister, Miriam Carrasco, she always did, as she was our contractor, since the time we arrived, we worked for her. And she always offered me her help. She would tell me, "If you need interpretation for anything, well, you just tell me." And I would receive papers, such as those for the food or papers to fill out like for Medicaid and those things, and she would help me fill them out. I was always there, going to her. And yes, she would help me and she would fill out my papers. And then, I just returned them all. Well, when my girls were still at the little school, and didn't know how to fill out the papers for me yet. That is why, the same way other people helped me, and I would also help another person who needed help.

At the end, Brenda mentions the fact that once her daughters grew up, they were the ones who acted as interpreters when needed, and the ones who would help her fill out forms. At some point, most participants allude to their children adopting the role of translators.

# Children as Interpreters

**Norma—*Y otra de las cosas más tristes [era] que a veces cuando necesitaba interpretación, eran mis hijos que me traducían.***
**(And another of the saddest things was that sometimes, when I needed interpretation, it was my children who translated for me.)**

In her in-depth study on this topic, Orellana (2009) documents the multiple ways in which immigrant children serve their families as language and culture brokers.

Placing phone calls, taking and leaving messages, scheduling appointments, filling out credit card applications, negotiating sales purchases, soliciting social services, and communicating for their parents with teachers, medical personnel , and other authority figures are part of everyday life for the children whom you meet in this book. (p. 1)

Several participants mentioned the fact that their own children had been asked to interpret for them; and some, namely, Susana, Brenda, and Sandra, express their pride in their children's skills. This arrangement was not favored by most women, who objected to their children taking up that role. In some cases, they did not believe their children were up to the task, because they were either too young and may not have understood exactly the ideas being discussed, or they were newly arrived in the US and could barely speak or understand English themselves. Especially if the communication at hand had to do with a situation involving the same child who might be asked to act as interpreter, Luisa, Silvia, Brenda and Norma expressed their preference for having someone else do the interpreting rather than the child who was the subject of the conversation.

## Norma's Sons

### Norma—*Se les hacía difícil cómo traducirlo.*
### (It was hard for them to translate.)

At different points of her account, Norma underscores the amount of effort she put into learning English through her work with English-speaking employers, so that now she can communicate in English, a bit better at least. But, she mentions how, at first, her sons had to act as interpreters, and she felt bad for them because they knew very little English at the time and did not always understand everything clearly.

> Lilian: Y ellos ¿habían ido a la escuela en México?
> Norma: Sí, el más grande vino a tercer grado. Estuvo en "kinder", primero, segundo…
> Lilian: Y ¿era mucho el contraste con cómo era la escuela allá?
> Norma: Sí, bastante fuerte porque yo podía ir. . . Allá no hay camión. Uno va y deja sus niños en la escuela y los recoge a la hora de salida. Entonces, siempre cuando yo iba por la tarde tenía la oportunidad de platicar un poquito con la maestra y le podía entender y podíamos conversar. Y aquí pues, no. Nada más me le quedaba viendo al maestro. Y otra de las cosas más tristes que a veces se me hacía, que a veces cuando necesitaba interpretación, eran mis hijos que me traducían. Y ellos se esforzaban, se esforzaban, porque ellos mismos me decían que no sabían mucho o que no sabían cómo traducirlo. Se les hacía difícil cómo traducirlo.
> Lilian: ¿En qué año era esto? Usted me dijo, en el noventa y…
> Norma: Pues, vine en el noventa y seis.
> Lilian: Se nota que ha cambiado bastante.

Norma: Pues, un poquito, por lo menos puedo, al menos, si ellos no hablan español, no podré conversar con ellos mucho, pero puedo entender qué quieren y decirles qué quiero yo, y antes no podía.

Lilian: And had they attended school in Mexico?
Norma: Yes, my older son came to third grade. He had done kindergarten, first and second.
Lilian: And was there a lot of contrast with how school was over there?
Norma: Yes, quite a marked contrast because I could go. . . Over there, there was no school bus. One goes and drops the kids off at the school and picks them up at the end of the day. So then, when I went in the afternoon I always had a chance to speak with the teacher a bit, and I could understand her, and we could talk. And here, well, no. I would just be looking at the teacher. And another of the saddest things was that sometimes, when I needed interpretation, it was my children who translated for me. And they made an effort, because they would tell me themselves that they didn't know much or that they didn't know how to translate it. It was hard for them to translate.
Lilian: What year was this, you told me, ninety?
Norma: Well, I arrived in 1996.
Lilian: It shows it has changed quite a bit.
Norma: Well, a bit, at least I can, at least if they don't speak Spanish, I may not be able to talk a lot with them, but I can understand what they want and tell them what I want; and before, I couldn't.

In this context, Norma introduces the dual frame of reference mentioned in the literature, by establishing a contrast between her situation in her place of origin and her new situation in the new context after immigration (M. Suárez-Orozco, 1990; Zentgraf, 2002). Norma remembers how different it was for her when she had just moved to the US, because in Mexico she used to talk to the teacher when she dropped off or picked up her children, but this was no longer possible, and when the teacher spoke to her she could not reply. Just after this, Norma describes how at first she despaired when she did not understand anything of what was being said to her. She comments that, in her frustration, at times she felt so bad that she had even wished she had been born here, so that she could speak and understand English. However, she explains, this was only a sign of her anxiety, since she is very proud of her Mexican culture, and shares how important it was for her to be asked to teach Mexican folklore ballet at her daughter's elementary school. Norma is now in charge of this extracurricular activity where she is able to share this part of her cultural heritage with the children she teaches.

## Brenda's Daughter: An Advocate for her Mother

**Brenda—*Como a los ocho años ella ya empezó a interpretar.*
(When she was about eight years old she already started
interpreting.)**

Immigrant children are often called on to assume the role and responsibilities
of problem-solvers for their families by mediating as interpreters. Such is the
case of Brenda's eldest daughter, Sara. Brenda explains how vulnerable a person who does not speak English is, for example, when at the mercy of a judge.
Later, she explains that she is referring to an occasion when she had to appear
in traffic court to appeal a ticket she had received for not carrying her current
insurance papers with her at the time she was stopped, even though she had
recently renewed her auto insurance.

> Pues, como para una corte, pues también está difícil para uno, porque si el juez no
> habla español y uno tampoco.... no habla el inglés, pues, entonces, ahí el juez va
> a hacer con uno lo que … lo que mejor le convenga, verdad. Ni cómo defenderse
> uno. Y entonces, pues, buscar una persona que hablara los dos idiomas. A veces, me
> llevaba yo a una de mis hijas y ya ella me decía: "Mamá, el juez dice esto y esto otro."
> "Ya, no, m'hija, dígale que … pues, yo voy a pagar lo que sea, pues, de todos modos
> el hecho ya está hecho." No, pues, en una corte siempre está más difícil porque ahí
> casi es lo que el juez diga. Sí, pero de todos modos sí se puede defender uno también,
> verdad. Pues, simplemente con llevar sus papeles todos en orden.

> Well, in a court, it's also difficult for one, because if the judge doesn't speak Spanish,
> and one doesn't speak English either, well, then, there the judge will do with one
> whatever is most convenient for him, right. No way will one be able to defend one-
> self. And then, well, to find a person that speaks both languages. Sometimes, I'd take
> one of my daughters, and she would say to me, "Mom, the judge says this and this."
> "Well, no, honey, tell him … well, that I will pay whatever it is, since the deed is
> done." Well, no, in a court it is always more difficult because there it's whatever the
> judge says. But anyway, one can defend oneself too, right? Well, simply by having all
> your papers in order.

Brenda's account of her experience in traffic court highlights the importance
of the job done by her daughters when acting as interpreters. As Brenda points
out, it would have been hard for her to defend herself and appeal a ticket without the mediation of a reliable interpreter, such as her eldest daughter, Sara.

> Porque una vez sí me pasó que tenía la aseguranza aquí. Y me paró porque, no venía
> muy recio, porque a mí no me gusta correr recio, pero yo venía como a 5 más arriba.

Pues, luego que me estaba cobrando creo que 45, no me acuerdo cuánto. Y le dije a mi hija en la corte: "No, pues, dígale que en tal tiempo me paró y la aseguranza está de tal tiempo. Es no más que no la traía ahí, pero..." Y ya le dijo ella al juez y dijo: "Ok." Y luego él ya miró ahí que sí la tenía. No más en ese rato no la traía. Sí, pues, si no se defiende uno y no sabe, pues, ahí tiene uno que pagar.

Because once this happened to me that I had my insurance here. And they stopped me, not because I was going too fast, because I don't like to drive fast, but I was going about five above. But, then he was charging me I think it was 45, I can't remember how much. And at the (traffic) court I told my daughter: "No, well, tell him that this is the date he stopped me and the insurance was effective at that date. It's just that I wasn't carrying it with me, but..." And she told the judge, and he said: "Ok." And then he saw there that I did have it. I just didn't have it at that time with me. So, yes, if one doesn't defend oneself, and doesn't know, well, one has to pay.

Although the context here is not that of the schools, this situation parallels one described in detail in an earlier chapter, in which Brenda's eldest daughter plays a similar role as an interpreter, mediator and advocate in an interaction with a figure of authority at the school.

The context of the first mention of one of her daughters acting as interpreter is a question on who were the first people in the school Brenda would usually talk to, in her first visits. She explains that when teachers were bilingual, there was no problem, but that when the teachers were not bilingual, the school would seek someone to interpret, and that, later on, her own daughters would be her interpreters.

> Brenda: Sí, pues, siempre ella nos ha tratado aquí de poner personas bilingües al frente, verdad, y, pues, así es más fácil para uno también.
> Lilian: Y ¿con la maestra, y los maestros, tenía lo mismo?
> Brenda: Y, con los maestros, cuando no eran bilingües los maestros, siempre me ponían una persona... O, ya cuando mi hija ya empezó a desempeñar los dos idiomas, porque la puse en bilingüe, ya empezó a desempeñar los dos; ya ella era la que me interpretaba.
> Lilian: ¿A qué edad empezó ella a interpretar, cuando ya podía?
> Brenda: Que sería, como a los ocho años ella ya empezó a interpretar.
> Lilian: La mayor.
> Brenda: Sí, la mayor.

> Brenda: Yes, well, she has always tried to put a bilingual person here in the front [office] for us, right, and, well, that way it's easier for us too.
> Lilian: And, with the teacher, or teachers, did you have the same?
> Brenda: And, with the teachers, when teachers weren't bilingual, they always put a person there... Or, when mi daughter already started to develop both languages,

because I put her in bilingual, she started developing both; she was the one who interpreted.

Lilian: How old was she when she started interpreting, when she was able to?

Brenda: What would she have been? When she was about eight years old she already started interpreting.

Lilian: The eldest.

Brenda: Yes, the eldest.

The second reference to children acting as interpreters was made by Brenda after describing being too embarrassed to speak up to offer her opinion in public meetings. In this case Brenda states the need to have a third person interpret at the schools once children grow up, in case there may be a temptation on the part of the student (one of her daughters) acting as an interpreter to misrepresent the teacher's words in order to defend her own interests, and prevent her mother from understanding exactly what is being said about her performance or behavior at school.

Lilian: ¿Y cuando tenía alguna cosa que consultar?

Brenda: Cuando tenía algo que preguntarles, así, pues si no tenían … si la maestra no sabía inglés y español, me ponían otra persona que hablara español. Como hasta ahorita, lo estamos haciendo así. Porque a veces, sus hijos de uno, dicen … "No, pues, si la maestra está diciendo algo y luego tú no me dices cómo es", verdad. Porque si la maestra no sabe español y luego yo no sé inglés, pues, mi hija me va a decir: "Oiga, Ma, pues, la maestra dice que voy bien," verdad. *(laughs)*

Lilian: Sí, porque está más grande.

Brenda: Pues, sí. Y ya son más inteligentes. *(laughs)* Sí, no, si a veces sí nos ponen personas así que son bilingües.

Lilian: And when you had questions?

Brenda: When I had something I needed to ask, then, well if they didn't have … if the teacher didn't know English and Spanish, they would provide another person who spoke Spanish. Right up till now we are doing that way. Because sometimes one's own children say, "No … well, if the teacher is saying something and then you are not telling it to me exactly as it is," right? Because if the teacher doesn't know Spanish and, then, I don't know English, well, my daughter is going to tell me, "Listen, Mom, well, the teacher says I'm doing well," right? *(laughs)*

Lilian: Yes, because she is older.

Brenda: Well, yes, and they are smarter. *(laughs)* Yes, sometimes they do provide someone who is bilingual.

In marked contrast to this comment on how in the past she might not have trusted as an interpreter the same child whose situation was being discussed,

Brenda refers to how now she often seeks the aid of her eldest daughter, Sara, who has already graduated from high school, as a reliable interpreter. More than once Brenda makes a point of highlighting how her three children benefited from the bilingual program they were enrolled in since this has allowed them to become skillful interpreters.

# Interpreters Provided by the School

The following cases illustrate how the outcome of critical decisions may be affected by the power asymmetry which, although present in most institutional situations, is highly intensified if the person serving as interpreter is also acting in an official capacity. In both these instances, it was a representative of the school who served as interpreter and conveyed a strong recommendation for a specific course of action.

## Norma's Name Change

**Norma—*"Estás en Estados Unidos ahora [...] Tú necesitas llevar el mismo apellido de tus hijos."***
("You are in the United States now," she said. "You need to use the same last name as your children.")

Norma's experience probably constitutes an extreme example of how an important decision may be taken during the process of filling out forms at a school, in a new country, as a new arrival, in a situation of vulnerability and without enough information. The first time Norma visited her children's school, when she had just arrived in the US, the wife of her husband's boss—who also happened to work at the school—acted as her interpreter. Norma's vulnerability in these early days is comparable to that experienced by Brenda, whose boss was the person entrusted with filling out forms for her and acting as interpreter and mediator in many of her interactions.

Norma's most salient memory of the day of her first visit to her children's school was that she was urged to permanently change the last name she had used until then, her own family name, or maiden name, to her husband's last name. Through the interpreter, the school secretary told her she needed to do so because, *"es que estás en Estados Unidos ahora"* (now you are in the United States). Norma was informed that from then on she always was to sign using the same name as her children. Adopting her husband's last name was not presented as a suggestion, or as an option among others, but as a common practice, and almost a requirement that she needed to comply with in order to function successfully in US society.

> Yo no conocía a nadie ahí. Pero mi esposo trabajaba en una lechería y el dueño de la lechería, su esposa trabajaba en la escuela. Entonces, cuando se enteraron que nosotros … que mi esposo vino con nosotros y eso, ella fue a mi casa y me dijo que ella me ayudaba para poner los niños en la escuela. Y sí, y ella nos tradujo. Asique no fui sola; ella fue conmigo. Pero una cosa que sí me acuerdo mucho es que yo… Mi apellido es Contreras, y en México cuando uno se casa, es Norma Contreras de Suárez. Entonces cuando yo vine aquí, que le preguntan a uno los datos para llenar las formas y todo, me preguntaron cómo se llamaban los niños y ya les dije; y luego, cómo me llamaba yo, y yo les dije que yo era Norma Contreras. Y me dijo la secretaria— bueno, era todo traducido, esta señora me estaba traduciendo y dice: "y es que estás en Estados Unidos ahora, no eres Contreras, eres Suárez. Y siempre tienes que firmar 'Suárez'". Sí. Me dijo: "Tú necesitas llevar el mismo apellido de tus hijos." Y desde entonces me acostumbré y lo cambié. Y ahora que ya me divorcié, se me hace difícil dejarlo, porque todos mis papeles, mi licencia, todo es "Suárez".

> I didn't know anyone there. But my husband worked at a dairy and the owner's wife worked at the school. So, when they found out that my husband had come with us, she went to my home and told me that she would help me to put my children in school. And yes, she translated for us. So I didn't go alone, she came with me. But one thing that I do remember well is that I… My last name is Contreras, and in Mexico, when one gets married, one is called Norma Contreras de Suárez. Then when I came here, when they ask you your information to fill the forms and all, they asked me my children's names, and I told them; and then, my name, and I told them that I was Norma Contreras. And the secretary told me—well, it was all translated, this lady was translating for me and she says: "It's that you are in the United States now. You are not Contreras, you are Suárez. And you always have to sign 'Suárez.'" Yes, she said: "You need to use the same last name as your children." And since then I got used to it, and I changed it. And now that I'm already divorced, it is hard to change it, because all my papers, my license, all say "Suárez."

In Norma's account of her first experience interacting with the schools in the United States, this was the first memory that came to mind, and one she described in great detail. Norma explains how she adapted to using her husband's name, and that she has maintained it even after her divorce because all her papers and documentation now bare her husband's last name. Norma's acceptance of such a drastic change is only understandable within the context offered in the narratives in this study, with the detailed descriptions of how unsettling it is to start anew with social interactions which follow a completely different set of rules.

In this situation, power asymmetry is intensified by the fact that Norma was accompanied by the wife of her husband's boss, who not only acted as interpreter but was also a school employee, and may be seen as acting as gatekeeper to the school. It is important to note that at the time of the interviews, Norma does not come across as a shy person, but rather appears to be one of the most outspoken, assertive and self-assured women in the group of participants.

## Patricia Signs the Forms

### *"Me los leyó y nada más lo firmé todo."*
(So, he read them to me and I just signed them all.)

Another example of the centrality of translation in the decision-making processes involving immigrant families and of the relevance of this resource to the access to information is offered by Patricia. In this case, the issue of how translation is handled arises in the context of Patricia's account of a visit to the school to discuss diagnostic testing for disabilities for one of her sons, Pedro, who is in kindergarten at the time.

> Lilian: Y ¿la atienden siempre bien cuando va?
> Patricia: Sí, siempre son muy amables, las señoras, cuando va uno de visita también. Como, ¿qué día fue? El jueves fui también a una visita para el niño, porque no puede hablar todavía bien y ya tiene cinco años. Y me habían mandado decir que fuera, el maestro, para llenar unos papeles. Pero, no, pues, estuvo bien. Ya fui y ahí llené ahí mismo, porque eran varios. Y yo dije: "Pues, por qué no me los manda para la casa, así puedo firmarlos." Pero, no, ya miré que sí eran muchos y hay veces que yo … esos papeles … hay veces que no vienen en español.
> Lilian: ¿Ah, estos estaban todos en inglés?
> Patricia: Pues, me los leyó él y yo nada más lo firmé todo.
> Lilian: Ah ¿Para qué era?
> Patricia: Era para que le hicieran otro examen sobre el habla, porque le hicieron uno y salió que no podía hablar bien. Y ese papel era para firmarlo y tenía preguntas así como: qué era lo que él hacía y que no podía hablar; o si había tenido algún problema que por eso que no podía hablar bien. "Pero, no," le digo, "es que él ya es así. Ya es así que él no ha podido hablar bien."

> Lilian: And do they always help you when you go?
> Patricia: Yes, they are always very kind, the ladies, when one visits also. Like, when was it? On Thursday I went to visit about my son, because he can't speak well and he

is already five years old. And they had sent word for me to go, the teacher, to fill out some papers. But, no, it was fine. And I went and there I filled them out right there, because there were quite a few. And I said, "Well, why don't you send them home to me, so that I can sign them." But, no, and I saw that yes, they were a lot, and there are times that I... those papers ... there are times that they don't come in Spanish.
Lilian: Oh, so these were all in English?
Patricia: So, he read them to me and I just signed them all.
Lilian: Oh, and what were they for?
Patricia: It was for them to give him another exam for his speech, because they gave him one and it came out that he couldn't speak well. And this paper was to sign, and it had questions like, about what it is that he does, that he can't speak; or if he had had any problem that may be why he can't speak well. "But, no," I said, "it's that he is like that. He's just like that, that he hasn't been able to speak well."

Patricia continues explaining how her middle son has problems pronouncing some sounds, and how he had already been tested once. She had been called to the school that same week, and this time there were many more papers to sign, with questions about the child's behavior and problems that might be related to his speech. Patricia mentions how, since she noticed there were a lot of forms, and they were all in English, she had asked the teacher if he could send them home for her to sign. This would suggest that she was asking if she could have more time to read them carefully before signing them, but the teacher read them out to her instead. As they were in English, he translated them for her in the process, and asked her to just give him the answers, so that he could fill out the forms and respond to the questionnaires, and she could sign them all then and there.

Patricia goes on to explain that what she had authorized at that time was a more in-depth exam. When asked if she had been informed about what might happen after her child was submitted to the testing or exam, Patricia noted that these have not been conducted yet, but she had not received any information, before signing all the paperwork, on the consequences of the results of the tests for her child. Then she went into greater detail about the reasons for the exam.

Patricia: Batallaba mucho antes, y ahorita ya lo puede pronunciar, pero hay veces que se le va y no puede. Pero no, sí, fui a eso, fui a llenar... Y así cosas, preguntas que me hicieron de él y su comportamiento. Pues sí, para que ellos puedan hacerle un examen más ... más a fondo de a ver por qué no puede hablar bien.
Lilian: ¿Y le explicaron qué pasaría después del examen, o...?
Patricia: Pues, todavía no se lo hacen. No más, para eso querían para que yo autorizara, autorizara para que le hicieran otro examen.

Lilian: Claro.

Patricia: Y no, le digo, está bien, todo por bien de ellos, verdad. Para que puedan hablar mejor. Es que cambia unas palabras. Como unas letras no las puede pronunciar,
no le salen bien. Sí, no es como que le falta, pues, no sé por qué no podrá pronunciar
bien unas letras, como la "r" la pronuncia por la "d". Entonces no puede hacer bien
las pronunciaciones. Pero, no, él puede hablar bien y decir, no más porque habla así.

Lilian: ¿Y era el maestro de él?

Patricia: Sí, es el maestro de él.

Lilian: Habló con él, no habló con otra persona.

Patricia: No, nada más con él.


Patricia: He used to struggle a lot before, and now he can pronounce it, but there are
times when he can't. But, yes, I went to do that, I went to fill out … and things like,
questions they asked me about him and his behavior. Well, yes, for them to be able to
conduct another exam, more in depth, to see why he can't speak well.

Lilian: And did they explain what would happen after the exam, or…?

Patricia: Well, they haven't done it yet. That's why; they just wanted me to authorize
it, so that they could conduct another exam.

Lilian: I see.

Patricia: And, I say, it's alright, it's all for their good, right. For them to be able to
speak better. It's that he changes some words. Some letters, it's like he can't pronounce them; he doesn't get them right. Yes, it's not like he is missing … well, I don't
know why he can't pronounce some letters, like the "r" he pronounces it like a "d".
Then he can't pronounce well. But, no, he can speak well and say things, it's just that
he speaks like that.

Lilian: And was this his teacher?

Patricia: Yes, it's his teacher.

Lilian: And you spoke with him; you didn't speak with anyone else.

Patricia: No, just with him.


Since this is Patricia's first experience with diagnostic testing, these are completely new circumstances in her relation to the educational institutions in
the US. Above all, the fact that she was not informed about the possible
consequences of the test results before signing the authorization forms renders
this decision-making process blind. Just as in Norma's case, in this incident it
is worth noting the multiple roles adopted by an authority figure. The person
translating for her, and conveying the information, expressed in a specific
tone, that would determine a consequential decision to be made on the spur
of the moment is someone associated with the school, who also happens to be
the same person who is making the recommendation for a certain course of
action, without offering other options. Regardless of whether the diagnostic
testing was the right decision or not at the time, what relevant information is

offered and by whom, as well as how it is presented, and how the decision is made are all critical factors which may weigh heavily on an important decision. In these circumstances, the asymmetry already existing in a situation of power imbalance is enhanced in such a way that it is likely to critically affect the decision-making process.

# References

Drew, P., & Heritage, J. (Eds.). (1992). *Talk at work*. Cambridge: Cambridge University Press.

Norton, B. (2013). *Identity and language learning: Extending the conversation* (2nd ed.). Tonawanda, NY: Multilingual Matters.

Orellana, M. (2009). *Translating childhoods: Immigrant youth, language, and culture*. New Brunswick, NJ: Rutgers University Press.

Suárez-Orozco, M. (1990). Migration and education: United States-Europe comparisons. In G. De Vos & M. Suárez-Orozco (Eds.), *Status inequality: The self in culture* (pp. 265–287). Newbury Park, CA: Sage.

Valdés, G. (2010). *Expanding definitions of giftedness: The case of young interpreters from immigrant communities*. New York, NY: Routledge.

Venuti, L. (1995). *The translator's invisibility: A history of translation*. New York, NY: Routledge.

Zentgraf, K. (2002). Immigration and women's empowerment: Salvadorans in Los Angeles. *Gender & Society, 16*(5), 625–646.

# PART IV

# FROM VULNERABILITY TO COMMUNAL AGENCY: FINDING, DEVELOPING AND BECOMING RESOURCES

# · 9 ·

# CRITICAL LINGUISTIC AGENCY

*Schools controlled by the dominant group comprise one important location where this di-*
*mension of the struggle for maternal empowerment occurs. In contrast to middle-class*
*children, whose educational experiences affirm their mothers' middle-class values, culture,*
*and authority, African-American, Latino, Asian-American and Native American children*
*typically receive an education that derogates their mothers' perspective. For example, the*
*struggles over bilingual education in Latino communities are about much more than retaining*
*Spanish as a second language. Speaking the language of one's childhood is a way of retaining*
*the entire culture and honoring the mother teaching that culture.* (Collins, 1994, p. 66)

Critical linguistic agency (Cibils, 2011) is defined here within the context
of critical theory as the proactive approach adopted by social actors—such
as the immigrant women in this study—in the negotiation of social spaces
with respect to access, development and maintenance of linguistic resources.
Why is it "critical" linguistic agency? As is the case for critical theory, in part
"critical" alludes to its contextualization, to intersectionality and attention
to social locations. "Critical" here implies a focus on social actors who would
often be marginalized or left out from so-called universal theoretical considerations, and their perspectives (Young, 1990, pp. 3–4). The qualifier also serves
to distinguish this concept from the traditional use of the term "agency" in
grammar and semantics. Linguistic agency, in this context, becomes actual-

ized by the participants in a variety of initiatives, some very specific and some broader, namely: in the energy directed to securing a translator, and sometimes, in the choice of who will play that role; in the efforts made to learn English; in the advocacy in favor of their children's biliteracy development; and, in the maintenance of Spanish as their home language, even when they may be instructed to only speak English to their children. The women in this study, for example, embrace their critical linguistic agency when they actively choose a bilingual program for their children and recognize its benefits but also when they struggle against all the odds and make extraordinary efforts to acquire the language of their new context.

Further, the concept of critical linguistic agency presupposes the workings of linguistic ideology, manifested, for example, in attitudes towards different languages. Taking into account linguistic ideology implies acknowledging the connection between linguistic practices and the underlying sociopolitical structures which encourage them and sustain them (García, 2009). In other words, it involves recognizing that "attitudes, values, and beliefs about language are always ideological, and are enmeshed in social systems of domination and subordination of groups, relating to ethnicity, class, and gender" (García, 2009, p. 84). Linguistic ideology is apparent in the schools, for example, in the value assigned to students' languages when different from English.

García (2009) stresses the difference that might be made by schools, depending on the language ideology they embrace: "The language choices available to children and their parents, as well as the discursive practices that are encouraged and supported in school, have an important impact on children's identity and their possibilities of developing agency or resisting" (p. 84). For instance, when a school system assumes a homogenizing and assimilative role, it may unknowingly become an instrument of symbolic violence (Bourdieu, 1991), given that "the dominant ideas are naturally assumed and the oppressed recognizes the dominant group as superior" (García, 2009, p. 84). Thus, the instances of critical linguistic agency in the stories of the immigrant women featured in this chapter mostly involve conflict with these structural assimilative forces. By exploring these moments of linguistic resistance and choice, we capture a glimpse of the tensions present in the articulation of agency and structure, as manifested in the micro processes of everyday interactions between social actors, of individuals and communities as they relate to representatives of institutions, in this case within the educational system.

# Seeking Resources in the Community

As García (2009) reminds us, "language is a place of resistance, of power and of solidarity" (p. 84). Each of these facets of language is illustrated in the seven women's narratives. Paradoxically, in the same school, one day a mother may experience the consequences of symbolic violence when faced with a teacher who refuses to speak Spanish even if he or she can speak it, while on her following visit she may experience linguistic solidarity, when a member of the school staff goes out of her way to offer her services as an interpreter, or to find someone who may serve in this role. The two experiences may alternate within a same meeting, for instance, in the case of the group of Spanish-speaking mothers virtually excluded from participating in a meeting until the very end when another mother, who is bilingual, is asked by the group to intervene on their behalf and summarize what has been discussed up to that point. In the midst of these incidents, which can be interpreted as instances of symbolic violence, emerge the most striking examples of resourcefulness and agency.

## Brenda—*Primero echo el ojo a ver cuál habla español.*
## (First I look around to see which one of them speaks Spanish.)

The context of the exchange that follows is Brenda's discussion of different types of informative meetings, and later, more specifically, of her daughter's involvement in some types of sports and not in others. The question followed up on a previous conversation when Brenda had remarked that sometimes she attended these meetings but other times she was discouraged and thought it was pointless, "What for … if I don't understand anything." As described earlier, on several occasions, Brenda recounts how during school meetings often she would spend most of her time trying to figure out who would be the best person to ask for a translation of the whole event, once it was over.

> Lilian: Y las … estas reuniones que hacen para informar, usted a veces va. Me decía que a veces va y a veces dice, "para qué si no…"
> Brenda: … Si no les entiendo. Sí, pues, a veces sí como cuando va a entrar al basquet. Hacen sus reuniones y ya nos dicen: "Tales y tales días van a jugar" y que si las podemos llevar y esto y lo otro. Y, luego, ya, palabras así que yo no entiendo, entonces, ya le pregunto a la maestra. Y ya me dice: "Pues, sí, vamos a meter tantos niños … (*as if starting an enumeration*) y los juegos van a ser tal y tal fecha … a tales horas…" Y ya me dice todo, verdad, y pues si ya mi hija quiere entrar, pues, entonces ya la anoto. Pero en las reuniones, pues, a veces yo también no más pelo los ojos pues, "¿qué es-

tarán hablando?" Pero, mientras están ahí yo les estoy echando el ojo a ver cuál me puede informar, verdad? *(laughs, aware of her resourcefulness)*.
Lilian: *(laughs)* Sí.
Brenda: Y ya después de la reunión, entonces, ya voy con esa maestra y ya le digo: "maestra, yo no entendí aquí, en esto, o en lo otro." Y ya ella me explica de cómo está el juego y las horas, el tiempo y qué días y todo.

Lilian: And the ... these meetings that they have for information, you sometimes go, but you were saying that sometimes you thought "what for if I don't..."
Brenda: ... if I don't understand them. Yes, well, sometimes yes. For example, when she is going to start basketball, they have their meetings and they tell us then: "Such and such days they are going to be playing" and that if we can drive them there, and this and that. And then, words that I don't understand, and so I ask the teacher. And she tells me: "Well, yes, we are going to take so many kids ... *(as if starting an enumeration)* and the games are going to be on such and such dates and at such times. And she tells me everything, right? So if my daughter wants to join, well, I register her. But at the meetings, well, sometimes I just keep my eyes peeled, thinking: "What could they be saying?" But while they are there, I am looking around trying to figure out who can give me the information, right? *(laughs, aware of her resourcefulness)*
Lilian: *(laughs)* Yes.
Brenda: And then after the meeting, I go straight to that teacher and I say, "I didn't understand this, and that" and she explains it to me, about practice, the times and days.

When asked to expand on this, Brenda explains how she figures out who to ask, by looking for any sign that points to a person knowing Spanish. There are some people who use only English during their presentation, but then there are others who intersperse a word in Spanish here and there. Then, that person will be who she seeks out at the end of the meeting.

Lilian: Usted se las arregla para encontrar la información.
Brenda: Sí, es que yo, como le digo, durante la conferencia estoy mirando la que ... porque hay personas así que ... que están hablando puro inglés pero luego hay otras que dicen una que otra palabra en español y entonces digo: "No, pues, esta sí habla español." De las mismas de ahí, verdad. Entonces, ya, acabándose la conferencia ya la ... la busco y le digo: "No, maestra, yo no entendí aquí, en esto" y ya me explica.
Lilian: Pero siempre ha tenido a alguien o si no lo busca.
Brenda: No, pues, como le digo, primero echo el ojo a ver cuál *(laughs)* ... cuál habla español. Aha, y si por algo no hay o así, yo le pregunto a mi hija, porque también va conmigo. Le digo: "M'hija, pues, yo no entendí aquí en esto, y en esto y lo otro" "No, mira, Mami, te dicen así y esto hacer..." Y, pues, ya, ya más o menos.

Lilian: So you manage to get a hold of the information.

Brenda: Yes, it's that, as I said, during the meeting I am looking around to see who …
because there are some people that … that are speaking only English but then there
are others who mix in one or two words in Spanish, and so I say: "Ah, well, she does
speak Spanish." The same women from there, right. So, once the meeting is over, I
go and look for her and ask her, the teacher: "I didn't understand this point and that,"
and she explains it to me.

Lilian: So you have always had someone or if not you look for someone.

Brenda: No, well, as I said, first I look around to see which one *(laughs)* which one of
them speaks Spanish. And if, by chance, there isn't anyone or something, I ask my
daughter, because she also goes with me. I tell her, "Honey, well, I didn't understand
this and this and that and the other." "Well, Mom, they are telling you this and to do
that…" So, more or less, then.

Finally, Brenda mentions how other times, when for some reason she doesn't
find anyone to translate for her at the end of a meeting, she turns to one of her
daughters for an explanation of what was discussed.

## Luisa—*Yo quiero que me lean bien todo.*
## (I want them to read it all out to me.)

Luisa explains how when she received letters from the school she would seek
help from neighbors. The daughters of her neighbor living across the street
from her, who are just a few years older than her sons, would often translate
for her. Luisa says her sons could understand but that they would not give
her all the details, instead they would just give her the gist. She trusted these
neighbors because they would tell her word for word what the letter said and
not leave out any information. Luisa made a point of finding someone who
would transmit effectively and thoroughly the communications received from
the school, in order to make informed decisions on whatever matter was at
hand.

Lilian: Me estaba diciendo que buscaba ayuda a veces para que le digan qué es lo que
necesitaba, cuando le mandaban a decir algo de la escuela. ¿Cómo hacía? ¿Cómo se
las arreglaba?

Luisa: Para que me ayudaran, para leer las cartas, y todo. Bueno, cuando estaba mi esposo, mi esposo sabía ¿verdad? Pero, como le digo, mi esposo no tenía tanta paciencia *(a sigh seems to stress the word)* para eso. No faltaba quien, como las muchachas,
enseguida me ayudaban. Las de en frente, también. Hay muchachas ya más grandes
que mis hijos y ellas me ayudaban, hasta porque, no sé si sepa, que ¿ya ve como man-
dan papeles? Muchas cartas que leer y muchos papeles que firmar, ¿verdad? Entonces,
las muchachas me ayudaban y luego … porque mi hijo el más grande cuando creció,

él ya sabía inglés, pero no me ayudaba igual, no me ayudaba bien. Me ayudaba ... me decía como ... no me decía bien las cosas de lo que decía la carta ...si no como, "pues, dice que no más le firmes porque vamos a jugar" (*imitating his casual tone*) y así, pero no todo bien. Entonces yo quería que me leyeran bien, todo. Igual que cuando mandaban cartas que les dice que si los dejo ver una película de violencia o que les hablen de sexo, de drogas, de todo, ¿verdad? Yo quiero que me lean bien todo. Y ellos no podían, así, o sea no me dicen todo completo. Y siempre yo busco a las muchachas de allá (*pointing out the window, in the direction of their house*), ellas, mis vecinas. O las de en frente porque ya son, ya están más grandes que mis hijos y me explican bien. Era la forma en que yo podía saber lo que me estaban mandando decir en los papeles.

Lilian: You were telling me that you sometimes looked for help to tell you what you needed, when they sent you something from the school. How would you do it? How did you manage?
Luisa: To help me read letters, and all. Well, when my husband was here, he knew, right? But, as I said, my husband wasn't too patient for that. There was always someone, like the girls, they would help me right always. The girls across the street, also. There are some girls that are older than my sons, and they helped me, because... I don't know if you know, but, you know how they send papers? Many letters to read and papers to sign, right? So, the girls would help me and then ... because my son, the older on when he grew up, he already knew English, but he wouldn't help me in the same way; he didn't help me well. He helped me ... he would say like ... he wouldn't tell me properly the things that the letter said ... instead he would like, "Well, it just says for you to sign because we are going to play," (*imitating his casual tone*) but he wouldn't tell me everything right. So I wanted someone to read it all, read it well. Just as when they sent letters asking if I allowed them to watch a movie with violence, or discussing sex, or about drugs, all that, right? I want them to read it all well to me. And they couldn't, like that, or they don't tell me everything fully. And I always seek the girls from over there (*pointing out the window, in the direction of their house*), them, my neighbors. Or the girls from across the street, because they are already, they are older than my sons and they explain it all well. It was the way that I could find out what they were telling me in the papers they sent me.

Not any translation will do; it needs to be complete and accurate. Luisa exercises her linguistic agency in her search among the people in her community for translators who will offer a thorough and careful rendering of the documents she needs to sign. Linguistic resources become communal resources, shared in solidarity.

# Learning English:
# Efforts Made to Attend English Classes

An eagerness to learn English emerges from all the narratives, as well as de-tailed accounts of the efforts made in that direction. The women's stories often stress the need to learn English, the lack of opportunities, and the obsta-cles they have to overcome to attend English classes. As Norton (2013) ex-plains, immigrant women often have few chances of acquiring the language of the new country through real life interactions given the types of job opportu-nities they encounter. They often find themselves in the paradoxical situation of needing to learn the language of the new context in order to participate fully in it and access important resources, while at the same time being unable to participate in everyday practices from which they would be able to learn faster through those same valued but inaccessible institutional interactions (Norton, 2013, p. 79). Opportunities for communication are often "limited to bureaucratic and gate-keeping encounters in which learners are doubly dis-advantaged by their limited competence in the target language as well as the power imbalance between the learners and their interlocutors" (p. 79).

According to Luisa, most language programs are offered during the sum-mer, which coincides with the time of year when there are more openings for agricultural work in that area. Most interviewees would be working long hours in the fields or the processing plants for the harvest. Besides, different occupations also imply varying prospects of learning English. The participants who mentioned having learned to speak English with a certain degree of flu-ency had worked at jobs where they have had more opportunities to interact with English-speaking co-workers or employers. Those women who did non-agricultural jobs were seen as having a greater chance of learning English; some jobs offered training, even if informally, to communicate more fluently in English.

Given the common assumption about a lack of interest on the part of immigrant parents to learn English, it is worth highlighting here the fact that all the women who were interviewed included detailed accounts of their ef-forts toward learning English without being asked directly. Aware of my own professional bias as a translator and a teacher of English as an additional lan-guage, in this study I deliberately avoided including direct questions about the role language played in their interactions, as it was important for the purpose of this study to leave it up to the participants to name those resources they considered most important. In spite of this, the interviewees brought up the topic time and again in their narratives. It is also worth noting that it usually takes several years of focused learning to move beyond conversational skills and develop the level of linguistic proficiency in a second or additional language required to communicate effectively in a formal situation, comprehend a speech, or actively participate in a meeting (Cummins, 1979, 1980).

### Patricia—*Sí me interesa aprender, porque sí le hace a uno falta.* (Yes, I am interested in learning, because one does need it.)

Patricia underscores the importance of learning English, after settling in the US. However, she often faces challenges to attend her English classes.

> Y la mamá de los niños que cuido sale ya hasta las cinco y media. Y el esposo de ella trabaja aquí, por aquí, pero ya llega tarde también. Entonces hay veces que no tengo mucha chanza de salir. *(laughs nervously)* Asique ahorita como voy a las clases de inglés *(high pitch, as sign of excitement)* hay veces que llego un poquito tarde. Son a las seis de la tarde. Pero siempre, siempre *(stretches out the word and repeats it to stress her frustration with this repeated situation)* llego un poquito tarde porque hay veces que ya vienen por ellos … como una ocasión me ha tocado que llegaron a las seis y media por ellos. Asique yo me alisto y todo, y ya no más llegan por ellos y vienen y yo me voy. Sí, le digo, porque sí me interesa, le digo, sí me interesa aprender, porque sí le hace a uno falta. Digo, mayormente, pues está uno en este país, digo, siempre se va a ocupar el inglés, siempre.

> And the mom of the children I take care of leaves work at about 5:30. And her husband works here, around here, but he arrives late also. So there are times when I don't have much of a chance to go out. *(laughs nervously)* So now that I'm attending English classes *(high pitch, as sign of excitement)* there are times when I arrive a bit late. Class starts at 6 pm. But I always, always *(stretches out the word and repeats it to stress her frustration with this repeated situation)* arrive a bit late because sometimes they come to pick them up … like it once happened that they came for them at 6:30. So I get ready and all, and as soon as they come and pick them up, I leave. Yes, I say, because I am interested, I say, I am interested in learning, because one does need it. I say, mainly, well if one is in this country, I say, one will always be using English, always.

There is obvious frustration in Patricia's voice with a situation which is out of her control. She is enrolled in an English program which offeres classes in the evenings but, because of her babysitting job, she can never make it on time. Invariably, some parents of the children she takes care of are late to pick them up, so this prevents her from meeting her objective of attending class. Yet, this does not seem to affect her determination.

## Luisa—*Pero se me hizo mejor aprender en ese trabajo.*
## (But I found that it was better to learn at that job.)

Throughout the series of interviews, Luisa frequently uses the words *"batallar"* (to struggle) and *"difícil"* (difficult) to refer to her communication experiences as a result of not having learned English. In the following excerpt, Luisa describes how the skills she has acquired to speak and understand English are mostly due to a job where she was able to pick it up and use it more often. By contrast, learning in a classroom seemed much harder to her and, in her opinion, it did not help her much.

> Luisa: Y a veces yo pienso que fue batalla y es batalla todavía porque uno no aprende. Yo no he aprendido inglés. Y he ido muchas veces a la escuela, pero no aprendo. Como que no, no, no, ya mi cabeza como que no. Y se me hace como que eso de estar allí en la escuela no me ayudó mucho. Me ayudó más un trabajo que tuve donde había mucha gente hablando inglés. Y yo con lo poquito que yo sabía y luego, ya oyendo más, ya aprendí más, no mucho, porque no. En primer lugar, no sé ni conversar en inglés. Pero, por ejemplo, si me hablan por teléfono, puedo decir poquito; poquito, no mucho. Yo les digo luego, luego, que no hablo inglés. Y así si me preguntan, por ejemplo, de mi hijo que es mecánico … me hablan mucho y me dicen que si está Jesús, que quiere arreglar una parte de un carro y yo ya sé muchas cosas, le entiendo cosas, pero no puedo decirle también mucho. Pero se me hizo mejor aprender en ese trabajo que … que. . .
> Lilian: que en las clases…
> Luisa: … que en la clase de la escuela. Y en la escuela, pues, ya le digo, pues, batallé y estuve así batallando mucho, muchas veces.

> Luisa: And sometimes I think that it was a struggle, and it still is, because one doesn't learn. I haven't learned English. And I have often attended school, but I don't learn. It's as if no, no, no, my head just doesn't. And I find that being there in the school didn't help me much. It helped me more when I got a job where many people spoke English. And with the little I knew, and hearing it more, I learned more; not much, because I didn't. In the first place, I don't even know how to carry on a conversation in English. But, for example, if I get a phone call, I can say a little; a little, not much. I tell them right away that I don't speak English. And if they ask me, for example, about my son who is a mechanic … they speak a lot and they ask if Jesus is here, that they want to fix a part of their car, and I already know a lot of things, and I understand a lot, but I can't say much. But I found that it was better to learn at that job than … than…
> Lilian: … than in class…
> Luisa: … than in the classes in school. And at the school, as I say, well, I struggled and I struggled a lot like that, many times.

In spite of the fact that she does not find learning in a classroom too useful, Luisa still wants to attend classes but it has been very uphill for her, because English and GED classes are always offered in the summer, during the months when most people in this area, who have agricultural jobs, are working long hours in the field. Since at other times of the year there is no work, during the summer Luisa takes on as many jobs as she can.

> Lilian: ¿Adónde fue esto? ¿En la escuela de los niños ofrecían clases de inglés?
> Luisa: No. Aquí hay, en esta primaria, ahí viene una maestra ... una señora—que hasta es mi amiga, también, mi amiga y de Norma—y ella es maestra, y da clases de inglés a los adultos. Pero, sabe, que cuando es tiempo que ella da clases para los adultos, siempre hay trabajo aquí. O sea, aquí no hay trabajo todo el año.
> Lilian: Ah, coincide. No puede ir, entonces.
> Luisa. Aha, no podemos ir a la escuela. Cuando es tiempo de que hay clases para adultos, nosotros tenemos que ir a trabajar. Y cuando ella ... Por ejemplo, ella da clases para agarrar el GED, eso, y enseña inglés, también, da clases de inglés. Y ya le digo, yo al menos, no he podido ir ni a agarrar mi GED, ni a aprender inglés, porque no, no puedo. No se puede, ya que en el tiempo así cuando ella pone la escuelita para aprender inglés o para agarrar el GED, nosotros trabajamos mucho. Ella la pone como, por ejemplo, en mayo, que ya son las vacaciones de los niños, ¿verdad? Y en mayo nosotros vamos a trabajar.

> Lilian: And, where was this? At the kids' school, did they offer English lessons?
> Luisa: No. Here there is, in this elementary school, a teacher comes ... a lady—who's also my friend and Norma's—and she is a teacher, and teaches English for adults. But, you know, when it's the time when she offers the classes for adults, there's always work here. That is, here there isn't work all year round.
> Lilian: Oh, so it coincides. Then you can't go.
> Luisa: Aha, we can't go to school. When it's the time when there are classes for adults, we have to go to work. And when she... For example, she also offers GED classes, and that, and she teaches English, she also offers English classes. And as I say, at least I haven't been able to take the GED or to learn English, because I can't, I can't. No one can, because at the time when she starts the school to learn English or to take the GED, we work a lot. She sets it up, for example, like in May, when it's the kids' vacations, right? And in May, we go to work.

An evident oversight in the organization of these language and education programs seems to be the fact that they do not take into account the reality of the population they are designed to serve. Unfortunately—as Luisa repeats several times—this valuable service offered in this area does not make much of a difference to those who would probably most benefit from it. It was unclear, from Luisa's account, who sponsors the adult ESL (English as a Second

Language) and GED (General Education Development) programs, which are sometimes offered in the summer, at the elementary school near her home. Although she knew that classes were free and assumed that the teacher got paid for teaching them, Luisa was not sure where the funds came from. Similar programs in neighboring school districts are offered as afterschool programs for parents and run by volunteers, either teachers or other members of the community, sometimes with the support of the ESL program at the local community college, who provides the curriculum and materials.

## Norma—*Pero se daba su tiempo para ayudarme. Y ahí fui aprendiendo un poquito.*
(But she would take the time to help me. And there I started learning a bit.)

Of all the participants in this study, Norma has sought and had the most opportunities to learn English in the workplace. Just after recounting her first visit to her children's elementary school, which had resulted in her changing her last name for good, Norma explains how since then she has made an effort to learn English.

> Norma: Después comencé a trabajar para americanos, gente que no sabía español, nada. Había una viejita aquí, de noventa años. Y yo me tenía que venir aquí a quedar con ella en la noche, pero ella era ... no sabía una palabra en español y yo no sabía inglés. Y la señora que estaba con ella en el día me ayudaba con frases. Me dijo: "Para que puedas aprender el inglés, al menos a entenderlo un poco y hablarlo. No tienes que preocuparte cómo se escribe, si no cómo se pronuncia." Ella me escribía las palabras como se pronunciaban, no como realmente se escriben.
> Lilian: ¿Y ella hablaba español?
> Norma: Ella hablaba español.
> Lilian: ¿Y ella trabajaba con usted?
> Norma: Ella se quedaba con la señora en el día y cuando yo llegaba, ella se iba. Pero se daba su tiempo para ayudarme ... como las cosas más importantes ... que si la señora quería ir al baño ... que si quería ella ir a dormir ... cómo ella me iba a decir. Y ahí fui aprendiendo un poquito.

> Norma: Then I started working for Americans, people who didn't know Spanish, nothing. There was a 90-year-old lady. And I had to come and stay the night with her, but she was ... didn't know a word of Spanish, and I didn't know English. And the lady who was with her during the day would help me with phrases. She said to me, "So that you can learn English, at least to understand a bit and speak it. You don't need to worry about how it's spelled, just how it's pronounced." She would write down the words as they are pronounced, not as they are really spelled.

Lilian: And did she speak Spanish?
Norma: She spoke Spanish.
Lilian: And she worked with you?
Norma: She stayed with the lady during the day, and when I arrived, she left. But she would take the time to help me … like the most important things … if the lady wanted to go to the bathroom … or if she wanted to go to bed … how she would say that. And there I started learning a bit.

Norma points out that she has worked for English-speaking employers for a long time, so this has helped her to learn English faster. In her first job, as a night-time caretaker for an elderly lady, Norma found the solidarity of a co-worker. Every evening, when Norma arrived to take over from her, before leaving, she would always take some time to teach her some basic phrases in order to help her out. She would write down the pronunciation of common expressions she would regurlarly need in her work routine. Later, Norma goes on to compare her experience with that of other women, friends of hers who have never worked outside the home and who, for that reason, have never developed the fluency that she now has in English.

Y hay gente en este pueblo, también, amigas mías, que nunca han trabajado, porque ellas no salen de su casa. Regularmente, en nuestra cultura, el hombre es el que trabaja y las mujeres nos quedamos en la casa, a atender la casa, los niños y eso … Y yo invito a una amiga a veces a mi trabajo, así, y ella también … donde vive Kathy, que casi hay puro americano, poquito, si acaso dos personas hablarán español. Y tenemos el mismo tiempo más o menos aquí, y ella está como yo hace muchos años … que muy poquita una que otra palabra, pero no entendía lo que le decían … Si yo le digo me ha ayudado comenzar desde un principio a tratarlos y esforzarme, porque es una motivación muy grande.

And there are people in this town, also, friends of mine, who have never worked, because they don't leave their home. As a rule, in our culture, the man is the one who goes out to work, and we, the women, stay home to take care of the house, the kids, and that… And I sometimes invite a friend of mine, to my job, and she also … where Kathy lives, where there's mostly Americans, very few, barely two people speak Spanish. And we've been here more or less the same length of time, and she is like I was many years ago … very little, just one or two words, but she didn't understand what they were saying to her. I say, it has helped me to start from the very beginning to relate to them and make an effort, because it's a very high motivation.

Norma stresses the fact that her motivation is very high, since she needs to be able to speak English for her work. But also, she cannot deny that she has made an enormous effort to learn, and she believes it has helped her get ahead. According to her own accounts, and Luisa's—who has been a close friend for many years, and babysits for her—Norma was one of the few women who started working for English-speaking bosses, and learned English faster because of this. In many respects, Norma emerges as a leader in the eyes of her friends who admire her.

## Sandra—"No quito el dedo del renglón. Sé que un día voy a tener la oportunidad de centrarme."
(But I don't lose sight of my objectives. I know that one day I will have the opportunity to focus again.)

In her first interview, Sandra mentions how she has had to stop attending English classes, momentarily, because she has nobody to take care of her two children. She still considers studying English one of her priorities, and has not given up on this idea (*"no quito el dedo del renglón"*), but she has decided to wait and focus on her children for the time being.

> Yo he intentado. O sea, paré de estudiar inglés. Lo paré, por los niños, por la escuela. Y yo sé que hay oportunidades pero eso requiere que yo deje a los niños. Y antes tenía gente de confianza que me los cuidaba, pero se ha ido esa gente y ya llega una etapa en que los niños no se quieren quedar con nadie, "que con esta no…" Entonces yo ya dije, ahorita, de momento hasta cierto punto lo más importante son los niños. Pero no quito el dedo del renglón. Yo sé que un día voy a tener la oportunidad de centrarme. Ahorita tengo una oferta de trabajo que me ha motivado. O sea, ya estaba muy así pero me dijo mi patrón: "Necesito que tú aprendas inglés para que trabajes en mi oficina." O sea, ¡lo único que me está deteniendo es el idioma! *(enthusiastic)* Ahora la motivación es muy alta. O sea, no que los niños no importen, sino que yo por no descuidar a los niños dije: "Lo más importante son los niños." Entonces, paré el inglés. Eran dos horas … cuatro horas a la semana, cuando iba al inglés. Y las tareas y que tiene uno que trabajar, atender la casa: todo. Dije: "Es mucho. No puedo abarcar tanto."

> I have tried. I mean, I quit English classes. I quit, because of the kids, because of school. And I know there are opportunities, but that requires for me to leave the kids. And I used to have some people I trusted who would take care of them, but they've left. And there comes a time when the kids don't want to stay with anyone, "… not with that person…" So I said, now, for the time being to a certain extent, the kids are what matter most. But I don't lose sight of my objectives. I know that one day I will have the opportunity to focus again. Now I have a job offer that has motivated me. So, I was motivated already, but my boss told me, "I need you to learn English so that you can work in my office." So, the only thing that is holding me back is language! *(enthusiastic)* So now my motivation is really high. So, it's not that the children don't matter, instead, so as not to neglect the kids I said, "The kids are what matter most."

> So I quit English. It was two hours … four hours a week, when I went to English. And homework, and that one has to work, take care of the house: everything. I said, "It's too much. I can't cope with everything."

Sandra's motivation to learn English is very high, she comments, as she shares her excitement over her prospects for advancement. One of her employers once mentioned that he would like to hire her to do administrative work for his office but there is one condition: she first needs to learn English. At the time, Sandra did housekeeping work for him and his wife, cleaning both their home and office space, as well as for several other families. On our last interview, several months later, Sandra shared that she had resumed her English classes and was back on track, working towards achieving one of her long-term goals.

# Linguistic Advocacy: Embracing Bilingualism and Biliteracy

Another common topic brought up frequently by the women who were interviewed had to do with the language or languages of instruction in their children's school experience. As part of their responses to questions on other issues, the women in this study often expressed their opinion as to what their preferences were. Several participants whose children were in bilingual programs were strongly in favor of encouraging them to become bilingual and biliterate, and spontaneously explained the benefits. Those with older children who had been enrolled in a bilingual program earlier in their schooling discussed the usefulness of developing bilingual skills.

In two separate cases, the womens' experiences with each of their children were contradictory, almost the exact opposite. For different reasons, one of their children was participating in a bilingual program and the other one was not. In all cases, Spanish was considered to be the child's first language. Both participants noted that they saw a difference in the progress of each child. According to their observations, the children who were learning how to read and write in Spanish first and worked on their English later, seemed to have advanced faster in their literacy development. Both mothers were strong advocates for their children to learn both English and Spanish.

**Patricia—*Yo sí quiero que aprendan los dos idiomas y escribir los dos idiomas.***
(I do want them to learn both languages and to write in both languages.)

Patricia's second son, Pedro, has just started kindergarten, and she is satisfied with his progress. After enumerating his achievements to date, she stresses the fact that she is glad he is in the bilingual program. Patricia also praises the teacher Pedro has in kindergarten and notes that he is well known for how the children who are in his class can read by the end of the school year. In this account about how proud she is of her kindergartner's achievements, she starts out by mentioning the preparation her son brought from Head Start.

Patricia: Sí, él ya sabe escribir su nombre y … ya ve que cuando salen de Head Start no saben mucho.
Lilian: Son chiquitos.
Patricia: Sí les enseñan pero no, no mucho.
Lilian: No. Es como preparación para la escuela, ¿no?
Patricia: Sí, no más como un entrenamiento, una preparación. Sí les enseñan como las figuras, los nombres, a saber contar, pero no, no saberse los números. Y ya ahorita, él ya sabe muchas letras, ya se sabe mucho el abecedario, a contar hasta el 20 y a hacer los números también un poquito, como hasta el 5, eso el que se sabe más.
Lilian: Ya está listo para la escuela.
Patricia: Sí. Y dice el maestro, dice, tiene que echarle ganas y ya cuando salga de aquí tiene que saber leer ya. Y he sabido por unas amistades, que ese maestro es muy bueno. Dicen que es muy bueno. Yo conozco una niña que ya salió de ahí de kinder con ese maestro y sabe leer muy bien. Sí, se ve que es bueno y él se… y ya ahorita le digo que donde quiera anda él pintando su nombre. *(laughs, with pride)* Cualquier cosa ya hasta en la pared me quiere andar poniendo su nombre. *(loud)* "No," le digo, "busca un papel y hazlo." Sí, anda él que donde quiera que … ya sabe y dice: "Mira, así se hace" "Pedro", pone "Pedro", así lo hace. Hace todavía la letra feita pero sí se le entiende bien que es su nombre.
Lilian: Pero es chiquito.
Patricia: Mmmm, por eso digo yo, que sí, o no sé, a lo mejor así están todos, verdad. Porque a todos les dan lo mismo que tienen que enseñarles. Pero no … es bueno, es bueno.
Lilian: Está contenta con él.
Patricia: Sí, estoy contenta con ese maestro. Sí es bueno.

Patricia: Yes, he already knows how to write his name and… as you know when they leave Head Start they don't know much.
Lilian: They are little.
Patricia: Yes, they teach them, but not much.

Lilian: No. It's like preparation for school, right?

Patricia: Yes, just like a training, a preparation. Yes, they teach them like the figures, the names, how to count, but they don't learn the numbers. And now, he already knows many letters, he knows the alphabet, how to count up to 20 and to write the numbers, a bit, up to 5, that's what he knows more.

Lilian: He's ready for school.

Patricia: Yes. The teacher says that he needs to give it his best and by the time he finishes he needs to know how to read already. And I've known, through friends, that this teacher is good. They say he's good. I know a girl who finished kindergarten there with that teacher and she can read very well. Yes, it shows he's good and he … and now, wherever he is, he is writing his name. *(laughs with pride)* Even on the wall he wants to write his name. "No," I say, "find a piece of paper and do it." Yes, he goes around … everywhere… He knows already, and he says, "Look, it's done like that. 'Pedro'," and he writes "Pedro," and he writes it like that. His handwriting is still a bit sloppy, but you can understand it clearly that it's his name.

Lilian: But he is very young.

Patricia: Mmmm, that's why I say, yes, or I don't know, maybe they're all at that point, right. Because they give them all the same that they have to teach. But no… he is good, he's good.

Lilian: So you're happy with him.

Patricia: Yes, I'm happy with that teacher. He is good.

At the end of this segment of her account, Patricia explains how students are placed in the bilingual program, according to their first language. Parents are not given a choice. To illustrate the process of placement, she shares an incident of a mother who had complained openly at a meeting because her child had been placed in a bilingual program although he knew English. But Patricia does not share that woman's views. Instead, she emphatically vouches for the bilingual program and insists on her preference for her children to be taught and to learn both in English and in Spanish, so as to become biliterate.

Lilian: Y cuando decidieron que fuera a bilingüe, ¿le dieron a elegir o le dijeron no más que iba a ir ahí?

Patricia: No *(pronounced emphatically prolonging the initial sound)*. Ellos los ponen, porque como saben que yo hablo español y que él no habla nada de inglés no lo pueden poner con una persona que hable puro inglés. No lo pueden poner así, entonces, ya ellos tienen sus grupos para esos niños. Porque una vez fui, en la primera vez que lo llevé para que aprendiera eso, lo de la comida de los niños, este, hablamos también con el supervisor de ahí. Y luego hablamos también con el maestro y tocó que dijo una señora: "Oiga, pero mi niño sabe inglés." "Pues, sí," dice, "sabe inglés pero está aquí y vamos a estudiar primero español." Pero como que la señora dijo: "Yo no quiero que estudie español, yo quiero que estudie puro inglés". Bueno, le digo, "yo sí quiero que aprendan los dos idiomas y escribir los dos idiomas." Le digo, pues, sí. Pero ella decía:

"Pero mi niño habla inglés," y dice: "Pues, bueno, tienes que hablar con el supervisor para que te lo cambie, si quieres."

Lilian: And when it was decided for him to go to bilingual, did they make you choose or did they tell you he was going there?

Patricia: No. They place them, because as they know that I speak Spanish and he doesn't speak any English, they can't put him with someone who speaks only English. They can't, so, they already have the groups for those kids. Because once I went, the first time I took him for him to learn that about the food for the kids, well, we spoke with the supervisor there. And then we also spoke to the teacher and one lady there said, "Listen, but my child knows English." "Well, yes," he said, "he knows English, but he's here and first we are going to learn Spanish." But the lady then said, "I don't want him to study Spanish, I want him to study only English." Well, I say, "I do want them to learn both languages and to write in both languages." I said, yes. But she kept on saying, "But my child speaks English." So he said, "Well, then, you need to talk to the supervisor for them to switch him, if you like."

Patricia's both school-age children participated in the bilingual program. Her eldest son, Alex, who is in fourth grade, and is now an avid reader, has already exited the program.

## Silvia—*Ella está en los dos idiomas. Yo digo que por eso ella va como muy avanzada.*
(She is in both languages. I say that that is why she is so advanced.)

In contrast, Silvia had a mixed experience, since only her daughter is in a bilingual class. Yet, she also believes the bilingual program has been the best choice. Silvia has had contradicting experiences with her children, as in each case, and in similar situations, she received opposite recommendations. She mentions how when her son, Juan Manuel, who is the older one of her children, first started school she originally wanted him to be enrolled in the bilingual program, but they asked her to pull him out. With her second child, Sarina, Silvia asked for her to be enrolled in an English monolingual class but the principal explained how it would benefit her daughter to develop her literacy in her first language, so she was placed in a bilingual classroom. Silvia now believes Sarina has advanced more and faster than Juan Manuel because of this. Ironically, in neither case did the school comply with her original request for the type of program she intended her child to attend.

Y la niña tiene una maestra…, pues, habla español. La maestra habla español. Así ha tenido, de español. Con ella no batallo, porque ella ahorita está en bilingüe, la niña. Porque quieren que aprenda los dos idiomas. O sea que ahorita, que el idioma que sabe más es el español y ella sabe leer en español. O sea que, cuando yo la he ido a poner, dije que me la pusiera en inglés. Pero el director dijo, "No se la puedo poner en inglés porque el idioma de ella es el español. Y cuando estén leyendo los libros, ella no va a entender." Dice él: "Es mejor ponerla ... y ella va a ir paso a paso aprendiendo." Dice: "Así como está aprendiendo en español, paso a paso, luego ya ... es más fácil que aprenda el inglés." Entonces, es lo que yo veo. Que sí, a veces trae papeles el niño, pues, en inglés, verdad. Y ella ya se pone ahí. Porque también le dan papeles en inglés y en español al niño. Y luego, dice la niña: "Que te leo," dice, "el inglés. También ya estoy aprendiendo inglés." Y agarra la hoja y se pone y ... batalla un poquito para el inglés, pero lo lee, también. O sea que ella está en los dos idiomas. Yo digo que por eso ella va como muy avanzada.

And my daughter has a teacher…, well, she speaks Spanish. The teacher speaks Spanish. She has had like that, Spanish. With her I don't struggle, because now she is in bilingual, my daughter. Because they want her to learn both languages. Because now, the language she knows best is Spanish and she can read in Spanish. So when I went to enroll her, I asked them to place her in English. But the principal said, "I can't place her in English because her language is Spanish. And when they are reading books, she won't understand." He said, "It's better if we place her ... and she will be learning step by step." He said, "Just as she is learning Spanish, step by step, then it is easier for her to learn English." So, that's what I see. That yes, sometimes my son brings home some papers, in English, well, in English, right? And she already starts. Because sometimes they send papers in English and in Spanish with him. And then, my daughter says, "Let me read it to you," she said, "the English part. I am learning English too." And she takes the sheet of paper and she starts ... she struggles a bit with English, but she reads it too. So she is in both languages. I say that that is why she is so advanced.

Silvia goes on to explain her experience with her first child in further detail, and how time and again she had insisted on enrolling her son in the bilingual program but that, inexplicably, he was removed from it. The reason she was given at the time was that they needed to change Juan Manuel's placement because he already knew Spanish. Silvia regrets the fact that he did not continue in the bilingual program, because although he is bilingual, she would have liked him to also learn how to read and write in Spanish, and thus become biliterate too.

Silvia: Y el niño, nunca me lo quisieron poner en bilingüe, que porque no lo necesitaba. Y entonces, yo lo metía en bilingüe y a la semana me hablaban que fuera a retirar las hojas para quitarlo de bilingüe. Que porque él no necesitaba el bilingüe. Como él hablaba español, él habla español, pero no sabe escribir el español. Y es el error, yo digo, que ahí han cometido ellos, porque; no digo que yo porque yo lo he puesto, lo he

puesto en bilingüe y ellos *(pause)* me lo han quitado. *(Emphatic, high fall)* Lo quitan, que porque no lo necesita … que porque sabe español…
Lilian: ¿Porque sabe inglés?
Silvia: … y sabe el inglés. Pero no saben que no sabe escribir español *(stress on "sabe" and "español")* ni leer en español. Ve, sabe hablarlo, sabe hablar el español porque su idioma es el español. Y yo noto la diferencia entre la niña y él. Sí. Sí, porque hasta para hablar el español el niño como que se atora. Como que … no lo dice correctamente. Aha, ve, porque puro inglés. No, no, me … que porque no lo necesita, que no-sé-qué … me lo han quitado, me lo han quitado de ahí. Porque no necesita bilingüe que porque él ya sabe español, y que no-sé-qué.

Silvia: And my son, they never let me place him in bilingual, because he didn't need it— they said. And then, I would enroll him in bilingual and a week later they would call me to go and pick up the form to remove him from bilingual—that he didn't need bilingual. As he spoke Spanish, he speaks Spanish, but he can't write in Spanish. And that's the mistake, I say, that they have made there, because… I don't say "I" because I enrolled him, I enrolled him in bilingual and they *(pause)* have removed him. *(Emphatic, high fall)* They remove him, because he doesn't need it … because he knows Spanish….
Lilian: Because he knows English?
Silvia: … and he knows English. But he doesn't know how to write in Spanish, or read in Spanish. You see, he can speak it, he speaks Spanish because Spanish is his language. And I notice the difference between my daughter and him. Yes. Yes, because even speaking Spanish my son sometimes gets stuck. Like … he doesn't say it right. Yeah, you see, because [he learns] just English. No, no, they've … that because he doesn't need it, that I-don't-know-what… they have removed him from there. Because he doesn't need bilingual, that because he already knows Spanish, and who-knows-what.

In an expression of frustration, Silvia repeats several times how in her son's school they removed him from the bilingual program and that, because of the school's decision, although Juan Manuel can speak Spanish he cannot read and write in Spanish. The argument used to place him in English classes did not seem to be consistent with the one used later, when she enrolled her daughter. The same reason was given by the school at different points in time to explain opposite decisions; her son was placed in a monolingual English classroom because he already was fluent in Spanish; while, her daughter was placed in a bilingual classroom for the same reason. In support of her view of the importance of developing biliteracy, she offers the example of one of her sisters who was deported and has had to return to Mexico with her children. Silvia's nephews had not studied Spanish in school and now are having a hard time adapting to school in Mexico.

Fíjese, como los niños que tiene mi hermana allá, que están allá. Pues, dice mi herma-na: "Si no puedo volver, me los voy a poner en la escuela aquí, mientras que podamos ir para allá." Dice el niño: "Yo no voy a ir a la escuela, porque yo no sé leer, ni escrib … bueno, leer poco, pero yo no sé escribir el español." Fíjese, ahí está un ejemplo, ahí está un ejemplo.

Look, like the children my sister has over there, who are over there. Well, my sister says, "If we can't come back, I am going to enroll them in school here, meanwhile until we can come back." And her son says, "I don't want to go to school, because I don't know how to read, or write … well, read a bit, but I don't know how to write in Spanish." So look, that's an example.

Silvia emphasizes the importance of maintaining and developing language skills in Spanish, as she contrasts both her children's experiences. Once again, Silvia points out the differences in achievement she observes between her two children, as her daughter who is in first grade learned how to read and write in Spanish first, and now is learning how to read in English, progressed faster than her son, who is now in fourth grade and was placed in a monolingual English classroom from the beginning.

Silvia: Yo cuando llevé a la niña digo: "Ay, por qué, si yo quiero ponerla en inglés, ¿por qué el director no me la quiere poner en inglés?" Y luego yo iba bien enojada, yo quería que la niña empezara a hablar inglés. No, pero ya cuando llegué, que me explicó el director cómo iban las cosas, pues, ya comprendí.
Lilian: Le explicaron bien.
Silvia: Lo que ella necesitaba. Es cierto, ahora yo veo los resultados en la niña. Sabe hablar inglés (*really loud, in assertive tone*), sí sabe hablar el inglés, pero fue muy im-portante porque sabe leer el español. La lectura que es muy importante.
Lilian: ¿Y ella trae libros en español?
Silvia: Sí, a ella le dan todos los días un libro. Todos los días trae un libro.
Lilian: ¿En español o en inglés?
Silvia: En español y en inglés no porque, en inglés tiene aquí, pero allá sí leen en inglés y leen en español. Hm. Pero sí sabe, sí lee. Ya le está agarrando al inglés en la lectura, también.
Lilian: Y usted dice que ve la diferencia, entonces, con el hijo.
Silvia: Sí. Veo la diferencia. El error, el error, que uno también dice: "Bueno, pues, si no lo necesita." También va uno y lo quita. Ahí está el error.

Silvia: When I took my daughter I said, "Oh, but why? If I want to place my daughter in English, why doesn't the principal want to place her in English?" And then I was very angry, I wanted my daughter to start speaking English. No, but when I arrived, and the principal explained to me how things worked, well, I understood.
Lilian: So they explained it well to you.

Silvia: What she needed. It's true, now I see the results in my daughter. She can speak English, yes, she can speak English, but it was very important because she can read in Spanish. Reading is very important.

Lilian: And does she bring Spanish books home?

Silvia. Yes, they give her a book every day. Every day she brings a book.

Lilian: Spanish or English?

Silvia: In Spanish, and English no, because she has books in English here, but over there they do read in English and they read in Spanish. But she does know, she does read. She is starting to read in English, too.

Lilian: So you say that you see the difference, then, with your son.

Silvia: Yes, I see the difference. The mistake, the mistake is that one also says, "Well, but he doesn't need it." They also go and pull him out. That's the mistake.

Silvia concludes that, since one never knows when they might have to return to Mexico, she intends to take on the job of teaching her son how to read and write in Spanish.

Y ahora le digo al niño: "Ahora te voy a enseñar yo a que leas en español y a que aprendas a escribir. Si no te enseñan allá, yo te voy a enseñar." Y "No," dice, "yo no quiero." "No si no es que no quieras, es por tu bien. Porque luego vas a batallar." Le digo: "Mira a tu primo, como está allá. Ya ves. Uno nunca sabe. Uno nunca sabe cuándo le va a tocar y lo van a llevar para allá, uno nunca sabe. Y te va a servir." Digo: "Si sabes escribir el español y si sabes leer el español, ya sabes escribir en inglés y leer el inglés," le digo, "sales adelante." Le digo "allá también dan clases de inglés, no te preocupes," le digo. "Pero es importante."

And now I tell my son, "Now I will teach you to read and write in Spanish. If they don't teach you there, I'll teach you." And he says, "No, I don't want to." "No it's not if you don't want to, it's for your own good. Later you are going to struggle." I tell him, "Look at your cousin how now he's there now. One never knows. One never knows when it's going to be one's turn and they'll take us over there; one never knows. And it'll be useful." I say, "If you can read and write in Spanish, and you know already how to read and write in English," I say, "you'll do well." I tell him, "Over there they also have English classes, don't worry," I say. "But, it's important."

Silvia often tries to stress the benefits of bilingualism and to remind her son of his cousins' situation. When you know how to read and write in both languages, she explains to him, you can progress, and it is an advantage.

## Brenda—*"Las mías lo aprovecharon y son muy buenas para interpretar."*
(My daughters benefited from it and they are very good at interpreting.)

At different points in her interview, Brenda mentions how she often asks her eldest daughter, Sara, who has already graduated from high school, to interpret for her. (See Chapters 5 and 8.) On many occasions, Sara is called upon to help her mother negotiate complicated situations. In the following excerpt, Brenda mentions how her daughters have all benefited from attending the bilingual program. As a consequence, she comments, they are now skillful interpreters.

> Lilian: Asique cuando recién empezaron ¿no había bilingüe o sí? Cuando empezaron las niñas, en el kinder, y eso…
> Brenda: Mmmm … pues … yo creo que ya había bilingüe, no más que siempre era acuerdo de los padres si querían que sus niños estudiaran bilingüe o no, verdad.
> Lilian: Eligen…
> Brenda: Porque hay unos que sí queríamos hay otros que no.
> Lilian: Y ¿pueden elegir ir a otro …? ¿Hay bilingüe y no bilingüe también?
> Brenda: Sí, pueden elegir. No más que hasta el año pasado fue que me dijeron que ya no iba a haber bilingüe, que porque se estaban confundiendo los niños… Y el año pasado fue cuando dijeron que ya no, quién sabe … Y de todos modos las mías lo aprovecharon. Y son muy buenas para interpretar…

> Lilian: So when they started, there was no bilingual [program], or was there? When your daughters started attending kindergarten and that…
> Brenda: Mmmm … well … I think there was bilingual, it just depended on the parents whether they wanted their kids to study in bilingual or not, right.
> Lilian: They choose.
> Brenda: Because there were some of us who wanted it and there were others who didn't.
> Lilian: And can they choose another…? Is there bilingual and non-bilingual?
> Brenda: Yes, they can choose. Just that last year they let me know that there wasn't going to be bilingual, because the kids were getting confused… And it was last year that they said that not anymore, who knows… Anyway, my daughters benefited from it. And they are very good at interpreting.

Brenda is one of the participants who can look back and reflect on the different stages in her experience with the schools, since by the time of our last interview she has two daughters who have already graduated from high school and one who is still in middle school. In her reckoning, Brenda chooses to highlight the value of the linguistic resources developed by her daughters in the school system, which have proved to be very useful to them, as they are all good intepreters. Orellana (2009) stresses the fact that the value of the translation work carried out by immigrant children is often not taken into account, as they are portrayed as being "a drain: they 'take' from the educational and health systems without giving anything back" (p. 124). The life stories of these seven women and their children helps support Orellana's call to recognize its value, "This is an assumption that bears reconsideration. The work immigrant children do is only as invisible as we allow it to be" (p. 124). Further, Brenda's daughters illustrate Valdés's (2010) argument "for the expansion of the definitions of giftedness that can include the special giftedness of young interpreters" (p. xxiii).

# References

Cibils, L. R. de (2011). *Immigrant women's narrative reconstruction of their interactions with their children's schools: A collective qualitative case study* (Doctoral Dissertation). New Mexico State University, Las Cruces.

Collins, P. H. (1994). Shifting the center: Race, class, and feminist theorizing about motherhood. In D. Bassin, M. Honey, & M. Kaplan (Eds.), *Representations of motherhood* (pp. 56–74). New Haven, CT: Yale University Press.

Cummins, J. (1979). Cognitive/academic language proficiency, linguistic interdependence, the optimal age question and some other matters. *Working Papers on Bilingualism, 19*, 197–205.

Cummins, J. (1980). The cross-lingual dimensions of language proficiency: Implications for bilingual education and the optimal age issue. *TESOL Quarterly, 14*, 175–187.

García, O. (2009). *Bilingual education in the 21st century: A global perspective*. Oxford: Wiley-Blackwell.

Norton, B. (2013). *Identity and language learning: Extending the conversation* (2nd ed.). Tonawanda, NY: Multilingual Matters.

Orellana, M. (2009). *Translating childhoods: Immigrant youth, language, and culture*. New Brunswick, NJ: Rutgers University Press.

Valdés, G. (2010). *Expanding definitions of giftedness: The case of young interpreters from immigrant communities*. New York, NY: Routledge.

Young, I. (1990). *Justice and the politics of difference*. Princeton, NJ: Princeton University Press.

# · 1 0 ·

# IMMIGRATION AS A GENDERED EXPERIENCE

## The Crucial Resource of Physical Mobility

*Gender is one of the fundamental social relations anchoring and shaping immigration patterns, and immigration is one of the most powerful forces disrupting and realigning everyday life.* (Hondagneu-Sotelo, 2003, p. 3)

In its complexity, immigration may involve the traumatic experience of loss and simultaneously carry an opportunity for transformation. The event of moving to a different country does not only affect the individual but often causes changes in the family structure (Hondagneu-Sotelo, 1994; C. Suárez-Orozco, 2000, p. 197). In their resettlement in a society different from that of their country of origin, members of a family often find their social roles to be shifting both within the family and in the outside world. The perception of this experience and the coping strategies used may differ according to the circumstances of migration and, especially, by gender (Ainslie, 1998). Immigration must be understood as a gendered experience, since in many cases "immigrant women occupy a particular and different location in society to immigrant men" (Norton, 2013, p. 52).

Some authors have stressed the significance of women's wage-earning occupation outside the home as a factor influencing the transformation of gender roles in immigrant families from Latin America. After migrating, women who had previously stayed home may start working outside the home; children may become interpreters or even social brokers; and men may go from being the sole bread-winner to becoming a partner in a redefined relationship where this responsibility is shared, and therefore find themselves socially "de-moted" (C. Suárez-Orozco & M. Suárez-Orozco, 2001). On the one hand, a woman who was exclusively devoted to being a housewife and a mother in a more patriarchal society may gain independence by starting to work outside the home. In turn, this autonomy may also redefine her role in the family and allow her to take a more active part in the family's decision-making pro-cesses (Hondagneu-Sotelo, 1994, p. 101). On the other hand, a man who may still wish to function by the scripted roles of a more markedly (or more uncritically) patriarchal society may resent these changes in gender roles, and marital tension may ensue (Hondagneu-Sotelo, 1994; C. Suárez-Orozco, 2000). In Hirsch's (1998, 2003, 2007) study, some men used the expression "*en el norte la mujer manda*, that in the US women are in control," to refer to this phenomenon of women gaining power as they adopt new roles once they cross the border (1998, p. 172).

Yet, these explanations cannot be generalized. The transformation of gender roles, as traditionally defined, cannot be attributed only to working outside the home for the first time, since before migrating many women were already employed in paying jobs in their country of origin. According to Zent-graf (2002), in some cases the women's sense of empowerment does not result from an overt challenge of their traditional roles either. Zentgraf suggests that it may have more to do with negotiating the challenges involved in transfer-ring their roles to the new context. Learning to function in the public sphere such as in schools and health clinics can be seen as a significant factor which contributes to an immigrant woman's development of self-confidence and self-assuredness. Especially empowering is the sense of freedom afforded by greater "spatial mobility" and "unregulated behavior" which results from be-ing or feeling less watched by family and community members than at home (Zentgraf, 2002, p. 636). This last observation would especially apply to wom-en who come from rural areas or smaller towns in their country of origin.

The transformation of gender roles within traditional families has been found to be affected directly by the different patterns of migrations: family stage migration, family unit migration and independent migration (Hondagneu-Sotelo, 1994, p. 39). The changes in gender roles within traditionally-structured families are often evident in cases of family stage migration, where historically men moved away first and women were left in charge of the chil-dren. As often women took over the role of head of the family during the husbands' prolonged absence, their responsibilities expanded, and so did their autonomy and self-esteem (Hondagneu-Sotelo, 1994, p. 101). In different periods, these patterns of migration fluctuate in response to changes in the global context.

The findings of Zentgraf's (2002) study coincide with Hondagneu-Sotelo's with respect to the partial effects of family stage migration on a more equitable distribution of household labor. Yet, in her study of immigrant Salvadoran women Zentgraf "challenges a unilinear, integrationist view that sees immigrant women's status and roles as changing along a traditional-modern continuum" (p. 625). Instead, she stresses the diversity and complexity of immigrant women's experiences, and the need to take into account "premigration class standing" and other differences, such as marital status, rural/urban contexts, and country of origin, in order to avoid "partial and distorted interpretations, including a tendency to view immigrant women's experiences ahistorically or as overly homogeneous" (p. 642). This contextualization is crucial for a more nuanced approach.

Although these experiences vary dramatically, researchers have consistently pointed to how, in some circumstances, the social and structural shifts accompanying migration may bring about conflicts in the family and between the spouses or partners, as well as divergent expectations when considering their future options. In particular, women and men may not share the same views or desires related to their permanence in the country where they have resettled (Ainslie, 1998; Hondagneu-Sotelo, 1994; C. Suárez-Orozco, 2000). In the case mentioned earlier of women whose relative social station has been transformed by migration, they may cherish their newly acquired roles and the autonomy these entail, so that they may not want to move back to their country of origin, while the men in similar circumstances may wish to recover some aspects of their previous lifestyle, and so may prefer to go back (Hondagneu-Sotelo, 1994, p. 98).

Yet, again, this perspective is complicated if different social class backgrounds are taken into account. In Zentgraf's (2002) study, middle-class immigrant interviewees who had never needed to work in their country of origin and found themselves in the obligation to work outside the home for the first time after migration expressed resentment about their change in social standing. They were not particularly pleased with their newly acquired double responsibility of working outside the home and in the home doing chores that in their country of origin they would never have done themselves but would have instead paid someone to do for them. Some of these women who saw their immigration experience as contributing to a loss of privilege expressed nostalgia for what they explicitly described as a more class-segregated social context at home (Zentgraf, 2002, pp. 642–643).

Similarly, Hirsch (2007) eloquently warns against any generalizations on the role of gender in the experience of migration, as she points to the need to take class and race into account.

> There is not, and never will be, just one answer to the question of how migration affects gender. A simplistic focus on how migration affects gender takes one back two decades in gender theory, to the idea of "woman" as a unified category. (p. 454)

The findings of these studies concerning the intersections of social locations in the experience of immigrant women may be seen as part of the social backdrop to the stories of the seven interviewees. Yet, more significantly, precisely those processes which are considered to be at the center of this social transformation are the same which are the focus of our exploration. As Zentgraf (2002) suggests, it is the negotiation of interactions with institutions such as those carried out within home-school relations which illustrate the challenges immigrant women overcome and which may largely contribute to role transformation. Within the stories of these seven women reside some of the key components of the redefinition of gender roles in the context of everyday experience, as they describe and define their own stances, resources and strategies in the negotiation of their interactions in the public sphere.

As Reay's (2004) work also reminds us, taking into account intersectionality, as reflected in the mothers' differences, permits a more subtle approach to the complexity of the social processes involved. She notes the need to incorporate gender, race, as well as class considerations to Bourdieu's concepts of habitus and cultural capital, to counteract the mainstream discourse of classlessness and gender-neutrality in considering the relations of parents and schools. These intersections become even more important if immigrant mothers are to be included when referring to parental involvement in institutions which replicate the power dynamics and hierarchies of the larger society.

## Physical Mobility and Gendered Migration

In the context of immigrant communities, restricted access to strategic resources contributes further to already existing situations of vulnerability and power imbalance. As mentioned earlier, when understood as dynamic and relational, power is closely connected to the development of symbolic and material resources. As examples of symbolic resources, Norton (2013) mentions language, education and friendship, which are all relevant to the seven immigrant women's stories. To Norton's list of material resources—goods, real estate and money—I will add access to independent means of transportation, as one of the most treasured resources in many immigrant Latin@ communities in the United States.

Transportation and the means of obtaining it constitute one facet of the adaptation to the new context after migration to the US which is often marked by gender in many Latin@ immigrant communities. Physical mobility is mentioned frequently in the literature on Latina immigrant women, especially by authors who focus on the gendered aspect of immigration, and the transformation of gender roles of immigrants from Latin America living in the Unites States (Hirsch, 2003, p. 194; Hondagneu-Sotelo, 1994, p. 117). In the Latin@ immigrant community which was at the center of her study, Menjívar (2000) observes how mostly men were the ones who owned cars at first, and women were often dependent on them for rides. The author observed that this became an issue for single women, who considered it necessary to make sure they paid for every ride they received from men, so as to avoid misunderstandings. Menjívar lists independent transportation and documentation to remain in the US among the highly valued resources men more often controlled and which contributed to women's dependency. Similarly, the significance of having a car and learning how to drive is underscored by the seven women at the center of this book. In their stories they refer to this as one of the crucial resources developed by them, one which affected most spheres of their life, including their interactions with the schools.

## Developing New Resources: Learning How to Drive

Independent mobility appears as a central resource in the seven women's stories shared here. This seemingly mundane process of acquiring a skill, or in some cases a vehicle, emerges in so many of the women's accounts and with such detailed descriptions that its meaning calls for special attention. Although this is a general resource not solely associated with interacting with the schools, it is included here, in the first place because, consistently, it was the women who brought it up and then offered minute descriptions of the development of this resource and of the difference it made in their everyday interactions. Secondly, most women refer to how at some point at an earlier stage they had had to walk to their children's school. Also, not being able to drive was mentioned as one of the obstacles which prevented them from attending some school functions.

Learning how to drive suggests itself as one of the vital aspects of adapting to life in the US and managing in the new context and as such it emerges as a central theme in each of the women's stories. Driving is seen as an indispensable resource to function fully in a society that seems to require being able to drive in order to belong and participate in it. Thus, these narratives are analyzed here not only in their literal meaning, as referring to a valuable resource but are further explored as a metaphor. The accounts about the importance of driving and acquiring this skill, beyond their literal sense of a valuable material resource, adopt metaphorical meaning as a parallel can be drawn between the stages undergone in the development of physical mobility, and those experienced in the development of stances, resources and strategies in the interactions in the new context. For instance, at the beginning of their time in the US, not driving or not knowing how to drive is associated with an initial intense sense of vulnerability. When this resource was absent, it left the women dependent on others for rides; this situation was called *"andar de ride"*. After migrating, walking in town, which had been the most common way of getting anywhere in their place of origin, made some of the women feel awkward and more keenly aware of their status as outsiders in their new environment.

Thus, when contemplated in its metaphorical meaning, an analogy may be drawn between the need to secure a ride in the early days after migration and those elements of the sociocultural script that are to be acquired in the new context. As is true of most aspects of this script, physical mobility derived from knowing how to drive is one of the fundamental resources that might be overlooked and taken for granted in most interactions of the newcomers with representatives of the receiving community, including institutions such as the schools. It is worth noting that the stories consistently include the word *"ride"* in English, even when hardly any other English words were interspersed in the rest of the accounts. This borrowing of the English word may be associated with the newness of the concept. Thus, it helps accentuate the novelty of the situations encountered in a new environment for which no direct equivalent is found in the home language. Further, for the women who mention it, in the long run, the process of learning how to drive or of acquiring that independent mobility by getting a car points to the development of resources to be shared with the community. When each of the women learned how to drive, this resource became available to others, and so it became a communal resource. Thus, the process of developing independent physical mobility becomes emblematic of communal agency.

These narratives stand as concrete examples of the development of agency from a situation of vulnerability. Each one of the women tells the story of their determination and of the efforts made to learn how to drive in order to become more independent. Most women share detailed accounts which comprise several stages, from the situations created by their dependence on other drivers, to the newly acquired freedom derived from learning how to drive, in some cases, or getting a car, in others. The circumstances of the learning process are shared in minute detail, followed by narratives describing the satisfaction of ultimately becoming a driver and a resource to others in the community, as insightful examples of the development of communal agency. It is worth noting that this communal aspect of resources and agency is closely connected to the concept of motherwork, found to emerge as the predominant ideology of motherhood underlying the women's narratives.

Close parallels can be observed among the lives of these seven women in how in each case driving became crucial in the way it affected all aspects of their interactions, and contributed to the process of acquiring agency and independence. The intensity of the narration as they each described the amount of energy they invested and the efforts they had to make to acquire access to such a valued resource suggests a level of perseverance and resilience in difficult circumstances which tells a very different story from some of the prevalent deficit narratives of Latin@ parental engagement (Valencia & Black, 2002). Although all seven women mention this resource, their focus is different.

### Brenda—*Antes a mí no me daba vergüenza caminar.* (I never used to be ashamed of walking.)

When asked about learning how to negotiate the new context, Brenda first establishes the link between driving and the new needs she encountered when she moved to the US. When confronted with the new challenges, she taught herself how to drive and developed more independence and self-reliance. In her account, it clearly becomes linked to her active roles in her family and in her community.

But initially, there was the more basic need of developing a sense of belonging. Brenda underlines the fact that when she first arrived in the US, and before she learned how to drive a car, she used to walk everywhere. She soon realized how embarrassing it was to walk because nobody else seemed to walk anywhere. In fact she stresses the contrast between her old habits and her new ones in pointing out how at the beginning, when she used to do everything on foot, she felt strange because she felt people were staring at her. In her view, they must have thought it was weird, since it is not so common to see people walking on the side of the road. The perception that she stood out for walking accentuated her sense of being an outsider.

Brenda contrasts her former habit of walking everywhere in her home town in Mexico with the need for private transportation experienced in the US. Even nowadays, when she goes back to Mexico to visit, she comments, she still walks long distances.

> Lilian: Y la emergencia, ¿no?
> Brenda: La emergencia, sí, la necesidad. A veces por la necesidad se hace. Sí, se hace uno más fuerte. Pero cuando yo empecé me temblaba. Me bajaba del carro y mis manos estaban así. (*Brenda shows how she was shaking, and laughs.*) Sí, pues, sí.
> Lilian: ¿Le cambió mucho eso?
> Brenda: Sí, pues, me cambió mucho porque de perdido ya no me miraban. Por ahí, cuando iba cruzando las calles caminando … (*laughs*) Le digo ya a mi esposo: "Antes a mí no me daba vergüenza caminar." (*lowers tone of voice*) Le digo: "Y ahora, ya me da vergüenza, si voy al correo caminando." Porque a veces sí hace falta caminar… Le digo: "Si voy al correo caminando, ya me da vergüenza que me miren." (*laughs*)
> Lilian: Uno se acostumbra, no…
> Brenda: Se acostumbra uno, sí. Pues, cuando vamos para México, uuu … caminamos bien lejototes, para ir al mandado, algo así, verdad. Y no me da vergüenza allá. No… (*high pitch*). No, pues, aquí sí. Como que la gente mira más a uno: "Mira, esa anda caminando." (*high-pitched, imitating voice of someone making fun of her, and laughs*) Me figuro, ¿verdad? (*laughs*)

> Lilian: And the emergency, right?
> Brenda: The emergency, yes, need. Sometimes one does things because of the need. Yes, one becomes stronger. But when I started I was trembling. I would get out of the car and my hands were like this. (*Brenda shows how her hands were shaking and laughs.*) Yes, well, yes.
> Lilian: Did this make a big difference for you?
> Brenda: Yes, well, it meant a big change for me because now at least they weren't looking at me. Sometimes, when I was crossing the streets, walking … (*laughs*). I tell my husband, "Before, I was never ashamed of walking." And I tell him, "Now, I even feel embarrassed if I walk to the post office." Because sometimes one needs to walk. I tell him, "If I walk to the post office, now I'm embarrassed because they will be looking at me." (*laughs*)
> Lilian: One gets used to it, right?

Brenda: Yes, one gets used to it. Because when we go to Mexico, we walk really far, to go shopping, or something, right. And I don't feel embarrassed there. No. No, but here, I do. It's as though people look at you more, "Look, that one's walking." *(high-pitched, imitating voice of someone making fun of her, and laughs)* That's what I imagine, right.

At first she even used to have to walk to school meetings, as usually her husband was not able to drive her there, because he was at work. Brenda shares how her husband had encouraged her to learn how to drive, and had eventually bought her an old little car, so that she would not worry if she crashed it. The words her husband used, literally, were, *"Te compré este carrito, para que te enseñes."* (I bought you this little car for you to teach yourself [how to drive].)

Lilian: Cuando usted llegó ¿cuánto tardó, después, en empezar a manejar?" ¿Unos años o unos meses?

Brenda: Como unos dos años...

Lilian: ¿Estaban en la escuela las dos más grandes?

Brenda: Sí, estaban en la escuela, pero, pues a veces hasta caminando venía a las juntas y a eso porque mi esposo trabajaba... Y, pues, caminando *(emphatic/rise-fall)*. Y ya me dijo él: "Tienes que enseñarte a manejar porque no vas a andar todo el tiempo así." "Y, no, pues yo tengo miedo." Y luego compró un carrito viejito, viejito. Y dijo: "Mira, para que no tengas nervios que porque el mueble," póngale que no nuevo, ¿verdad? pero más o menos. Dijo: "Te compré este carrito, para que te enseñes. Así, pues si le das un golpe, pues, ya." *(tone of voice imitating husband's and gestures brushing it off, as not important)* Ahi, pues, sí, ya gracias a Dios. Pues, echándole ganas, sí ... Sí, sale uno, pues, más adelante.

Lilian: When you arrived, how long was it until you started driving? A few years, a few months?

Brenda: About two years.

Lilian: Were your older daughters already in school?

Brenda: Yes, they were in school, but sometimes I even went walking to the meetings and things, because my husband worked. And, well, walking *(emphatic/rise-fall)*. And he told me, "You need to teach yourself how to drive because you're not going to go on like this all the time." "And, no, well, I'm scared." And then he bought an old, old little car. And he said, "Look, so that you're not nervous about the vehicle," as if it was, not new, but kind of. He said, "I bought you this little car, so that you teach yourself. So that if you crash it, so what." *(tone of voice imitating husband's and gestures brushing it off, as not important)* There, well, yes, thanks be to God. Well, making an effort, yes... Yes, one does progress.

Being able to drive is one of the resources that Brenda mentions first as one of the most important changes she has made. When asked about how she had learned to navigate her new context, Brenda responds with a detailed narration of how she learned how to drive a car, as one of the main skills that she developed in order to function in the US. As a sign of how significant an achievement this is for her, she devotes a considerable amount of time to the discussion of the decision and process of learning how to drive.

> Lilian: Después ¿qué le contaría a una amiga de cómo aprendió a moverse aquí en Estados Unidos? Sabe, a moverse, que uno se mueve diferente...
> Brenda: No, pues, aprendí a manejar ... que era lo que yo no sabía. Y, pues, ahí en el parqueadero donde nosotros vivíamos, cuando mi esposo se iba a trabajar yo no más movía el carro para atrás y para adelante, para atrás y para adelante y así... Y así empecé. Y luego iba y lo parqueaba en la sombrita y luego dijo él: "Ahora te voy a sacar a manejar a la carretera." Y yo le dije: "No, en la carretera yo no, porque tengo miedo encontrarme los carros." Y luego me dice: "Y luego, pues, ¡tampoco te vas a meter sola a la carretera...que no haya carros!" *(laughs)* Y, no, pues ya con todo y mis nervios, pues, así, me tuve que meter. *(laughs)*

> Lilian: Then, what would you tell a friend about how you learned how to manage *(literally "move")* here in the United States? You know, to manage, that one needs to manage differently.
> Brenda: Well, I learned how to drive ... which was what I didn't know. And, well, there in the parking lot where we used to live, when my husband left for work I used to just move the car back and forth and back and forth, and so. And that's how I started. And then I would park it in the shade, and then he said, "Now I am going to take you out to drive on the highway." And I said, "No, on the highway no, because I'm afraid of coming across other cars." So he said, "And then, well, you're not going to expect to be alone on the highway... for no other cars to be there!" *(laughs)* So, well, nervous and all, well, I had to get on. *(laughs)*

There are several parallel expressions in the explanation of how she learned how to drive, and how she learned how to negotiate the new context. To highlight the connections with other aspects of her account, it may be useful to compare some elements of Brenda's description of her learning how to drive side by side some of the language used in her description of how she learned how to interact in the schools. In both contexts she refers to how she learned, little by little, even when it was scary. Brenda describes how she taught herself how to drive, with the phrase *"movía el carro para atrás y para adelante,"* to explain how she learned, as she practiced going backward and forward. This expression is similar to the phrase Brenda used in talking about what she would recommend someone to do if they were planning to come to the US, *"poquito a poquito una va aprendiendo para seguir adelante con sus problemas"* (little by little one learns how to push on [and deal] with one's problems). The phrase *"poco a poquito"* (little by little) is used in reference to learning both how to drive and how to navigate the new context, which in Spanish may be expressed literally in terms of *"aprender a moverse"* (learning how to move about). Another phrase used both to describe the way she learned how to drive as well as to allude to the progress in the new environment is *"echándole ganas,"* which implies a combination of the willingness and the effort necessary to succeed.

## Physical Mobility as a Communal Resource: Solidarity as Self-Realization

**Brenda—*Y me pedían "ride" y a mí se me hacía malo decir que no.
Y de ahí empecé yo a superarme más*.**
**(And they would ask me for rides and I felt bad saying "no".
And from then on I started progressing more.)**

In Brenda's story, solidarity contributes to personal growth in community. So that the person who receives help is not the only one who benefits, but the helper feels grateful for the chance to develop skills through helping someone in need. Selflessness leads to self-confidence, but it is more of a self-in-community-confidence, not a source of individual pride, as much as something that became a resource for the community and was born from the community, from a need or a desire to help.

Vulnerability and agency remain tightly intertwined throughout the narratives. Once again, Brenda offers the most detailed account of their different facets, ranging from the feeling of standing out as an outsider at first when she walked everywhere, to the satisfaction of finally being able to offer a ride to a friend in need, through the self-confidence developed in the process of teaching herself how to drive. One of the reasons which compelled her to gather the courage to start driving was the need to help a friend in an emergency. Brenda views this incident as a decisive factor in her learning process. She also gives her friend credit, because at the time she had encouraged Brenda with reassuring words, telling her that she could do it.

> Y luego, también yo tengo bien presente una amiga, que ella ya tenía tiempo aquí, y ella tuvo un aborto. Y entonces esa amiga tenía que ir a la clínica y no podía manejar. Y luego me dijo a mí: "Brenda, usted me hace el favor de llevarme a la clínica." (*rising, as a question*) Le dije: "Yo no puedo" (*stretched out as if indicating a big or serious impediment*), le digo: "Yo no sé manejar." Dijo: "Usted puede, Brenda, usted puede".

Y luego, pues, a mí se me hizo malo que ella necesitaba, verdad, porque ella a mí me había ayudado también mucho. Entonces, ya, dije: "Pues en el nombre ya de Dios, Señor que tú seas quien lleve este volante y no yo." Y saqué el carro y me vine. Y vivía ella aquí por ... Ay, no me acuerdo la calle, pero está como a cuatro cuadras de aquí. Pues, así me vine por ella.

And then, I remember well a friend who had been here for quite some time; she had a miscarriage. And then that friend had to go to the clinic and she couldn't drive. So she asked me, "Brenda, would you do me the favor of taking me to the clinic." (rising, as a question) I said, "I can't. (stretched out as if indicating a big or serious impediment) I don't know how to drive." She said, "You can, Brenda, you can." And then, I thought it was bad that she was in need, right, because she had also helped me a lot. So then I said, "In God's name, Lord, may you be who guides this steering wheel and not me." And I got the car out and came. And she lived here, around ... oh, I can't remember the name of the street, but it's about four blocks away from here. So, then I picked her up.

After giving a detailed description of that episode, about when she had to drive a friend who had just had a miscarriage to a clinic, Brenda says: "Yes, that helped me a lot, a lot." This may refer both to the fact that her friend had offered to take her out every day to drive on the highway, and learn little by little, as well as to the decisive incentive to finally start driving created by her need to help her friend in an emergency.

Y me dijo: "Ya ve, que nada le pasó, no más con sus nervios. Y luego ya la llevé a la clínica" (Her voice sounds happy; you can sense her satisfaction.) y regresamos a la farmacia y ya me regresé yo a mi casa y me dijo: "Y ¿cómo está?" "No, pues, bien." Y dijo: "Ya ve, así, poco a poquito todos los días va a venir conmigo para que se le quite el miedo a andar por la carretera." (laughs) Y también eso me ayudó mucho a mí, mucho. Sí. Y ya después así, amigas que no tenían carro yo manejaba, poco a poquito (said fast, as if explaining, not all of a sudden, of course, as a clarification) verdad, empecé, pero ... Y me pedían "ride" [raide] y a mí se me hacía malo decir que no. Y de ahí empecé yo a superarme más. Ahora, ya, gracias a Dios, ya voy a Puentes.(laughs with satisfaction) Sí, ya, gracias a Dios. Sí ... pues, poco a poquito, pero se va superando uno ... no más el inglés no lo puedo desarrollar todavía. (laughs)

And she said, "You see that nothing happened; it's just your nerves. And then I took her to the clinic." (Her voice sounds happy; you can sense her satisfaction.) And we went to the pharmacy and I returned home and she asked, "So, how are you?" "No, I'm fine." And she said, "You see, like that, little by little every day you're going to come with me so that you lose your fear of going on the highway." And that also helped me a lot. Yes. And then, with friends who didn't have a car, I drove, little by little, (said fast, as if explaining, not all of a sudden, of course, as a clarification) right, I started. And they would ask me for rides and I felt bad saying "no". And from then on I started progressing more. Now, thanks be to God, I already go to Puentes. *(laughs with satisfaction)* Yes, now thank the Lord. Yes, little by little, one goes making progress ... it's just English I haven't been able to develop yet. *(laughs)*

Brenda repeatedly points out that she taught herself how to drive, and mentions how learning on her own was much better than having someone bossing her around. Thus, she relates the development of this resource, and sharing it, to her sense of achievement and self-realization.

Brenda: [...] Pero esa es más mi experiencia, aquí, pues que me enseñé a manejar.
Lilian: Y sola al principio...
Brenda: Sí, sola. Es mejor que ... a que le digan a uno: "Mira, dale para acá"; y "no te metas a la raya"; y "no la pises"; y "no vayas a ir para acá". *(Said very fast and in nervous tone, in high pitch, suggesting yelling.)* Lo ponen a uno más nervioso. *(laughs)* Y así, pues, uno solo, pues, está mejor. Verdad, ni qué nos regañen. Uno solo sabe que si se pasó un "stop" o algo, sabe que hizo algo mal, ¿verdad? *(laughs)*

Lilian: And on your own, at first...
Brenda: Yes, on my own. It's better than ... them telling you, "Look, go this way"; or "don't go on the line"; or "don't go over it"; or "don't you go this way". *(All said very fast and in a nervous tone, in high pitch, suggesting yelling.)* They make you more nervous. *(laughs)* This way, well, on one's own, it's better. Right, without their scolding. You already know that if you crashed a stop sign, or something, that you did something wrong, right? *(laughs)*

By way of conclusion, at the end of this part of her account, Brenda establishes a connection between driving and learning English, as she mentions that she still needs to work on the latter. So, in her view of what is significant learning that affects a person's functioning in the States, and more specifically, in interacting with schools, Brenda equates these two apparently very different experiences: learning how to drive and acquiring a new language, even though these ideas were not connected in the interview questions. These emerge as the top two resources for the immigrant women who shared their stories, considered essential to their new needs in this new context. This section seems to hold the key to interpreting Brenda's words. *"Y ya, después, yo manejaba, poco a poquito. Y de ahí empecé yo a superarme más, gracias a Dios, ya voy a Puentes."* (And then, I would drive, little by little, right, I started. And from then on I started progressing more. Now, thanks be to God, I already go to Puentes.) Again, she relates learning how to drive with *"salir adelante"* (progressing or moving ahead) and achievement. Brenda is not an exception in the central role transportation plays in her story. As mentioned earlier, each of the seven women devotes a significant amount of time to expressing the importance of getting rides, learning how to drive, knowing how to drive, or owning a car.

## Susana—*Así es que era indispensable que aprendiera a manejar. Ya después ¡a ver quién me detiene!*
(So I just had to learn how to drive. Afterwards, who would stop me!)

In her first interview, Susana mentions two of the first things a newcomer must obtain in order to survive in the US, and compares these with some aspects of the lifestyle she left behind in Mexico.

Lilian: ¿Qué le contaría sobre cómo aprendió a moverse aquí en los EE.UU?
Susana: Como en las primeras veces…
Lilian: De cómo aprendió a abrirse camino…
Susana: Como por aquí es difícil, lo primero que tiene que conseguir es un carro y teléfono. Porque si no … si no tiene teléfono, haga de cuenta que no tiene boca. Porque aquí todo es por teléfono. Carro es indispensable. Para ir a la tienda, para llevar a los niños a la escuela … (*as if starting a long list, implying that it is necessary for everything*). No es como allá en México, pues, que hay camiones. Paga uno el boleto, se sube al camión, y lo lleva donde quiere, verdad. Aquí, no. Hay que … si tiene carro, si no tiene que andar pagando "ride" /rai/ que luego sale más caro. Asique tiene que conseguirse un carro y un teléfono, luego luego. (*laughs*) Pues, sí, para ir a trabajar, para … pues, sí, para llevar a los niños a la escuela, para ir cuando tiene a traer mandado o algo, verdad. … ir a la clínica. Uhm. Es algo que aquí, pues, les digo, aquí tener teléfono y carro no es un lujo, es una necesidad. Aha. Le digo que si no tengo carro, haga de cuenta que me mochan los pies. (*laughs*) Porque no puedo salir a ningún lado. (*high rise*) Me quedo aquí.

Lilian: And what would you tell her [a newly immigrated friend] about how you learned how to manage in the US?
Susana: At the beginning?
Lilian: About how you learned to find your way around things…
Susana: As here it is difficult, the first thing you need to get is a car and a phone. Because if not, if you don't have a phone, it's as if you had no mouth because here everything is [done] on the phone. A car is indispensable. To go to the store, to drive the kids to school … (*Intonation suggests a long list, implying that it is necessary for everything.*) It isn't like over there, in Mexico where there are buses. You pay your ticket, you get on the bus, and it takes you wherever you want to go, right? You have to … if you have a car, if not you have to be paying for rides, which are more expensive. So you need a car and a phone, right away (*laughs*). Yes, to go to work, to take the kids to school, to go shopping or something, right? To go to the clinic. Uhm. I tell you that if I have no car, it's as if I had my feet chopped off (*laughs*) because I can't go anywhere. I have to stay right here.

Susana uses hyperbole to underscore how a phone and a car are not only necessary but indispensable. You might as well have no mouth, or no feet, she comments, if you are without a phone or a car once you are living in the US. In the first few minutes of her second interview, Susana refers to driving and learning how to drive. For a while, her older brother was the main driver in the family but, soon after he left, Susana had to learn how to drive. Again, the amount of detailed attention devoted to this resource may be seen as an indication of its centrality. Susana lists all the reasons that made it necessary for her to learn how to drive. First, she comments on the fact that here there is no public transportation. She then describes how it came to a point when she had no one she could count on to drive her to doctor appointments, or to pick up a child when they called from the school.

> Yo aprendí a manejar el día que se me fueron todos los choferes de la casa. Se me fue mi mamá para México. Mi papá, como él siempre andaba tomado, pues, no podía confiar en él. Si yo tenía una cita, no podía confiar en que él iba a estar a tiempo, o si me hablaban de la escuela, o para ir a la iglesia, o si tenía que ir a llevar al niño al doctor, pues, no. Y hasta que él apareciera… Y mi hermano, que era el que manejaba, pues, se había ido a buscar trabajo a otro estado del oeste. Asique, pues, no me quedó otra opción más que agarrar el volante y: "Señor ¡ahí voy!"

> I learned how to drive the day all the drivers left home. My mom left for Mexico. My dad, as he was always drunk, well, I couldn't trust him. If I had an appointment, I couldn't trust that he was going to be on time, or if they called me from the school, or to go to church, or if I had to take my child to the doctor, no. And, for him to show up… And my brother, who was the one who could drive, well, he had left to look for work in another western state. So, I had no choice than to take over the wheel and: "Lord, here I come!"

Then, she presents the most detailed account of how the system of *"rides"* works. Susana explains that these rides she relied on until she was able to drive herself are paid trips provided by neighbors, who offer what amounts to an informal cab service. She stresses the fact that this system of transportation lacks flexibility and provides limited mobility, since when a passenger pays for a ride, it is assumed by the driver that they will go to only one specified destination and back.

> Susana: Cuando aprendí a manejar tenía a los dos niños chiquitos. Uno tenía dos años y la niña tenía tres. Y tenía a mis hermanos. Tenía a Mari, Gladis, Vivi, Gabriel. Y Miguel, que era el que se me había ido, era el chofer. Y se me había ido, asique pues tenía cuatro hermanos en la casa y mis dos niñitos. Así es que era indispensable que

aprendiera a manejar. Ya después, ¡a ver quién me detiene! Sí pero tuve que aprender a manejar porque pedía "ride" y cinco dólares. Y, pues, no más a donde iba. No podía desviarme a otro lado. Si iba a la tienda, iba a la tienda. Nada que "ahora vamos para acá o para allá". No, va de "ride" uno y a lo que va, va. Y ¡no te entretengas mucho! Y, pues, a esperar a que tengan tiempo de darle el "ride" a uno. Así fue cómo empecé a manejar, por necesidad. Y me dio la libertad de que puedo ir, si se me ofrece, y ya no tengo que esperar, a ver quién viene.

When I learned how to drive, I had both my young children. One was two and my daughter was three. And I had my brothers and sisters. I had Mari, Gladis, Vivi, Gabriel. And Miguel, the one who had left, was the driver. And he had left, so I had four siblings at home and my two little kids. So I just had to learn how to drive. Afterwards, who would stop me! Yes, but I had to learn how to drive because I would ask for a ride, and it was five dollars. And, then, it was straight to where I was going. I couldn't make a detour. If I was going to the store, to the store I went. There was no "now we go here or there." No, if you get a ride wherever it is you are going, that is it. And, no dawdling! And also having to wait for them to have time to give you a ride. That's how I started driving, out of necessity. And it gave me the freedom of going, if I need to, without having to wait and see who can come.

This excerpt reveals the importance of gaining access to independent mobility for Susana, who at the time was in charge of four siblings and her own two young children. Susana captures the possibilities offered by her newly acquired skill, which had become a vital resource, in the following words, "*Así es que era indispensable que aprendiera a manejar. Ya después ¡a ver quién me detiene!*" (So it was indispensable to learn how to drive. Afterwards, who would stop me!) There is a new sense of freedom of movement that came with being able to decide on her own when and where she could go, without having to wait around for a driver to be available or willing to give her a ride, which she needed to pay for. This freedom would often be taken for granted by many adults in the US.

### Patricia—"*Ahora que empiezo a manejar, un poquito más me relaciono así con la escuela y todo.*"
(Now that I'm starting to drive, I relate a bit more with the school and all.)

Although the seven women interviewed devote a significant amount of time to expressing the importance of getting rides, learning how to drive, knowing how to drive, or owning a car, it is Patricia who explicitly points to it as a factor which has contributed to changing her relationship with the schools.

When Patricia lived in another western state, she sometimes walked to school meetings. At one point, she also had to walk her eldest child to school, because she lived outside the bounds of the bus route.

> Lilian: ¿Le parece que ha cambiado cómo usted interactúa con la escuela, o no? Como usted se relaciona con la escuela o la escuela con usted, la comunicación... ¿Cómo le parece que es?
> Patricia: *(laughs)* No, pues, siempre ha sido así, igual. Un poquito ahoritas me relaciono más con la escuela, porque ... ah ... *en el estado* [name of state deleted] adonde vivíamos antes, yo no manejaba, así es que no podía ir mucho que a las conferencias y reuniones y que todo eso. No podía ir mucho. Y había veces que en una sí me podía ir, porque me iba caminando. En uno de los apartamentos que vivimos, estaba cerca la escuela, tenía que llevar yo al niño caminando a la escuela, porque estaba cerquita y el bus no los levantaba.

> Lilian: Do you think that the way you interact with the schools has changed, or not? The way you relate with the school, or the school with you, in your communication... How do you see this?
> Patricia: *(laughs)* No, well, it's always been like this, the same. A bit now I relate more with the school, because ... uhmmm ... *in the state* [name of state deleted] where we used to live before, I didn't drive, so that I couldn't go much to the conferences and meetings and all that. I couldn't go much. There were times where I could go, because I walked there. At one of the apartments where we lived, it was close to the school, so I had to walk my son to school, because as it was near, the bus didn't pick him up.

Although she does not yet think she can drive perfectly, and still does not go on the highway, Patricia says she has lost her fear of driving, and manages well. Now she can interact more freely with the school. Among other things, she can now schedule her parent-teacher conferences, choosing the times, knowing that she will be able to attend because of the autonomy that driving brings.

> Pero aquí, pues, ya cuando hay siempre conferencias, yo pongo mi horario a qué horas quiero y yo voy a la hora que yo puedo, porque pues ya manejo *(laughs)* un poquito, verdad. No sé manejar todavía mucho, pero ya he perdido ... no tengo miedo ... por ejemplo para ir a la tienda. Para Los Puentes, yo no voy casi; siempre me anda llevando mi esposo. Pero no, se me hace que un poquito más, ahora que empiezo a manejar, un poquito más me relaciono así con la escuela y todo. Y, como le digo, no voy mucho si hacen cada rato así que de padres que vayan, pero yo con los niños que cuido no puedo ir mucho, no puedo salir. Y ya en los tiempos de tarde, que está muy frío, como el año pasado que tenía al niño por este tiempo, estaba chiquito y batallaba mucho yo con él y su tos.

But here, well, when there are conferences, I choose the schedule I want and I go at the time I can, because I already drive *(laughs)* a little, right. I can't drive a lot yet, but I have lost... I'm not scared ... for example to go to the store. But to Los Puentes, I hardly go; my husband always drives me there. But no, I think that a bit more, now that I'm starting to drive, I relate a bit more to the school and all. And, as I said, I don't go if they have things all the time for parents to attend, because with the kids I babysit I can't go much, I can't go out. And then in the evening, when it's very cold, like last year when I had my baby, he was very young and I struggled a lot with him and his cough.

At the beginning of this first interview, Patricia shared a vivid description of a day on a weekend soon after her family had arrived in the semi-rural area where they now lived, which coincided with one of the largest harvest festivals in the region. Although at the time this seemed like a digression from the main points of the interview, it soon became clear that this was a story of how she had used her newly acquired skill of driving to negotiate her new context. That day she managed to get out of a complicated situation with unusually heavy traffic in an area she was barely familiar with, at a time when she was just learning how to drive. Within the context of Patricia's whole account, this story pointed to her intense awareness of the significance of being able to drive.

## Luisa—*Aunque tenía miedo o nervios, tenía que hacerlo.* (Even if I was afraid or nervous, I had to do it.)

For a long time, Luisa had only been able to manage by depending on her network of friends, acquaintances and family to move around. Again, in Luisa's case, learning how to drive did not only mean gaining physical mobility but it also represented becoming a resource for others. This example reflects another aspect of communal agency. Luisa learned how to drive, by a combination of being taught by the person who was her boss at the time, and her own effort in teaching herself to drive in the open spaces surrounding her house. At the time, Luisa was employed as an agricultural worker, and also took care of her boss's children. So, driving became important for her, not only personally but as part of her job, to be able to drive the children who were under her supervision to sports practice and other after-school activities.

> Lilian: Y le iba a preguntar de vuelta ¿cómo le contaría a su amiga cómo aprendió a moverse aquí en los EE.UU.? ¿Qué cosas aprendió? ¿Cómo aprendió?
> Luisa: ¿Yo, cómo aprendí?
> Lilian: Sí, cuando llegó, ¿cómo aprendió?

Luisa: Híjole, oiga, cuando llegué aquí, para mí ... el moverme, el saber moverme ... fue muy difícil porque, pues, no conocía. Y ... no manejaba. (*sing-song/rise-fall intonation*) No sabía manejar y estaba tan acostumbrada a lo de México, verdad, y luego venir aquí que yo no hallaba nada de las cosas que yo estaba acostumbrada a usar. Pero sí hay. Pero no sabía. Y, sí se me hizo muy difícil porque por aquí, por ejemplo, no hay camión, verdad? Como en Puentes, que puede uno andar en el bus. Pero aquí no. Entonces aquí si no... Por ejemplo, mi esposo se iba a trabajar y yo no podía ir a ningún lado, ni a la tienda ni nada, porque no tenía dos carros, teníamos uno no más. Y, fue muy difícil. El me decía: "Tienes que aprender a manejar para que me dejes en el trabajo y vayas a hacer lo que tienes que hacer tú." Pero para mí fue muy difícil eso, moverme, ir a las tiendas, o al trabajo, a trabajar. Eso se me hacía, pues, difícil porque yo no sabía mover el carro. (*sing-song*) Y mi hijo el más grande, a los 13 años ya andaba ahí manejando y él era el que nos movía. Pero, imagínese: nos movía aquí al trabajo, no lejos, porque él no tenía ni edad ni nada para ... para ... movernos, verdad. Entonces: "No, no," dijimos. "No, él no puede." No más porque él quería aprender y todo, pero, no. Pero sí fue duro para mí, yo ... un tiempo pues batallaba porque él me tenía que llevar al trabajo y luego hablarle para que me recogiera. (*stretches words*) Pero sí fue difícil eso, sí fue duro acostumbrarme a ir a las tiendas y hasta allá y... Y que aquí no hay, tenemos que ir hasta Puentes. Y así. Pero sí, eso sí se me hizo difícil.

Lilian: And I was going to ask you again, how would you tell your friend how you learned how to manage here in the U.S.? What things did you learn? How did you learn them?
Luisa: How did I learn?
Lilian: Yes, when you arrived, how did you learn?
Luisa: Wow, listen, when I arrived here, for me ... managing, knowing how to move about...was very difficult because, well, I didn't know. And ... I couldn't drive. (*sing-song/rise-fall intonation*) I didn't know how to drive, and I was so used to everything in Mexico, right, and then when I came here I couldn't find any of the things that I was used to. But they have them, but I didn't know. And, well, I found it very difficult because around here, for example, there's no bus, right? Like in Puentes, where one can ride the bus. But here you can't. So, here if you don't... For example, my husband would go to work and I couldn't go anywhere, not even to the store or anything, because we didn't have two cars, we only had one. And it was very difficult. He used to say to me, "You need to learn how to drive so that you can drop me off at work and then go and do what you need to do." But for me it was very difficult, that, moving about, going to the stores, or to work. I found that very hard, well, because I didn't know how to move the car. (*sing-song*) And my son, the older one, was already driving at 13, and he was the one who drove. But, imagine, he would drive us to work here, not very far, because he wasn't old enough to to take us, right. So, then. "No, no," we said. "He can't." It was just that he wanted to learn and all, but no. But it was hard for me, I ... There was a time when I struggled because he had to take me to work and then I had to call him so that he would pick me up. (*stretches words*) But that was hard, yes, it was hard getting used to going to the stores and over there and...

And some things you can't get here, we need to go to Puentes. And so on. But, yes, I found it very difficult.

As was the case with the other women, Luisa mentions how important it was to learn how to drive in order to become more independent. At first, she depended completely on her husband, to go shopping and everything. As an illustration of her dependency on others before learning how to drive, Luisa shares a story of an emergency. Her older son, Manuel, broke his hand while at school, and needed to be taken for surgery and treatment to a hospital in the largest city in the state, El Palenque, that was three hours away by car. The weight of having to depend on others at a time of emergency becomes clear as she lists one by one who she had to rely on: First, she had to depend on the husband of a co-worker, then on her husband, and later on a transportation service to drive her. She repeatedly comments on the added complication of not knowing how to drive in such circumstances.

Lilian: Asique aprender a manejar le fue muy importante.
Luisa: Sí. Sí, porque yo no sabía manejar.
Lilian: ¿Y pudo ir a la escuela también así? ¿Empezó a ir, o no tanto, la llevaban a usted?
Luisa: No, no, cuando ya yo aprendí a manejar… Yo me acuerdo que cuando apenas andaba aprendiendo que nada más sabía ir para allá, yo estaba trabajando y me hablaron que mi hijo el grande se quebró una mano. Imagínese, yo sin saber … manejar. Y lo bueno es que llegó este señor y le dije … y la esposa de él … "Le hablaron a Luisa que a Manuel se le quebró una mano. Ve, llévala." Y él fue el que me llevó. Pero imagínese, yo sin poder manejar. Pero ya ahí empecé. Y luego de allí, "Oiga, se le quebró el brazo." Y luego, no me acuerdo. Se me hace que no lo enyesaron. Algo le pasó, desde aquí, desde este dedo y lo tuvieron… tuvimos que ir hasta El Palenque a llevarlo hasta el hospital, porque quién-sabe-qué le hicieron. Y le enyesaron y luego le quitaron el yeso y le hicieron como una cirugía. Pero teníamos que ir allá, imagínese, sin manejar. Nos llevaba una caminoneta, como del "Safe Ride". Y él, mi esposo, no más una vez fue y dijo: "No, ya ve tú. Que te lleve la camioneta." Porque, pues, yo no sabía manejar. Y a él no le gustaba ver cómo le picaban.

Lilian: So learning how to drive was very important.
Luisa: Yes, Yes.
Lilian: So, were you able to go to the school too, that way? Did you start driving there, or not so much, did they drive you?
Luisa: No, no, when I had learned how to drive… I remember once when I was starting to learn, when I only knew how to go over there, they called me because my eldest son had broken his hand. Imagine, and I didn't know how to … drive and the good thing is that this man arrived and I said … his wife told him, "They called Luisa

to tell her Manuel broke his hand. Go and take her." So he was the one who took me. But imagine, without knowing how to drive. But there I started. And then, from there, "Look, he broke his arm." And then, I can't remember. I think they didn't put him in a cast. Something happened to him, all the way up from here, from this finger, and they had to … We had to go up to El Palenque, to take him to the hospital, because who-knows-what they did to him. And they put his arm in a cast and then they took it off, and he had surgery. But we had to go all the way there, imagine, without driving. We took a truck, like Safe Ride. And he, my husband, went only once and said, "No, you go. The van can take you." Because I didn't know how to drive. And he couldn't stand watching how they gave him shots.

Luisa points out how she had struggled after her husband's death but that she finally overcame these difficult circumstances. Luisa weaves the sequence of important events in her life into the account of becoming self-reliant by learning how to drive.

Lilian: Y ¿cómo fue resolviendo eso usted?

Luisa: Bueno, lo resolvimos, aprendiendo a manejar. Aprendiendo a manejar y, luego, teniendo otro carro para, pues, para mí. Ya cuando aprendí, pues, ya fue más fácil, porque ya no dependía de mi esposo, asique "Llévame para aquí, llévame para acá" … o de Norma de así… "Norma necesito ir a tal parte" o ella también, verdad, así: "Oiga, présteme su carro que voy para …" Ya, y yo también así, verdad: "Oiga, ahora necesito esto y lo otro." Pero ya le digo, sí resolvimos eso, cuando yo aprendí a manejar. Yo aprendí a manejar ya y yo al principio no más iba aquí cerca. Pero ahora no, si ahora, no me gusta mucho andar allá, porque tengo muchos nervios, andar allá, pero sí, pues, fue del modo que aprendí, porque tenía necesidad de hacerlo porque no, nadie lo iba a hacer por mí. Y, cuando mi esposo se murió como que también se me hizo como un poco difícil, no sé por qué, si yo ya sabía moverme, sabía todo, pero como que estaba acostumbrada a él. A que: "Oye, voy a ir para tal parte" esto y lo otro. Y "Cuida a los niños," y así. Y cuando él ya no estuvo como que ¡hasta me encerré! Así a no ir ni al mandado ni nada. Así fue algo difícil para mí, ya quedarme sola aquí, ya así como que yo me sentía insegura de estar sola. Pero, pues salí adelante. Salí adelante y ahorita también, verdad. (very high pitch, high rise) Ahí sola yo y ahorita ya no, pues no, no batallo así para … pues para nada.

Lilian: And, how did you solve that?

Luisa: Well, we solved it by learning how to drive. Learning how to drive and then having another car, well, for me. Once I learned, it was easier because I didn't depend on my husband, so, "Take me here. Take me there." Or Norma, also, "Norma, I need to go to this place." Or she also, "Lend me your car that I am going…" And I also, like this, "Listen, now I need this and that." But, as I said, we solved this when I learned how to drive. I learned how to drive and at first I only drove around here. But now no, even now, I don't like much going over there, because I'm very nervous, to go over there, but yes, well, it was how I learned because I had the need to do it because nobody was going to do it for me. And when my husband died it was also a bit difficult for me, I don't know why, because I already knew how to move about, I knew everything, it was as if I were used to him. Like, "Listen, I'm going here," this and that. And, "Take care of the kids," and so on. And when he wasn't there, it's as if I even became withdrawn! I didn't go shopping, or anything. So it was something hard for me, being left on my own, it's as if I felt insecure of being on my own. But, well, I managed to get through it. I got through it and now, also, right? (*very high pitch, high rise*) Well, alone and now I don't struggle so much for ... well, for anything.

In this chronological narration of the sequence of important moments in her life in the United States, and as a backdrop to the story of how she learned how to drive, Luisa begins by describing how she managed at first, walking for miles. She used to go from the house where she worked as a nanny and housekeeper, to the chili processing plant, where she worked for the same boss, cleaning chili peppers. She would walk up and down a hill to accompany the children she took care of to their extracurricular activities. And, she would pick up her own son from school on foot as well.

> Lilian: ¿Usted ya había aprendido a manejar cuando su marido falleció, no?
> Luisa: Sí, sí, ya. Mi esposo, hace seis años que murió; seis años y medio. Y yo aprendí a manejar, sí, hace como ... ¿qué será? Como unos 10, 11 años.
> Lilian: ¿Cuando recién vino?
> Luisa: Cuando recién vine. Ándele.
> Lilian: ¿Tardó un poquito, o no?
> Luisa: A ver. Sí, yo creo como un año. Porque cuando recién llegué fui a trabajar con la familia Prieto, que vive para allá, a cuidar dos niños así como el niño y otro más grandecito. Y duré ... Ese señor tiene ... como una chilera. Siembra chile, lo levanta y lo limpia acá en una bodega. Entonces ellos viven allá, por donde se ven aquellos pinos, allá lejos, aquellos árboles, aquella loma, por ahí viven. Entonces, yo venía de allá, desde allí, así, por todo este camino, caminando, hasta allá, hasta atrás de esa loma, a ... cuidaba los niños, limpiaba la casa, hacía comida y cuando acababa me venía a limpiar chile. Pero me traía los niños, caminando. Y luego ya el mío, a las tres, yo me subía la loma y lo agarraba por ahí, para...
> Lilian: Ah, todo caminando.
> Luisa: Sí, caminando.

> Lilian: You had already learned how to drive when your husband passed, right?
> Luisa: Yes, yes, already. My husband died six years ago, six and a half years. And I learned how to drive, about, what would it be? About 10, 11 years ago.
> Lilian: When you'd just arrived?
> Luisa: When I'd just arrived, yes.
> Lilian: It took you a little while, right?

Luisa: Let's see. Yes, about a year, I think. Because when I first arrived I went to work with the Prieto family, who live over there, to take care of two children, one as young as my grandchild (almost two), and an older one. And it took me… That man has a chili pepper processing plant. He sows chilies, and he harvests them, and he cleans them here in a warehouse. So they live over there, where you see those pine trees, over there, those trees, that hill, that's where they live. So, I used to come from over there, all this way, walking, up to there, behind the hill … to take care of the kids, clean the house, cook the meals, and when I finished I would come and clean chilies. But I would come walking with the children. And then, mine, at three o'clock, I would climb up the hill and I would pick him up over there.
Lilian: All walking.
Luisa: Yes, walking.

The details in this story once again show the significance of the learning process. Luisa associates having independent physical mobility with her job, with driving the kids to school, and with visiting her family in Mexico. Again, she stresses the fact that previously she had depended on many people to give her rides. Since Luisa's extended family still lives in a border city in Mexico, to be able to visit them she used to depend on someone to drop her off at the border, about an hour and a half away from where she now lives, and then she would walk across the border.

Luisa recalls how her boss had urged her to learn how to drive, and had even given her driving lessons. She recounts, step by step, how she started, first driving along the country roads, and then on the main roads.

Luisa: Entonces, él, el señor ese, un día me dijo· "Oiga, debería de aprender a manejar, porque cuando hace frío o algo." Y le decía yo: "No, es que, Manuel, mi esposo, no me tiene paciencia. Quiere que aprenda rápido y me dice que 'Así no' y que esto y que el otro." Y él me enseño a manejar. Ese señor. Ese señor de repente un día me dijo: "Véngase, súbase al carro." Tenían un carro chiquito y me subió y me dijo: "Préndale y…" Y él me enseñó.
Lilian: Su patrón sería, no?
Luisa: Sí, era mi patrón. Y él me enseñó y … sin gritarme, sin desesperarse conmigo. Primero me traía así por aquí (a quiet unpaved country road), por toda la terracería. Me sacaba así, no más para venir de la casa aquí. Y, luego, ya en la tarde, ya me traían y me venía yo y ellos se iban. Y luego ya me sacó para el camino. Y ya, ya después, estaban los niños en la escuela y yo iba por ellos a la escuela y ya venía. Pero no más aprendí aquí no más, así. Pero ya, como le digo, íbamos necesitando. Tenía que moverme yo y empecé a irme yo sola allá, para Greenfields o para Gamesville, adonde yo pudiera ir. Y para Puentes, apenas hace poquito que empiezo a ir. Como siempre, me llevaban los muchachos, mis hijos… Bueno, primero mi esposo y luego los muchachos, mis hijos… Y luego, mis hijos, como que no me querían acarrear tanto para

allá, siguieron mis nueras. La mamá del niño, ella siempre… hasta para La Vía [*a large border city in the next state*]. Decía, "Quiero ir para México" y ella iba y me dejaba a La Vía, y ya yo me iba … caminando para México. Y ahí me esperaban, pasando el puente. Pero así aprendí. El me enseñó, sí.

Luisa: Then, he, that man (*or gentleman*), one day said, "Listen, you should learn how to drive, for the cold or something." And I said, "No, it's that Manuel, my husband, isn't patient with me. He wants me to learn fast and he says, 'No, not like that,' and this and that." And he taught me how to drive. That man. Suddenly, one day this man said, "Come, get into the car." He had a small car and he made me get in and said, "Start it and…" And he taught me.
Lilian: That was your boss, right?
Luisa: Yes, he was my boss. And he taught me and … without shouting, or despairing of me. First he would bring me this way (*a quiet unpaved country road*), along all the dirt roads. He would take me like this, just to come from his house here. And, then, in the afternoon, they'd bring me, I would drive up to here, and they left. And then he took me out to the road. And then, when the kids were in school, I would go and pick them up and come back. But mostly I learned around here. But, as I said, we needed it. I had to manage and I started to go on my own, to Greenfields, or to Gamesville, wherever I could go. And to Puentes, I've only started going recently. Because, the kids, my sons used to take me always. Well, first my husband, then my sons. And then, my sons didn't want to keep driving me there, so it was my daughters-in-law, the child's mother, she always … even to La Vía [*a large border city in the next state*]. I'd say, "I want to go to Mexico," and she would go and drop me off at La Vía, and I would cross over to Mexico, walking. Over there they would wait for me, on the other side of the bridge. But that's how I learned. He taught me.

The thread of Luisa's story of learning how to drive weaves in and out of the tapestry of her lifestory. There is a parallel between how Luisa made progress learning how to drive, and how she had to manage parenting as a single mom once her husband died. In her conclusion *"así tuve que aprender"* (that's how I had to learn), Luisa seems to be referring both to driving and to raising her teenage sons single-handedly. Luisa's is a story of managing and of progress through effort (*"salir adelante"*).

Y sí pero, ya le digo, así fuimos … fui … pues, saliendo ¿verdad? Tenía que aprender y, aunque tenía miedo o nervios, tenía que hacerlo. Y más cuando me quedé sola, pues, más. Tuve que, como que, tener más cuidado con los muchachos en la escuela (*fall-rise*). Porque ya estaban con… el más chiquito todavía estaba en … apenas iba a ir a la … se me hace que estaba en la middle school cuando mi esposo murió. Entonces, ya, usted sabe que cuando están creciendo, ¡híjole! Tiene uno que estar cuidándolos y viendo a ver con quién andan y todo… Pero, ¡así! (*assertive, as if saying, "so that's the way I did it"*) Y no … Así tuve que aprender. Porque ya no había quién, verdad, quien: "Mira esto, mira lo otro." No, ya uno tiene que… salir adelante.

And, yes, that is how we started… I progressed, right? I had to learn and, even if I was afraid or nervous, I had to do it. And once I was on my own, well, more so. I had to, like, be more careful with the kids at school. Because they were already … the youngest still was in … he was about to go to… I believe he was still in middle school, when my husband died. So, then, you know when they are growing up, Jeez! One has to be taking care of them and looking to see who they hang out with and all. But, yes! (*assertive, as if saying, "so that's the way I did it"*) And, well. That's how I had to learn. Because there was no one to say, "Look, this or that." No, one just has to … manage.

Solidarity and community make up the backbone of Luisa's story. Within her account of how she learned how to drive, Luisa mentions that she still works for the same boss during the chili season, but she refers to her work in the processing plant in terms of "helping out" her old boss (*"le ayudo a limpiar"*). At the time of the first interview, Luisa was helping her son out, so that he and his wife could graduate from college. So, it was hard for Luisa to go and work for her boss because she was taking care of her grandchild, and she could mostly work on weekends.

Y ahorita todavía, cuando es como noviembre, le ayudo todavía a limpiar [chiles]. Cada temporada voy y le ayudo a … Ahora fue muy difícil porque todavía estaba el niño. Y mi nuera trabajando y yo tenía al niño así es que iba los fines de semana, o a veces le decía a ella: "Llévate al niño con tu mamá para que te lo cuide, para yo irle a ayudar a este señor."

And even nowadays, around November, I help him clean [chilies]. Every season I go and help him … Now it was difficult because the child was still here. And my daughter-in-law was working and I still had the child with me, so I went only on weekends, or sometimes I'd tell her, "Take the child with your mom for her to take care of him so that I can go and help this man."

Although it has been hard for her to manage, Luisa can always count on her neighbors and friends. Introducing a recent example of how she had just asked the attendant at a store, probably the gas station, to help her fill up the tires of her car, Luisa stresses the fact that she lives in a community marked by solidarity in these terms, *"lo que tiene que la gente, la comunidad, sabe, que son amables"* (the thing is that here people, the community, you know, are kind).

Y, pues, ya le digo, sabe qué, aquí lo que tiene que la gente, la comunidad, sabe, que son amables, saben que uno… Por ejemplo, yo ahorita que estoy sola, si a mí se me ofrece algo, alguien, algo, no me dicen "no". Son así, que qué necesito… Como ayer, me fui a Puentes, y yo no sé echarle aire a una llanta. Tengo miedo. Y fui a la tienda y le dije al hombre de la tienda, le dije: "Gerardo, necesito un favor." Y me dijo: "Sí, ¿qué necesita?" "Necesito que le ponga aire a la llanta." Y: "Sí." Imagínese. Allá fue. Y siempre así, muy amables…

And, well, I tell you, you know what, the thing is that here people, the community, you know, are kind, they know that one… For example, now that I am alone, if I need anything, someone, something, they don't say, "no." They are like that, like what do I need… Like yesterday, I went to Puentes, and I don't know how to fill up the tires of my car. I'm scared. So I went to the store and I asked the man at the store I said, "Gerardo, I need a favor." And he said, "Sure, what do you need." "I need to pump air into my tires." And, "yes." Imagine. There he went. And it's always that way.

Just as she can count on her neighbors and friends, they can count on her. In an example of her own role in this communal solidarity, on the afternoon of one of the interviews, Luisa had a friend over, whom she was helping to get a job by sharing information on several agencies that provide home care, who occasionally hire her.

Once she learned how to drive, Luisa became a resource for others. She explains how she became a chauffeur to the children in the family she worked for, as she drove them to all their games, to sports practice, and to social events. As she reflects back on those days, Luisa cannot begin to imagine what it would have been like without knowing how to drive.

Lilian: Pero igual se manejaba, era la que llevaba a los chicos a todos lados…
Luisa: Sí. Sí, cuando ya empecé a manejar yo llevaba hasta esos niños que yo cuidaba. Los llevaba al juego, los llevaba a la práctica. Pero fueron niños que jugaban siempre. O sea, que se acababa una temporada de un juego y seguía el otro y el otro y así. Nos la pasamos siempre en juegos, o en convivios que hacían de los juegos, que los torneos, creo que le dicen, todo eso. Y ya era yo la que los llevaba. Y que si ellos iban a ir a tal parte a jugar, por ahí, lejos, teníamos que vender burritos para darles dinero o para la gasolina del camión que los iba a llevar. Y todo eso teníamos que hacerlo. Y para los juegos, pues, siempre andaba yo llevándolos, trayéndolos, en la práctica y todo. Teníamos que ir, pues, yo, a llevarlos, verdad. Sí, pues, fue muy importante aprender a manejar. Porque si no, imagínese. Fíjese que aquí sí hay mucha gente, oiga, que nunca aprendió a manejar. Se me hace tan… así tan difícil, digo yo. Imagínese que uno no maneje. Y luego, aquí hay mucha gente que llegaron primero que yo y no aprendieron a manejar. No se han animado. Como que todavía tienen ese miedo y yo pienso que ya ahorita… Pero no, imagínese como yo que ya me quedé sola y que no sepa manejar ¿Qué haría? No, ya me hubiera ido de aquí, para estar más cerca, con mi familia.

Lilian: But you still managed, you were the one who took the children everywhere…
Luisa: Yes. Yes, when I started driving I would take even the children I took care of. I took them to the games; I would take them to practice. But they were kids who were always playing [sports]. So, the season for one sport finished, and then another one, and another one, and so on. We were always at games, or going to socials they organized for the games, or the tournaments, I think they call them, and all that. And I was the one who would take them. And if they were going to go and play somewhere else, somewhere, far away, we had to sell burritos to give them money, or for the gas for the bus that was going to take them. And we had to do all that. And for the games, well, I was always taking them back and forth, to practice and all. We had to go, well, I, to take them, right? Yes, it was very important to learn how to drive. Because otherwise, imagine. And here there are many people, you know, who never learned how to drive. It seems so … difficult, I think. Imagine not knowing how to drive. And then, here there are many people who arrived before me and didn't learn how to drive. They haven't found the courage. They sort of still have that fear, and I think that by now… But no, imagine like me, that I'm on my own, if I didn't know how to drive. What would I do? No, I would have already left, to be closer, with my family.

Luisa reflects on how difficult it must be for those people who never learned how to drive after migrating. This comment mirrors Norma's comment on the limitations experienced by her neighbors who have not learned English since their immigration. In her case, Luisa especially wonders what would have become of her, when her husband died, if she had not already known how to drive. She would probably have moved back, she concludes, and returned to live with her family in Mexico. This final comment reveals the value Luisa assigns to this resource and her view of it as crucial and closely linked to survival in the United States.

# References

Ainslie, R. (1998). Cultural mourning, immigration, and engagement: Vignettes from the Mexican experience. In M. Suárez-Orozco (Ed.), *Crossings: Mexican immigration in interdisciplinary perspectives* (pp. 283–305). Cambridge, MA: Harvard University Press.

Hirsch, J. (1998). *Migration, modernity, and Mexican marriage: A comparative study of gender, sexuality and reproductive health in a transnational community* (Doctoral dissertation). Johns Hopkins University, Baltimore, MD.

Hirsch, J. (2003). *A courtship after marriage: Sexuality and love in Mexican transnational families.* Berkeley, CA: University of California Press.

Hirsch, J. (2007). "En el norte la mujer manda": Gender, generation, and geography in a Mexican transnational community. In D. Segura & P. Zavella (Eds.), *Women and migration in the U.S.-Mexico borderlands: A reader* (pp. 438–455). Durham, NC: Duke University Press.

Hondagneu-Sotelo, P. (1994). *Gendered transitions: Mexican experiences of immigration*. Berkeley, CA: University of California Press.

Hondagneu-Sotelo, P. (2003). Gender and immigration: A retrospective and introduction. In P. Hondagneu-Sotelo (Ed.), *Gender and U.S. immigration: Contemporary trends* (pp. 3–19). Berkeley, CA: University of California Press.

Menjívar, C. (2000). *Fragmented ties: Salvadoran immigrant networks in America*. Berkeley, CA: University of California Press.

Norton, B. (2013). *Identity and language learning: Extending the conversation* (2nd ed.). Tonawanda, NY: Multilingual Matters

Reay, D. (2004). Gendering Bourdieu's concepts of capitals? Emotional capital, women and social class. In L. Adkins & B. Skeggs (Eds.), *Feminism after Bourdieu* (pp. 57–74). Oxford and Malden, MA: Blackwell.

Suárez-Orozco, C. (2000). Identities under siege: Immigration, stress and social mirroring among the children of immigrants. In C. Robben & M. Suárez-Orozco (Eds.), *Cultures under siege: Collective violence and trauma* (pp. 194–226). New York, NY and Cambridge: Cambridge University Press.

Suárez-Orozco, C., & Suárez-Orozco, M. (2001). *Children of immigration*. Cambridge, MA: Harvard University Press.

Valencia, R., & Black, M. (2002). "Mexican Americans don't value education!"—On the basis of the myth, mythmaking, and debunking. *Journal of Latinos and Education, 1*, 81–103.

Zentgraf, K. (2002). Immigration and women's empowerment: Salvadorans in Los Angeles. *Gender & Society, 16*(5), 625–646.

# · 1 1 ·

# BECOMING A RESOURCE

## The Articulation of Agency and Structure

*Subjects are not only conditioned by their positions in structured social relations; subjects are also agents. To be an agent means that you can take the constraints and possibilities that condition your life and make something of them in your own way.* (Young, 2002, p. 101).

The notions of agency and structure adopted throughout this book draw on the theory of structuration put forward by Giddens (1984). In it the concept of agency means not only acting but also being capable of doing so, and carries the implication, as well, that at any point in their behavior the person(s) could have chosen to act in a different way. Being capable of exercising power to bring about transformation is described as the sine qua non of agency:

To be able to "act otherwise" means being able to intervene in the world, or to refrain from such intervention, with the effect of influencing a specific process or state of affairs. This presumes that to be an agent is to be able to deploy (chronically, in the flow of daily life) a range of causal powers, including that of influencing those deployed by others. Action depends upon the capability of the individual to "make a difference" to a pre-existing state of affairs or course of events. An agent ceases to be such if he or she loses the capability to "make a difference", that is, to exercise some sort of power. (Giddens, 1984, p. 14)

As the construct of agency emerges most clearly in instances of articulation with structure—especially, in the context of analyses based on critical theory—a better understanding of agency for our purposes also requires an exploration of the notion of structure which Giddens defines in terms of properties of social systems:

> [...] social systems, as reproduced social practices, do not have "structures" but rather exhibit "structural properties" and [...] structure exists, as time-space presence, only in its instantiations in such practices and as memory traces orienting the conduct of knowledgeable human agents. (Giddens, 1984, p. 17)

Finally, a definition of institutions also becomes relevant to an examination of the significance of structure in social reproduction and of the power dynamics involved. Again, Giddens establishes the connection between structural principles and institutions in these terms: "The most deeply embedded structural properties, implicated in the reproduction of societal totalities, I call *structural principles*. Those practices which have the greatest time-space extension within such totalities can be referred to as *institutions*" (p. 17, Italics in the original). The term "structure" adopted here and applied to the analysis of the narratives is closer to the definition of "structural principles" offered by Giddens in this context. Giddens's theorization, in combination with Young's, is central to our analysis of the narratives of the seven immigrant women, mainly because it sheds light on the macro and micro issues in their interconnection.

# Communal Agency

In his analysis of the articulation of agency and structure, and the dialectic relationship between social reproduction and transformation, Giddens (1984) indirectly suggests the need to understand the dynamics of power as pertaining to collectivities as well as individuals and their social interaction (p. 16). The construct of agency is expanded in the context of the analyses presented here so as to apply to a collective; this notion encompasses not only the actions of an individual in her interactions with institutions as she develops and acquires resources but further captures how these become communal resources. Thus, agency emerges as an intrinsic quality of the community. Agency and solidarity are conceptualized as inseparably interwoven and thus combined they become "communal agency" (Cibils, 2011; Martin, 2007). As an extension of the concept of "collective agents" (Sztompka, 1991), communal agency emphasizes the building of community through the continuous cycle created by the sharing of valuable resources once access to them is gained by members of the group.

## Communal Resources: A Characteristic of Motherwork

By way of conclusion, this chapter expands on the stories introduced earlier on acquiring and sharing the most valued resources—physical mobility, access to language resources, information on how institutions work, and access to these institutions. Thus, the narratives below serve as illustrations of communal agency in action by focusing on the way the seven immigrant women who were interviewed secured resources for themselves and their community, either by developing them or by seeking help to access them, and on how they eventually shared them.

In the stories of these seven Latina immigrant women, what in other contexts might be seen as personal gain is underscored here instead mainly for the way it affects the people around the person who initiated the change. Invariably, when a participant mentions developing or obtaining a resource, almost in the same breath she mentions how it was shared with others. Although the changes they brought about may appear to be insignificant from the outside, as they involve resources often taken for granted by members of mainstream society, these shared resources affect the lives of many and contribute significantly to the building of the community of immigrant mothers and the gradual transformation of their interactions and everyday functioning.

"I am a resource to others" is a motif which emerges from the seven women's narratives as they describe their own role in their community. This sharing of resources and becoming a resource for the survival of the community reflects the ideology of motherwork (Collins, 1994) driving the lives of these women. Quite distinct from the dominant ideology of motherhood, motherwork is not limited to the nuclear family, to an interest in the wellbeing of close relatives only but involves instead a sense of availability for whoever might need help in the community. The sense of urgency and eagerness to contribute to each other's survival is not described in heroic terms or as an out-of-the-ordinary overextension of the individual's generosity but as a way of life within a communal circle of shared resources.

## Becoming a Resource: Helping a Newcomer

An illustration of this process is offered in the response to a hypothetical case presented to each interviewee which involved the arrival of a newcomer to the community. The detailed experiences and recommendations shared here are just a sample of the communal support a newcomer would receive. Based on her experience of what a newly arrived immigrant mother could expect in the new context, Brenda lists the types of information she would share to help reduce her anxiety.

> Lilian: Y si ella le pregunta a usted de su experiencia con las escuelas, específicamente, cómo le fue, cómo se las arregló usted, qué necesita ella saber, y qué puede esperar. ¿Qué le contaría usted, de su experiencia? Si ella piensa venir ¿qué tiene que saber?
> Brenda: No, pues, yo le diría que aquí sí es bueno que los niños estudien aquí porque aprenden los dos idiomas, se superan más. Y, pues, por lo difícil de que ella se comunique con sus maestros, pues, que no se preocupara porque hay personas bilingües y personas buenas que le ayudan a uno, sí.

> Lilian: And if she asked you about your experience with the schools, specifically, how you did, how you managed, what she needs to know, and what she can expect. What would you tell her about your experience? If she is thinking of coming here, what does she need to know?
> Brenda: Well, no, I would tell her that it is indeed good for children to study here because they learn both languages, they progress more. And, well, as to how difficult it would be for her to communicate with their teachers, well, she shouldn't worry because there are bilingual people and good people who help you, yes.

Previously, Brenda introduced the basics of interacting with the schools with the phrase: "*Y luego, pues, yo le diría que sí se viniera y que yo le ayudaría.*" (And then, well, I would tell her to come and that I would help her). The choice of the two issues she would focus on offers an insight into what Brenda considers to be some of the most urgent issues to learn and the deepest sources of anxiety about managing in the new situation. She anticipates that the newcomer will wonder, "How will I communicate with the schools?" and "Will my children be ok?" To the first question, Brenda responds that there would be help for the adults, from "*personas bilingües*" (bilingual people) and "*personas buenas*" (good people).

The basis of her reassurance is communal solidarity which is also linked here to linguistic resources, as indicated by the use of the parallel phrases "bilingual people" and "good people". This may be a suggestion that some people will be able to assist her by speaking Spanish, and others, who may not be bilingual, will try and help her anyway—maybe by finding someone else who can interpret for her.

## Brenda—*"Hasta si no sabía manejar, yo le enseñaba a manejar."* (Even if she didn't know how to drive, I would teach her how to drive.)

As she lists the ways in which she would help a fellow immigrant woman who had just arrived in the country with school-age children, Brenda suggests that she would even offer to teach the newcomer how to drive if she did not know how to. As mentioned earlier, driving was one of the first aspects of life Brenda associated with the new sociocultural script and the new needs she encountered when she arrived in the US. As she accepted the new challenges, she taught herself how to drive and she developed this new independence and self-reliance. Further, once she had learned, driving was a way of becoming a resource to others.

> Lilian: ¿Habría otra cosa que le diría a su amiga imaginaria?
> Brenda: No, pues, que se viniera que yo la ayudaba. Hasta si no sabía manejar, yo le enseñaba a manejar, verdad. Le enseñaría … porque uno cuando llega aquí ni el dinero conoce. ¿Verdad que no? No lo conoce y pues, uno no más apronta el puño: "Pues, ahí, agarre" *(laughs, at own vulnerability)*, porque uno no lo conoce. Y, no, pues, le ayudaría a ella en lo que ella necesitara. Sí, porque yo ya sé lo que se sufre cuando uno llega sin … a ciegas, como luego dicen, verdad, sí. Sí la ayudaría y la apoyaría en todo eso. *(short silence)*
>
> Lilian: Would there be anything else you tell your imaginary friend?
> Brenda: Well, no, [I would tell her that] if she came I would help her. Even if she didn't know how to drive, I would teach her how to drive, right? I would teach her … because when one arrives here, one doesn't even know the money. Right? One doesn't know it and you just put your hand out and say, "There you are, take it" *(laughs, a sense of vulnerability is transmitted in this moment of complicity)*, because one isn't familiar with it. And I would help her in whatever she needed. Yes, because I know how you suffer when you have just arrived without … in the dark *(literally: blind)*. Yes I would support her and help her with all this.

Besides the need to acquire this skill, there are other issues related to driving that are mentioned in connection to adapting to the new context. An important piece of advice Brenda offers in her "survival kit" is the recommendation to drive carefully and not to speed. A detailed explanation of how to sign out a child during the school day is followed immediately by the advice to slow down, especially in front of the school, so as not to attract the attention of the police.

> Lilian: Y ¿qué le contaría usted de cómo hizo para arreglárselas? Algo que necesitaría saber ella … vio … estaría preocupada porque no sabe nada de cómo es aquí.
> Brenda: No sabe nada … *(laughs)* Bueno, pues, ya si no sabría ella cómo, dónde, porque ya ve que a veces no sabe uno en qué cuarto están, o cómo comunicarse, adonde va a llegar a procurarlos, cuando tiene que ir a recogerlos. Pues, entonces, yo ya le explicaría: "Pues, mira, hay una oficina, donde va a llegar primero y va a firmar para poder sacar su hijo, en caso que lo tenga que sacar, ¿verdad? Y, pues, si lo tiene que llevar y recoger, pues, no más irse al límite para que no la pare el 'chota' *(laughs at the word)*. Y tener cuidado, verdad, de manejar bien, despacio, mayormente en frente de la escuela o cuando ande ahí, verdad. Los niños, pues, poco a poco ellos … se van a ir haciendo amigos, verdad, y poco a poco van a ir aprendiendo el inglés, sí. Y, pues, siempre, sí, se supera uno más en este país. Sí." *(laughs)*. Tengo poco que comunicar, pero… *(laughs)*

> Lilian: And, what would you tell her about what you did to manage? Something that she would need to know. You see, she would be worried because she knows nothing about how things work here.
> Brenda: She knows nothing … *(laughs)*. Well, if she didn't know how, where— because you see, that sometimes one doesn't know in which room they are, or how to communicate, where one has to pick them up, when one has to go an pull them out. Well, then, I would explain to her, "Well, look, there's an office where you are going to go first and you are going to sign to be able to take your child—in case she had to pull the child out, right? And, well, if she has to drop off and pick up her child, just to drive at the speed limit, so that the cops *(laughs at the word she used)* don't stop her. And to be careful, right, to drive well, and slowly, especially in front of the school, or when she is around there, right? The kids, well, they are going to start making friends, little by little, and little by little they are going to start learning English, yes. And, yes, one progresses in this country. Yes." *(laughs)* I have little to communicate, but … *(laughs)*

In this context, the vulnerability of the participants centers on the possibility of being stopped by the police. Some time before the interviews took place, a sense of fear prevailed in the Borderlands as raids of immigrant communities by ICE (Immigration and Customs Enforcement) had intensified, and deportations had reached unprecedented numbers. Families were being separated, and there were reports of immigrant children being handcuffed outside of their elementary schools in different towns across the state. In a similar passage of her interview, Susana also mentions as a reason to be careful when driving the likelihood of being asked for documentation as proof of immigration status during a traffic stop. In fact, one of her sisters had recently been deported with her children after one such stop. According to Susana, this had happened mainly because her sister had attracted the attention of the police officers for having her children with her in the car during school hours. "I had warned her against it," Susana comments. But her sister had not listened to her, instead, that afternoon she had signed her children out of school early, to take them shopping before school got out.

**Brenda—*Y así, pues, nos ayudábamos las unas a las otras.***
***Pero esa es mi experiencia, aquí, pues que me enseñé a manejar.***
(And that is how we helped each other. But that is my experience, here, that I taught myself how to drive.)

As soon as she acquired this prized skill, Brenda became a resource to her community. Her husband jokingly calls her "el taxista" ("the cabby"), since she has become a driver for many of her friends, to whom she often offers rides to go shopping, to the post office, or the clinic. She is aware of the significance of her role, which is understandable, considering her description of how uneasy it used to make her feel at first to have to walk everywhere, because she stood out as different in her village.

> Lilian: ¿En qué le cambió? Por ejemplo, ¿qué cosas pudo empezar a hacer cuando empezó a manejar, que no hacía antes?
> Brenda: Mmm, pues, como le digo, había amigas que no tenían a veces en qué moverse y me decían: "Brenda, ¿me lleva al correo?" "¿Me lleva a la tienda?" "¿Me lleva a la clínica?" Mi esposo ya me decía "el taxista".
> Lilian: *(laughs)* Porque llevaba a todas...
> Brenda: *(laughs)* Dijo: "Mira, de primera no te podías enseñar a manejar, ahora ya te pareces taxista." *(continues laughing)*
> Lilian: *(laughs)* Sí, no la para nadie.
> Brenda: No, le digo, "Pues, que Fulano no tenía su mueble, que lo tenía descompuesto. Y pues, que la amiga, la otra, no tiene en qué moverse. Y, pues, que la otra que el esposo se llevó el mueble y, pues, no más tienen uno." Y así, pues, nos ayudábamos las unas a las otras. Sí, ya le digo. Pero esa es mi experiencia, aquí, pues que me enseñé a manejar.
> Lilian: Y sola al principio...
> Brenda: Sí, sola. Es mejor [...]

> Lilian: And how did it change things, for example, what things were you able to start doing that you couldn't do before, when you started driving?
> Brenda: Mmmm, well, as I said, there were friends who sometimes didn't have any means of mobility and they would ask me, "Brenda, can you take me to the post of-

fice?" "Can you take me to the store?" "Can you take me to the clinic?" My husband already called me "the cabby".
Lilian: *(laughs)* Because you gave everyone rides…
Brenda: *(laughs)* He said, "Look, at first you couldn't teach yourself how to drive, and now you are like a taxi driver." *(continues laughing)*
Lilian: *(laughs)* Yes, no one can stop you.
Brenda: No, I say, "Well, so-&-so didn't have her car, it broke down. And then, my other friend doesn't have mobility *(literally, what to move in)*. And, then, the other one's husband took the car and, well, they only have one." And that is how, well, we helped each other, yes, as I say. But that is my experience, here, that I taught myself how to drive.
Lilian: And on your own, at first…
Brenda: Yes, on my own. It's better […]

Brenda synthesizes her experience in developing this valuable resource through her own efforts, and its significance as she becomes a resource to others in this phrase: *"Y así, pues, nos ayudábamos las unas a las otras. Sí, ya le digo. Pero esa es más mi experiencia, aquí, pues que me enseñé a manejar."* (And so, well, we helped each other, yes, as I say. But that is my experience, here, that I taught myself how to drive.) Thus, Brenda's willingness to share with a newcomer one of the most valuable resources she has developed herself serves as an example of the transformation of vulnerability into communal agency which emerges in each one of the narratives of the group of women who participated in this study.

## Luisa—*"Yo iba con ella, porque aquí en la escuela, en la primaria, yo conozco a la gente."*
(I would go with her, because here, at the elementary school, I know the people.)

Luisa's response to the question of the potential newcomer compares closely to Brenda's, as she also introduces a sense of community and agency, interwoven in her words of reassurance. Although, Luisa has reiterated how hard it was at the beginning for her, and how anxious she was for not understanding and not being able to manage on her own, when thinking of someone in her same situation, she presents a communal solution.

First and foremost, Luisa suggests this person should come to her own town, so that her experience could be of use to the newcomer, and so that she could help her in person. So she opens with the phrase, *"yo iba con ella"* (I would go with her). Further, when referring to matters she still needs help with herself, Luisa suggests she would offer her support, and the support of her close friends, in finding the needed help. She anticipates telling a newcomer, *"podemos encontrar quien te ayude"* (we can find someone to help you). Luisa offers a whole list of people who would be of help at each of the schools in the area.

Lilian: Y si viniera aquí ¿por dónde le diría que empiece?
Luisa: Bueno, ¿si traería niños en la escuela?
Lilian: Sí.
Luisa: ¡Yo iba con ella! *(laughs)*
Lilian: *(laughs)* ¡Claro!
Luisa: Yo iba con ella porque aquí en la escuela en la primaria yo conozco a la gente: a la secretaria, que habla español *(as if starting an enumeration, rising intonation)*, Prieto habla español. Mucha gente habla español. De las maestras, muchas no, pero muchas sí, y yo le ... iría con ella. Igual que allá en la escuela de allá también, porque conozco igual a la gente. Las secretarias no hablan español pero los maestros hablan español. En la high school, Prieto habla español, Claudia habla español, esta cómo se llama ... Roxana, también habla español. Muchas, bueno, muchas no. Y es cuando uno necesita ayuda. Sí. Si viniera aquí, pues, conmigo tendría ... conmigo y con Norma. Sí, pues, yo y Norma llegamos yo creo como en el mismo tiempo y así. Norma tiene una gran ventaja: que ella siempre trabajó con pura gente que habla puro inglés. Y Norma aprendió.

Lilian: And if she came here, where would you tell her to start?
Luisa: Well, if she brought school-age kids?
Lilian: Yes.
Luisa: I would go with her! *(laughs)*
Lilian: *(laughs)* Of course!
Luisa: I would go with her, because here, at the elementary school, I know the people: the secretary, who speaks Spanish *(as if starting an enumeration, rising intonation)*; Prieto speaks Spanish. Many people speak Spanish. Of the teachers, many don't but many do, and I would ... go with her. Also at the other school, because I also know the people there. The secretaries don't speak Spanish, but the teachers do. At the high school, Prieto speaks Spanish, Claudia speaks Spanish, this other person, what's-her-name, and Roxana also speaks Spanish. Many, well, not many. And that is when one needs help. Yes, if she came with me she would have ... with me and Norma. Yes, because, Norma and I arrived more or less at the same time. Norma has a great advantage: that she always worked only with people who only speak English. And Norma learned.

At this point, as Luisa mentions each person by name, she is offering access to the whole social network she has built within each of the schools in her area at all levels of education, elementary, middle and high school.

Yo le diría: "Sí, vente, acá. Sí, puedes … podemos buscar quien te ayude con los niños aquí." Aunque no traiga papeles, ¿verdad? Pueden ir los niños a la escuela. Sí, yo diría: "Vente y aquí hay quien te ayude." Pues, me ayudaron a mí. Aunque no hablo inglés, yo siempre estuve … hay gente que le ayuda a uno a comunicarse, a traducir, cuando hay una junta o algún problema, verdad? Que con los niños, cuando están niños, ellos… Pero sí le diría que sí podría, no batallaría, yo pienso. Yo, así, anduvimos y dondequiera nos ayudaron. Decía: "¿Me puede ayudar a ver qué me está diciendo?" o "¿Me puede leer este papel?" Y todavía lo hago, porque si no hay nadie, hasta cuando voy por Verónica, tengo que firmar un papel. Y la secretaria me dice: "Dice que no más tú te vas a llevar a Verónica a tales horas." Y ya. Pero siempre ayudan. Y yo le diría: "Sí, vente, vente."

I would tell her, "Yes, come, here. Yes, you can … we can find who can help you with the kids." Even if they have no papers, right? The kids can go to school. Yes, I would say, "Come and here there are those who can help you." Well, they helped me. Even if I don't speak English, I was always … there are people who help you communicate, translate, when there's a meeting or some problem, right? That with the kids, when they are young, they… But I would tell her that she can; she wouldn't struggle, I think. I did it, like that, and everywhere they helped us. I would say, "Can you help me understand what she is saying?" or "Can you read me this paper?" And I still do it, because if there is nobody, even when I go and pick up Veronica, I have to sign a paper. And the secretary tells me, "It just says that you are picking Veronica up at such-and-such a time." And that's it. But they always help. And I would say: "Yes, come, come."

The solution offered by Luisa to the challenges for the newcomer mostly involved her own direct help, and sharing her network of acquaintances from within the schools. In this list, she is also offering access to one of the most valuable resources, interpretation or translation, through the people she would introduce her to. Added to her social relationships which she has built and nurtured throughout the years, Luisa offers all the knowledge and information she has gathered, which she would leave at a newcomer's disposal. Finally, Luisa insists that she and her friend, Norma, who has learned more English, would also be there to support her; thus, in her narrative, Luisa includes herself as a valuable resource.

# From Extreme Vulnerability to Communal Agency

**Sandra—*Ya se va uno abriendo camino, y todo a pie*.**
**(One starts making one's way, and all on foot.)**

If one of the seven women's stories were to be chosen to epitomize the passage from vulnerability to communal agency it would be Sandra's. She begins her account of how she learned how to manage in the new context by mentioning that her sister-in-law had been the first person to help her. She took Sandra shopping and also drove her to the school to get her children enrolled.

> Lilian: Y qué le contaría sobre cómo aprendió a moverse aquí en Estados Unidos, si ella le pregunta, cómo aprendió a moverse en todo sentido.
> Sandra: Con todo, ¿verdad? Pues, poco a poco. Llega uno al lugar y, pues, siempre hay alguien, un familiar… Por ejemplo, nosotros cuando llegamos a La Vía mi concuña era la que: "Vente, vamos a la escuela para que inscribas al niño. Y vente, acá está la tienda, vamos a la tienda." Y ella era la que hacía las compras y todo, verdad.

> Lilian: And what would you tell her about how you learned how to manage here in the United States, if she asked you how you learned how to manage (literally "move about") in every sense.
> Sandra: With everything, right? Well, little by little. One arrives in a place and, then, there's always someone, a family member. For example, when we arrived in La Vía, my husband's sister-in-law was the one, "Come, let's go to the school so that you enroll your son. And come, here's the store, let's go to the store." And she was the one who went shopping and all, right.

When they had just arrived, Sandra and her family spent some time in the largest city in the area, La Vía, a border city in the neighboring state, about an hour and a half away from the village where she now lives. At the time, some of her family's difficulties derived from the fact that she and her husband were living with and depended on her brother-in-law (her husband's brother). According to Sandra, he had not been willing to help them and this had created tensions.

The extreme vulnerability of Sandra's situation in those early days is captured in her concluding words, *"Por ser gente sin documentos, piensa uno que no tiene derecho a vivienda, derecho a nada."* (When you are a person without documents, you think that you have no right to housing, no right to anything.)

> Entonces estábamos viviendo con ellos. Sí, pero, yo digo, muchas oportunidades se le van a uno. Porque si vive uno con gente egoísta, no le dicen a uno que haga o que

deje de hacer o cómo hacerle. ¿Sí? Yo sé, yo pienso a veces, digo, si, por ejemplo, le dije a mi cuñado: "Es que necesito una carta adonde diga que vivo con usted para que me den el WIC." Pero dijo, "No, pero que quién-sabe-qué." *(imitating yelling or complaining tone of voice)* Dije "ya". Y bueno, no más eso. Entonces, yo quería ir a aplicar a los departamentos… Sí, me entiende, una vivienda o algo. Y él no me quiso firmar. Asique fue mucha presión y estar viviendo bajo presión es bien difícil. Y ahí fue donde se vinieron los problemas con mi esposo y todo. Y él tronó y aventó y se fue. Entonces, pero, si vive uno con gente egoísta, no, va a salir … y lo más importante es salir de ahí y a ver, que Dios le abra camino, buscar gente que la oriente, ¿sí? Pero, fueron dos ocasiones y las mismas me pasaron: que no, no hubo apoyo, no hubo quién la orientara. Por ser gente sin documentos, piensa uno que no tiene derecho a vivienda, derecho a nada.

Then we were living with them. Yes, but one loses many opportunities. Because if one lives with selfish people, they don't tell you to do or not to do or how to do things. Right? I know, I sometimes think, I say, if for example I said to my brother in law, "It's that I need a letter where it says that I live with you so that they give me WIC." But he said, "No, but who-knows-what." *(Imitating yelling and complaining tone of voice)*. And I said, "Ok". And so, that was it. Then, I wanted to go and apply for apartments… You understand, for housing or something. And he refused to sign. So it was a lot of pressure and living under a lot of pressure is very hard. And that is when our problems started with my husband and all. He snapped and exploded and left. Then, if one lives with selfish people, one is not going to progress … and the most important thing is to leave and see, that God opens your way, to find the people who will guide you, right? But those were two occasions that the same thing happened to me: that no, there was no support, there was no guidance. When you are a person without documents, you think that you have no right to housing, no right to anything.

Sandra tells the whole story of how she went from an experience of utter vulnerability to a period in which after seeking support, she was able to find her way. At first, when they had just arrived in the US, only her sister-in-law (the wife of her husband's brother) had been supportive. Soon after that, the situation in her family became so grave that Sandra had to move out with her children, and spent a few months at a shelter for victims of domestic violence. Sandra stresses how much help she received there to get back on her feet and start out her new life independently in a new country; she points out the significance of finding the right people to guide you at the beginning.

Entonces, ya, cuando yo llego al shelter, entonces, ya, rápido, el lunes me llevan: "Vamos a aplicar para el Medicaid de los niños, y las estampillas." Y es más hasta ayuda de dinero por emergencia. Dice: "Tienes dos niños." O sea, ahí fue donde yo me orienté más, donde aprendí, se me abrieron los ojos: "Ah, bueno," y luego, "que tiene que ir usted a la clínica, a checarse, a hacerse... ¿Sí me entiende?" O sea, voy y me toca una doctora muy buena, muy fina persona. Me habló, me dijo: "Mira, estás en el país de las oportunidades. De tí depende. De tí depende, tienes la puerta abierta, a lo grande," me dijo. "No vuelvas para atrás, échale ganas, no te va a faltar nada..." Haga de cuenta que ... pues, yo salí muy fuerte. *(laughs softly)*

So, then, when I arrived at the shelter, then, right away, on Monday they took me, "Let's go and apply for Medicaid for your children, and stamps." And they even gave me monetary help for an emergency. They said, "You have two kids." So, that's where I got more guidance, where I learned, my eyes were opened. "Oh, I see," and then, "You need to go to the clinic, to get a check-up, and have... Do you understand?" So I go and a very good doctor sees me, a very fine lady. She spoke to me, she said, "Look, this is the country of opportunity. It depends on you. It depends on you, the door is wide open," she said. "Don't go back, give it your all, you are not going to go without." Imagine... I came out [of there feeling] very strong. *(laughs softly)*

Sandra offers a chronology; she describes the sequence of her first steps toward settling independently in the United States. Her story of survival is punctuated by the mention of key moments and key people who offered her their support during harsh times. First, there was the doctor at the clinic where she was taken for a check-up right after she arrived at the shelter, who spoke to her and encouraged her not to give up and to keep going for her children's sake. Of her visit to the doctor, Sandra comments, *"Pues, yo salí muy fuerte"* (Well, I left there feeling very strong).

Then, there was Norma, her friend, who encouraged her to seek safety, just as she had done, by moving to this semi-rural area, about 50 miles away from there, the city of Los Puentes and the shelter where they had met. Next, it was the staff at the shelter who helped her. The social worker, for instance, had interceded on her behalf with the manager of the apartment complex where Sandra would eventually move. There was also the emotional and material help she received at the shelter throughout this process.

Entonces, estuvimos tres meses ahí, juntando, juntando, mandado, juntando poquito de todo, y salimos. Salimos equipadas, y ahí mismo, conocí a esa señora Norma y ella fue la que me trajo. Entonces, el trabajador social me acompañó para apoyarme con la manager, para que me dieran el departamento. ¿Sí? Pero ya desde ahí ellos ya habían hablado a Sandville [another city in the same border state], para ver si me podía ir a Sandville, porque estaban buscando donde ubicarme, porque yo no me quería quedar en Puentes. Entonces, ya con esa ayuda es como uno sale adelante, ¿sí? Pero... pero si uno llega como, como en el caso anterior, llega con su misma familia, es egoísta, es egoísta, no quieren. A mí, eso me pasó. Entonces, le digo, bueno, pues, ni modo. Eso hicieron. Pero de todas maneras yo salí adelante. ¿Sí me entiende? Si no que luego, luego, hubiéramos conseguido donde vivir quizá no hubiéramos tenido los problemas que tuvimos. Pero, bueno, así pasó. ¿Sí?

Then we were three months there, collecting, collecting, collecting, shopping, collecting little by little, and we left. We left equipped, and right there I met Norma, and she was who brought me. And then, the social worker came with me to help me with the manager, so that they'd rent me an apartment. Right? And from there they had already called Sandville [another city in the same border state], to see if I could move to Sandville, because they were looking for a place for me to settle down, because I didn't want to stay in Puentes. So, it's with that help that one gets by. Right? But ... but if one arrives as, as with my previous experience, arrives with one's own family, and they are selfish, selfish, they don't want to. That's what happened to me. Then, well, no way. They did that, but anyway I got by. Do you understand? If instead we had found where to live right away, maybe we wouldn't have had the problems we had. But, well, that's what happened. Right?

In a sort of catalog of practical reasons to be grateful, Sandra goes down the list of material donations she received at the shelter in order to be able to move out on her own before mentioning the counselor's visits to her in her new home.

Por eso llegué ahí, y duré tres meses ahí. Y ellos me apoyaron para salir de ahí. Me dieron muebles, ropa. Nada menos, estaba viendo, esta blusa salió de ahí. Ya va para siete años. O sea, todos salimos con, o sea, muebles, con trastes, con mis cajas de mandados que yo fui comprando, comprando los tres meses, y cajas de mandado y todo eso. Entonces ya cuando me vine, después vino la consejera y estuvo dándonos consejería, apoyándonos, porque sí era empezar solos. Y luego, ya, le conseguí gente a ella. Y así, le digo, siempre tratando de ayudar a otros.

That's why, I got there, and I spent three months there. And they helped me to get out. They gave me furniture, clothes. I was thinking, this blouse, came from there. It's been seven years. So, we all left with, like, furniture, pots and pans, with my boxes of things I had been buying, for three months, and with my boxes and all that. And then, when I moved here, afterwards the counselor came and gave me counseling, and gave us her support, because for us it was starting out on our own. And then, I also found people for her. And that way, I tell you, I always tried to help others.

In her account of struggles and help received, Sandra uses many idiomatic expressions related to finding her way and progressing: *"Entonces, ya con esa ayuda es como uno sale adelante"* (So, it's with that help that one gets by.) At one point, Sandra uses an idiomatic expression combining both an allusion to finding her way and a concrete reference to managing without a car: *"Ya se va uno abriendo camino, y todo a pie."* (One starts making one's way. And all on foot.) It is quite telling how Sandra uses figurative language about making her way and getting by, and in the same breath describes literally having done it all walking.

One of the aspects of her time at the shelter that Sandra chooses to highlight as most helpful is a goal-setting exercise. After describing how she had set these goals for herself in consultation with her counselor at the shelter, Sandra mentions how she kept on working on them after that. Specifically, she had resorted to them again during an interview at her child's Head Start program, when they had asked her about her goals. One of the goals she had set for herself was buying a car. In the context of her story of survival, Sandra refers in passing to the fact that it had not taken her too long to meet this goal, as she had only remained without a car for exactly a year and two months. Before that, she would depend on rides, or do everything on foot, walking long distances, even carrying all her shopping bags, and having to stop to rest along the way. Pointing out the window at the road that led to the village, Sandra stresses the fact that she and her children had often walked back and forth the length of that road, *"Este caminito lo teníamos bien caminado."* (This was our well-trodden little path.)

Sandra: Entonces, ya ahí en Puentes fue adonde ellos me llevaron y arreglaron todo. Ya llegando aquí ya sabe uno dónde está la clínica y dónde está, bueno, pues ya. Ya se va uno abriendo camino. Y todo a pie. *(laughs)* Todo era mucho a pie. *(laughs)* Y no duré mucho a pie. Yo creo que duré, qué sería un año y dos meses a pie. Y al poco tiempo, ya teníamos nuestro carro. *(laughs with satisfaction)*
Lilian: Las distancias son grandes
Sandra: Sí. Este caminito lo teníamos bien caminado. Porque allá estaban los departamentos, los que se inundaron. Entonces, así que este era nuestro caminito a la clínica, *(rising intonation, as if starting a list)* o a llevar al niño, había veces, a la escuela, o así, pero el siempre viajaba en el camión, por eso no teníamos mucho problema, ¿ve? A la tienda pues ahí conseguíamos "rides" o nos veníamos con las bolsitas, descansando y descansando y hasta que llegábamos.

Sandra: Then, in Puentes was where they went with me and made all the arrangements. When I arrived here one already knows where the clinic is and where, well, that. One starts making one's way. And all on foot. *(laughs)* It was all on foot. *(laughs)* I wasn't on foot for long. I think it was, about a year and two months on foot. And shortly after that we already had our car. *(laughs with satisfaction)*
Lilian: Distances are long.
Sandra: Yes. This was our well-trodden little path. Because the apartments were over there, the ones that got flooded. So this was our way to the clinic, *(rising intonation,*

*as if starting a list)* or to take my son, sometimes, to school, or so. But he always took the bus, that's why that wasn't much of a problem, you see? For the store, we would get rides, or we would carry our shopping bags, stopping to rest and stopping to rest, until we got here.

While she describes the difficulties of starting on her own once she moved out of the shelter, she makes a point of mentioning how some of her neighbors had gone out of their way to help her and offer her guidance. Her counselor's follow-up home visits had been crucial, not only for her, as she was not the only one who needed support in such a vulnerable situation. When the counselor from the shelter checked in on her, sometime after she had moved out, Sandra referred some of her neighbors to her for help. They were also immigrant women who were in situations of domestic violence.

> Entonces, sí ... a mí me tocó cuando mucha gente empezó. . . algunas personas vecinas empezaban ... que llegaban: "Y no, hágale así. Y no, vaya aquí, y hable con fulano." Y así. Orientándolo así. *(voice reflects a smile, and sounds like gratefulness, or happiness)* Hubo una señora, dos ... yo estaba recibiendo la asistencia de la consejería porque después de que salí de allá del "shelter", había una consejera que venía cada dos semanas, creo, y después una vez al mes. Después, y ella ... entonces, cuando ... así que yo ... me tocó, *(lowering voice)* conocer gente, mujeres maltratadas. *(lowers voice to almost a whisper)* Yo les ayudaba.

> And then, yes, I went through this when neighbors would come to me and suggest, "No, do this. And, no, go over there, and speak to so-and-so." Like that, guiding us that way. *(voice reflects a smile, and sounds like gratefulness, or happiness)* There was a lady, two... I was receiving counseling support because when I left the shelter, there was a counselor who used to come every two weeks, I think, and afterwards once a month. Then, and she ... then, when ... then I... I happened *(lowering voice)* to meet people, battered women. *(lowers voice to almost a whisper)* I helped them.

It becomes evident that Sandra struggles when speaking about these experiences, as her narrative appears punctuated by repeated pauses and hesitation especially as she is about to refer to the women she helped out. The contrast with the rest of her account is striking, as Sandra up to that point has shared her story in a clear and articulate style, and in a voice which exudes self-confidence. Even as we spoke in the privacy of her home, in a rural area outside of the village, and no one else was present at the time, Sandra noticeably lowers her voice to a whisper when she refers to the fact that some of her neighbors were also survivors of domestic violence, and especially when she mentions having provided them with help in these circumstances. Sandra's hushed voice as she recounts how she secretly arranged for other women in her neighborhood to meet with her counselor contributes to emphasize the vulnerability of their situation and Sandra's awareness of it.

These moments in the narrative are clearly distinguished in the interviews through prosodic markers and, as mentioned above, stand in noticeable contrast to Sandra's general self-assured tone of voice. Just as Brenda's voice lowers to a whisper as she refers to the racism and discrimination experienced by her daughter (Chapter 5), Sandra whispers when she refers to domestic violence, to the way she asked for help and to how she offered it to her neighbors. In the narrative strands, these shifts can be seen as markers of *the unspeakable*, instances which simultaneously point to these women's agency in moments of extreme vulnerability.

Lilian ¿En el shelter?
Sandra: No, aquí, ya. Entonces, yo le decía: "Mire, si quiere, aquí en secreto, mi consejera viene tal fecha," le digo "si quiere la contacto." (*speaks in lowered voice, hushed*). Y, una de ellas fue orientada y ya hasta tiene sus papeles. Y a sus hijos, alcanzó a arreglarles. La otra, no quiso la ayuda, pero finalmente, ya esta semana la vi y se quedó sola, finalmente. Pero hasta en eso yo estaba, yo le conseguía gente a la consejera (*with a smile and satisfaction in her voice*) porque, pues, yo veía la necesidad.
Lilian: Era del shelter, ¿no?
Sandra: Del shelter, Beatriz. El shelter es como una asociación, es una asociación, alguien la sostiene, para mujeres maltratadas.
Lilian: Sí, sí, es una fundación.
Sandra: Aha, sí, y entonces, tiene trabajadoras sociales, consejeras…
Lilian: Y, usted estaba allí, fue el primer contacto que tuvo … ahí.
Sandra: Tres meses, sí. Fue el primer … sí, duré ahí tres meses.

Lilian: At the shelter?
Sandra: No, here already. So I would say, "Look, if you like, here in secret, my counselor comes such-and-such a date," I said, "If you like I can contact her." (*speaks in lowered voice, hushed*). And, one of them received guidance and she already has papers. And for her children, she managed to fix that. The other woman didn't want the help, but finally, this week I saw her, and she's on her own, finally. But even in that I was, I got people for the counselor (*with a smile and satisfaction in her voice*) because, well, I saw the need.
Lilian: She was from the shelter, right?
Sandra: From the shelter, Beatriz. The shelter is like an association, someone sponsors it, for battered women.
Lilian: Yes, yes, it's a foundation.
Sandra: Aha, yes, and then, they have social workers, counselors…
Lilian: And you were there, it was the first contact you had … there.
Sandra: Three months, yes. It was the first… Yes, I spent three months there.

Sandra points out that in a situation of domestic violence, the help of an institution such as the shelter and its counselors is crucial, since women suffer from deep depression. Sandra mentions that among the factors which heighten the vulnerability of many immigrant women is their complete dependence on their husbands after migration, given the power which their immigration status sometimes gives them. She refers to how in cases when they are the only ones in the family who have "papers", legal documentation necessary to remain in the US, the husbands may use this as a means of control. By withholding their signature, they deny their support for their wife's application for a visa, the first step towards a green card, the paperwork needed for them to regularize their legal status in the US. Similarly, Susana and Silvia offered the example of their father, who had denied them and most of their siblings this support, leaving them open to deportation.

> Y, le digo, y esa señora, le digo, pues, bueno que pudo arreglar sus … sus … pudo arreglar sus papeles, ella. Porque el esposo sí tenía … papeles. Nada más que muchos tienen ellos papeles y ella no. Y es como las controlan (stressing the word). Depende de él (rise-fall)
> Lilian: Ah, y esta señora no tenía y el marido sí.
> Sandra: Y él … aha … y el marido no le quería firmar. No le quería firmar para poderla controlar. Y triste, triste, pero… Y no, otras, recibieron nada más apoyo, de hablar con alguien (lowered voice) que necesitan ayuda. Porque si … cuando sufre la gente violencia doméstica, se deprime mucho. Se deprime. Y, ya le digo, asique fue una de las cosas, como … a mí también me ayudó, el hecho de que la consejera viniera y: "¿Qué necesita?" y también: "Hágale así." Uh … Recibí mucho apoyo de ella. Ve. Fue un paso especial (rise-fall) o sea que ya nos quedamos solos después de la violencia doméstica. Pero alguien que llega, este, pues, sí necesita ayuda. Sí necesita apoyo … de cómo le haga. Orientarlo, cómo se mueva… asique… Pues, hemos tratado de hacer eso. (laughs lightly, and says this as if announcing the conclusion of this section of her sharing with this statement.)
> Lilian: Asique a quién encuentra es lo importante, con quién se encuentra cuando llega.
> Sandra: Sí, es muy importante. Sí.
>
> Sandra: And I say, this woman, as I said, well, she was able to fix her … her … she was able to fix her papers, hers. Because her husband did have … papers. It's just that many have papers themselves, but the women don't. And it's how they control (stressing the word – articulating it slowly) them. The woman depends on him.
> Lilian: And her husband had papers and she didn't.
> Sandra: And he … right … and her husband didn't want to sign. Didn't want to sign for her, so as to control her. And, sad, sad, but… And, others just received the help of speaking to someone (lowered voice) because they needed help. Because if … when people suffer domestic violence, they get very depressed. They get depressed. And,

as I say, so this was one of the things, that ... that also helped me, the fact that the counselor came and, "What do you need?" and also, "Do this." Oh,... I received a lot of help from her. You see. It was a special step... Because we were on our own after the domestic violence. But someone who arrives, well, does need help. They need help ... on how to go about things. Guidance, on how to manage.. so ...Well, we've tried to do that. *(laughs lightly, and says this as if announcing the conclusion of this section of her sharing with this statement.)*
Lilian: So who you meet is important, who you meet when you arrive.
Sandra: Yes, it's very important. Yes.

Although Sandra's and Brenda's experiences differ in many ways, a common factor between them is the role of solidarity and sharing resources. In Sandra's story, her state of vulnerability goes hand in hand with a period in her life when she managed on foot. In Brenda's case, once she learned how to drive she became her friends' driver, thus sharing the most valuable resource she had developed by herself. Whereas in Sandra's case, the vital resource she counted on to get by in the hardest of times was the help and guidance she received from the shelter, or as she put it, *"gente que la oriente"* (people who will guide you), which she also shared with those around her whom she noticed were also in dire need of help.

As mentioned in the previous chapter, in these stories references to physical mobility and driving appears to carry more than their literal meaning. In Sandra's case, she uses the metaphor of *"abrirse camino"* (making one's way) to tell her story of survival, which involved prodigious amounts of energy, courage, and collective resources. Sandra's situation was slightly different from the rest of the women in that she came from an urban area in Mexico and she already knew how to drive. Yet, references to physical mobility are also woven into her whole story. The different stages marked in Sandra's comments on her physical mobility or lack thereof run parallel to her development of agency. There are references to walking, driving, getting rides, all embedded in her narrative of survival from domestic violence. She continues with the stories of other women she knows, her neighbors, who were in similar situations, and that she supported and secured help for. Sandra's account describes a collective form of agency, not for her own survival only, but to contribute to the well-being of those around her who shared her same circumstances, best synthesized in the concept of communal agency.

Sandra stands out from other participants, and may be compared to Norma, in the leadership role she has adopted among her friends and acquaintances. The concept of parental involvement is redefined in her agency, which does not concentrate only on her children, but includes the concept of communal solidarity and of communal resources. Collins's (1994) concept of "motherwork" applies to Sandra's mode of motherhood, which extends from the nuclear family to the extended family and, further, to the community.

In these stories, in the long run, and despite the narrative tensions, the interactions with some institutions are not seen as relations between "them" and "us" but as a collaborative endeavor where the individual who is being helped will be, in turn, contributing in the effort to meet the needs of the community, based on their development of a sense of belonging. In Sandra's narrative, for instance, the shelter for victims of domestic violence is an example of an institution where the blurring of the "them" and "us" distinction through this communal form of agency is observed. Sandra found there the support she needed to put her life back together, but she also found help for other women by acting as a bridge between the shelter and these women in need. This same blurring of the "them" and "us" appeared in Luisa's narrative as she shares the list of the acquaintances she has made among the school staff that have always been helpful to her and that she refers to as a valuable resource which she would generously share with a newcomer.

## Communal Agency and Motherwork in the Narratives of Mexican Immigrant Mothers

The stereotypical image of the powerless and indifferent parent who remains in isolation unwilling to participate does not match the experience of the Latina immigrant women whose stories are the focus of this book. The characteristics of motherwork as an ideology of motherhood—as as defined by Collins (1994) and briefly outlined in Chapter 4 above—apply to them. First, the dichotomy of family and work does not stand, since these two spheres are closely interconnected in the experience of working-class women. As has long been challenged by Black and Chicana feminists, in many cases the private/public sphere dichotomy does not apply to Latina mothers, since employment and motherhood are not seen as incompatible (Hondagneu-Sotelo & Avila, 2003; Segura, 1994). Second, the experience of mothering/motherhood goes beyond the individual and nuclear families, and extends to the whole community. Third, physical survival is not taken for granted, as it is in middle-class views of mothers, but instead it figures at the center of motherhood, as illustrated in the accounts of each participant in this study.

The immigrant women who shared their stories perform their mother-work as othermothers in a context which includes not only their nuclear family but their extended family and their community. One participant specifically comes to mind: Luisa. Beyond the support and interest Luisa manifests towards her own sons' wellbeing and education, at the center of her narrative shines the motherwork she exerts in caring for her extended family and community. At the time of the first two interviews, Luisa is taking care of her grandchild for her son and daughter-in-law to be able to attend college. Besides, Luisa had been in charge of her teen-age nephew for some time, while he was attending high school.

Earlier in life and for many years, Luisa worked as caretaker for the children of her boss—who employed her not only as a nanny, but also as an agricultural laborer. Thus, Luisa is an example of an immigrant woman whose motherwork extends to the community through her social motherhood (Collins, 1999). These children Luisa took care of, and drove to their games and sports practice, all became teachers as they grew up. Years later, it would be them Luisa would trust to help her sons catch up with work in high school, when they had fallen behind. Her boss, the father of the children she took care of, was also the person who helped her develop a much valued resource: he taught her how to drive. Luisa exemplifies how through "motherwork" family and community are intricately interwoven, with shared resources and the development of agency (Collins, 1994).

But Luisa is not the only one of the participants who has exercised responsibilities beyond her immediate family or her own children. Susana took care of her siblings for extended periods of time, first, when their mother left Mexico for the United States to look for their father, and later when she returned to Mexico. Susana was also in charge of one of her nieces for two years. However, it is the story of Susana and Silvia's mother that stands out as the embodiment of motherwork, as her daughters recount how she has struggled for years, looking out for her children and grandchildren. Although she is not one of the participants in this study, she adopts the role of protagonist in her daughters' accounts, as she appears repeatedly and is often praised for her strength, her hard work, and her resilience.

Both Silvia and Susana, in their separate interviews, start out by sharing an account of the circumstances of their migration. Silvia offers more details of how their family migrated in stages; and shines a brighter spotlight on the figure of their mother. Silvia credits her own relative well-being and that of her siblings to their mother's efforts. When her father first left for the United States, their mother stayed back with her 10 children in Mexico. At the time, their youngest sister was around one or two years old. After 10 years, her mother decided to travel to the United States to look for their father—for them to be able to see him after so long—and stayed on to work in the US. When she found him, their father was very sick, so she stayed to take care of him and started sending for her children, Silvia, Susana and their siblings, gradually.

> Pues, ella se vino. Mi papá estaba aquí, pero nosotros teníamos más de 10 años que no lo conocíamos ya, no lo habíamos mirado. Pero mi mamá vino para acá porque le dijeron que él estaba aquí. Y mi papá estaba muy grave. Entonces, lo que ella quería era que, de perdido, sus hijos vieran a su papá, verdad; que no dijeran: "No, pues, mi mamá nunca lo buscó." No, siempre ella luchó porque nosotros viéramos a mi papá. Nada más que mi papá, no más él nunca… No sabíamos ni dónde encontrarlo. No más que mi mamá, pues, tomó la decisión de buscarlo, por nosotros, por sus hijos. Entonces, cuando lo encontró, pues, él estaba muy malo. Y fue cómo ya ella empezó a traernos, de poco a poco.

> Well, she came over. My dad was here, but we hadn't seen him in over 10 years. But my mom came here because they had told her he was here. And my dad was seriously ill. So, what my mother wanted was that, at least, her children saw their father, right; so that they wouldn't say: "No, because our mom never looked for him." No, she always struggled for us to be able to see our dad. It was just that my dad, he never… We didn't even know where to find him. But she just decided to look for him, because of us, because of her children. Then, when she found him, he was very sick. And that was how she started bringing us here, little by little.

Silvia's account centers on her mother's qualities—her strength, her hard work, and her determination to overcome all the difficulties she encountered in her life, as an immigrant woman and the mother of 10. She highlights the fact that they had always lived in their own home, and that if they worked it was because they were old enough. According to both Silvia and Susana, their mother was the person who held their family together, through hard work, as they could not count on their father, because he did not keep in touch with them or contribute to their support, and struggled with alcoholism. Even at this stage in their lives as grown-ups, their mother is always there for her children and grandchildren, Silvia says.

> Trabajó primero. Porque eso sí, para salir adelante uno tiene que trabajar. Para tener con qué traernos, ella trabajó y trabajó. Y nosotros en México estábamos. Pues teníamos casa allá, porque mi mamá siempre nos ha tenido casa. A ella casi no le ha gustado vivir de renta o nada. Ella lucha y pone su terreno, su casa y sale adelante. En-

tonces, ella no nos dejó en la calle: teníamos casa, estábamos trabajando. Entonces, decidió venirse, encontró a mi papá y de poco a poco ya fue trayéndonos. Pero ella, como quien dice, ella también que salió porque mi papá, pues, era un alcohólico, borracho. Y malo, pues, no aportaba a la casa. Asique ella todavía aquí siguió luchando por sus hijos. Aunque con unos ya traía nietos ella. Ya traía sus primeros dos nietos de allá. Así es que ella estaba luchando no más no por sus hijos, sino hasta por sus nietos, porque no les faltara el alimento. O sea que ella siempre ha luchado por sus hijos, pues, es lo más importante que uno tiene en la vida. Así es que por los hijos uno no debe derrotarse, sino salir adelante, cueste lo que cueste. Y sí se puede.

She worked first. Because to be able to succeed, yes, one has to work. To be able to bring us over, she worked and worked. And we were in Mexico. We had our home there, because mi mom always made sure we had a house. She has never liked to rent or anything. She struggles and gets some land, sets up a house and progresses. Then, she didn't leave us in the street: we had a home, we were working. So, she decided to come over and then she found my dad, and little by little she brought us. But she left for my father, because he was an alcoholic, a drunk. And mean, because he didn't contribute to the home. So here she kept on fighting for her children, even when she already brought grandchildren with her. She already brought her first two grandchildren. So she wasn't only fighting for her children but also for her grandchildren, so that they wouldn't lack food. So that she has always fought for her children, because it's the most important thing in life. So, for one's children one shouldn't give in, but make headway, whatever it takes. And, yes, it is possible.

When her mother left and her eldest sister, Susana, was left in charge of all her siblings, her mother would send them remittances regularly to Mexico, to help support them. Silvia also emphasizes the importance of family unity and strong kinship links and points out how close to each other her siblings, herself and her mother have always remained.

The underlying purpose of Silvia's description of her family's migration appears to be to stress the central role her mother had played in her family's well-being. She admires her mother's work ethic, stamina and willingness to sacrifice for her family. A woman here in the US can do well, through hard work; she can succeed in achieving her goals, and overcome hardships, Silvia says. If her mother was able to do it, alone, and with 10 children, then it is possible for anyone who is willing to work hard. Silvia is proud of her mother and considers her a role model.

Muchas oportunidades aquí de salir adelante en este país, eso sí. Porque trabajo hay y no más es tener ganas de trabajar, salir adelante, verdad. Si viene uno aquí es para venir a salir adelante y a trabajar. Así es que yo creo que sí, hay muchas posibilidades de que salga una mujer con sus hijos adelante. Y lo digo porque mi mamá salió adelante.

¡Ella, con 10! Tenía 10 hijos cuando mi papá la dejó, y estábamos bien chiquititos. Mi hermana, la que está ahorita en el hospital, y está por tener su bebé, tenía acaso como uno o dos añitos cuando nos dejó mi papá. ¡Y mi mamá con 10! Una mujer sí sale adelante. Si ella quiere luchar y sacar a los hijos adelante, sale adelante, porque mi mamá lo hizo. Eso es un ejemplo que yo tengo de mi mamá: ella con 10 hijos y ella salió adelante. Aha. Y ella no tuvo ni que robar, ni que hacer cosas que … que no verdad, que no iba para nosotros; no, ella con su sacrificio, con su trabajo. Puro trabajar y trabajar. Y ella … pues sí, estoy muy orgullosa de mi madre, porque ella fue una de las que pudo salir adelante con tanto sacrificio. Y es un ejemplo muy importante para nosotros.

Many opportunities to get ahead in this country; that is true. Because there is work and one only needs to be willing to work, get ahead, right. If one comes here it's to come and get ahead and work. So I believe there are many opportunities for a woman and her children to get ahead here. And I say it because my mother got ahead. She did, with 10! She had 10 children when my dad left her, and we were very young. My sister, the one who is now in the hospital, about to have her baby, was about one or two years old when my dad left us. And my mom with 10! A woman can get ahead. If she is willing to struggle and get her children ahead, she gets ahead; because my mom did it. That is an example I have in my mom: she had 10 kids and she got ahead. And she didn't have to steal, or do anything … anything that wasn't right for us; no, with her sacrifice, with her work. Simply by working and working. And she, well, yes, I am very proud of my mother, because she was one of the ones who was able to get ahead with such sacrifice. And she is a very important example for us.

Just as the boundaries of family and community are blurred in these women's stories, in their motherwork, so are the boundaries of parental involvement extended, in the sharing of resources with neighbors and friends, and in looking out for them as well as their children. Similarly, the blurring of borders can be applied to the public and private spheres comprising the realm of maternal involvement. A close analysis of the accounts by this group of immigrant mothers suggests the need to question the mainstream construct of parental involvement, reflected in the official discourse of education policies and practices. If the official approach to parental involvement is to move towards greater inclusiveness, any attempt at its redefinition should seriously take into account the ideology of motherwork.

# References

Cibils, L. R. de (2011). *Immigrant women's narrative reconstruction of their interactions with their children's schools: A collective qualitative case study* (Doctoral Dissertation). New Mexico State University, Las Cruces.

Collins, P. H. (1994). Shifting the center: Race, class, and feminist theorizing about motherhood. In E. N. Glenn, G. Chang, & L. R. Forcey (Eds.), *Mothering: Ideology, experience, and agency* (pp. 45–65). New York, NY: Routledge.

Collins, P. H. (1999). Producing the mothers of the nation: Race, class and contemporary US population policies. In N. Yuval-Davis (Ed.), *Women, citizens and difference* (pp. 118–129). London: Zed Books.

Giddens, A. (1984). *The constitution of society: Outline of the theory of structuration.* Berkeley, CA: University of California Press.

Hondagneu-Sotelo, P., & Avila, E. (2003). "I'm here, but I'm there": The meanings of Latina transnational motherhood. In P. Hondagneu-Sotelo (Ed.), *Gender and U.S. immigration: Contemporary trends* (pp. 317–340). Berkeley, CA: University of California Press.

Martin, J. (2007). Educating communal agents: Building on the perspectives of G.H. Mead. *Educational Theory 57*(4), 435–452.

Segura, D. (1994). Working at motherhood: Chicana and Mexican immigrant mothers and employment. In E. N. Glenn, G. Chang, & L. R. Forcey (Eds.), *Mothering: Ideology, experience, and agency* (pp. 211–233). New York, NY: Routledge.

Sztompka, P. (1991). *Society in action: The theory of social becoming.* Chicago, IL: University of Chicago Press.

Young, I. (2002). *Inclusion and democracy.* New York, NY: Oxford University Press.

# CONCLUSION

The reproduction of social inequality by schools and their practices in the United States and elsewhere has been widely studied and well documented in the literature for decades starting by some classics in education (Bourdieu & Passeron, 1977; Bowles & Gintis, 1976; Davidson, 1996; Rist, 2000; Willis, 1977). Instead of becoming spaces of equal opportunity and social mobility, schools have long been seen as sociocultural institutions which have tended to strengthen the status quo by mirroring the patterns and hierarchies which contribute to structural racism and social injustice present in broader society. Critical pedagogues have long denounced the connivance of the education system in the values of the utopia of globalization, and have stressed the need for educators and researchers to embrace hope by thinking and acting against the grain in an era of social injustice (Cole, 2005; Fischman & McLaren, 2005; Giroux, 2001). The official discourse and practices of parental involvement, strewn with allusions to home-school collaboration and partnership, due to a tendency to stem from a cultural deficit model, often leave out the perspectives of those whose exclusion they are precisely intended to address, at least purportedly (Auerbach, 1990; Dantas & Manyak, 2010; De Carvalho, 2001; Delgado-Gaitán, 1993, 1994; Fine, 1993; Hurtig & Dyrness, 2011; López, 2001; Luttrell, 1997; Olivos, 2006; Olivos et al., 2011; C. Suárez-Orozco et al.,

2008; Valdés, 1996). Latina immigrant women, who have undergone one of the most challenging situations in a person's life—such as the uprooting from their country of origin and resettling in an unknown context, often subject to exploitation and inhuman working conditions, in an environment of generalized hostility towards poor immigrants—are further faced with the challenges of daily negotiating their existence and their children's survival in an unfamiliar education system (Ainslie, 1998; C. Suárez-Orozco, 2000). If each child is to enjoy the human right to an education, and each parent the right to have a say in it, immigrant mothers must be taken into account.

According to Fraser (2005), "Overcoming injustice means dismantling institutionalized obstacles that prevent some people from participating on a par with others, as full partners in social interaction" (p. 73). For any changes in the home-school relations to have long-lasting transformative effects in the lives of immigrant mothers, their experiences, perceptions and opinions are to be sought out and heeded. This need not involve the display of showy gestures by the schools. Instead, for these efforts to make a difference requires that attention be paid first to the everyday interactions in which power asymmetry impedes the full participation of parents in decisions which affect them and their children directly.

The study at the center of this book and especially the stories generously shared by seven immigrant women point to the persistent need for the implementation of culturally and linguistically sensitive approaches to home-school relations, with genuine efforts at two-way communication at their center. In practical terms, it may well be worth reconsidering some of the traditional ways of inviting parents to participate and the nature of some of the forums commonly used to make decisions, and more frequently to inform about those which have already been made, such as assemblies, presided by authoritative figures addressing a group of parents from the front of a large room. To find out what the best way to encourage mothers (and all parents and caregivers) to be part of decision-making processes, it may also be necessary to ask more questions, not just through standardized written surveys, but in more informal environments, in groups or small circles, or other spaces specifically designed so that immigrant mothers may be more comfortable participating. If parent involvement continues to be listed as a priority in education, linguistic resources, considered among the most valuable symbolic resources in the community, would also need attention. Leaving these to contingency and taking care of them only as an afterthought contributes to diminishing the quality of family-school relations and produces informal exclusion of many individuals and groups of parents from the same information and decision-making forums which are often used to measure and assess parent involvement. Among material resources, access to transportation, which also plays a crucial role in many immigrant communities, must also be set as a priority.

Although immigration may be considered a deeply traumatic experience, in many cases, the same social processes involved in meeting the demands of the new situations are taken as opportunities for transformation, for agency in the midst of vulnerability. This has been observed to be the case for many Latina women who immigrated to the United States (Hondagneu-Sotelo, 1994; Zentgraf, 2002). Communal agency, this collective and collaborative form of solidarity, is the most striking feature which characterizes the stories of the seven women at the heart of this book: Brenda, Luisa, Norma, Sandra, Patricia, Silvia and Susana. Interlocked throughout their narratives are moments of struggle and survival, of vulnerability and agency, of strength and resilience. Tightly woven into the fabric of the life stories shared by them we can find the threads of each of their counter narratives, of their full engagement with their children's schooling and education, as well as with the well-being of their community.

To move away from the view of mothers prevalent in public policy as people who mainly need to be educated, it would be valuable for schools to engage immigrant mothers as the resourceful and active members of the community they prove to be. It behooves school administrators to tap into their ingenuity and their strategic communal agency instead of continuing to operate on the basis of deficit thinking and the stereotyped portrayal of the uninvolved parents who need to be changed, i.e. improved, which is perpetuated in the official discourse of parental involvement. This image of the powerless and indifferent parent who does not care enough about her children's education to participate does not match the strong, engaged, caring and proactive women I met and who chose to share their stories because they wanted to make a difference.

# References

Ainslie, R. (1998). Cultural mourning, immigration, and engagement: Vignettes from the Mexican experience. In M. Suárez-Orozco (Ed.), Crossings: Mexican immigration in interdisciplinary perspectives (pp. 283–305). Cambridge, MA: Harvard University Press.

Auerbach E. (1990). *Making meaning, making change: A guide to participatory curriculum development for adult ESL and family literacy*. English Family Literacy Project. Boston, MA: University of Massachusetts.

Bourdieu, P., & Passeron, J. (1977). *Reproduction in education, society and culture* (R. Nice, Trans.). London and Beverley Hills, CA: Sage.

Bowles, S., & Gintis, H. (1976). *Schooling in capitalist America*. London: Routledge.

Cole, M. (2005). New labour, globalization and social justice: The role of education. In G. Fischman, P. McLaren, H. Sünker, & C. Lankshear (Eds.), *Critical theories, radical pedagogies, and global conflicts* (pp. 3–22). Lanham, MD: Rowman and Littlefield.

Dantas, M. L., & Manyak, P. (Eds.). (2010). *Home-school connections in a multicultural society: Learning from and with culturally and linguistically diverse families*. New York, NY: Routledge.

Davidson, A. (1996). *Making and molding identity in schools: Student narratives on race, gender and academic engagement*. Albany, NY: State University of New York Press.

De Carvalho, M. E. (2001). *Rethinking family-school relations: A critique of parental involvement in schooling*. Mahwah, NJ: Lawrence Erlbaum Associates.

Delgado-Gaitán, C. (1993). Researching change and changing the researcher. *Harvard Educational Review* 63(4), 389–411.

Delgado-Gaitán, C. (1994). *Empowerment in Carpintería: A five-year study of family, school, and community relationships*. Report No. 49. Baltimore, MD: Center for Research on Effective Schooling for Disadvantaged Students, The Johns Hopkins University.

Fine, M. (1993). [Ap]parent involvement: Reflections on parents, power, and urban public schools. *Teachers College Record*, 94(4), 682–710.

Fischman, G., & McLaren, P. (2005). Is there any space for hope?: Teacher education and social justice in the age of globalization and terror. In G. Fischman, P. McLaren, H. Sünker, & C. Lankshear (Eds.), *Critical theories, radical pedagogies, and global conflicts* (pp. 343–358). Lanham, MD: Rowman and Littlefield

Fraser, N. (2005). Reframing justice in a globalizing world. *New Left Review*, 36, 69–88.

Giroux, H. (2001). *Theory and resistance in education: Towards a pedagogy for the opposition*. Westport, CT: Bergin & Garvey.

Hondagneu-Sotelo, P. (1994). *Gendered transitions: Mexican experiences of immigration*. Berkeley, CA: University of California Press.

Hurtig, J., & Dyrness, A. (2011). Parents as critical educators and ethnographers of schooling. In B. A. U. Levinson & M. Pollock (Eds.), *A companion to the anthropology of education* (pp. 530–546). Oxford, UK: Wiley-Blackwell.

López, G. (2001). The value of hard work: Lessons on parent involvement from an (Im)migrant household. *Harvard Education Review*, 71(3), 416–438.

Luttrell, W. (1997). *Schoolsmart and motherwise: Working-class women's identity and schooling*. New York, NY and London: Routledge.

Olivos, E. (2006). *The power of parents: A critical perspective of bicultural parent involvement in public schools*. New York, NY: Peter Lang.

Olivos, E., Jimenez-Castellanos, O., & Ochoa, A. (Eds.). (2011). *Bicultural parent engagement: Advocacy and empowerment*. New York, NY: Teachers College Press.

Rist, R. (2000). Student social class and teacher expectations: The self-fulfilling prophecy in ghetto education (HER Classic Reprint). *Harvard Educational Review, 70*(3), 257–301.

Suárez-Orozco, C. (2000). Immigration, stress and mirroring among the children of immigrants. In C. Rubben & M. Suárez-Orozco (Eds.), *Cultures under siege: Collective violence and trauma* (pp. 194–226). New York, NY and Cambridge: Cambridge University Press.

Suárez-Orozco, C., Suárez-Orozco, M., & Todorova, I. (2008). *Learning a new land: Immigrant students in American society.* Cambridge, MA: Belknap Press of Harvard University Press.

Valdés, G. (1996). *Con respeto: Bridging the distances between culturally diverse families and schools—An ethnographic portrait.* New York, NY and London: Teachers College Press.

Willis, P. (1977). *Learning to labor: How working class kids get working class jobs.* New York, NY: Columbia University Press.

Zentgraf, K. (2002). Immigration and women's empowerment: Salvadorans in Los Angeles. *Gender & Society, 16*(5), 625–646.

# EPILOGUE

## Educational Motherwork Beyond Grade School

Educational motherwork and all the support it involves do not end with high school graduation. The seven women I interviewed had dreams for their children's future and were already witnessing the results of their hard work. Some of the stories which stood out the most for the evident excitement and pride in the mothers' voices were about their hope and support for their children's education beyond high school. We will conclude with Silvia, Brenda, Patricia and Luisa sharing theirs.

Throughout her interviews, Silvia spoke with pride about her young daughter's qualities and her progress in school, stressing her high level of motivation. Silvia described Sarina's constant curiosity and keen awareness of everything that is going on around her, often manifested in incisive questions or comments. On our last interview, Silvia ended her story about her first-grader by mentioning how on her own Sarina has already made up her mind that she will be going off to college once she graduates from high school.

> Silvia: Ella dice que cuando ella salga de la "high school", dice: "Mami, cuando yo salga yo no voy a vivir aquí." Le digo: "Y ¿dónde vas a ir a vivir?" Dice: "Me voy a ir vivir a Puentes porque voy a ir a estudiar. Voy a ir al colegio a estudiar. Yo no voy a estar aquí," dice. Y le digo: "Y ¿qué vas a hacer sin tus papás?" "No" dice "pues, se mudan allá conmigo." (laughs)

Lilian: Ah, pero lo tiene todo pensado.

Silvia: Ya, ella lo tiene todo calculado. ¡Todo! Y va a estudiar para doctora o para maestra, para …Sí, y dice: "No, Mami, pero ya te dije, yo no voy a vivir aquí." Le digo: "Pero m'hija, pero no, aquí es nuestro hogar ya, nuestra casa. Tu papi compró aquí, ya no rentamos, ya estamos, ya tenemos nosotros nuestra casa." Dice: "Pues, no le hace, Mami. Yo me voy para Puentes." Ella se va para Puentes. Y dice, "Yo salgo de mi escuela, de la 'high school' *(pause)* y me voy para Puentes." ¡Qué nos espera con ella, si apenas tiene seis años!

Lilian: Lo tiene claro.

Silvia: She says that when she finishes high school, she says, "Mom, when I finish high school I'm not going to live here." I say, "And where are you going to live?" She says, "I'm going to live in Puentes because I'm going to study. I'm going to go to college to study. I'm not going to be here," she said. And I ask, "What are you going to do without your parents?" "You can move there with me." *(laughs)*

Lilian: Oh, she's thought about everything.

Silvia: Yes, she's got it all figured out. Everything! And she's going to study to be a doctor, or a teacher, or… Yes, and she says, "No, Mom, I've already told you, I'm not going to live here." And I say, "But, honey but, here's our home already, our house. Your dad bought it, we're not renting any more, we've settled down here, and we already have our house." She says, "Well, it doesn't matter, Mom. I'm going to Puentes." She's going to Puentes. "She says, "I finish school, high school, and I go to Puentes." What are we in for, if she is only six years old!

Lilian: She's made up her mind.

By the excitement in her voice while she is retelling her conversation with her daughter it becomes evident that Silvia is extremely proud of her young daughter's determination to attend college. Her first reaction, though, when she asks Sarina about whether she would leave her parents and their home is similar to Brenda's comments on how at first she, her husband, and even Luz had felt unsure about their daughter leaving for college.

In Brenda's case, the misgivings she had expressed early on in the interviews about whether Luz would or would not attend college after graduation had vanished by the last interview, when she shared the news of her daughter's enrollment at a four-year university. Luz was participating in a program which supports first-generation students from migrant families, and Brenda, who had attended meetings for parents organized on the campus of the state school, expressed her satisfaction with the support her daughter and her family were receiving, as well as with her daughter's hard work.

At the time of her first interview, Brenda was not sure about what Luz, who was then a senior, would do after graduation. Brenda mentioned her daughter's distress at the recent death of her high school counselor, who had been instrumental in helping her with her college applications. Besides, there were also Brenda's and her husband's doubts about letting one of their daughters leave for college on her own.

Lilian: Y de su hija que está por recibirse, me dijo que estaba averiguando para seguir estudiando, ¿no?

Brenda: Pues, todavía no sabe. Como yo miro que tiene miedo de salir sola. Porque, pues, todo el tiempo, está aquí con nosotros. Y ella, de a ratos, dice que sí se va a ir a estudiar y, de a ratos, dice que, pues, cómo lo va a hacer sin nosotros.

Lilian: About your daughter who is about to graduate, you had said that she was finding out about continuing with her studies, right?

Brenda: Well, she doesn't know yet. As I see it, she is scared of leaving on her own. Because, she is here with us all the time. So, sometimes, she says she'll go away to school, and, other times, she wonders, well, how's she going to manage without us.

By our last interview, Luz was attending college at the state university, an hour away from their home, and was participating in a program especially designed for first-generation college students who are the children of migrant agricultural workers. The representatives of this program had visited her school, and had provided her and her classmates with information, but Luz had mostly made all the arrangements herself, filling out all the forms and collecting all the documentation she needed for her application.

Lilian: Estuve con Sandra ayer y me dijo que su hija entró al colegio, a la universidad.

Brenda: Sí, la del medio.

Lilian: Ah, cuénteme.

Brenda: Sí, entró a la universidad. Y entró a ese programa, es buen programa. Está muy contenta ella. Ella sola se puso de acuerdo con ellos y todo. No más ella me explicaba: "Mira, Mamá, aquí me van a ayudar en esto, a estudiar. Y si subo mis calificaciones, puedo agarrar otra beca, la de la lotería." Si sale bien en su primer semestre. Le digo, pues, "Échele ganas." Ella quería trabajar, pero yo le dije, "M'hija, no. En estos tres meses échele ganas, a ver si puede calificar para esa otra beca. Y luego, quizá agarra trabajo en las horas que no esté estudiando, según cómo esté." A mí se me hace imposible, porque a veces le hablo y dice, "Mamá, estoy estudiando. Estoy haciendo mi tarea." Es mucha tarea. Y le dan libros enteros que lea y que haga el resumen. Se está esforzando mucho.

Lilian: ¿Y está allá, viviendo allá?

Brenda: Allá está, en la misma universidad. El primer año en ese programa le dan cuartos y la comida.

Lilian: ¿Y está contenta usted?

Brenda: Sí, estoy contenta, porque yo veo que ella está bien.

Lilian: I was with Sandra yesterday, and she told me that your daughter got into school, into college.

Brenda: Yes, the middle one.

Lilian: Oh, tell me all about it.

Brenda: Yes, she got in. And she got into that program, a good program. She is very happy. She arranged it all herself with them. She just explained to me: "Look, Mom, here they're going to help me like this, to study. And if my grades go up I can get another scholarship, the lottery one. If she does well in her first semester. I tell her: "Give it your all!" She wanted to work, but I told her, "Honey, no. These three months, put in all your energy, to see if you can qualify for the other scholarship. And then you can see if you can get a job for the hours when you are not studying, depending on how you're doing." I find it impossible, because sometimes I call her and she says, "Mom, I'm studying. I'm doing my homework." It is a lot of homework. And they give her whole books to read and to summarize. She is working very hard.

Lilian: And is she living there?

Brenda: She's there, at the university. Her first year, they give her food and board.

Lilian: And, are you happy?

Brenda: Yes, I am happy because I see that she is doing well.

Brenda expresses her joy as she shares how she and her husband had been invited to participate in several events and meetings held on the university campus, especially organized for parents of the students who have joined this program which supports children of families of agricultural workers. Now that she has met the people who run the program, who have explained to them what to expect, and how the program supports their children in school, she feels more comfortable with the idea of her daughter attending college. She was especially grateful to find out about how the support system they have in place for students worked. Brenda also assesses the event favorably because the leaders had planned activities so that they got to meet other parents who also have students in the program. In this space, they were able to share with the other parents and the organizers their experiences about getting used to their separation from their children in their first year away from home. Brenda's pride and excitement with her daughter's prospects shine through in her words.

In Patricia's case, it is her eldest child's teacher who has started to bring up with them the topic of Alex furthering his education, as she has high hopes for him. Although he is only in fourth grade, Patricia discusses her hope that Alex may attend college one day, since his teacher has emphasized how well he is doing and how she would like to see him go on to high school, and beyond. Patricia is very proud of what an avid reader he is. At the beginning of the interview, this is one of the first topics she brings up in reference to her children's schooling.

> Patricia: Ya le digo, como él trae muchos libros para leer. Y él siempre, lleva un libro y le saca los puntos, y casi siempre se saca los cien puntos, el 100% bien de lectura. Le digo que está bien. Y me dice la maestra de él: "Está muy bien; es muy buen estudiante," dice. "Yo quisiera que cuando él saliera fuera al bachillerato". ¿Bachillerato? *[In Mexico, this usually refers to the high school program for college-bound students.]* Algo así. Sí, dice: "Ha de estudiar." Le digo: "Pues, ojalá." Pues a veces los niños no más crecen y ya tienen la mente en otra cosa. Oh, él está chiquito, él tiene apenas nueve años. El nada más se ha enfocado en la escuela y en el juego. Sí, ojalá. Él es bueno para leer, lee muchas palabras en un minuto. No recuerdo cuántas me dijo la maestra, pero muchas. Los ponen a leer y luego les miden qué tanto leen. Y dice que él es uno de los mejores y de los mejores estudiantes. "Sí, yo quisiera que estudiara cuando estuviera grande," dice.
> Lilian: ¡Qué orgullo! ¿No?
> Patricia: Sí, se siente uno bien.

> Patricia: As I said, he brings many books to read. And he always takes a book and gets the points, and he almost always gets 100 points; 100% on reading. I tell him that that's good. And his teacher tells me about him: "He's doing very well; he's a very good student," she says. "I would like him to go on studying, to attend a college-bound high school program. *[In Mexico, 'bachillerato' usually refers to the high school program for college-bound students.]* Or something like that. Yes, she says, "He should study." I say, "I hope so," because sometimes kids grow up and have their mind on something else. But he's very young, he's barely nine years old. He has just focused on school and playing. Yes, I hope so. He is very good at reading, he reads many words per minute. I can't remember how many the teacher told me, but it was a lot. They make them read and then they measure how much they've read. And she says he's one of the best and one of the best students. "Yes, I would like him to study when he grows up," she says.
> Lilian: How proud [you must be]! Right?
> Patricia: Yes, one feels good.

It is evident from her narrative that Patricia is quite aware of how well Alex is doing in school, as his teacher has often told her that he is very good at reading and that he is one of the best students in his class. Above all, Patricia expresses her gratitude and her satisfaction with her children's schooling, and comments, *"Se portan bien; siempre me han tocado buenos, buenos maestros con los niños."* (They [the school] are good to us; I have always had good, good teachers for my kids.)

Going above and beyond the basics, Luisa, again, stands out as the epitome of motherwork. Luisa supported her sons throughout their school years and helped them overcome all the tough times. For instance, when her younger son, Jesús, fell behind in high school, she actively sought out assistance for him. Luisa was determined not to allow her son to be held back and waste a year. So she turned to the children she had taken care of, and who had grown up to be teachers, for help.

> Pero, como le digo, siempre hubo quien me ayudara. O me decían: "No fíjate que no te puedo… pero ve con fulanito y él te puede ayudar." Aquí en esta escuela, ¡tremendos para ayudar! Porque yo me acuerdo que mi hijo un tiempo tuvo como dos clases atrasadas. Y yo no quería que él se quedara, verdad. Yo quería que pronto acabara. Porque decía: "No, no quiero que esté perdiendo el año." O que dijeran, "para el año próximo va a venir a hacer esas clases. Va a estar en su año pero va a ir para atrás a hacer…" No, eso no quería yo. Entonces, pues, le digo que trabajaba con ese señor, y él me decía: "Pues, pregúntele a los muchachos a ver en qué le pueden ayudar." Y ya ellos me decían: "Pues, no, mándelo aquí a la escuela. Cuando se baje del bus, dígale que venga. O que venga a la casa." Ahí viven atrás. Entonces, decían, "Que venga a la casa y yo le ayudo. Yo le digo esto." Y así.

> But, I said, there was always someone to help me. Or they'd say to me, "No, I can't but go to so-&-so who can help you." Here at this school (the elementary school), they're great at helping! Because I remember that my son once was behind in two classes. And I didn't want him to fail, right. I wanted him to finish soon. Because I said, "No, I don't want him to be held back a year." Or for them to say, "Next year he's going to be taking those classes; he'll be in his grade, but he'll be behind, by re-taking those classes." No, I didn't want that. So, then, you know how I mentioned that I worked for that man, and he'd say, "Ask my kids to see what they can do to help him." And they'd tell me, "Just send him over. When he gets off the bus [on the way back from the high school], tell him to come by the school. Or tell him to come home." They live over there. So, they'd say, "Tell him to come over, and I'll help him. I'll tell him how to…" And so on.

At different points in her life, Luisa says, she has had to overcome her shyness in order to support her sons and help them advance in their studies. In her modesty, Luisa tends to point out the helpfulness of different people who have stepped in at difficult times. However, when the fact that she was the one who proactively reached out for help is mentioned, she acknowledges it, and expands further on how she continued offering her support to her children even beyond high school.

Luisa recalls visiting the community college for an interview to discuss financial aid for her younger son, Jesús. Although Luisa was the one who generally attended to any business concerning her children's school, if her husband had still been alive, on this occasion she would probably have asked him to go, since he understood and spoke English.

> Lilian: Pero usted buscó la ayuda también, ¿no?
> Luisa: Pero sí.
> Lilian: Usted tuvo que salir a buscar.
> Luisa: Sí, sí, ándele. Todavía ahora cuando mi hijo fue al colegio a La Vía [*the largest city in the area, on the border, in a neighboring state*], también yo anduve allí. Como la vez que tuvo una entrevista para la beca, que les ayudan y todo, yo tuve que ir. Y no le entendía al hombre, y me estaban traduciendo. Pero bien...
> Lilian: Y usted no lo hubiera hecho quizá antes, ¿no?
> Luisa: Pues, sabe que antes, tal vez hubiera dicho, si estuviera mi esposo, yo le hubiera dicho: "Anda, ve tú. Porque tú sabes, tú entiendes bien." Eso hubiera hecho.

> Lilian: But, you also looked for help, right?
> Luisa: Oh, yes.
> Lilian: You had to go out and find help.
> Luisa: Yes, yes, exactly. Even now when my son went to college to La Vía [*the largest city in the area, on the border, in a neighboring state*], I also went. Like the time he had an interview for his scholarship, that they help them with, and all, I had to go. And I couldn't understand the man, and they were interpreting for me. It was good.
> Lilian: And maybe before you wouldn't have done this, right?
> Luisa: Well, you know before, if my husband was here I probably would've said, "You go, because you know, you understand well." I would've done that.

Luisa describes in detail her participation in the process of her son's application to college. To begin with, she was even surprised that she was needed, since he was already 18. Then, she recalls having needed someone to interpret for her at the interview, and her initial shock at the figures they were showing her. Finally, she was relieved to learn that the amount mentioned for the cost of her son's education was not what she would have to pay, but that most would be covered by financial aid because of her low income. The vividness with which Luisa retells the details of this interview and of how this information had been communicated to her suggests the intensity of the moment. Again, as had been the case with many of her interactions during her sons' schooling, this entire interview had been mediated by an interpreter, recruited on the spur of the moment.

> Lilian: Y esta entrevista para la beca ¿Cuándo fue? ¿Cuando terminó la secundaria?
> Luisa: Cuando terminó la "high school", que iba a entrar a la escuela allá en La Vía. Entonces, habló a la escuela y que cuánto le iban a cobrar y ya le dijeron: "Tal día tienes una cita para una entrevista y tienes que llevar los 'income tax' de tus papás

y esto y lo otro." Y ya, dijo: "Ma, necesito tus 'income tax' y necesito que vayas tú."
Entonces, yo pensaba que porque ya estaba grande que ya tenía 18, ya no necesitaba
de mí. Pero sí tenía que ir yo. Entonces ya fuimos. Ya le digo, tuve que ir yo y el
hombre ya me estaba diciendo a mí, me preguntó que si hablaba inglés y yo le dije
que no y la otra mamá del otro muchachito le dijo que sí, verdad, que sí le entendía.
Entonces, ya el otro señor me decía: "Pues, bueno, mira, le están diciendo a tu hijo
que le va a costar... creo que 90.000 dólares." Y yo decía: "¿Con qué voy a pagar todo
ese dinero?" *(very high pitch, in surprise)*. Y decía yo: "¿Con qué lo voy a pagar?" Pero,
entonces, él dijo, "Pero como no más tienes mamá y tu mamá no trabaja tanto y todo,
con esto que gana ella, tú no puedes pagar." Me estaba diciendo que iba incluido todo,
verdad, adonde vivir, que no más tenía que conseguir trabajo en las horas que no iba
a la escuela, para su comida, para su gasolina; que fuera a trabajar porque la escuela y
los departamentos estaban ahí mismo y eso estaría todo pago. Entonces, todo eso me
estaban traduciendo.

Lilian: And this interview for his scholarship, when was it? When he finished high
school?
Luisa: When he finished high school and he was going to go to school in La Vía.
Then, he spoke to the school, to ask about how much they would charge him and
they told him: "On such-&-such-a-day you have an appointment for an interview
and you need to take your parents' income tax receipts and this and that." And so he
said, "Mom, I need your income taxes and I need you to go." So, I thought that as he
was older now, since he was already 18, he wouldn't need me. But I did have to go. So
we went. I tell you, I had to go and the man was talking to me, and he asked if I spoke
English, and I said that I didn't, but another mom of another kid said she did, that
she understood. So the man was telling me, "They are telling your son that it's going
to cost him" ... I think... 90,000 dollars." So I said, "How am I going to pay all that?"
*(very high pitch, in surprise)*. So I said, "What am I going to pay with?" But then he
said, "As you only have your mom, and your mom doesn't work so much, with what
she earns, you can't pay." He said that it was all included, right, housing, and all, that
he only needed to find a job for his free time, for his food and gas; to work because the
school and the apartments were right there, and that would be all covered. So all of
this was being translated to me.

In spite of the fact that he was admitted and was offered financial aid, Jesús
almost decided not to go to college, as he got married a short time before leaving for college, and his wife got pregnant. Luisa recalls in detail the sequence
of events that followed, and how she persuaded her son to attend college
anyway.

Y luego ya él decidió casarse poquito antes de ir a la escuela. Y de todos modos, según
él se iba a ir a la escuela y la muchachita se iba a quedar ahí con los papás. Pero, ya en
eso encargó al niño y ya no fue. Que no le podía dejar a esa muchachita embarazada.

Y decidió no ir allá. Que iba a buscar ... Yo le decía que fuera en Puentes, verdad. Para qué iba tan lejos. Pero dijo que en Puentes tenía que ir cuatro años a la escuela y que él no quería ir tanto porque ya tenía que trabajar y todo. Entonces, decidió buscar en La Vía y de repente le hablaron. Fue cuando apenas había nacido el niño, asique vino y me dijo: "Ma, sabes que no voy a ir a la escuela porque necesito trabajar y pagar renta." Porque vivían en Puentes ellos primero. Entonces, dijo: "Cuando Cynthia acabe su carrera, entonces, yo voy."

And then he decided to get married just before going to school. And anyway, according to him, he was going to go to school and his wife was going to stay with her parents. But then they were expecting a child and he didn't go. He said he couldn't leave her now that she was pregnant. So he decided not to go, he was going to look for something ... I told him to go to Puentes, right. Why go so far? But he said that in Puentes he had to go to school for four years, and he didn't want to go for so long, he needed to start working and all. So, he decided to look in La Vía and they called him. It was when his son was newly born, so he came and told me, "Mom, you know, I'm not going to school because I need to work and pay my rent." Because they first lived in Puentes. And he said, "When Cynthia finishes her studies, then I'll go."

Jesús had decided to support his wife until she finished her studies, and once she graduated, it would be his turn to attend college. But Luisa could not let another opportunity pass by for one of her sons to attend college. Although Luisa, a widow, struggles to make ends meet on seasonal agricultural work and sporadic jobs as an in-home caretaker, she would do whatever was within her means for her younger son to be able to attend college.

At this crossroads, Luisa stepped in and offered the young couple her full support: her son and her daughter-in-law could save on housing and bills by living with her; she would help them out with money for gas, since school was over an hour away; and she would take care of their newborn until they were out of school. Thus, at the time of our first interview Luisa was taking care of her grandson. Although this may seem a natural situation, in Luisa's case this was a measure of how important her son's education was, since it did imply making a significant sacrifice on her part, as she sometimes had to miss some opportunities for work, given the responsibility she had undertaken.

Lilian: Claro, fue cuando usted lo apoyó.
Luisa: Entonces, yo le dije: "No, m'hijo. Si usted no va ahorita a la escuela, nunca va ir a la escuela." Le dije: "No." Si quieren, hable con esa muchacha y dígale, vénganse para acá. Para que no tengan que pagar "biles" y yo te ayudo para la gasolina. Yo les cuido al niño y se van. Y ya, mire, se vino para acá, se quedaron y ahora ya está. Pero si yo lo hubiera dejado que: "Sí, m'hijo." No... Así pasó con el grande.
Lilian: Ah, no hubiera ido a estudiar.

Luisa: No. Mi hijo el grande se iba a ir a un estado del sudeste a estudiar y fue cuando mi esposo se murió. Entonces como estábamos tristes, deprimidos y todo, entonces, dijo: "Ma, yo no voy a ir al colegio este año, hasta el año que entra porque mira, mi papá se acaba de morir" Mi esposo… él se tenía que ir para allá el día 13 de agosto y mi esposo murió el 24 de agosto. O sea que cuando él se tenía que ir, estábamos en El Palenque *(the largest city in the state)*, en el hospital. Entonces, ya, a los pocos días murió mi esposo, entonces, pues, ya no fue. Dijo, que el año que entra y mire nunca más fue. Nunca fue.

Lilian: Right, that was when you helped him.
Luisa: Then I said, "No, Honey. If you don't go to school now, you'll never go to school." And I said, "No. If you like, speak it over with your wife and tell her, and you come over here, so that you don't have to pay any bills and I'll help you with the gas. I'll take care of your son and you can go." And so, look, he came over, they stayed here and now they're done. But if I had agreed and said, "Ok, my son." No… That's what happened with my older son.
Lilian: Oh, he wouldn't have studied.
Luisa: No. My older son was going to go to the Southeast to study and it was when my husband died. Then as we were sad and depressed, and everything, he said, "Mom, I'm not going to college this year, until next year because, look, my dad has just died…" My husband… he had to leave on August 13 and my husband died on August 24. So when he had to leave, we were in El Palenque *(the largest city in the state)*, at the hospital. So, a few days later my husband died, then, well he never went. He said next year, and look, never again. He never went.

Luisa had learned from her experience with her older son, who once postponed attending college—at the time when his dad was in the hospital, dying—and, finally, never went. This time around, Luisa was determined to do whatever was in her power to prevent this from happening again. By the last interview, her son had graduated and had already moved out.

# INDEX

## Studies in Criticality

*General Editor*
*Shirley R. Steinberg*

Counterpoints publishes the most compelling and imaginative books being written in education today. Grounded on the theoretical advances in criticalism, feminism, and postmodernism in the last two decades of the twentieth century, Counterpoints engages the meaning of these innovations in various forms of educational expression. Committed to the proposition that theoretical literature should be accessible to a variety of audiences, the series insists that its authors avoid esoteric and jargonistic languages that transform educational scholarship into an elite discourse for the initiated. Scholarly work matters only to the degree it affects consciousness and practice at multiple sites. Counterpoints' editorial policy is based on these principles and the ability of scholars to break new ground, to open new conversations, to go where educators have never gone before.

For additional information about this series or for the submission of manuscripts, please contact:

Shirley R. Steinberg
c/o Peter Lang Publishing, Inc.
29 Broadway, 18th floor
New York, New York 10006

To order other books in this series, please contact our Customer Service Department:

(800) 770-LANG (within the U.S.)
(212) 647-7706 (outside the U.S.)
(212) 647-7707 FAX

Or browse online by series:
www.peterlang.com